*The Collected Papers*

OF

OTTO FENICHEL

**FIRST SERIES**

*Books by Otto Fenichel*

The Psychoanalytic Theory of Neurosis

The Collected Papers of Otto Fenichel: First Series

The Collected Papers of Otto Fenichel: Second Series
*(in press)*

# THE *Collected Papers*

## OF

# OTTO FENICHEL

FIRST SERIES

---★---

W · W · NORTON & COMPANY · INC · New York

PRINTED IN THE UNITED STATES OF AMERICA

FOR THE PUBLISHERS BY THE VAIL-BALLOU PRESS

23456789

# Contents

# Introduction

THE twenty-six years that closed with the death of Otto Fenichel in January, 1946, marked a very special time of development in the world of psychoanalysis. In its first half Freud was still productive, and his work was being eagerly studied, discussed, elaborated, and tested by the small groups of analysts who were gathered about the newly formed psychoanalytic institutes. These groups were foci of an intense psychoanalytic life, and as time has shown, potentially extraordinarily expansive. It is this period which Zilboorg has called "the erudite period" of psychoanalysis. Psychoanalysts followed an inner calling; their psychoanalytic life was dedicated to observation, study, and learning.

This same quarter-century is the period in which Otto Fenichel lived his professional life, and of all his contemporaries he was perhaps its best example and avatar. An eager and alert intellect, an indefatigable worker and student, an avid and incisive observer, digester, elaborator, and systematizer, Fenichel possessed the ideal ear and pen of his time. The present volume shows at a glance the extent of his capacity to observe, to think, and to shape his thoughts; but besides the essays here collected and besides the books which brought him fame, a constant and extraordinary number of reviews which appeared in the psychoanalytic journals attests to the breadth and depth of his reading and knowledge. These reviews were soon discovered by his colleagues to be of the highest value. Not only were they often clarifying where the author might be obscure; they also contained comments and judgments that in themselves were original contributions. We could all of us rely on Fenichel to point out what was new and sound in our colleagues' thinking, and we were sure of a definite and mature opinion on its importance.

Fenichel had that rare integration of personality and activity which is indicated by the word *sincerity*. His interest in "sociology," to give an example, was not pallidly abstract. Not at all: Fenichel played a real social role; he functioned in the group constantly, effectively, absorbing from it and giving back to it. No one was ever a better citizen. I recall one of the many committee meetings at which we both sat. Fenichel had some policy to advocate, which seemed important to him at the time. He put his all into this advocacy. With the passion and intellectual persuasion of a great lawyer, he argued, explained, reasoned, and rebutted; one would have thought that the defeat of his measure would leave him a malcontent and a rebel. On the contrary: after an unfavorable vote, there was Fenichel, smiling, joking, relaxed, entirely content that he had adequately stated his point, without any personal disappointment and without any thought that he would do other than follow honestly and conscientiously the decision of the majority. He was absolutely trustworthy, free of personal resentments and grudges, equally free of any partisanship that stemmed solely from friendship.

This same quality permeates his writings. Fenichel is solid to the core. Independent in his convictions, as a person and as a psychoanalytic journalist, he was a carrier and a bond. The same holds for his more permanent and systematic authorship, as the reader of the present book will easily see. There was nothing in the analytic atmosphere for which he did not serve as a condenser, no currents for which he did not serve as a medium; and *nihil tetigit quod non ornavit.*

I should not like to persist in mechanical metaphors in this sketch of Fenichel's qualities and functions. More accurate would be the biological tropes of growth and production. The great storage and transmutation which Fenichel's solid clinical experience and erudition represented came to fruit in significant and prodigious fashion, with a burgeoning and efflorescence that amazed us all. In the analytic world, it passed as self-evident that a textbook of psychoanalysis was impossible, even if this textbook covered only the field of the neuroses. Fenichel accomplished the impossible—and twice. His first textbook, in English called *The Outline of Clinical Psychoanalysis,* first published serially and then in book form, was an immediate success. All that psychoanalysis had said specifically about the special neuroses, skillfully digested, clarified by original comments, was presented in a convenient arrangement. In eleven chapters, the material was ordered according to the individual neuroses, an arrangement that is obviously somewhat arbitrary, which made necessary the omission of much related theory and much analytic material of related fields (for example, dream psychology), yet at the same time the book was incredibly complete in the fulfillment of its practical intention. For a decade it was read eagerly by students, in all senses of that word, to their great profit. Its effect was not limited to the narrower psychoanalytic world; it became standard reading for the larger world of psychology, psychiatry, and the mental and social sciences. It was shortly out of print, it became hard to buy, and there was a great and growing demand for its reissue.

Fenichel's revision and rewriting, prolonged because of the war, produced a totally new book, even though the older *Outline* served as a point of departure. This was his justly famous large work, *The Psychoanalytic Theory of Neurosis,* the more remarkable of the two impossible accomplishments. This book, with its immense erudition, its textual profusion, and its vast bibliography, was not a mere exposition but, in the words of Hanns Sachs's review, "an encyclopedia of stupendous completeness," compared by the same reviewer to the great digests of law and jurisprudence, specifically to the most famous of them all, the Code of Justinian. Nor was the book merely monumental, a satisfying demonstration of brilliant scholarship, to be viewed with sterile admiration. Fenichel always "functioned." The book proved consistently and intensely useful. It shortened and eased the work of everyone who has, since its appearance, engaged upon the study of a clinical psychoanalytic subject, or who has written a psychoanalytic paper. It is at once a work of reference for the advanced and a trustworthy guide for beginners. In fact, for a few years after its appearance, there was some danger that the uninitiate might mistake this book for *all* of psychoanalysis, an idea which its scholarly author would have been the first to combat.

With so much of Fenichel's work available in these books (and there is also a monograph on psychoanalytic technique), it might be asked with reason why the present collection of individual essays should see the light. The answer is not hard to find. Fenichel's books, for all their sinewy bulk, did no more than touch upon many subjects cultivated in these essays. Psychoanalysis is more than a theory of neurosis, however broadly this theory may be conceived, and Fenichel contributed to many other fields. Indeed, in the narrower clinical field itself, even Hanns Sachs's review found one source of dissatisfaction. "The only point in which the book gives less than complete satisfaction is the abbreviated rendering of case histories." The present collection in many ways corrects this omission. Many of Fenichel's case histories deserve attention and study for themselves and not merely as part of a general exposition, where many niceties are lost in the generalizations. The reader's attention is therefore called to some of the fine case reports in the individual articles; it is difficult to single out one more than another.

Besides the extension of case reports and subject matter in general, another merit characterizes the separate articles. Many of them are brief but comprehensive monographs in themselves. The brilliant and useful essays on "Identification" and "Isolation" come to mind. Even when the essay deals with new, original conceptions (the counterphobic attitude, for example, or transvestitism), so much is brought to bear on the central topic from so many sources and then packed so trimly into the context that these essays become convenient compendia and works of reference for a much larger field. The discussion of the counterphobic attitude and its clinical application is a minor treatise on anxiety in general; the article on transvestitism is a major contribution to the psychology of the perversions. The articles that deal with screen memories give much more than is to be found in Fenichel's books. His essay on boredom gives promise of setting a standard for the study of moods. Indeed, many of these essays have served younger colleagues as models for their investigations and presentations. It would have been a great pity if they had met the usual fate of papers that are printed in scientific journals, where they become items in the kind of file which newspapermen have called the "morgue." Because they are "old" it comes to be assumed that they are drained of meaning, outdated, or that all that is good in them has been copied and preserved in current books and teaching. The numerous instances in many sciences that contradict this prejudice are well known. Yet for all that, the old journals are insufficiently used. Hence, a book of the present type is to be welcomed for its simple function of preserving much that will undoubtedly be useful and for making it conveniently available. It is thus for the most part that Freud, Abraham, and Ferenczi are preserved for us as continuous forces in psychoanalytic life.

Fenichel is a writer of great forthrightness and little ornamentation. His style is spare, with no superfluities; where his sentences are complex, so are the thoughts. With his gift for extracting the meat of a subject, he has performed great feats of clarification in matters of first importance. We must be indebted to him for such successful tasks as his compact exposition of the work on depressions, for his incisive formulations of the cathectic situation in hypochondriasis and the narcissistic neuroses, and for many often unnoted organizations of subject matter which bring large segments of analytic observation and thinking immediately into unitary view. His concentrated exposition always results in a great clarification of issues, as for example the problem of interpreting preoedipal material, for which Freud expressed his appreciation.

Hanns Sachs, in his comments on *The Psychoanalytic Theory of Neurosis*, remarked that the book's real value would be demonstrated when a new edition was required: "Then it will appear that the mere reëditing and bringing up to date of the task he accomplished single-handed, can be done only with the coöperation of several experts." Such a revision is apparently not yet necessary, and now fortunately, thanks especially to Dr. Hanna Fenichel and Dr. David Rapaport, a more immediate task has been successfully carried through. We are all indebted to the editors of this volume for the result of their labors, which have been very great, for their dedicated and thorough job of collecting, translating or retranslating, organizing and revising, and doing all they could to make these papers more useful and convenient. The publishers too must be praised for their wise appreciation of the importance of this task.

The editors, after careful consideration, came to the conclusion that the best arrangement of the papers is that based on chronology. This seems to me a happy decision. The papers do not lend themselves to the artificial rubrics of an arbitrary and stiff "classification" by subject matter; they would lose much by such an arrangement. For, as I have tried to explain, time and growth were synonymous in Fenichel's life and productivity—the growth of his own powers and of the science of which he was so sensitive a part. The collection therefore is a cross section, and a solid one, of a quarter-century of fine personal and psychoanalytic development. Fenichel was a builder and constructor; he gave much more than he received. It is odd, considering the difference in the two men, that Anatole France's praise of Rémy de Gourmont should apply so well to Fenichel: "Il a touché tout, il n'a cassé rien."

BERTRAM D. LEWIN, M.D.
NEW YORK PSYCHOANALYTIC INSTITUTE

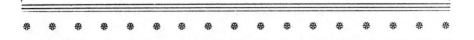

# Preface

THE publication of the two series of Otto Fenichel's *Collected Papers* is the result of the concerted efforts made by those who felt that this book would at once be a memorial to Otto Fenichel and the fulfillment of a public need. My sincere appreciation goes to all those who have contributed to the completion of this project.

This new collection will now make easily available all those papers written in English which had previously appeared in many different periodicals, and besides it will make accessible those papers which had not been translated before.

These papers were written over a period of 24 years and though changing views are expressed in them no attempts at unification were made, as it seemed essential to me to preserve their original form.

In all references to Freud's work the latest editions are given. This procedure makes for easy recourse for those interested in the context of the quotation but inevitably obscures the actual chronological sequence of Freud's writings.

There are a few papers of Otto Fenichel which are not included in the two volumes: early publications of his which deal with Jewish, youth movement, and social problems and which seemed to me not to belong to his strictly psychoanalytic writings.

These two volumes, however, together with his previous books, represent Otto Fenichel's life work, his contribution to psychoanalysis.

HANNA FENICHEL

# Acknowledgments

GRATEFUL acknowledgment is made to the publishers of the following periodicals for permission to print those papers of which they control the copyrights: *The Psychoanalytic Quarterly, The International Journal of Psycho-analysis, The Psychoanalytic Review, The American Imago, Psychosomatic Medicine,* and the former *Zeitschrift fuer Paedagogik.*

I am greatly indebted to Dr. David Rapaport for doing the rough translations of the previously not translated papers and to Mrs. Alix Strachey, who took the responsibility of the final English form; to Miss Suzette Annin, who with Dr. Rapaport's help is responsible for the completion and unification of the bibliographic footnotes; to Miss Annin and Mrs. Ruth Shippey, secretaries of the Austen Riggs Center, Stockbridge, Mass., who did the work of typing and assembling through all its phases with the help of Miss Sarah Austin, librarian of the Riggs Center for the bibliographic work; to Drs. Alfred Goldberg and Milton Wexler for assistance with the index.

I also wish to thank the publishers for their patience and continuous support during the many months of preparation.

Most of all, however, I want to express my deep gratitude to my friend David Rapaport, without whose unending and devoted help and efforts this publication could not have been achieved.

HANNA FENICHEL

*The Collected Papers*

OF

OTTO FENICHEL

FIRST SERIES

## *ONE*

# Two Brief Clinical Contributions*

### I. THE DISCOVERY OF A PRECONSCIOUS FANTASY OF RAPE

A FEMALE patient found out that her man friend had not told her about the existence of a woman with whom, as she found out, he had sexual relations. She was deeply hurt by this concealment, and, as a consequence—so she related in the analysis—she became indifferent to the friend, as well as to all other people and interests. She had read that in mental disorders there occur conditions in which the patients withdraw completely from the external world: that is how she felt. She had only had the impulse to reproach her friend for his silence. I commented: "Then your loss of interest was not so complete?" She replied that she did not quite trust her so-called loss of interest either, because though she had completely cooled off towards him, she nevertheless felt bound to him. "You probably," said I, "feel indifferent towards your real friend in order to replace him in your fantasy with one who fulfils your wishes better." About this she said she did not know. Following Ferenczi's active methods a little further, I now asked her whether she had any daydreams of the last few days to relate. Yes, she daydreamed of reproaching him, but of nothing else. Then she shifted to other topics and the hour proceeded under the sign of resistance. Suddenly the following memory emerged: she had read a case history in a medical book in which the word "stuprum" † occurred. She did not know the expression and took it for "stupor," the word for the condition of loss of interest which occurs in mental disorders. The whole thing made no sense to her. She asked me what "stuprum" meant and when I now replaced stupor and loss of interest by

* This paper was first presented at Vienna in March, 1922. Dr. Fenichel's manuscript has been translated into English, in conformity with the other papers, but no attempt has been made to give it the final form Dr. Fenichel might have given it if he had prepared it for publication.

† "Stuprum," unlawful connection with or defilement of a woman (Funk & Wagnalls).—Trans. note.

"stuprum" in her story, it began to make sense. "Why are you telling me this?" I asked.

"I do not know."

"Perhaps it is the key to the understanding of your behavior. Let us also try substituting 'stuprum' everywhere where you spoke of stupor, that is, loss of interest; then perhaps it will make sense too."

The patient did not want to accept this suggestion. Immediately after this, however, she began to talk about having been overtaken in the last few days by a fear of going into the Grunewald in the evening, as she used to with her friend. Now she had to agree that the continuation of the fantasy in which she scolds her friend was as follows: that he asks for her forgiveness, declares his love for her, and that there then follows a "stuprum." Her "stupor" was her concealed passive readiness to let him do whatever he liked with her.

## II. DOUBT AS A GENITAL SYMBOL

Another woman patient suffered, among other things, from compulsive doubting. At the time in question the analysis had already progressed far and had brought a considerable improvement in her condition. She recognized that her doubts were rooted primarily in the castration complex (she wondered whether she was a woman or a man and whether she was castrated or did not after all have a penis somewhere hidden inside her). At this point the patient made the following reflection about her state: This solution did bring her considerable relief, but she still had a remnant of doubt about everything. This remnant, she felt, would always remain with her, even if the analysis were to go on for years. She could not get rid of it, it was grown in fast to her, was a part of herself. It would stay with her even after she had long since come to terms with her feminine sexual role. "What is your association to this piece of doubt?" I asked. It was a grinning little man, a scornfully laughing dwarf with a magic cap of invisibility, or at least with a pointed cap. She recognized him to be the penis. One consolation I could give her, namely, that even after her uncertainties as to her sex were resolved, that is, after the analysis had definitively done away with her hopes for a penis, a "remnant of her doubt" would remain to her in the shape of her clitoris, which was "grown fast to her," truly a "part of herself."

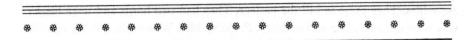

## TWO

# Fear of the Dead*

THE fear of the dead, who return to take away with them the living, has found an explanation from the point of view of individual and social psychology in the unconscious death wishes which the survivor harbored against the dead person while he lived, because of which he now fears that person's vengeance. In a schizophrenic whom I observed, I found a different determination of this fear.

Rosa H. became ill in her twentieth year. She showed restlessness and anxiety, heard voices, and had ideas of reference and persecution. The voices said that she was immodest and had to look at the genitals of men. The patient believed that there were ghosts in her bedroom. Brought to the psychiatric clinic, she was anxious and confused and hallucinated fearsome ghosts. She said emphatically and repeatedly that she had wished the ghosts on herself and now could not get rid of them. Fourteen days later she fell into a catatonic stupor, during which she did not speak for five months, and had to be forced to eat and to eliminate, and her tremendous salivation could not be influenced by atropin. After five months she again took part in her environment, was oriented and ordered. But she scarcely moved; her mood was apathetic and her facial expression dull; she collected herself with difficulty, spoke very slowly, and between question and answer there were long pauses. Speaking about her hallucinations and delusions, she believed at times that they were sick imaginings and at others that they were factual reality.

From what she said the following may be gathered: The patient felt herself persecuted by horrible animals, which crawled like snakes, yet had legs like

* This paper was first presented at Berlin in November, 1922. Dr. Fenichel's manuscript has been translated into English, in conformity with the other papers, but no attempt has been made to give it the final form Dr. Fenichel might have given it if he had prepared it for publication.

crocodiles. They came to kill the patient. They had two horns and were black; they were not animals at all but devils. Probably Mrs. W. sent these devil-animals to bring the patient to her in death.

Concerning what the patient related about Mrs. W., the following is of interest: She was a twenty-year-old woman who died of tuberculosis. The patient used to nurse her, shop for her, and clean her house. Mrs. W. paid her 10 marks weekly. This made the patient's mother angry because she thought that with that much work the patient could earn more money, and she forbade her to go to Mrs. W. The patient went nevertheless—allegedly out of pity. But Mrs. W. found out that the patient's mother disliked her, and she was abusive. What her words were the patient did not want to remember. Finally, in the face of strong resistance, she related that Mrs. W. had said: "The devil take your mother." On one occasion Mrs. W. even sent her husband to beat up the patient's mother. This old drunkard came "like a wild beast, like a devil." I commented, "So at the time Mrs. W. sent the devil against your mother, now she sends him against you," and the patient laughed and agreed.

The patient further related that she too found her mother's prohibition unkind. When Mrs. W. died the patient was sorry that she had not made her peace with her own mother before she died. Her mother often prohibited things the patient would have liked to do, so they often fought. For instance, when the patient was 16 she went out with a young man of 20; the mother prohibited it because he was too young. On the other hand the mother of the young man was very nice to the patient; but she died soon after.

The patient's father died when she was six, in an insane asylum (diagnosis: chronic hallucinatory paranoia). The patient remembered that her mother left her and her siblings, now dead, alone with the mentally ill father: he had beaten on the wall and broken it. Mrs. W.'s husband did the same to the window panes when he was drunk.

The situation, then, was this: Mrs. W. was taking the patient to her in death. While she was alive, however, she had fulfilled the oedipus situation on behalf of the patient: she wished her mother dead ("the devil take her"; she sent the devil to her in the form of her husband; and the good mother did indeed die—in the form of the young man's mother); and she was married to the patient's father (her husband is the dangerous and violent father-imago). Her death was thus the punishment for the oedipal sin.

It is plausible to assume that the patient sentenced herself, on grounds of the same etiology, to the same fate as overtook Mrs. W. Her fear of death thus arose from a hysterical identification with Mrs. W. It is possible, but not proven, that the patient had death wishes against Mrs. W. also.

There are, however, two more points to be considered. First, the circumstance that it was the dead Mrs. W. who sent the death-bringing devil against the patient, and also the specific characteristics of the devil; second, that the patient was in fact not a hysteric, but a schizophrenic.

Some light is thrown on these points when we learn that the patient associated to the devil that "he is the one who leads into temptation," who "lets one fall into sin," when we remember that she said that she had wished him on herself, that he was shaped like a snake, and when, too, she related a dream in which such devil-animals break all the windows. Clearly, the devil was Mr. W.; Mr. W., however, behaved violently towards the patient's mother and was a father-imago (the patient's father broke the wall). We are thus justified in considering that the devil-animal was the violent penis, and that the death which the patient feared was at the same time sexual intercourse with her father. It was not only punishment for, but also the repetition of, the sin (the *snake*like creature breaks the window). This is expressed not only in the above sadistic language, but also in oral terms: the patient's only association to the crocodile was that it devoured people. But then she was in turn under the impression that while she was sick she ate up the devil-animals. Later on she corrected this and said that it was not the devil-animals that she swallowed, but a steamlike mass they ejected, and as a consequence the patient was swollen all the time; she had something in her abdomen. In her psychosis she conceived the child which she wished for from her father.

If we remember that the devil-animals came at the command of the friend who was a narcissistic object choice of the patient, and that she abandoned her only man friend on the first demand of her mother; and when we hear further that she never had sexual intercourse, "never paid any attention to men," but that she had deeply loved a girl schoolmate who, too, died of tuberculosis later on, then it seems plausible to assume the presence in her of a strong repressed homosexual impulse—perhaps based on her love for her father. This would support the thesis that persecutions always originate from a love object of the same sex. When her mother forbade her to meet the young man, she obeyed; when she forbade her to visit Mrs. W., she did not obey. In accordance with this love, the patient's psychosis attributed to Mrs. W. also that violent and satisfying organ in which—so the very first accusation of the persecuting voices asserted—she was all too interested. Perhaps, too, her excessive salivation was an attempt to compensate for the lacking organ by an oral production of fluid.

## *THREE*

# Psychoanalysis and Metaphysics*

## *A Critical Inquiry*

### I

In his paper on "The Unconscious" Freud says: "The psychoanalytic assumption of unconscious mental activity appears to us, on the one hand, a further development of that primitive animism which caused our own consciousness to be reflected in all around us, and, on the other hand, it seems to be an extension of the corrections begun by Kant in regard to our views on external perception. Just as Kant warned us not to overlook the fact that our perception is subjectively conditioned and must not be regarded as identical with the phenomena perceived but never really discerned, so psychoanalysis bids us not to set conscious perception in the place of the unconscious mental process which is its object. The mental, like the physical, is not necessarily in reality just what it appears to us to be." [1]

It seems to me that this passage allows of no misunderstanding. In accordance with it, psychoanalysis has taught us to seek behind our conscious thought contents the unconscious contents which determine them. In an important respect this doctrine closely approaches that of Kant, which similarly holds that behind phenomena presented to us lie concealed metaphysical entities which determine them. Thus, Kant and Freud agree in that both look beyond that which is given to that which is hidden behind it and which they consider the more real of the two. But this does not at all mean that the metaphysical reality of Kant and the unconscious reality of Freud are identical—especially since in another place we read Freud's statement that "Whether any *reality* is to be at-

* First published in *Imago*, Vol. 9, 1923, pp. 318–343.
[1] S. Freud, "The Unconscious," *Coll. Pap.*, Vol. IV, London, Hogarth, 1948, p. 104.

8

tributed to the unconscious wishes, and if so, in what sense, I cannot say off-hand. Reality must, of course, be denied to all transitional and intermediate thoughts. When we have tracked down the unconscious wishes to their final and true expression, we should still have to say that *psychic reality* is a special form of existence which must not be confounded with *factual reality*." [2]

Thus when Schilder, referring to the first of the two passages quoted above, once expressed the opinion that Freud makes his world of the unconscious coincide with the metaphysical world of Kant, and conscious perception with phenomenality, this appears to us to mistake Freud's meaning, and to suppose that he was postulating an identity between things where he was only making an analogy. In this paper Schilder polemized against this interpretation of Freud's view. Other psychoanalysts making a similar interpretation have adopted this conception, which they mistakenly believe to be Freud's, thus identifying the system Ucs. with Schopenhauer's metaphysical "will," and consciousness with its phenomenalistic presentation. When, therefore, Freud goes on to say: "It is, however, satisfactory to find . . . that the inner object is less hard to discern truly than is the outside world," [3] such interpreters conceive this to mean that psychoanalysis opens a way into the metaphysical world, alleged by Kant to be inaccessible. In this way only am I able, for example, to understand Spielrein's statement at the last Congress, that psychoanalytic investigation has taught us that the concept of time in children is not an *a priori* one. Much the same is true of Pfister's point of view. When he says, for example, that Freud had long known that "the sex problem is on the one hand a psychological problem and, on the other, a metaphysical (metapsychological) one," [4] it indicates that for him metapsychology belongs to metaphysics. Furthermore, his essay on "Psychoanalyse und Weltanschauung" [5] presents the relationship of metapsychology to metaphysics very unclearly.

But anyone who attempts to break through the barriers separating us from the-thing-in-itself may not argue on an empirical, inductive basis. He is subject to the critique of epistemology. To equate the psychic reality of the Ucs. with the metaphysical reality of the-thing-in-itself calls for an epistemological critique of this kind. If such a critique should also lay down limitations to the validity of psychoanalysis, these would differ in no way from those which obtain for every science. And if we were to succeed in defining more narrowly the field of

---

[2] S. Freud, "The Interpretation of Dreams," *The Basic Writings*, New York, Modern Library, 1938, p. 548.

[3] S. Freud, "The Unconscious," *Coll. Pap.*, Vol. IV, p. 104.

[4] O. Pfister, *Zum Kampf um die Psychoanalyse*, Vienna, Int. Psa. Verlag, 1920.

[5] In *Zum Kampf um die Psychoanalyse*. In this work Pfister also discusses in detail the studies so far published by psychoanalysts on metaphysics; among others, the studies of Putnam, Jung, and Maeder, which are not considered in this paper.

validity of psychoanalytic theories, this would seem to us to be a service to psychoanalysis, rather than the reverse.

## II

The idea basic to Kant's critique of all metaphysics is this: Our "experience" is dependent not only on the object which is being perceived, but also on the subject who is perceiving it. We experience in the *a priori* forms of space and time, we think in categories, causal and final, although neither space nor time, neither causality nor finality, is in the nature of things. A recognition of the nature of things would therefore require that we exclude the categories, an achievement impossible for the human mind.

Some psychoanalysts, attempting to evade this logically compelling train of thought, make appeal to Bergson, whose philosophy has much—some of it actual and some apparent—in common with psychoanalytic knowledge. Bergson considers metaphysical truth possible; the train of thought in question, he believes, only proves that *rational* metaphysics is impossible, not metaphysics per se. Intuition, he thinks, does better than reason. He argues thus: Intuitive certainty is possible. It is possible to immerse one's self in the undoubtable pure existence of one's own self, as "pure duration" free from all "extension." Therefore it is possible to put oneself in the place of things, the existence of which thereby becomes as certain for one as was in the first place only one's own existence.

This is not the place to enter into a detailed refutation of Bergson. Since, however, there is a close relationship between his metaphysics and that allegedly professed by psychoanalysis, in so far as the psychoanalytic method of free association is assumed to correspond to the immersion in Bergson's "pure duration," we must, before examining the relationship of psychoanalysis to metaphysics, draw up a scheme of things with which to refute Bergson's line of reasoning.

First of all, then, there is no intuitive certainty of a metaphysical sort. Judgments which have intuitive certainty are either categorical (e.g., arithmetical ones and those belonging to Euclidian geometry), in which case they certainly cannot lead us into metaphysics; or else they refer to experience. In the latter case it remains open to question (1) whether the feeling of certainty is justified in regard to what is phenomenal; (2) whether such judgments depend any less upon categories than syllogisms.

As to (1): The feeling of certainty alone is no proof of objective validity. It makes no difference that the knowledge in question originally sprang from intuition. Only its subsequent standing up to rational reality testing is decisive for its factual reality.

As to (2): Since such judgments refer to experience, they refer to what is perceived in space and time, or to what is causally or finalistically deduced, and therefore are useless from a metaphysical standpoint.

Moreover, a complete intuitive "immersion" in things outside of one's own self ("empathy") is impossible. True, it is demonstrable within the phenomenal realm that people occasionally make correct statements about the thoughts and feelings of other persons, without knowing whence they have come by such knowledge; for these statements can be verified by the assertions or the later acts of the persons about whom they were made. But the mechanism of such "empathy," such "narcissistic identification," as it is called, does not guarantee the objective correctness of its results. Obviously, the tendency to perceive all reality as being like the self subserves the pleasure principle. (The first object relation is introjection; identification precedes object love.) Love was learned in relation to the self: if the outside world is to be loved, it must be perceived as being like the ego. Animistic doctrines, however, have no phenomenal or factual validity. Where actual similarities exist, empathy is possible; where they do not, supposed empathy goes astray. But we have no objective criterion for the existence of actual similarities except verification after the fact. If, for example, we believe in other people's consciousness, this belief is justified not because our naïve judgment assumes such a consciousness, but because there are in fact analogies between our ego and other persons. "Empathy" with animals, plants, and inorganic matter, however, seems to me to be less an assimilation of the ego to those objects than a falsification of them by assimilating them to the ego without justification. Instead of the requisite introjection a projection takes place.[6] In any case, like all intuitive judgment, "empathetic" judgment, too, is dependent upon categories, and would thus be useless as a means of gaining metaphysical knowledge, even if it were to prove valid within the phenomenal realm. It may be mentioned at once here that the compulsion to identify has its roots in the Ucs. But the examination of factual reality is a function of the Cs. Thus, "empathy" versus experience and investigation means the pleasure principle versus the reality principle. It is a regression to the period of pure pleasure principle, to psychotic thinking; but such thinking cannot attain a knowledge of reality.

Should, nevertheless, Buddhistic meditation be valid as a second source of

---

[6] Freud, in his study "Certain Neurotic Mechanisms in Jealousy, Paranoia and Homosexuality," (*Coll. Pap.*, Vol. II, London, Hogarth, 1948), shows that even paranoiacs do not project arbitrarily, but rather by exaggerating minute objective signs. But, firstly, it seems questionable to me whether the intuitive knowledge of the nature of inanimate things, as reported by the older animists and new occultists, is sustained by objective signs arising from the inanimate objects in question. Secondly, it seems to me that the statement of the paranoiac that he is pursued, though it has a psychic reality, is not a source of knowledge of factual reality; for objectively he is not loved enough, but he is by no means persecuted.

knowledge, made possible by such regression,[7] it would by no means be a source of external knowledge of the nature of *things,* but at most a source of internal knowledge of the nature of the *ego.* (Of this, more later.)

Finally, "immersion in pure duration" is also impossible. For "pure duration" is a property, a quality, of the act of consciousness, which, as such, can never become a content of consciousness. Such an immersion no more exists than does "consciousness of an act" as distinct from "consciousness of an object," as some psychologists assume. When the judgment "I exist" is a content of consciousness, the content is not identical with the quality of thought "it is I who judge that I exist" which accompanies this act of consciousness; this also holds for the quality of thought "it is I who judge that A exists" which accompanies the judgment that A exists when that judgment is the content of consciousness.

But this eliminates the possibility of making the evidence of internal perception the basis of wider metaphysical conclusions. For these contents of consciousness, perceived in time, may be as deceptive as externally perceived objects. They, too, are phenomenal. The "intelligible I," and therefore the metaphysical "I," is simply and solely that qualitative coloring, that adjectival property, the *act* of consciousness in contradistinction to the *content* of consciousness. Certainty of one's own being is not only the starting-point of all metaphysics; it is all it ends in.[8]

### III

We thus conclude that an intuitive system of metaphysics is as impossible as a rational one. And now we may turn to our theme proper, the critical investigation of the possibility of relationships between metaphysics and psychoanalysis.

Kant has taught us that no natural science, from its very character, can ever reach the metaphysical world which lies beyond the categories. Thus, our first question must be: is psychoanalysis a natural science in this sense, or is it not?

"Natural science," for which Kant's view holds, includes all efforts at systematic description or "explanation" of natural phenomena, thus all that takes account of spatial and temporal conditions. That psychoanalysis aims at explanation is no less indubitable than that, for instance, "development of the libido" or "regression in time" are terms which refer to the temporal. Were a serious attempt made to consider a part of the subject matter of psychoanalysis, namely, the

---

[7] F. Alexander, "Der biologische Sinn psychischer Vorgaenge," *Imago,* Vol. 9, 1923.

[8] Pfister, who also praises Bergson because with him the "intellect lets itself be drawn by the eternal feminine of intuition up to the true heights of life," thinks that metaphysics "contains the true coin of valid knowledge for all who have broken with Kant's dualism and relative agnosticism." ("Psychoanalyse und Weltanschauung," *Zum Kampf um die Psychoanalyse.*) But we have by no means broken with Kant, and we consider Bergson's attempt to justify this break a complete failure; nor, as far as we know, has Pfister made any such attempt.

Ucs. system, as not being a mere phenomenon, on the strength of the fact that Freud himself lists "timelessness" as one of the characteristics of that system, we should answer this by pointing out that such "timelessness" is nothing more than "indestructibility in time," or in other words "durability," and that there-fore not only is the Ucs. not lacking in relationship to temporal extension, but what its "timelessness" refers to is precisely its position in regard to the temporal dimension.[9] In *Beyond the Pleasure Principle* Freud says: "We have found by experience that unconscious mental processes are in themselves 'timeless.' That is to say, to begin with: they are not arranged chronologically, time alters nothing in them, nor can the idea of time be applied to them. . . . Our abstract concep-tion of time seems rather to be derived wholly from the mode of functioning of the system Pcpt.-Cs., and to correspond with a self-perception of it."[10]

But the system Pcpt.-Cs. alone can test reality. Therefore to say this is to say no more than that, since every reality can be perceived only in a distorted way through self-perception of the perceiving system, there can be no knowledge of the-thing-in-itself.

Psychoanalysis is a natural science in the strictest sense of the term, based as it is upon extending the application of the concept of the strict validity of the law of causality to things that were previously regarded as "accidental." Such a basis, however, implies the giving up *ab initio* of the metaphysical validity of conclusions built upon it. Little as this militates against the value of psycho-analysis, and wrong as the assumption would be that there is no causality in the realm of the psyche, this fact does, nevertheless, set limits to the sphere of validity of psychoanalytic inference. In this respect the position of psychoanalysis is ex-actly the same as that of physics, chemistry, and biology. An "analytic experience" is no more metaphysical than the experience of an astronomer who observes the occurrence of an eclipse of the sun at the hour calculated in advance.

Nevertheless, psychoanalysis is invoked on behalf of metaphysics in three dif-ferent connections: twice by disregarding these principles and once in deliberate contradiction to them. In the first instance, it is said, in disregard of them, that what psychoanalysis calls the Ucs. is identical with the metaphysical; in the second, that psychoanalysis has demonstrated how pitifully narrow conscious-ness is, and that it is ridiculous to expect much of reason: while, in contradiction to those principles, it is asserted that psychoanalysis is a science unlike astronomy, since its working method is not reason but intuition. From this, both the validity of intuition as a method of acquiring knowledge and the metaphysical character

---

[9] When we speak of the "timeless unconscious" we mean that in the Ucs. there is no such thing as time. For the observer, however, the Ucs. is within time.

[10] S. Freud, *Beyond the Pleasure Principle*, London, Hogarth, 1948, p. 32.

of the results of psychoanalysis are inferred. We shall now make a critical examination of these three points of view.[11]

1. The Ucs. is allegedly identical with the metaphysical.

Here the Ucs. is presumed to be metaphysical in two respects. First, as a content, inasmuch as the unconscious ideas exist as such, apart from perception and categories; and second, as a method, in that intuition, as a derivative of this metaphysical content, conveys metaphysical truth to the possessor of it.

It is true, I should say, that what we call "intuition"—that is, the sudden appearance, due to motives unknown to us, of images, judgments, and thoughts— derives from the Ucs. But the more important question whether the Ucs. is metaphysical in content or is a method of acquiring metaphysical knowledge is, I think, problematical. It seems to me that to consistent thinking the opposite would at first glance appear much more likely, for the following reasons. What undoubtedly gave intuition its metaphysical air before the advent of psychoanalysis was not only the affective coloring which accompanied it, but its inexplicability. To the minds of naïve thinkers causality applies to our conscious actions in the same way as it does to the mechanical occurrences of the external world, except that "motivation" takes the place of "cause." But in the case of "intuition," in creative imagination, inspiration, ecstasy, dreams, symptoms, and hypnosis, motivation seems to be absent. Whence come the inspiration, the idea, the value, and the details of the dream-content? Certainly not from our conscious ego. Thus people had to come to the conclusion that all these phenomena were transcendental.

It is, however, psychoanalysis which has exposed the allegedly transcendental as being merely the immanent. It teaches us that even these phenomena of intuition are—phenomena; they have a *cause* like everything else, and they do not fall outside the categorical laws. Just as our need for causality has made necessary the assumption of the ether, which seems to explain light, electricity, and magnetism, so it has made necessary the Ucs. as the cause of otherwise causeless intuition. Psychoanalysis has taught us that creative imagination, inspiration, ecstasy, dreams, symbols, and hypnosis, all derive from a power which is inherent in man, within his psyche, and that they, no less than his conscious actions, are at bottom motivated by his will. And it seems to me that, once the difference in principle between intuition and other psychic and physical phenomena is eliminated, its transcendental character vanishes.

But psychoanalysis goes much further. Approaching these seemingly spontaneous phenomena with the heuristic maxim "causality must obtain," it is able not only to elucidate the necessary existence of the Ucs., but to throw much light

[11] The same objections would stand if the metaphysical character should be attributed not to the system of unconsciousness but, following Freud's *The Ego and the Id,* to the id.

upon its nature. Once its discoveries are accepted, all claims as to the metaphysical nature of the Ucs. fall to the ground.

a. *Concerning Method*. In "The Unconscious" Freud writes: "The kernel of the system Ucs. consists of instinct-presentations whose aim is to discharge their cathexis; that is to say, they are wish-impulses. These instinctual impulses are co-ordinate with one another, exist independently side by side, and are exempt from mutual contradiction. When two wishes whose aims must appear to us incompatible become simultaneously active, the two impulses do not detract one from the other or cancel each other, but combine to form an intermediate aim, a compromise. There is in this system no negation, no dubiety, no varying degree of certainty. . . . [The unconscious contents] are subject to the pleasure-principle; their fate depends only upon the degree of their strength and upon their conformity to regulation by pleasure and pain." [12] In addition to this there is the fact that words are alien to the Ucs.

A system knowing no negation and whose content is wishes, is supposed to be a means of acquiring knowledge! It is as though a person trying to prove the existence of God were to say: "How sad it would be if there were no God!" A system in which the law of contradiction does not obtain is to be a source of knowledge! The pure pleasure principle is alien, and often contrary, to valid knowledge. This obvious fact leads Freud to the conclusion that "this function of orientating the individual in the world by discrimination between inner and outer must now, after detailed dissection of the mental apparatus, be ascribed to the system Cs. (Pcpt.) alone." [13]

Knowledge, however, including the metaphysical kind, means orientation in the world. The "test by reason" to which intuition must be subjected in order to attain validity, is nothing else but this "reality testing" which supersedes the pleasure principle. If it is omitted and intuition remains untested, there results a hallucinatory confusional state, which we know is phenomenologically false, from which we may conclude that it is also metaphysically false. *Knowing,* even knowing by the Ucs., is a conscious process. The emergence of derivatives of the Ucs. of a sort to whom A can be not-A, and the pleasurable the same as the true, is no method for grasping reality; it is neither a scientific nor a metaphysical method.

b. *Concerning Content*. That the unconscious content is itself not metaphysical or, in other words, is not in-itself-existing can be shown in two completely different ways, from general considerations and from specific ones.

(a) General Considerations: Reason *only,* and no immediate evidence, leads us to assume the existence of a Ucs. However much the feeling of its possessor

---

[12] S. Freud, "The Unconscious," *Coll. Pap.,* Vol. IV, pp. 118–119.
[13] S. Freud, "Metapsychological Supplement to the Theory of Dreams," *Coll. Pap.,* Vol. IV, p. 148.

may contradict this, after he has consciously thought in psychoanalytic terms, the fact remains that the Ucs. still remains a *working hypothesis;* our only reason for believing in a Ucs. is that by assuming it *phenomena* become explicable. And something that is assumed for the sake of causality, for the sake of a category, *cannot* be metaphysical. The existence of the Ucs. thus remains limited to the phenomenal realm, even if, or rather *because,* it has been arrived at by inference.

Freud justifies the Ucs. in the following words: ". . . both in healthy and in sick persons mental acts are often in process which can be explained only by presupposing other acts, of which consciousness yields no evidence. . . . A gain in meaning and connection, however, is a perfectly justifiable motive, one which may well carry us beyond the limitations of direct experience. When, after this, it appears that the assumption of the unconscious helps us to construct a highly successful practical method, by which we are enabled to exert a useful influence upon the course of conscious processes, this success will have won us an incontrovertible proof of the existence of that which we assumed," [14] which proof, however, is by definition, confined to the phenomenal field.[15] Either one agrees with Freud that the Ucs. (even if it was conceived by an intuitive idea) is proved by its usefulness, in which case one gives up its metaphysical nature, since usefulness is not metaphysical, and nothing which is true only for the sake of causality is metaphysical truth; or one is of the opinion that the Ucs. is metaphysical, by virtue of a metaphysical intuition, in which case one is arguing in a circle.

(b) Specific Considerations: The discoveries of psychoanalysis likewise speak against the metaphysical nature of the Ucs. We have heard that the content of the Ucs. is wishes which are always represented as fulfilled. The formula is: "Substitution of external by psychic reality." In this formula "external" is not in any sense a spatial concept, but means nothing more than "factual," whereas "psychic reality" means a *reality which is regarded as such only by the subject and therefore need not be factual.* If, however, metaphysical reality is that reality which exists independently of the person who apperceives it, then psychic reality is, by definition, not metaphysical reality. Since, however, according to psychoanalysis, the only reality in the Ucs. is "psychic," the Ucs. is not a metaphysical reality.

Two more points should be mentioned. The contents of the Ucs. are altered by the unconscious mechanisms of *condensation* and *displacement,* and these alterations depend solely upon the mechanisms at work in that system itself. Thus, even if the unconscious ideas had not been wishes to begin with, but

14 S. Freud, "The Unconscious," *Coll. Pap.,* Vol. IV, p. 99.

15 We agree with Knopf ("Fiktionalismus und Psychoanalyse," *Annalen d. Philosophie,* Vol. 3, 1923) that psychoanalysis works with fictional assumptions. The unconscious—that is, the id—too, is a fiction if everything else is fiction that is justified by its usefulness.

corresponded to metaphysical realities, they would no longer correspond to them after condensation and displacement had occurred. We might also mention that "verbal dissimilation" disparity is a natural sequel of the reality principle being displaced by the pleasure principle.[16]

Let us repeat, then: A thing need not be true just because it is pleasurable. But it may be true, nevertheless. This point, however, can be decided only by conscious reality testing; and since conscious reality testing is only concerned with what is phenomenal, human beings have no criterion for metaphysical reality. *In no case is it permissible to regard a field of concepts created to explain phenomena, as metaphysical.* If, however, the metaphysical nature of the Ucs. is discredited, the inference that intuition, as a derivative of the metaphysical Ucs., transmits metaphysical knowledge, is discredited too. Instead, intuition, in the realm of truth (i.e., apart from its role in the realm of "ought" *) becomes amenable to explanation.

It has been pointed out, however, that, according to psychoanalytic experience, the Ucs. systems of two people may communicate with each other without the people themselves knowing about it, and also that, once more according to psychoanalytical experience, there is such a thing as unconscious knowledge, which, for instance, manifests itself in symbolism.

But either this unconscious knowledge is intuitive knowledge, whose validity is only vouched for once more by intuitive certainty, in which case the proof of its metaphysical nature by such means is circular; or else—and this is probably what is meant—it is a knowledge whose validity is later on substantiated by experience and demonstrable understanding. Without doubt, the symbolic coital activity of the child to whom the "facts of life" have not been explained presupposes a vague "knowledge" of coitus in him, and his symbolic representation of the penis by a mushroom presupposes an unconscious comparison between them on his part. There is no doubt that thinking without the participation of consciousness does exist.

But why should thinking unattended by consciousness have more metaphysical validity than thinking attended by it? Whence does the Ucs. draw the knowledge it acquires, for instance, in the course of ontogenesis? Freud, in his paper on "The Unconscious," says: "But the Ucs. is also affected by experiences originating in outer perception. Normally all the paths from perception to the Ucs. remain open."[17] It is known that even perceptual stimuli which are below the

---

[16] One could, however, conceive of a position that would attribute to the Ucs. not metaphysical *knowledge,* but metaphysical *reality* as being a sum of wishes whose objective fulfillment or nonfulfillment was beside the point. This view would not be affected by our second argument (b). But our first argument (a) suffices to disprove it.

* The "categorical *imperative.*"—Trans. note.

[17] S. Freud, "The Unconscious," *Coll. Pap.,* Vol. IV, p. 126.

threshold of the Cs. can reach the Ucs. (See Poetzl's tachystoscopic experiments, and the dream as premonitor of illness.)

But if such a communication from perception to the Ucs. is possible, whence does the archaic, the *phylogenetically* inherited unconscious knowledge, in so far as it can be verified by secondary experience, originate? Is it not more plausible to assume that it comes from the experience—that is, the *perception*—of ancestors, rather than to have recourse to metaphysics?

I refer to the basic idea of Semon's theory of the Mneme. According to this, "knowledge" is but the possibility of activating memory traces (or "engrams"). But only if a trace has been laid down can it be activated. If there are inborn symbols, that is no more surprising than that individual development is a "brief recapitulation of phylogenesis." This is surprising enough; but it does not necessitate transplanting these phenomena into the realm of metaphysics. We need only get used to the fact that neither mnemonic capacity nor external perception is tied to consciousness.[18] But whatever has its roots in external perception cannot, as we have seen, be metaphysical.

Even if we were to equate the Ucs. of psychoanalysis with the biological "unconscious" of Eduard v. Hartmann—an equation which has been attempted more than once and which does not seem altogether unexceptionable to me—even so, exact biological experiments demonstrate that this "unconscious knowledge" is obtained through sense-perception. The salamander turns yellow on yellow ground, black on black ground. But he loses this faculty if his eyes are removed. The salamander's "intuitive knowledge" is nothing but *what he has seen,* is spatial and phenomenal, not metaphysical.

Unconscious knowledge, no less than conscious knowledge, rests on categories, and is thus metaphysically useless.

But even if this knowledge were metaphysical, we would still lack criteria to decide what part of the arising idea corresponds to such knowledge, and what to a hallucinatory fulfillment of a wish; thus even then it would be useless as a method of attaining metaphysical knowledge. For instance, a primitive has the "intuitive idea" that in the puberty rite he is eaten by a monster. His unconscious knowledge, however, is this: "Many generations ago I killed my father." Even if the latter is correct (in the phenomenal realm), the former is still wrong, and he is eaten by no monster. Only reflective reason, however, can reach the knowledge that this is so, and reflective reason cannot attain any metaphysical knowledge. Such knowledge, too, remains limited to the realm of the phenomenal, both because it originates in perception, and because its criterion is reflection; for neither perception nor reflection reaches into metaphysics.

[18] I learned of W. Gutmann's book, *Psychomechanik, Freud und Semon*, Vienna, Heller, 1922, only after the completion of this study.

Thus it is not at all clear why there should be anything metaphysical in the phenomenon of direct communication between the Ucs. systems of two people. It is a phenomenon which was unknown before its discovery, as was America. The fact that we must assume America, too, to have existed prior to its discovery, does not imply that America's existence was, or is, metaphysical.

*The Ucs. is not metaphysical.*

2. The Cs. is allegedly insufficient.

What then? If this is true, would it follow that the Ucs. is sufficient? Consciousness is not sufficient; I admit it. But I must add: how much less sufficient are unconscious and intuitive methods! Yes, consciousness is insufficient. Freud writes: "In all cases, however, the news that reaches your consciousness is incomplete and often not to be relied on; often enough, too, it happens that you get news of what has taken place only when it is all over and when you can no longer do anything to change it. Even if you are not ill, who can tell all that is stirring in your mind of which you know nothing, or are falsely informed? You conduct yourself like an absolute sovereign who is content with the information supplied him by his highest officials, and never goes among the people to hear their voice. Look into the depth of your own soul and learn first to know yourself." [19] That is to say, we are never logical, our "reality principle" is infested with the pleasure principle. Basically, we never see things consciously as they are, but only as we want them to be.

But what of it? Does it follow that when even that little bit of reality testing which we have at great sacrifice achieved is out of action, when pure pleasure principle reigns, that then there is more truth than when truth is being falsified by the remnants of the pleasure principle? Does it not follow, rather, that when there is no rational truth available to man, no truth at all is available to him?

There should exist only two criteria for a science which ventures to challenge the pleasure principle and find out the truth: [20] the agreement between its laws and phenomenal experience subsequent to their discovery on the one hand, and, on the other, its practical usefulness as technique.

But who would still dare to spin metaphysics wherein these two methods of subsequent validation do not apply, now that Freud, like a new Copernicus, has shown that our "truth" is not truth but wish? Reason and intuition both fall short. Humble resignation is man's share.

3. Psychoanalysis is allegedly not a natural science; its method is intuitive.

Let me say, first of all, that I consider this an irrelevant proposition. Either psychoanalysis is a natural science—i.e., it works with categories—in which case

[19] S. Freud, "One of the Difficulties of Psycho-Analysis," *Coll. Pap.*, Vol. IV, p. 355.

[20] S. Freud, "Contributions to the Psychology of Love: A Special Type of Choice of Object Made by Men," *Coll. Pap.*, Vol. IV, p. 193: "For science betokens the most complete renunciation of the pleasure-principle of which our minds are capable."

its results cannot be metaphysical; or it does not concern itself with "proofs," maintaining that what is essential is the "analytic experience," and not the proofs, in which case its results would be of the same order as all professions of faith, and psychoanalysis could command no more credibility than can dogma and theosophy.

There actually are some authors who do more or less hold this of psychoanalysis. Thus Groddeck writes: "When I am told that all this is nonsense, I have to accept it, but I go right on believing, even without proof, or even, possibly, *because* there is no proof; because the longer one deals with proofs, the more suspicious one becomes of them." [21] Does not every religious man say the same of his faith?

We must also sharply object to Jacobi's recent view [22] when, in contrasting intuitive and imaginative psychology with scientific psychology, he classes psychoanalysis with the former, maintaining that it attempts to understand the individual human psyche in a creative and intuitive fashion, and when he asserts that an "unconscious" which is fully justified in an intuitive psychology could have no place in a scientific psychology. We may quote Freud in this connection, who writes as follows about an article by Havelock Ellis which attempts "to show that the writings of the creator of analysis should be judged not as a piece of scientific work but as an artistic production": [23] "We cannot but regard this view as a fresh turn taken by resistance and as a repudiation of analysis, even though it is disguised in a friendly, indeed in too flattering a manner. We are inclined to meet it with a most decided contradiction." [24]

We assert that psychoanalysis is a science. Our thesis is that even if psychoanalysis cannot do without intuition, its tendency is toward reason.

In "The Unconscious" Freud writes: ". . . we have no other aim but that of translating into theory the results of observation . . ." [25] According to Hoefler, "logic" is "the science which comprises the completest possible and most systematically ordered collection of all certain judgments (or at least near-certain ones having the highest possible degree of probability) that are accessible to human thought." [26]

Since, as we have shown, only "reason," that is, logic, can decide upon certainty and probability, there are no sciences except those working by reason and the Cs. Since "observation" presupposes sense perception and reality testing, and

[21] G. Groddeck, "Der Symbolisierungszwang," *Imago*, Vol. 8, 1922, p. 80.

[22] W. Jacobi, "Ueber die Bedeutung extrem eingestellter psychologischer Forschungsrichtung in der Psychiatrie," *Med. Klin.*, Vol. 18, 1922.

[23] S. Freud, "A Note on the Prehistory of the Technique of Analysis," *Coll. Pap.*, Vol. V, London, Hogarth, 1950, p. 101.

[24] *Ibid.*, p. 101.

[25] S. Freud, "The Unconscious," *Coll. Pap.*, Vol. IV, p. 122.

[26] A. Hoefler, *Grundlehren der Logik und Psychologie*, Leipzig, Freytag, 1902.

"theory" presupposes logic, it goes without saying that analysis, too, is a natural science and works by reason and the Cs. The concept of the Ucs. as a purely scientific auxiliary assumption, has been sufficiently justified by Freud.

But what is the actual role of intuition in psychoanalysis? Since it is used in order to make observations which are then subjected to reality testing and translated by the Cs. into theory, intuition in psychoanalysis is subservient to reason, and not vice versa.

It is correct, then, that the understanding which the psychoanalyst brings to the patient stems from an intuitive source. But this can only be so because experience has confirmed the usefulness (or probability) of the knowledge thus gained. The goal remains the causal explanation of so far unexplained phenomena, that is, a rational goal. Here, like everywhere else, only Cs. reality testing decides the validity of judgments gained by means of unconscious identification.

In the case of the "analytical blind spots" [27] it is not intuition which is paralyzed by repression and has to be liberated; it is reason which is paralyzed by it, in that the striving to avoid the unpleasure which would be aroused by one's own complex becoming conscious—that is, the pleasure principle—prevents the operation of reality testing in that place. The Cs. is paralyzed by resistance, in order to keep what is unconscious out of the Cs.

There can be no doubt, however, that the goal of psychoanalysis is to gain knowledge of (phenomenal) reality. Reality testing, however, is conscious. The goal of psychoanalysis is, and remains, to make conscious what is unconscious.

But even if that were not so, the intuitive "knowledge" concerning the Ucs. would still belong to the phenomenal realm, and would have nothing to do with metaphysics, since the Ucs. is not metaphysical. When Alexander described at the Psychoanalytic Congress the intuitive knowledge of Buddha, he demonstrated that the path of inward-turning which goes as far as catatonia leads, at most, to recollections of experiences, that is, only to unmetaphysical and absolutely subjective matter.[28]

Two different positions may be adopted toward psychoanalysis, as toward any other science. The first is that of the epistemologist for whom reason can never reach reality. Seen from this position, the Ucs. is a "working hypothesis" for the explanation of the phenomena of consciousness which has no reality of its own, and the "bias" of psychoanalysis toward "conscious reason" is taken for granted. The second position is that of the naïve realist, who takes the results

---

[27] W. Stekel. (The term "blind spot"—skotoma—was introduced and used ubiquitously by Stekel. —Trans. note.)

[28] F. Alexander's study (op. cit.), excellent though it otherwise is, seems to err in that, accepting the proposition *ordo et connexio idearum idem est ac ordo at connexio rerum* as a dogma, it concludes that subjective knowledge always has general objective validity. This dogma, however, is dubious. True, "the self is only a special case of reality," but it is precisely only a *special* case.

of science for entities. This position holds that the psychic phenomena are in themselves unconscious.

Even if we were to adopt the latter position and even if psychoanalysis shows us the enormous discrepancy between that which we call Cs. and that which we call Ucs., even if we knew that the former is to the latter as a grain of sand to the bottom of the ocean, one thing would remain unchanged: that the starting point as well as the ultimate goal of psychoanalysis as a science, is this grain of sand.

If we assume the Ucs. to exist, then it was and is existent, whether or not it is recognized. The only thing that has changed is this recognition. Psychoanalysis, possessing only a grain of sand, makes from that grain inferences concerning the whole ocean bottom. Even if this would seem overdaring and presumptuous, it is because of this quality of psychoanalysis that progress in it can mean nothing else than the making conscious of the Ucs. Psychoanalysis aims at consciousness; its farthest, highest goal is to attain a complete, conscious, logical, scientific understanding of the Ucs., and to be able to predict how a given person will act under given conditions at a given time, with the same certainty with which the astronomer predicts an eclipse of the sun. In principle psychoanalysis has no more to do with intuition than have biology or physics or chemistry. Psychoanalysis is a wedge driven by the Cs. into the realm of the Ucs., not the other way around.

## IV

We shall now proceed to make a few remarks on the psychoanalysis of metaphysics. These are necessary because we must seek to answer the question why, against their better judgment, men continue to succumb to metaphysical needs, and why they continue to regard intuition as metaphysical. The psychoanalysis of intuition, although it cannot attack an idea of an "ought" as such, may be able to attack the objective credibility of intuitive ideas.[29] There is an existential affective experience of this sort which may most aptly be used as an example here; for it possesses unmatched strength in this line and can certainly serve as a model of supposedly metaphysical intuition. I refer to the "analytic" experience, to the experience of one's own Ucs. Psychoanalysis shows that it has phenomenal reality, but only within us, not outside of us. Kant's *Critique* shows that it has

---

[29] The psychogenic character of metaphysical theories would not alone invalidate them, and we will turn to it only after we have succeeded in invalidating them epistemologically. Psychoanalysis is not a method of polemic. Pfister is right when he says that agnosticism, too, stems from complexes. But it is not only a "projection into the outer world of neurotic disinclination from deeper self-knowledge, a persisting fixation on the father, etc." (O. Pfister, "Psychoanalyse und Weltanschauung," *Zum Kampf um die Psychoanalyse*, p. 265); it also holds up under the objective test of reason—which, to our mind, cannot be said of metaphysical theories.

no metaphysical reality. And—as psychoanalysis once again shows—not everything that appears together with the judgment as to the existence of the Ucs. has phenomenal reality. Precisely that particular item which would be the most essential for the interpreter of the metaphysical view has no phenomenal reality —namely, the validity of the Ucs. above and outside of the ego, the validity of the feeling that it is the All.*

Let us ask ourselves whence comes this false judgment, why should the phenomenal appear to be metaphysical precisely here, whence comes the feeling that we stem out of the All, if there is no such thing? The answer is close at hand. Everything the "patient" says is somehow right. If it has no external reality, it has *psychic* reality.

Let us recall again in brief what we know about the ontogenesis of the mind. To the development of the libido from auto-erotism to object love via narcissism, there corresponds an at least equally complicated development of the ego. At first there is no differentiation between ego and non-ego; no ego boundary exists as yet, only (unconscious) emotions. Cruel feelings of unpleasure establish the difference between ego and non-ego. Unpleasure of external origin is recognized as "external," because the will does not control it; unpleasure of internal origin is recognized as such because muscular action does not free one from it.[30] And now: "Under the sway of the pleasure-principle there now takes place a further development. The objects presenting themselves, in so far as they are sources of pleasure, are absorbed by the ego into itself, introjected . . . while, on the other hand, the ego thrusts forth upon the external world whatever within itself gives rise to pain. . . ."[31] The first stage of the [undifferentiated] All is thus followed by a second stage of the "pleasure-ego and unpleasure-reality." In the meantime auto-erotism grows into narcissism, that piece of the external world which is the "own body" is recognized to have a mysterious interaction with the inner world, and an "ego" is built up.

But reality demands recognition more and more, and the process of introjecting its pleasurable aspects becomes ever more complex. At first, in the "cannibalistic phase," this takes the crude form of an attempt to incorporate the beloved object *per os*. The next attempt to change the object back into ego— an attempt which is already more adapted to reality—is that of narcissistic identification, whose domination marks the ego phase of animism. In so far as it is in relation to his own ego that the individual has learned to love, if he is to love objects those objects must be like his ego. The animist sees only ego-imagos

* *"Das Pan."*—Trans. note.
30 S. Freud, "Metapsychological Supplement to the Theory of Dreams," *Coll. Pap.*, Vol. IV, pp. 148–149.
31 S. Freud, "Instincts and Their Vicissitudes," *Coll. Pap.*, Vol. IV, p. 78.

in the world, and he is concerned to see the objects as more like the ego than they are.[32] This is described by Roheim: "The libido avenges itself upon the external world. Adaptation and the reality-principle were imposed on it only by force. Now it tries to remodel this external world in its own image." [33] Thus, if what was originally inimical—reality—is to be loved, then, as a consolation and to make things more familiar, as it were, it must be falsified into something that resembles the ego. Nor must it be forgotten that the libidinization of the external world arouses once more the illusion of the primeval All. Again I quote Roheim: "The universal animation is a secondary libidinization of the fear unleashed by the external world; it is a narcissistic libidinization of the universe." [34] Eisler correctly says: "The feeling for nature is thus a negative picture of the delusion of grandeur." [35] We know that, hand in hand with the further development of narcissism into object libido and the accumulation of pleasurable and unpleasurable experiences, animism advances to adaptive logic through the establishment of Cs. reality testing. (Since logic cannot enter the realm of metaphysics either, "advance" is meant here in the sense of achieving better adaptation.)

Does this survey of the development of the ego from the All via the pleasure-ego and animism to logic contribute toward answering our problem?

Yes. Because we have seen that an All really exists. But in what sense "really"? Endopsychically, within the mind of the infant. It is not true that the infant was once one with the world. But it is true that the infant was once one with its mother, and that it *feels* itself one with the world. Undoubtedly, transformism can extend this oneness of mother and child to a oneness which encompasses every living thing. But this changes nothing in what we have already recognized and it does not prevent the longing for an All from being a longing for a purely psychic reality—for the return of a time in which the boundaries between Ego and World, even though they existed, were not accepted ("omnipotence of thought").

Perhaps this has only become quite clear to us from the lucid exposition of Lou Andreas-Salomé [36] who, more than anyone before her, stressed the fact that the establishment of reality testing, and with it the subjective separation of ego and non-ego, is not only a (narcissistic) pleasure gain, but also causes unpleasure, as being a limitation, a circumscription, a renunciation. Thus, the eternal longing for the limitless, the unbounded, the all-powerful, is to be comprehended as a longing for the opposite of this—as a longing for the absolute, for the primal

[32] Freud's *The Ego and the Id* has further elucidated this narcissistic identification.

[33] G. Roheim, "Das Selbst," *Imago*, Vol. 7, 1921, p. 466.

[34] *Ibid.*, p. 457.

[35] M. J. Eisler, "Ueber einen besonderen Traumtyp. Beitrag zur Analyse der Landschaftsempfindung," *Imago*, Vol. 6, 1920, p. 343.

[36] L. Andreas-Salomé, "Narzissmus als Doppelrichtung," *Imago*, Vol. 7, 1921.

beginning whence we have arisen. Lou Andreas-Salomé has discussed how love, as loss of ego, how ethics and works of imagination are longings of this sort. So, too, is the need for metaphysics. It forever strives to attain the impossible, to transcend the boundaries of the ego, to submerge itself in the All, and, in doing so, to feel with certainty: "Thus it was once before."

This certainty is correct. It was so once before. But not in reality—only in the psyche which was not yet able to grasp reality.

At that time we did not distinguish between objective and subjective. And adults who believe that their deepest intuitions are objectively founded are still doing the same. Intuition must appear to be objectively founded since it stems from a depth of the psyche in which the objective and the subjective are not differentiated—and which is for that reason completely useless as a source of knowledge and metaphysics.

Thus we see that it is in the *interest* of intuition to be regarded as metaphysical and absolute. For in that guise its conditional character is safe from detection. Intuition stems from "beyond the reality principle"—but from this side of the pleasure principle.

The development of the mind began with the All. Metaphysical intuition wants to return to its starting point.

This All which existed at the beginning, that is at the beginning of the individual's life, and which was then endopsychic and not real—this is the *true* object of metaphysical longing. There is no indication that what was in me at my beginning, was also outside the world at *its* beginning. On the contrary, all indications speak against it. Metaphysics mistakes endopsychic ontogeny for real phylogeny.[37] If people could remember the first years of their life, they would have no need to go in for metaphysics.

And they would spare themselves much suffering. For despite their longing it is not granted to them to attain metaphysical truths.

Metaphysics is an unjustified assimilation to the ego of what is alien to it. "Ignorabimus."

It would be nicer, more optimistic, more pleasant, if it were otherwise; ethics too could again be transcendental. But the criteria of truth are neither beauty nor goodness, nor the desire to explain the inexplicable. We, who are neither infants nor schizophrenics filled with the All, nor animistic occultists and mystical dreamers, who are logical men, have by dint of hard struggle created for ourselves the new criterion of "Cs. reality-testing." And, so that we shall not be painfully oppressed by the renunciation of pleasure which this criterion im-

[37] This point has already been made by Freud in his *Psychopathology of Everyday Life.* "As a matter of fact, I believe that a large portion of the mythological conception of the world . . . *is nothing but psychology projected into the outer world.* . . . We venture . . . to transform *metaphysics* into *metapsychology*" (*Psychopathology of Everyday Life,* New York, Macmillan, 1948, p. 217).

poses on us, we have established a new ethics which affords a high pleasure premium for the original renunciation of pleasure. This new ethics makes no other demands but these: that one should make judgments as to reality or unreality only according to one's understanding; and that once one has accepted a piece of knowledge, one should hold on to it as long as the reasons which led one to accept it continue to exist, but that, at the same time, one should always be ready to revaluate all those reasons anew. This new virtue, this virtue of the adult, of the conqueror of the pure pleasure principle, is what Nietzsche called "the youngest of all virtues, 'integrity.'"

Bearing this in mind, we shall perhaps realize that he who applies reason to whatever it can be applied to is not in flight from what is foreign to reason, but, on the contrary, is struggling to grasp it more persistently and faithfully than he who, free of doubts, gives facile credence to his intuition.

Reflection is not always "sober"; it is at times a profounder exaltation than the cheap glow which a thoughtless person feels on a mountaintop. The experience of logical thinking is no less holy than that of a lyric poem. I may, therefore, close with Beer-Hoffmann's words on the longing for God:

> And closer to His throne is my hatred
> Than all the love of his cherubim.

## FOUR

# From the Terminal Phase
# of an Analysis*

A FEW months after the publication of Rank's *The Trauma of Birth* I made a detailed critique of the book. In my criticism I regarded the assertion of the unique significance of birth as, to say the least, unproved, and I felt even more strongly about other features of the volume. Since then I have had a case in which Rank's assertions—that toward the end of the analytic treatments mother-transference comes to the fore, and that the treatment is projected as an intra-uterine state, and its termination as birth—have received such a striking and surprising confirmation that I think I may be permitted to present a brief communication of the pertinent material. I should like, however, to preface my remarks by saying that we do not know at all whether these intrauterine and birth fantasies have any basis in reality (the criteria for this decision which I have set up in my critique of Rank being no more satisfied by my material than by his). Furthermore, it will be seen that the relevant material is so interwoven with material belonging to the oedipus complex that they cannot be isolated from each other; and we must bear in mind Freud's attempt to regard intrauterine fantasies as regressive representations of the primal scene.

The patient was a twenty-eight-year-old woman who had lost her mother two weeks after birth. Subsequent mother-figures were frequently reincarnated in the person of the analyst in her transference to him during her analysis. The mother herself played a minor role. Her early death not only made it possible for the patient to regard herself as a disadvantaged exception, but also, it is true,

* This paper was first presented at Berlin in November, 1924. Dr. Fenichel's manuscript has been translated into English, in conformity with the other papers, but no attempt has been made to give it the final form Dr. Fenichel might have given it if he had prepared it for publication.

27

as a privileged one since she remained the only child of her mother, all her siblings being half-siblings. Her childhood oedipus complex, which came into the analysis in its full scope only after a long passage through the most strongly repressed and primitive stages of libido organization, and which appeared in its most commonplace form, was staged around an aunt, a younger sister of the patient's mother, who lived in the house.

After fourteen months of analysis, the patient was sufficiently improved for a termination of the treatment to be thought of. Instantly birth fantasies and birth dreams appeared. The first of these characteristically took the form of a transference fantasy: the therapist invites the patient to a mountain tour, they climb a steep mountain, it is a volcano with a big crater. Arrived at the top she pushes the analyst into the crater. He dies. But she too falls into the inside of the mountain, and has to crawl through fiery lengths and narrows until, after great efforts, she reaches daylight through a narrow opening and is free and rid of analyst and analysis. The fantasy, which took its departure from several contemporary events, plainly reflected in the death of the analyst the history of the patient's own birth, although her mother's death actually came after her birth, while the analyst's was made to precede it. This point, however, is explained by another realm of ideas, pertaining to the oedipus complex, which also entered into the formation of this fantasy and in which the analyst represented the patient's half-brother. Between birth and termination of analysis, moreover, there was interpolated the memory of the trauma of learning to walk: in it too the child was let go from the arms of the mother to make, anxiously and irresolutely, her first steps into the unknown world.

The birth fantasies and dreams reappeared promptly once more when in the eighteenth month of the analysis, termination of the treatment threatened in earnest and was speeded up by the patient. (No date of termination was set by me.) For an understanding of the libidinal situation I must mention that just about this time an acquaintance of the patient came to me in analysis. The patient was able to exploit this circumstance to repeat a problem of her early oedipal situation: "whom will Father choose to replace Mother, me or my aunt?" The patient's acquaintance had sought analysis at her instance, and upon his entering on his treatment she wished to leave hers. In this way she would have given the analyst (her father) a child. This wish was brought to naught by the analyst: her acquaintance did not become her son but her brother, newly included in the family circle. This forced her to repeat the trauma of her oedipal frustration, in which the analyst played the role of the father. When even her attempt to make her rewarding symptoms disappear at one blow did not avail her, the patient one day brought an association which she felt was in contrast to and a consolation for the idea that her acquaintance was her younger brother.

This association was that her acquaintance was her twin brother. She felt that the acceptance of her acquaintance for analysis threatened her with the loss of the only two advantages which were left to her, discriminated against as she was, viz., that she was the youngest child of her mother, and that she was the only one. The twin brother idea eliminated this threat. As regards the second advantage, she had always been impressed with the thought that her mother became pregnant for her sake alone. This marvelous revolution took place only once, never again, and that for her! And now the mother-transference broke through all at once with the thought that when her analysis was finished I must give up my work as an analyst and must never have any more patients. Promptly thereupon she dreamed next night that as her analysis ended I died. Though by this time another interpretation was also at hand, we at first only understood this much about the twin brother idea: that if by assuming that the acquaintance was her twin brother her privilege of being the only child was preserved, then that brother was herself, her masculine ego. Identifying herself with her acquaintance, she repeated her whole analysis over again and experienced in a new form her old idea that death and birth coincided. Thus, at the end of her analysis she did after all fulfill her old wish to become a man, in all probability because her feminine wish to make her acquaintance her child had failed. (In doing so she recapitulated a long-since analyzed infantile regression from object love to identification.) She felt that everything would begin again from the beginning, and she did actually make a start at this with single symptoms. This brought much important material, which, however, is not relevant here.

The recurring symptoms, after being at first very diffuse and mixed, became concentrated into pure anxiety or anxiety equivalents, such as palpitations and diarrhea. They were accompanied by a longing to be mothered, to be in bed and to be nursed like a little child. She admitted, against strong resistance, to having a fantasy in which it was I who nursed her. It is with this fantasy that the above-indicated material broke through and a complete shift from the father- to the mother-transference was made. And curiously enough, the patient said, it occurred to her that her anxiety was related to this and only to this. At my interpretation that I was her mother she experienced a bottomless, entirely primitive anxiety quite different from all other fears which had already come up in the course of her analysis. It occurred to her that what she was actually so very afraid of was that I should discharge her from analysis and she would have to get along without it. On my pointing out that she had already previously compared leaving analysis with birth, the patient spontaneously made the interpretation of the "twin brother"—an interpretation which I had overlooked: If I am the mother, my office is the uterus. The acquaintance who is also in treatment with me is therefore her twin brother. And now an old fantasy came to the fore again. She had fantasied that she would have liked to bite off her mother's breast while nursing on it, in order to have something to remember her by. The fantasy took this form: I should write a scientific paper about her and she would keep it as a keepsake of the treatment. Thus, she no longer wanted to give me a child; rather I, the mother, should give her one. The following symbolic equation presents itself: *the mother's birth-death—weaning—girlhood—learning to walk—various experiences of a castration character—menstruation—leaving analysis.*

These discoveries, however, did not dissipate the patient's anxiety. On the contrary, it became more intense and did not let her sleep. She felt, too, that all the other not yet solved questions were infinitely irrelevant in comparison with this anxiety, which was the essential thing. She felt it as a finish, a kind of final spurt before the ending of the treatment. It had no object, it was, she said, anxiety-in-itself. For a long while she refused to associate to it and wanted only to be protected and consoled in a motherly fashion. Then she had a vision of two rooms. She was to go from the smaller one through a very narrow door into the bigger one; she defended herself against this amidst most intense anxiety, but was forced to do it by grown-ups who were too strong for her and pushed her through the door. The omnipresent connection with the oedipus complex now once again made its appearance, in that the next anxiety objects were fleas, that is, younger siblings, whose birth she feared. She told me that she had been itching violently and since a few days she had noticed petechiae on her breast and neck. Her earlier birth fantasy, too, was permeated by oedipal ideas and ideas to do with primal scenes. In the big room into which she was forced there were wild grown-ups dancing and shouting (the aunt who was her mother-substitute used to dance and sing in company). She did not want to go in, and hung onto a woman, crawling under her skirt, and would not let go; but something pulled her away by force, the whole room danced, they were wild giants performing grotesque dances. She did not want to leave the woman, who was dark and warm, while the giants were light and cold. Now there came a sensation which lasted only a moment and did not recur, but shook the patient deeply: a sort of pressure on the head—as if a ring should press very hard against the back of her head, giving her an indescribable feeling. The whole thing lasted but an instant and with it the anxiety was gone for good.

Later on childhood experiences were discovered which were points of departure for the particulars of the above-described fantasy, and which belonged to the themes of the oedipus and castration complex. The anxiety pertained to going to say "good night" to guests at parties in the house, at which her aunt used to dance. Occasionally she was even taken from her bed where she was already dreaming, to do this. She had to look on at her father spending the nights with the dancing aunt instead of with her. To demonstrate how birth and oedipus fantasies merge with each other, let us take one more fantasy from the following days: After recalling various poems learned in school the patient came to *Johanna Sebus,** the woman who rescued all from the water but herself perished. This brought to her mind the idea of myself who rescues people by analysis. The goats come across, but Johanna drowns. Had she gotten on a he-goat she too would have gotten across the water. The he-goat would have run away with her and would have put her in a carriage. Then there would have been a mad ride with the father as driver. The ride goes through a tunnel underground; it goes through the water like a Noah's Ark. In the tunnel it is bumpy, the father falls off the goat and is dead. Then he comes back with a woman whom he chases to death, and must thereafter chase about forever as a wild hunter. (The motif here is the patient as the avenger of her mother, in that she kills her father in intercourse. The other woman, who is also killed, is the aunt.)

When asked, the patient related that she had heard that her birth had lasted four days because of acute weakness of labor; finally she had nevertheless been delivered spontaneously without forceps. Her mother had been terribly weakened and had died fourteen days later of an embolism. The patient had read the *Introductory Lectures to Psychoanalysis,* but had heard nothing about Rank's theory.

* A ballade by Goethe.—Trans. note.

*FIVE*

# An Infantile, Preliminary Phase of "Defiance by Lack of Affect"*

THERE is a type of patient, as Ferenczi has quite recently pointed out, who produces no fantasies invested with affect, nor indeed any genuine affect at all, and who speaks of the most agitating experiences and recollections without becoming in the least agitated. A patient of mine uses this lack of affect entirely for purposes of resistance. He expresses his defiance of the rules of analysis by a complete indifference to analysis itself and to the analyst. I have been able to ascertain that this stoical equanimity has always been his most powerful weapon throughout the rest of his life as well. He has been in the habit of tormenting father-substitutes almost to death; he works them into a violent passion in order that he may express his own superiority by remaining entirely without emotion.

The patient came for treatment on account of obsessional characteristics; in spite of numerous sexual relationships he is wholly on the anal-sadistic level of libidinal organization. The sadistic nature of his unemotional defiance is obvious: it is designed to annihilate his father; but the anal roots of this attitude could at first only be inferred by the analyst, until at last the following recollection emerged: In his childhood, when he happened to be engaged in games of an obsessional character and his father told him to come for a walk, he used to elude this order by going to the water-closet and continuing to sit there with perfect equanimity for hours at a time, until his father outside had exhausted his anger and had gone for a walk without him.

The equanimity of this patient is only occasionally disturbed by a feeling of strangeness, akin to depersonalization. When this comes upon him the whole world seems more than ever a matter of indifference, not to be taken seriously;

* First published in *Int. Z. Psa.*, Vol. 11, 1925, pp. 95-96.

indeed, as he makes haste to add, people who insist on taking it seriously seem ridiculous, and so funny that he cannot help laughing at the thought of how they have been taken in by the swindle this world implies. Surely it is ridiculous, he says, to take anything seriously, whatever it may be. For instance, the tragic poet seems to him ridiculous for regarding human suffering as a serious matter; so, too, the busy merchant, for whom success and honor are serious aims; the lover, whose love is a matter of life and death to him, and the analyst, who listens to all manner of nonsense with serious attention. For the patient nothing in this world is serious, or rather (he adds) some things in music are so. When he is playing Beethoven or is engaged on some musical composition, it is a serious matter—possibly, he volunteers, because music is the form of art most remote from reality. To be sure, in order to be a serious matter, music must be engaged in autoerotically, so to speak; public performances are always ridiculous, and above all it is ridiculous to think of any of his own compositions being performed in public. At this point I explain to the patient that this is a manifestation of introversion. Reality and the society of his fellow men are to him ridiculous, while fantasy is serious; the feeling in question amounts to a depreciation of reality and an overestimation of fantasy: he regards the reality principle as ridiculous and the pleasure principle as serious. The patient confirmed this and gave the following specific associations: Most ridiculous of all are the people who interfere with everything, bother him and interrupt his autoerotic fantasies. (He is constantly engaged in obsessional tricks which give him pleasure: reality is simply a great hindrance to this pleasure.) Why will they do it? The analyst is ridiculous (as the patient remarks for the second time), for he interferes with these pleasurable fantasies and, by laying upon him the compulsion to relate them, turns an autistic process into a social one. Finally, the great figures of reality are ridiculous: for instance, Napoleon; to think that Napoleon must either have gone to the closet or else have soiled his trousers! Here we have the source of this remarkable feeling: the child regards grown-up people, with their important doings and their prohibition of everything pleasant, as ridiculous; they behave in accordance with reality and social requirements, and yet all the time they indulge in forbidden pleasure. The infantile preliminary phase of the feeling of depersonalization is the same as that of the "unemotional" defiance: the father who interferes with the child by demanding that he shall go for a serious walk becomes (together with all the real world) ridiculous, for all his rage, when he is powerless before the boy locked in the water-closet, and need no longer be taken seriously.

# SIX

# The Appearance in a Dream
## of a Lost Memory*

A PATIENT came to me for treatment on account of difficulties arising out of his character, which was of the obsessional neurotic type. At the bottom of his trouble was the influence exercised on his mind by repressed sexual observation of the parents in early childhood. The dominating factor in his neurosis was the conflict between the positive and negative sides of the oedipus complex. He had identified himself with each of the two partners in the act he had witnessed, and could not definitely renounce either of the possibilities of pleasure which it presented. In childhood he had identified himself principally with his father, and this had kept him well on the whole; at the same time, from his sixth year onwards, he had had a regular love-relation with a younger sister. Later, however, in the homosexual *milieu* of war service the hitherto repressed mother-identification broke through and he fell ill with every indication of a heavy sense of guilt. The neurosis became manifest in his relations with a mistress who had previously belonged to an officer of a higher rank than himself. I must mention that, when we were analyzing the castration anxiety, the idea of a *vagina dentata* which might swallow the patient up reawakened a peculiar sensation, which he had known in childhood but had forgotten until his analysis. He could not express it in words, but the attempt to do so ran as follows: "with tremendous speed—in feces—downwards."

When the analysis had already reached an advanced stage the patient heard that his younger sister had become engaged to be married. The material which came up as a result of this current event threw a new light on the extraordinarily strong sadism of the patient. This was no longer directed, as we had hitherto

* First published in *Int. Z. Psa.*, Vol. 11, 1925, pp. 226–229.

supposed, towards the two parents. His cruel impulses towards them included not only the idea of killing either of them, in order to make sexual intercourse possible with the other, but also that of coitus itself conceived sadistically. We now found that the sadistic tendencies were also aimed at a brother who existed merely in fantasy. Not only had the patient suddenly torn out the hair of a dog which was very much attached to him, and caused it to bite him, but he had furiously and persistently killed little beetles which crawled out of an ash-pit, and he dreamed that he was thrusting playmates over a precipice. It was suggested that some gynecological illness of his mother, to which he had often referred, might possibly have been a miscarriage, and that his hatred was raging against a brother who had never been born. He then had a very dim memory: he thought he really had been told that he was going to have a brother, and afterwards his mother fell ill.

After another letter from his engaged sister he produced a peculiar "dream of down below" which he recounted with extraordinary affective disturbance and which he associated with the sensation of "with tremendous speed—in feces —downwards"; the whole dream, he said, had been accompanied by this sensation. This dream which the patient, whose mother-tongue is not German, subsequently wrote down may be literally translated thus:

"Suddenly I hear a loud cry. I run in the direction of the sound and open the door of the room whence the cry comes. There I see a naked woman, whose genitals are being bitten by a small white dog, so that they are bleeding. I drive the dog away and chase it. As I overtake it, it turns into a very disgusting kind of beetle, which when I was a child used to live in our ash-pit, but this one is red, swollen with blood, and about thirty centimeters long. I tread on its tail and it wriggles. I leave it there and want to go back to the woman whom I have rescued. But I am in the city and I cannot find my way. I go into a lavatory and there I see in the pan an enormous mass, like a brain. It is a brain or feces. It is dark red in color. As I look at it, it suddenly vanishes. It is so heavy that it pushes down the trap of itself. I suddenly become conscious that I am very ill. I am 'ill of feces'; I have to go to a watering-place and so I go to G., a little watering-place near my home. There is a woman doctor there who can cure people who are 'ill of feces.' When I get there I see written up on a board that three out of five of these patients have died. I dream something else as well: I think, memories of bathing in childhood."

It is not to be wondered at if at first no associations would come to a dream of this sort. But the patient cleared the way to a complete understanding of it by selecting one part to be discussed more in detail: the mass in the lavatory, which looked like a brain. His association to this was a dish of brains cooked with eggs. But it was not brains of this sort: it consisted at the same time of blood and excrement, and it was dark red. He could not get rid of this impression. It was also a loaf of bread, or at any rate something to eat—something between brains, blood, feces, and bread. He still saw the form quite clearly in front of him. It was not like bread because there were excrescences with holes between, all over it, as there are over the cerebrum, but the excrescences and holes were only on one side; the back of it was smooth and covered with something like a dark-red skin. He saw this skin, which was smeared with blood and excrement, fall down. It was a darker red than the mass itself, which was spotted with white. This description could not be misunderstood. "Do you know what the placenta is?" I asked the patient. "Yes, it is what comes away after the child at birth. Why do you ask?" "Do you know what it looks like?" "I have not the slightest idea." I fetched a book with anatomical plates and showed him a placenta. "But that was what I dreamt," he cried; he was tremendously excited and looked upon it as a marvel which he could not explain that he could have dreamt of something which he did not know. I told him that he must have known it once, and that there was nothing so very remarkable in repressed impressions from the subject's third year emerging without change in a dream.

After this discovery it is not difficult to account for the complete absence of associations to the first part of the dream. It was a repetition-dream, which gave us the history of the infantile trauma, whose existence we had already hypothetically inferred from the analysis. His mother had given birth to another son, but he was stillborn. In real life the patient again received a brother in the person of his brother-in-law. The wish in the first part of the dream was: May it end as well as it did the other time! Clearly, on the earlier occasion he had heard his mother cry out and had run into her room. The white dog, which he saw at first, perhaps represented white linen. The fact that a newly hatched beetle, which in the guise of the dog had bitten the mother's genitals and made them bleed, is red and exactly 30 centimeters long, would seem to show that the child saw not only the placenta but the prematurely born fetus. (It could not have been anything else.) He trampled on and crushed this beetle; i.e., he held himself responsible for his little brother's death, because he had wickedly wished it might happen. When he wanted to return to the woman he had rescued (his mother), he was in the city and could not find his way. This meant: "I don't understand what is happening." While he was brooding on it he found "in the closet" the placenta, which made the matter even more mysterious. He probably saw it in some receptacle, with other objects which he must have taken to be feces.

The patient at once confirmed this analysis by producing further associations, which explained the second part of the dream. We now learn the meaning of the "illness of feces." As a child he had often dirtied his knickerbockers, and he was told that only children who were ill did that. And, sure enough, his mother proved to him that to have a child meant a bad illness. He himself bore not children but feces. When he noticed in the dream that he had an "illness of feces" he was identifying himself with the mother in childbirth. Afterward his mother did actually go to get well at the watering-place which, later in childhood, he constantly yearned to visit and which he went to in the dream, thus putting himself in every respect in his mother's place. The woman doctor who cured the "feces-illness" was an old cook, who used to play with his genitals, and probably also washed him when he had made himself dirty—thus curing his "feces-illness." The element in the dream, "Three out of five have died," meant that of the five brothers and sisters (besides his younger sister he had two elder ones, so that, counting the untimely-born infant, they were five altogether), three were to die; only he and the younger sister, with whom he had had a sexual relation, were to survive. (Or possibly he disregarded the elder sisters and meant that his mother, the baby, and the younger sister were to die, and he and his father to survive.)

As we should expect, the further associations to the "feces-illness" led straight to the castration complex. He had anticipated that his mother would die at the watering-place. If, identifying himself with her, he wanted a child from his father, he himself, like his mother, would have to die. He had been threatened that he would die if he dirtied his knickerbockers. Hence the symbolic equation *to be "ill of feces"—to have children—to die—to be castrated.* Once he was given a big sailor-cap like his sisters', and he made a great fuss, because he did not want to be a girl, and ended by throwing it into the water-closet. Thus, if one is identified with the mother, one catches the illness from the father. As long as he threw the sailor-cap (the instrument of castration), like the beetles, straight into the closet, in order to remain a male and like his father, he kept well. Indeed, in his seventeenth year he brought about a repetition of the primal scene by having coitus with a nursemaid in the presence of a little child, that is, in complete identification with his own father. When, during his war service, the temptation was too great for him and he found himself under two kindly superior officers in contrast to many hostile ones, his homosexuality broke through and, in his longing to have a child, he regressed to the old mother-identification, which brought with it a new form of illness; he immediately developed an obsessional neurosis which, inasmuch as it belongs to the anal-sadistic level of organization, really did represent an "illness of feces." What wonder that, when he longed to be cured, he thought it could only be by way of identification with the father, and therefore in his dream substituted a woman for the male physician who was treating him.

The patient never had a feeling that he remembered his mother's miscarriage, which we inferred from the analysis and supposed him to have witnessed. But we had a whole series of indications and indirect confirmations of our hypothesis.

## SEVEN

# Introjection and the Castration Complex[*]

### I

In 1921 Pfeifer called attention to vicissitudes undergone by the libido after a disappointment in love during the course of an analysis, and called for a discussion of this theme.[1] After an abrupt rejection by his sweetheart, which forced him to give up the love object, his patient made all imaginable attempts to recover the gratificatory situation, in the course of which the movements of his libido, as was to be expected, stood under the sign of regression. The most far-reaching regression to objectless primitive narcissism was followed by oral, anal, and genital-incestuous trends, representing brief recapitulations of the entire development of the libido. The patient first reacted to his object loss with depressive mourning, with complete loss of interest, suicidal thoughts, insomnia, and refusal of nourishment. The first nourishment which he finally accepted had to be liquid. On subsequent days various anal symptoms came to the fore; later on, infantile incestuous wishes toward his sister and cousins were rekindled, and finally a positive homosexual transference to the analyst was also reinforced.

In these pages I propose to report a case which, in the first place, fully confirms Pfeifer's observations, but which, owing to the nature of the precipitating disappointment in love, made possible a detailed study of the subsequent vicissitudes of the libido and thereby the uncovering of the infantile development, and which finally led to a full analytic clarification of the neurosis. Since it was a case of hysteria with prominent oral symptoms, the relationship of the genital to the oral libido could be well observed, and the symptoms, which were strati-

[*] First published in *Int. Z. Psa.*, Vol. 11, 1925, pp. 261–296.
[1] See S. Pfeifer, "Liebesenttaeuschung waehrend der Analyse," *Int. Z. Psa.*, Vol. 7, 1921.

fied according to the depth of regression, could be studied in their relation to one another; insight was gained into the relationships between depression and hysteria—that is, identification and object love—and the interesting observation could be made of two series of object relations running side by side, one taking the form of identification, the other that of object love.

## II

The patient, a young woman of twenty-eight, was in analysis for eighteen months. The "disappointment" which was to attain so crucial a significance occurred in the eighth month of treatment. From the preceding period only what is most indispensable will be communicated here.

The patient came to treatment with hysterical symptoms. She suffered from an irremovable fear of making a fool of herself and blushing, and this actually happened to her frequently. Thus, she felt extremely insecure in the presence of superiors, for instance at examinations, and she often did in fact behave very awkwardly. She was most uncertain where manual skills were required. Besides anxiety, or in place of it, she would vomit or have diarrhea, occasionally of such intensity that she had to withdraw from the examination. The urge to urinate and defecate, as well as fear of these, encroached particularly on the patient's social contacts. Her insecurity compelled her to make continuous comparisons with other, healthy people, and laid the foundations for an intense feeling of inferiority. But fear of disgracing herself in some terrible way completely dominated the original clinical picture.

The patient was the fourth and youngest child of a well-to-do merchant. The siblings, a brother twelve years older than herself, a sister, six years older, and a brother, four years older, came from the father's first marriage and were thus only half-siblings of the patient. Her own mother died two weeks after her birth. Thus, in her unconscious she considered herself "an exception," who had the right to expect of fate a substitute for the early loss of her mother. After having been fed by her mother during her first days of life, she was brought up on the bottle without a wet nurse. Until her fourth year, an aunt, a sister of her mother, took her mother's place. This aunt, whom the patient preferred on every occasion to her siblings, was somewhat peculiar. We shall hear more about her. She was followed by a governess, who remained in the house for eleven years. This person was a strict and extremely anal character, who compelled the children to the most painful cleanliness and punctuality, and forced on them all kinds of compulsory regimentations, managing thoroughly to spoil their most innocent pleasures. Throughout the time the patient was very ambivalent toward her. This governess stayed in the house until the patient was fifteen. In the first period of the analysis the father was little talked about. The patient had an intense admiration, but one not free from fear, for her twelve-years-older-brother, who was a quiet, inward-turned man, suffering from a chronic illness. With the other two siblings, fights and scenes of jealousy were the order of the day.

To begin with, in the analysis the patient's behavior was in keeping with her general insecurity. She was shy, unaccustomed to talking, afraid she might say too much or too little or the wrong thing; she wanted to be reassured by the analyst and to be told that she was a worth-while person. She was afraid that she might behave ineptly, and would be punished for it by the analyst, thus identifying him with the governess who used to spank her. Behind this façade there lurked an enormous defiance which occasionally kept the patient silent for hours. In her long withholding of material, in her fear of punishment for it, in her explosive giving-out-too-much, and the like, anal traits were perceptible. An intense exhibitionism manifested itself at first negatively in her external behavior: the patient kept her hand in front of her face in order not to be seen, had dreams of inhibited nakedness, etc. Several dreams and unequivocal associations made clear to the analyst, long before he could discuss this with the patient, that the disgrace which threatened her if she should exhibit herself was the discovery of her lack of a penis. Remarkably enough all her insecurity disappeared in one particular situation, namely when she was acting on the stage. She appeared repeatedly in amateur performances; in these she was altogether self-assured and secure, and had the feeling that only on the stage was she herself, while in everyday life she was play-acting.

Her manifest shyness corresponded to a marked sexual inhibition. She was a virgin. Her relations with men regularly suffered the same fate: she chose men who were either tied up erotically, or such as did not reciprocate her feelings in the least. She often used not to notice the coolness of the man at all for a remarkably long time, and then suddenly she would be horribly disappointed. On the other hand, she noticed just as little if a man was interested in her. Sexual approaches, to which she was repeatedly exposed, came to her entirely unexpectedly, and never from a man from whom she wanted it. Indeed, the ideas "sexual approach" and "unexpected surprise" seemed to her to belong together. After such surprises she would withdraw with a reinforced longing for the unreachable objects. Her persistently unhappy love helped to nourish her feelings of inferiority. A particular interest in cripples, and in the care of the blind, pointed to a strong castration complex.

The transference did not present a unified picture. The father, both brothers, above all the punishing governess, and other people in her childhood, too, were reincarnated in the analyst. Finally, the older brother, who had consoled her in her childhood, became the leading model in the transference. Her unhappy choices in love also seemed to follow his model. A fairly deep disturbance of her positive transference brought with it the interpretation of her penis envy, although at first this was made in connection with memories of experiences with exhibitionists, and did not touch upon her ideas of castration. The first mention of the penis in analysis had an outright traumatic effect. The patient immediately forgot the interpretation and responded with weeks of resistance, in which she made strong attempts to deny the reality of analysis and the analyst. It was very painful for the patient on arrival and departure to see the analyst and to be thus convinced of his existence. At the same time a neurotic hunger made its first appearance.

Still under the influence of this resistance, the patient fell violently in love with a young man whom she met at a party. She transferred to him all the libido she withdrew from the analysis. Nevertheless, it was a success for the analysis that she permitted him to kiss her and enjoyed it for the first time in her life. He lived in another town and left Berlin soon, but promised to return in a few months. Although he did not write, the patient pinned all her expectations on him and hoped that he, whom she had seen but twice, would marry her.

In the meanwhile, the analysis discovered repressed memories of sexual scenes with the younger brother, in whom the patient acquired her penis envy; these we will discuss later in detail. This coincided with the date of the expected return of the patient's friend. He did not come. The patient asked acquaintances, and learned that the man did not take the brief adventure as seriously as she. This was the disappointment mentioned above which compelled the patient once more to withdraw her libido which she had brought to the object with such difficulty.

### III

Those forms of reaction which Pfeifer's case passed through appeared here also in quick succession. Their subsequent analysis, which took months, provoked in part a second and slower repetition of them.

The patient's first reaction to her object loss was a state of mourning, which may be described as a transitory melancholia, since it fulfilled all the criteria of this illness. The patient sank into a low mood, lost her appetite, reproached herself continuously, and expressed suicidal ideas. At first, she seemed to have no interest whatever in the analysis. Her self-reproaches were aimed precisely at this lack of interest, activating old ideas of inferiority: she worked at nothing, only did her job mechanically and without thought, had not achieved anything recently, etc. This latter self-reproach gave a hint to the analyst. A question as to why she felt that she had done no work sufficed to reveal the accusations against her object which were hidden in her self-reproaches: *he* had occupied her whole mind so much that she was left with no other interest. The patient grasped, with violent affect, that her self-reproaches were directed against the object, with whom she identified herself, though we did not as yet know how and why.

When her mourning disappeared, other regressive phenomena came to the fore. The patient began to vomit and felt like the continually vomiting infant of an acquaintance. The vomiting diminished, but the regression to the infantile stage was not yet overcome. In a children's home which she visited, she asked for milk, and had the wish to drink up the children's milk as well. She wanted to sleep all day long, or to take a warm bath, and had vivid imaginings about the warm baths of her childhood.

With the longing for motherly care, there arose a strong impulse to make up for everything that had been withheld from her as a child. This was particularly so in the oral field. She imagined that all the cakes whose enjoyment the governess had ever forbidden her were now spread out in front of her, whole mountains of cakes, and she was allowed to eat them. It was easy to see that the kindly counterpart of the governess, who permits anything, was her older brother and therefore the analyst. She wailed in the analytic hour to be sympathized with and consoled. When she did not succeed in this, she made transparent allusions to how consoling and helpful she herself was.

The flow into the transference of the libido which had been freed was noticeable in other things too. The patient had the (not unfounded) feeling that in the months of her infatuation the analysis had run dry, and was only now once more becoming serious, and of interest to her. In her resistance she reproached herself—though these reproaches were actually aimed at the analyst—for her hitherto unsuccessful analysis. Her silence, which she rationalized as a persistent tiredness, turned out to be defiance against the analyst, who refused to show her consoling tenderness. It became increasingly clear that she expected an oral present from him. In the analytic hour, she experienced hunger more frequently and intensively than before, and longed for sweets and cakes. Cakes were what her father used to give her, and what her governess used to forbid. When, by her father's order, her sister was given particularly good and plentiful food, because of a mild tubercular pulmonary infection, the patient's jealousy knew no bounds. The food which she expected from the father (the analyst) meant in her unconscious a child. Later on, her hunger became so intense that on her way to or from the analysis she had to buy herself cakes. Simultaneously, diarrhea and vomiting appeared. It soon became clear that in these symptoms wishes from various levels of libido organization found their expression. Since the transference did not gratify these wishes, the patient became dissatisfied with analyst and analysis: they did not succeed, she thought, in catching "the unconscious." This unconscious she perceived as something slippery and soft, which ran away and withdrew "into the inside" when one wanted to grasp it. Later on she recognized in it the "fecal column" and with it, the fecal meaning of cake: they had to be chocolate cakes or other dark cakes. In a sudden vision, she saw these cakes as outright piles of feces. Finally there emerged a memory of an attempt at coprophagy in her early childhood, which was thwarted by the grownups. Her neurotic nausea could be traced, to begin with, to the repressed wish to drink urine.[2] The nausea also often appeared on the first day of menstruation, that is, at a time when she was as a rule excited and filled with feelings of inferiority. This happened particularly when she was rinsing her mouth, and occasionally when she was drinking water. It became clear that water meant for the unconscious of the patient her own menstrual blood mixed with urine, which she was to drink so as to conceive a child without a man. Her feelings of inferiority during menstruation suggested that the child which she longed for in fantasy took not only the form of milk, urine, and feces, but also of the penis. In prepuberty she had heard a sexual theory which included "cutting open the abdomen," and which she did not like, and had asked her older brother about it. He had reassuringly explained to her the falsity of those theories, and had told her something about the "seed." Thereafter, in keeping with her repressive tendencies, she had imagined that children grew in flowerpots. But there arose spontaneously a very vague memory from earlier times, which showed that for her having children was somehow connected with eating: a maid, who later had a child and was dismissed for this, had given the patient chocolate; she thought it might have been a bribe to be silent about a secret she had seen.

These memories brought a brief repetition of her infantile sexual inquiries. Her ever-renewed complaints of being no good at anything proved to be determined not only by her feeling that she was castrated, but also by her infantile inability to solve the sexual riddle by herself. Her restlessness, her lack of understanding, her confused train of associations, all represented a repetition of the sexual unclarity of her childhood.[3] But one day as she was saying about some people that they "came from there," she associated the word "seed," and then for a while she was compelled to talk in doggerel rhyme until she herself found the solution of this peculiar symptom. This was that in the last hour she had complained that what she was saying was without *rhyme* or reason. The answer she had got was "It depends on you. You can do differently." Now she brought

[2] Much later we discovered an infantile sexual theory, according to which the woman drinks the man's urine.

[3] Cf. S. Freud, "Recollection, Repetition and Working Through," *Coll. Pap.*, Vol. II, London, Hogarth, 1948.

rhymed words. The meaning was: "I can make a rhyme about it all right: the children came from seeds." *

This break-through of genital libido made finding a new object possible, and this, like the first, was undoubtedly an act of defiance against the analyst. The new object was a man who, resembling her older brother externally, was married and suffering from the consequences of an earlier illness. The patient's infatuation with him was as sudden and as intense as it had been with her previous object. We shall have more to say later about the course of this love.

## IV

It was only in the further course of the analysis that the meaning of this rapid repetition of libido development could be properly understood. The patient, in keeping with her inclination to action, produced renewed regressions. There were "melancholic" phases with brief periods of depressive moods and occasional mild paranoid symptoms, such as an inclination to have ideas of reference and motor hallucinations—these latter being, incidentally, the most frequent hallucinations of all to appear in non-psychotics as well. There were also anal periods and unalloyed incestuous ones. All these phases were naturally not sharply separated. Some of the material I shall proceed to give appeared earlier in the analysis, but could only now be fitted into its proper place.

We must approach the situation from two sides: from that of hunger, and from that of penis envy and the castration complex.

The patient's hunger persisted stubbornly for several months, even after she had gone through the described affective period. Its intensity fluctuated, reacting with extraordinary vehemence to partial analytic solutions. The time of its appearance also fluctuated. At first it appeared immediately after the analytic hour, with a feeling of disappointment, which was easily related to her ungratified transference wishes; later it appeared at all times of the day. Finally, we succeeded in forcing it into the analytic hour. The object of her desire to eat also varied: while during the time of her most intense hunger it made no difference to the patient what she ate, at other times she especially craved for sweets and cakes, milk and chocolate, eggs, or particularly fat meat.

At first the hunger did not vanish, though the symbolic equation *object of hunger—proof of affection—milk—urine—sperm—child—feces—penis,* the validity of which had already been recognized, was discussed in detail and repeatedly confirmed; but the intensity of the hunger and its choice of object were amenable to influence, and whatever term of the equation was being activated at the time gave rise to transitory symptoms. In view of the strong latent anal character of

---

* What the patient said in German for "came from there" was *"daher kamen";* and the German for "seed" (and "semen") is *"Samen."*—Trans. note.

the patient, the origins of which will be further discussed later on, it was no surprise that this became particularly clear on the occasion when she recognized the longed-for cakes as piles of feces. At that time she not only withheld psychic material, to burst forth with it later on all at once, but for the first and only time forgot to pay her fee punctually, and then left the money by mistake with her friend.

To begin with, only vague surmises could be made about the relationship between the patient's hunger and her identification with the lost object. One day, as she was speaking about having once wanted to drink away the children's milk, she was gripped with violent fear of her hunger, which set in with full intensity, and which she suddenly personified and separated from herself. It was not she who had the hunger and wanted to eat; the hunger had her and wanted to devour her. The hunger appeared to her as a huge dragon with horrible jaws, who was so black that he darkened the sun. The hunger was the Minotaur; he, too, lived in a labyrinth, in her intestinal labyrinth. He dwelt there as a man-eating parasite; he ate everything she ate and thus devoured her from inside; she must eat continuously in order to feed this insatiable creature, otherwise he would devour her bowels. Thus her hunger appeared to her as a dangerous monster, which threatened her now from the outside, now from the inside (from her intestines). His threats came discontinuously, in a certain rhythm which she experienced acoustically as a rising and falling roar. In the "crescendo," which corresponded to a spatial closeness, something had to be put into his mouth; then he would withdraw in the "decrescendo."

The patient recognized relatively easily that this monster which was feeding on her in her intestines, represented a tapeworm and that the tapeworm stood for feces and child. She said that her father used occasionally to give her sweets and fruits; when one swallows the kernel of fruit, a tree grows in one's stomach.[4] The nature of the monster—which, after all, had threatened at first to penetrate into her as well as to devour her—showed, too, that the object which she desired in the shape of hunger had not only the meaning of feces and child but of penis. Later on, the hunger appeared to her no longer as a dragon, but as a dog. The patient had already spoken about sexual observations which she had made on dogs, which represented in her consciousness observations made on exhibitionists (and—as we shall soon relate—on her brother). Hunger, however, was not a common dog; he was rather the dog in Hans Christian Andersen's story "The Tinderbox"—which was actually a set of three dogs, each with eyes bigger than the others'. Those of the first dog were as big as saucers, those of the second as big

---

[4] The story of the apple of the Garden of Eden made a great impression on the patient. When she was once jokingly told about an apple that it came from there, she ate it up secretly. More about this later on.

as a mill-wheel, and those of the third as big as clock-towers. Those towers the patient imagined to be steep and pointed, like church towers. (That this erection symbolism represented by the eyes made such an impression on her pointed to visual observations on her part.) This erection-dog lived in the patient's bowels and wanted to be given food there, or rather, wanted, through incessant eating, to be always entering the intestine anew, to dwell there as feces, penis, and child. One more step had to be made. If the hunger-dog was a threatening penis, then it was also a man who threatened with his penis. As a last interpretation of the patient's hunger, which had still to be fitted into the symbolic equation, unequivocal cannibalistic tendencies appeared. These referred entirely to her younger brother, with whom the patient had never got on well, and who had died when she was twenty-one. The patient took his death with relative equanimity, but reproached herself for this. For beneath this manifest equanimity, she unconsciously celebrated a triumphal feast, at which the dead brother was devoured. And now a whole series of earlier, not-understood symptoms was remembered and analyzed. The fat which the patient also wanted to eat proved to be the fat of the corpse. It is no accident that at the beginning of the analysis she had exemplified her feelings of inferiority by comparing herself with a woman physician of her acquaintance who worked as a pathologist and anatomist. Now her long-standing affective attitude toward the legend of *Antigone* also became understandable. When she had tried to talk about it in analysis, she had mixed up *Antigone* with *Andromeda,* who was threatened by a devouring dragon, and she could not in the least remember the content of the legend. Only now was this forgetting understandable and thereby eliminated: *Antigone,* by burying her brother, had prevented him from being devoured by dogs and birds.

We shall stop here for a moment to fill in the material belonging to the castration complex which we have already touched on. From the beginning this complex stood clearly in the foreground of the patient's analysis. We have already seen that the main content of her fear of disgracing herself was the fear that her lack of a penis might be discovered. As a child, she used to urinate standing up. She was interested in, indeed she liked, cripples of all sorts, particularly the blind. During her periods of menstruation she was depressed and extraordinarily irritable. We need not report here any further material, which again and again yielded the familiar idea that originally both sexes possessed a penis, but that the man robbed the woman of hers either in intercourse or as punishment for masturbation. It need only be added that the patient also came into analysis with the complaint that she had a compulsion to look at men's genitals, and then felt an impulse to grab at them. This proved to be a weakened expression of the impulse to tear out the penis and thus to recover it.

The patient's repression of her intense exhibitionism also fitted in with her fear of disgrace. As has been said, to begin with she held her hand in front of her face all the time in order not to be seen, and she had, too, a great liking for acting on the stage. To be photographed, and better still—as once happened— to be painted, was the greatest pleasure she experienced as a child. Wherein the nature of her bliss in stage acting actually lay became clear through the following transitory symptom, the analysis of which awakened an important memory. When this sort of topic was discussed, the patient had an intense urge to urinate. She had long suffered from enuresis. Her younger brother taught her that one can hold one's urine by pressing the hand against the genital. She also used this method in her occasional actual masturbations. In "displacing upwards" in her analysis, she put her hand on her face instead of her genital. Her erythrophobia too was rooted in this genitalization of the face. The patient's need to urinate increased steadily during several following analytic hours. It reached its climax in the hour in which she related how she had been painted; she had to interrupt the analysis to go and urinate. She came back looking very much ashamed, as though she had completely disgraced herself. From then on, the symptom did not occur *in* the analysis any more, but *before* it, in that the patient took care to urinate just before the hour, in order to prevent the repetition of such an embarrassment. Her impulse to repeat the infantile enuresis disappeared when it was made clear to her that the real aim of her intense exhibitionistic strivings was that she should be seen while urinating. But then the observer could not fail to notice that she had no penis, and would laugh at her, and that would be the great disgrace. The patient supported this interpretation by associating to "theater," "monkey-" and "dog-theater," * and finally produced the following memory:

Her first appearance on the stage occurred when she was only about two years old. It was at a wedding, and she was dressed as Cupid. She was given breeches to wear and two wings, and recited a little verse about how her power united the couple. This magnificent gratification of her exhibitionism was the source of her love for the stage and of the feeling of absolute security which she experienced when she was on it in contrast to actual life. In her unlimited narcissism, she had at the time believed that she was not only *dressed* as a boy, but actually *was* a boy. As a result, she had as a child considered, logically enough, that sex was something which changed from time to time on festive occasions. Naturally, just as a change from girl to boy seemed possible to her, so did a change from boy to girl. This, to her mind, was connected with urinating.

Already, early in the patient's analysis, un-understandable fragments of early infantile memories had cropped up about this. Now a memory came to the

---

* German *"Affentheater"* = farcical situations in real life; and *"Hundetheater"* = (possibly) a wretched kind of show. But this may be a made-up word.—Trans. note.

fore, that once some boys who were competing at spitting out cherry stones told her that girls could not do that. We could now establish the connection with the old material, and, behind her experiences with exhibitionists and dogs, which have already been mentioned, we were able to reconstruct those totally repressed scenes in which her femininity came most painfully to her consciousness. It happened that sometime in her fourth year, while the family were on a trip, she shared a bedroom with her younger brother. In the morning he noticed her urinating into the chamberpot, made fun of her to her greatest dismay, demonstrated how one should urinate, and showed her that she could not do it. On another similar occasion, the same brother gave her a drastic piece of sexual enlightenment accompanied by the demonstration of a penis and a bloody bandage, which she, however, immediately and completely repressed. Instead of the repressed, there appeared in the analysis characteristic substitutive ideas. She imagined that her brother had looked out or pointed out through the window, in front of which there stood an uncannily big tree; the brother himself was at the same time uncannily small, much smaller than ordinarily. As an introduction to this, she had a memory of a hotel room, with all its details, which she could not identify. The plasticity of this memory was the more striking since as a rule the patient was unable to describe what she saw, even rooms she had inhabited for years. The breaking through of this inhibition to look pointed to the voyeuristic character of the forgotten scene. The affect of frightened surprise, which—according to the memory that emerged—accompanied both scenes at the time, and furthermore, the total inability to act which followed them, suggest that the patient had already on some previous occasion discovered the existence of the penis, but had successfully repressed her knowledge. For fright and surprise, as we know, are indications of an arousal of the repressed out of repression. Even if she had attempted to defend herself against the disturbing scenes by new repression, her experience of the reality of castration shook her belief that sex could change, and thereby laid the foundations of her lasting sense of inferiority.

As was to be expected, the patient had fought with all her might against accepting this humiliating fact. As we know, she forgot both scenes and replaced them by a later memory, which assured her of exactly their opposite: the same brother had showed her how, in order to combat enuresis, she ought to press her hand on her genital organ, and had thus seduced her into masturbation. In this, she had not thought of the difference between the genitals, and had assumed that she urinated just like her brother. She had imitated him in his enuresis, his way of fighting it, and in masturbation. Thus she had identified herself with him in these things, denying her castration (as, for instance, when she urinated standing up).

Her relations to her brother remained tense till his death. In her unconscious, she never fully believed the new discoveries she had had to make through him, and in the deepest strata of her mind she never gave up her conviction that a change of sex was possible. Indeed, we discovered that she had come into analysis *with the unconscious expectation that here she would be made into a man again;* and when she found that these hopes could not be fulfilled she was disappointed and angry. (This was seen in her equating the analyst with her younger brother, and having castration wishes against both.) But the patient had to prevent this relation of rivalry with her brother from becoming too clear. It was noticeable that on the very days when her recollections of being shamed by her brother appeared in succession, she produced a special hatred against her sister, with whom she otherwise got along fairly well, and picked quarrels with her on the slightest occasion. We know that she had always had a competitive attitude toward this sister in relation to her father and her older brother. This hatred of her competitor could quite inconspicuously include her hatred of her younger brother as well. This displacement was facilitated by the circumstance that at later marriage ceremonies, and other occasions, the sister repeatedly played the breeches-wearing role, while the patient had to be satisfied with the role of the onlooker. Memories of envy also emerged from the time when her sister had already developed breasts, but she had not. She equated the developed breasts with the penis, once more condensing her penis envy with her milk envy.

Environment and sexual curiosity took care that the patient's repression of the disagreeable experiences and her identification with the more fortunate communicator of them (her brother) did not last. Already at the age of seven she had the first of her above-mentioned encounters with exhibitionists; more followed at puberty. These obliged her to convince herself definitely of the existence of the penis and its erigibility. The memories of these encounters, which were also in part repressed, emerged very early and served as screen memories for the still earlier scenes with her brother. She gradually managed to become reconciled to the fact of the difference between the sexes; but the narcissistic wound and her defiant thirst for revenge persisted in her unconscious. Thus, filled with envy, she had also attempted to identify herself with the exhibitionists because they had a penis. Her own exhibitionism—which mounted transitorily to a point at which she felt that she had lost a piece of her clothes or underlinen—was on this pattern: "What these men may do, I may also do." These identifications also explained her symptom of urinatory urge.

Between the brother and the exhibitionists was interpolated the memory of the frequent and guilt-laden observation of urinating dogs. Thus it was confirmed that her exhibitionistic instinctual aim was to urinate in front of observers, that her inhibition and shyness corresponded to her certainty that she could not do it so successfully as her brother, and that her anxiety corresponded to the fear that her castration might become patent. This ambivalence also disclosed the meaning of her erythrophobia. A long-drawn-out analysis of this symptom, carried on in the face of violent resistances, showed that her blushing was a condensation of these two opposed tendencies. On the one hand, blushing was a "displacement upward" of the erection. She had ideas of women with red Jacobian caps, revolutionary and violent in their behavior. On the other, it was the great bleeding after castration (her associations were, bleeding from the head—bloodletting from the abdomen—the revolutionary women are guillotined —bleeding to death in menstruation). We shall only add that behind the idea of the "revolutionary women," too, there lay her sisterly rival who wore the breeches and who was to be castrated. Here, once more, in the deepest strata we have an identification with the younger brother. A characteristic detail from one of her encounters with an exhibitionist was by its nature remembered only considerably later. This was that the man had asked her to put his penis into her mouth. Under such circumstances it is understandable that her first menstruation mobilized her entire guilt feeling, and that she should have considered herself incurably ill. Her subsequent enlightenment as to the true nature of the bleeding could, needless to say, in no way alter the persistence of the already described menstrual symptoms.

The person, however, toward whom her fear of castration was directed to begin with, was a mother-substitute, the governess, and behind her, the aunt. Being castrated meant for the patient first of all a decrease of the ability to urinate —and according to the law of talion, there is no doubt that the guilt must have been one of urinating. And now, the memory of a scene emerged with all the vehemence of an affect suddenly liberated from long repression. She was six years old, and was learning to write, and she wrote the word "jackass." At this, she wet her pants, obviously because of the rebellion implied by her behavior; and after that she had a terrible fear of punishment by castration. "I will drive this out of you," the governess would say, and the patient had no doubt that "this" could only mean the penis. When, on one occasion, she wetted herself in public and dirtied a chair, she was told that a man would come to take away her money for the stained chair. Another time, when she told the governess that a young uncle had touched her genitals (we shall hear more about this), the governess answered, "One gets ill from that." She said the same when the patient stayed too long on the toilet, or when—following her brother's example— she masturbated. Occasionally the governess would also beat her in solemn style after sundry preparatory ceremonies. The analysis showed that being beaten meant castration to the patient. She also had the masturbation fantasy "a child is being beaten." We could confirm here too—even if not in all its stages—Freud's description of the genesis of this fantasy. It developed as follows: "My father (the governess) shall beat my brother (the sister). He (she) will beat me as a punishment for this wicked wish. He (she) will beat me for pleasure." Later on she reacted with defense and anxiety to a tender approach by the man she loved, which seemed to her to threaten her genital integrity. She feared defloration with its flow of blood as a renewed castration. When the storm of ambivalent libido thus evoked discharged itself in masturbatory activity, she had fantasies which corresponded to the revival of her infantile masturbation. She pictured to herself a scene of rape in a brothel, in which she—the untouched girl—was first beaten and then cohabited with. Later on the beating was omitted and the brothel changed into an institution for crippled and blind girls. The patient's masochistic masturbation fantasy thus betrayed its secret meaning: she wished to be castrated by the sexual act. She appears, therefore, to resign herself to her feminine role, but only because by extensive identification with the castrator she can partake in his masculine sadistic pleasure. She always masturbated with her clitoris and never with her vagina. The patient's fear that if she withheld the correct material the analyst would beat her—as the governess had done before—thus proved to be a fear of being castrated; in the final analysis it was this anxiety which made her keep her hand protectively in front of her face. Behind this castration anxiety, however, was hidden the wish to be made into a boy by the analysis and at the same time actively to castrate the analyst. But the patient believed that she had invited the fate of castration not only through the sins of masturbation and of enuresis and the withholding of feces which were related to it. Her fear of becoming blind and her zeal in helping the blind, as well as her already described inhibition in observing, showed clearly that important scenes of voyeurism, which must be older than those already discovered, had succumbed to repression. This was also indicated by her early developed overpowerful exhibitionism, by the compulsion to look at men's genitals, and above all, by the rhythmic restlessness—the crescendo–decrescendo—which she ascribed to her "hunger-dog." The scene with her uncle, who at an early age touched her genitals, could not have been the ultimate source of her great feeling of guilt either, though several details bespoke its reality. The uncle's attack —just like the brother's scorn—came utterly unexpectedly to her. Until her analysis, the patient reacted to every physical approach by men with the same paralyzing and dumbfounded surprise (surprise = paralysis = castration). In reproducing the scene with the uncle, she stressed particularly her white (innocent) dress, and his dark black suit, the good and the bad principle. The song about the white and the black lamb ("and when the child does not want to sleep, then comes the black one and bites it"), which was—according to a very early childhood memory—sung to her once, confirmed her in her belief that the surprising black thing was the castrating power; but it also indicated the anxiety-laden observation of an adult's pubic hair. This contrast of black and white brought forth early memories which made her aunt, who was the predecessor of her governess, into the castrating person. Black is night, white the nightgown. To the accompaniment of intense anxiety, which was manifested in palpitations and an urge to defecate and which broke through only gradually, the patient had a memory of herself as a child, seeing from her bed how her aunt got up in the night and went about some mysterious business. There emerged in her memory the picture of her aunt leaning over her and her overdeveloped and anxiety-arousing breasts suddenly hanging just above her, as though she meant to do something to her with them. The same aunt was supposed—and vague memory traces of this were met with in the analysis—to have danced in the presence of the children, while undressing, half-naked, or perhaps completely naked (the black lamb?) in front of the mirror. From objective sources we were told that this aunt, who suffered from "nerves" and insomnia, used to wake the patient's sister, who was at the time at most ten years old, to play cards with her in the night. On one occasion, the sister had fainted, and so the father heard about it. An association of the patient's showed that this hearsay story coincided with the memory of the aunt's over-large breasts. It is possible that her sister's fainting aroused in her the impression that killing equaled castration. It is, however, more probable that yet other experiences with this aunt aroused her feelings of guilt and fear of castration. But even this does not make the assumption of an even earlier sexual observation on a man superfluous, since the memory of the too-big breast in its turn clearly betrays a knowledge about erection. This expectation was confirmed. With great difficulty and much uncertainty there finally arose, first without any details, a very hazy memory that as a small child, quite early in life, she had once seen her father's penis (the black sheep) and had been tremendously scared by it. This observation was probably the true cause of her excessive seeing-inhibition and her feeling of guilt. Much later, at first without any sense of remembering, came the association that she asked at the time what it was and was told that it was none of her business and that one did not ask such things. Later still, we were able to obtain complete certainty as to the reality of this scene. It turned out, first as a reconstruction, then with a sense of remembering, that the scene took place on a Sunday morning during a walk with her father, when she was about two years old. The father, disregarding her presence, had urinated. This attracted the interest of the little observer; she may have reached for his penis and asked what it was; and then, as we have heard, followed the rebuff. The significance of this experience will only be able to be completely appreciated later on.

It is possible that besides this, the maid who linked for the patient's mind the idea of sexuality with that of eating had given her the opportunity to make an early observation of intercourse, since the material makes such an observation probable. But nothing certain could be established in this respect. A much later association of the patient seemed also to recall that on that exciting night in which her aunt's threatening big breast had leaned over her, she had had occasion to see her father's penis as well. The nature of this association as a screen memory for a primal scene or primal fantasy was clear: her father and her aunt showed each other their genitals, he the penis, she the breast. She (the patient) spied on this and would therefore be castrated. The Sunday morning scene must have taken place earlier. The aunt's nightly activities aroused her repressed memory of that scene and gave rise to the idea that her father gave the aunt what he withheld from the daughter. This was the basic idea of the patient's oedipus complex. Experiences with the maid may have provided a basis in reality for this primal fantasy.

The screen memory of the overdeveloped threatening breasts shows us that— if we equate the threatening with the threatened—the patient's penis envy coincided in its roots with her milk envy, with which we are already acquainted, for, as we know, she considered herself handicapped for life because fate had robbed her of her mother and so of the mother's breast. The loss of the breast proved to be a sort of predecessor of castration, as has been described by Staerke and Alexander. To this we shall return later on. But it should be mentioned at once that the patient's penis envy later on hid itself, among other things, behind her envy of her growing sister's breast; that her sexual curiosity was directed almost entirely toward mother-figures (for instance, toward the aunt who danced in front of the mirror); that she remembered how, even later on, she spied lustfully on her governess when the latter undressed (the observation that she had no penis either gave her satisfaction); and finally that although she felt that the threat of castration came from male persons, (her younger brother, exhibitionists, the deflorating sexual partner), she also felt that it came, and perhaps primarily, from the side of women.

It is natural that the patient, having these attitudes, wanted in revenge to castrate the man. It should be briefly mentioned that once, after having been with her friend, and having feared that she might lose her virginity, she suddenly had the idea that should it come to intercourse, she must rob him of his penis during it. Later, after she had parted with this friend, and was sitting alone and deserted in the theater watching a performance of Hebbel's "Nibelungen," she had to break out in loud sobs at the moment when the dead Siegfried was brought in and Kriemhilde threw herself over the body; immediately afterwards she felt extremely ashamed about her lack of control. It was easy to find the source of her pain in what she and Kriemhilde had in common: both were

robbed of their lovers. The subsequent associations showed that for her unconscious, Siegfried personified the penis of which the black Hagen robbed Kriemhilde. Kriemhilde's throwing herself over the body, that is, over the penis, is
the first act in cannibalism, that is, in swallowing the penis.

V

Surveying the material presented so far, we see all too clearly how the patient
imagined the retributory castration of the man. She wanted to bite off and
swallow his penis. This establishes the link with the hunger-animal, where we
stopped our discussion. The dangerous hunger-dragon raging in the patient's
abdomen is the penis which she had swallowed, obviously out of revenge. Her
revenge is directed primarily against the younger brother, who so blatantly
demonstrated his superiority to her (and behind him, of course, against the
father). By devouring this brother after his death, she incorporates his entire
personality, including his penis. We may surmise that, later on in her pseudo-
depressive phase, by introjecting the object she executed a distant repetition of
this revenge on the younger brother.

Through this explanation, too, the double nature of the personified hunger—
that is, its being simultaneously outside and inside the patient, its wanting to
devour and its being devoured—loses its peculiarity. The penis, which corresponds to it in the patient's unconscious, plays the same double role: after
being devoured, it is to be used as means of further castrations.

A second nexus of ideas, widely ramified in the analysis, concerning flames
and a sword of flame, proved to be a full equivalent of the hunger and its
double nature. In her inside, the patient believed, there burned a fire, which,
as a fire of love, first consumed her herself, but which now threatened to con-
sume anyone who approached her sexually. It was the redness of this fire which,
besides the redness of the erect penis and the castration wound, spread over her
face when she blushed. This fire had nearly the same properties as the hunger:
the patient thought of it as a "fire child" of magic power, and it had many similarities to the fire child of the schizophrenic described by Schilder.[5] The patient
would compare herself with a seething caldron, which, outwardly, showed
nothing wrong but which, when the tension inside it had risen still further,
would one day explode to pieces. That this fire too had phallic significance was
demonstrated by its change into a sword of flame, which was lodged partly
in the breast and partly in the genitals, and whose destructive point was directed
both inward and—in defense against attackers—outward. Behind the sword of
flame was concealed first the executive tool of the governess, then in a deeper
stratum, the flaming sword of the cherubim, who guard the entrance to the

[5] P. Schilder, *Seele und Leben*, Berlin, Springer, 1923.

garden of Eden, that is, to her genitals; it was also interwoven with the sword of flame of the Jewish legend with which the angel, on Passover night, puts a bloody sign on the door of believers. The full analogy with hunger, however, was established only after the oral nature as well of the incorporation of this sword became patent. The patient produced fantasies of sword-eaters and fire-eaters, which she equated in her childhood with man-eaters—cannibals—and whom she immensely feared and respected. As a child, she had owned a picture of a clown depicted as a sword-swallower, which came from wrappings of a chocolate bar. Thus, both her coprophagy and her cannibalism could hide behind her hunger for chocolate.

We see to what a high degree milk envy and penis envy were condensed in this patient into a single unity. The first loss she sustained, the loss of the mother's breast, made her into an underprivileged and revengeful human being, who could conceive of revenge only in oral terms. Of a similar nature was her triumph when she ate up whole mountains of cakes, which the governess had forbidden her to eat, at one sitting. In the same way, too, she devours the man's penis, or rather, the penis-possessing man, so as to become like him. Her fellatio fantasy —which came to utterance in connection with her encounters with exhibitionists and which screened the more unacceptable fantasy of biting off the penis—was a cover for the idea of drinking from the mother's breast. But this idea, full of longing, also changed later into the wish to bite off the mother's breast or to devour it entirely.

The fantasy of oral incorporation of the penis always appeared in connection with the endeavor to repress the idea of the penis altogether. It was an attempt to eliminate the hated penis from the world. This attempt, however, failed, since the introjected penis continued to threaten her from the inside, in the same way as authoritative persons who have been introjected do in the form of the superego.

We have already learned that before her latency period, the patient went through a stage of intense sexual explorations, but that these were doomed to failure, owing to strong repressive pressure. These explorations, too, proceeded entirely on oral lines. Her favorite play was "cooking." In this period of exploration her hunger found its final object of preference in eggs. Highly significant egg meals played a great role in her fantasy. (The patient asserted that she did not know that testicles were called eggs.*) On one occasion, she had a memory, which was entirely disconnected from anything else, of a mysterious arrangement, an egg hovering in a glass of water. Later on she recognized it as the equipment of a magician, who can make things out of nothing. When the

---

* Common German slang.—Trans. note.

patient decided to renounce her second friend also, she did not get up the next morning, but had herself brought an egg in bed, so as to introject the lost object in that form. To be given a meal in bed after a bath, to be served by others in sweet idleness—these were signs of a renewed regression into babyhood.

Underneath these isolated cannibalistic features we then came upon the fantasy of a great and ceremonial sacrificial meal, which the patient had formed on the pattern of the religious Jewish customs on the evening of Passover. She spoke repeatedly of the lasting impression which this festival had made on her. By degrees, her repressed ideas connected with it came to the fore. She had related the feast solely to the death of the first-born, of which the holy tradition reports, and which she perceived as the death of her brother. The strangely prepared dishes, the eating of which the rites prescribe for Jewish believers at Passover, and the solemnity of the proceedings had created in her unconscious the fantasy idea of a sort of "totem meal" which was somehow connected with the idea of the death of her brother. Then the angel with his sword of flame must come and castrate her as a punishment for her wishes.

In the course of Passover the father of the family is required to explain to the family the historical meaning of the feast. This takes the form of an answer to an inquiry by the youngest son. Both inquiry and answer have a text fixed by ritual. At her father's wish, the patient had to read the inquiry formula, the meaning of which she understood. She did not understand, however, anything of the long and rambling story which the father recited in answer. She felt disappointed, dissatisfied, and hurt. Finally she had a chance to ask: "What does all this mean?" and the answer he gave her was utterly incomprehensible stuff. We can recognize that the patient equated Passover with her earlier observation of the paternal penis. At that time, too, she had got an evasive and unclear answer to a clear and unequivocal question. Her association, that the Passover bread was made with children's blood—that therefore the brother whom her evil wish had killed was eaten in it—elicited an intense anxiety attack. Her anxiety corresponded to the fear that she herself was the killed child that was being eaten, as a retaliatory punishment for her crime. Now we understand her change from activity to passivity, which consisted in the hunger she had devoured devouring her, and her outwardly turned sword of flame being directed inward. This is the punishment which the introjected object inflicts on her ego after the introjection. In this way it has become a superego. Finally, from behind the anxiety of being devoured as a revenge, unmistakable ideas of birth broke through: a narrowing passage, through which she must pass under increasing pressure and lack of breath. Between the eliciting idea and the idea of birth, the memory material of the oedipus complex was interpolated as something dynamically essential and form-giving. Whether behind these there was an active memory of her actual birth could not be decided.[6]

## VI

It is time at this point to add the most important things that occurred in the patient's external experience during the last few months of the analysis. Her psychic life was so much subject to the repetition compulsion that only the most thorough observation of her recent behavior in life could bring the final and most important solutions. We have already heard that the patient's new love object richly fulfilled her unconscious requirements. He was an unusually intelligent but very neurotic married man, whose marriage was not happy and who was shut in and turned inward upon himself. Although he seemed to need the consolation and love of the patient, he permitted her no glimpse into his psyche, and his irrational ideas and actions drove her into ever-increasing inability to understand him. This object was undoubtedly chosen after the type of the older brother; like him, he had a bodily defect. The patient, who fell in love partly as a result of turning away libidinally from the analyst, and partly in defiance of him, hung with the same full passion on this man with which she had already leaned earlier on images of the older brother, and which was only increased by the analysis. In him the infantile imago was more completely achieved than ever before.

In this period there occurred an episode which clarified several things that had so far remained unclear. The patient's anxious family had already made attempts to marry her off at the beginning of the analysis, and in its first period. The patient had suppressed these attempts in their inception, rejecting them without hesitation as below her dignity. Now at about this time, there appeared on the scene a young man, whom the patient was forced to meet; and all her aunts urged her strongly, in view of the difficult real conditions of her life, not to reject his approaches out of hand. Although the patient did not for a moment think seriously of marrying the young man, this encounter affected her much more closely than could have been surmised from previous experiences of that kind. She was able neither to encounter this man freely, nor to refuse further meetings. Her entire ambivalence broke forth again. Behind her conscious

---

[6] It is true that in the last days of her analysis, the patient produced in a fairly unequivocal and surprising fashion the birth symbolism described by Rank: The analyst became the mother, the analysis itself the pregnancy, and the dismissal from analysis the birth. But analysis of this fantasy did not succeed in demonstrating any direct relations between it and her birth. Consequently, we had to be satisfied with viewing these fantasies in their analytically clear meaning of distorted oedipus fantasies. Between the idea of dismissal from analysis and birth there was interpolated the *trauma of learning to walk;* on that occasion, too, the child was let go from the arms of the mother, to make its anxious and halting first steps into the unknown world.

rejection an unconscious assent became noticeable, and, surrounded by a family which was talking her into it, she longed for somebody who would give contrary advice and who would help her in the struggle against her unconscious will. Her internal struggle manifested itself as a fear of reality—a reality which her suitor, as contrasted with her friend, seemed to embody. Though she disdained the former as a philistine, she still asked herself whether his secure income might not promise real gratifications, while her longing was but flight and estrangement from the world. She thought that she was wavering between the demands of the reality principle and those of the pleasure principle. She longed to be reinforced from the outside in her choice of the pleasure principle, and pressed me for advice.

Upon her stormy questioning, I reminded her that she had agreed to postpone for the duration of the analysis all crucial decisions about her life, and I advised her to let her importuning relatives know of this agreement. She took my attitude as equivalent to an approval of the pleasure principle, and was grateful to me for being the only one who "was on her side."

There was no doubt that the contrast between pleasure and reality covered only part of the contrast between friend and suitor. The patient felt that in comparison with her friend, her suitor was crude, inconsiderate, and violent, though this last at least he certainly was not in reality. Finally, besides anxiety she also felt hate against him, and she eventually found the solution of this attitude in the association that he reminded her of her younger brother. Thus here the older and the younger brother were opposed as candidates for her love; this was the unconscious cause of her conflict.

Now it was easy to recognize that this opposition of her imagos was typical for the patient. We remember that all approaches made to her by men were always surprising and unexpected to her and that afterwards she always hated those men. These were younger brothers and their approach was always a repetition of his aggressions. On the other hand, she always loved men who were not interested in her, who had a wife or other women friends and who were more or less crippled, and thus she was always once again disappointed by them. All these were older brothers whose womenfolk corresponded to her sister and who were disabled just as he was ill. The fact, too, that these men seemed to represent the pleasure principle while the others stood for the reality principle was now easily explained. It was the effect of the opposite kind of sexual enlightenment she had received from the two brothers. From the elder, the idea of the flowerpot; from the younger the drastic, realistic demonstration of the penis, which at the same time gave her her feelings of inferiority.

The contrasting fates of these two imagos was even more interesting. It struck me that the patient never mentioned the name of her suitor. Finally I asked her what it was. It was "Food." * Now it was clear enough why this man aroused more excitement than other similar kinds of suitors. The younger brother had been "food" for the patient; for she wanted to devour him for daring to possess a penis and superior knowledge, so as to punish him and to have him and his penis inside her, and thus to become like him.

The sexual disorder of the patient could now be characterized as follows. All men appeared to her either as the older or the younger brother. Only for those who were like her older brother could she feel manifest love. This love was, however, *a priori* inhibited, turned away from reality, and without sensuality (the man is a cripple). She had to be unhappy, because the repetition-compulsion demanded rejection and disappointment. The men who were like her younger brother unleashed a storm of ambivalence. In regard to them, the patient regressed to oral-sadism, in fantasy she bit off their penis so as to devour it and them. Thus she regressed from object love to identification, and, by virtue of introjection, she herself became a possessor of a penis, and therefore like the devoured object. The incorporated object continued the conflict of ambivalence, and raged inside her against her ego, as a punishing superego. In this way every object relationship ended either as an unhappy love or as an identification; happy love was prohibited to the patient.

There is no doubt that the women who threatened her with castration were treated like the younger brother, since they were like him in what was essential, namely, in the threat of castration.[7] The traces of these identifications are

---

* *"Nahrung"* in German.—Trans. note.

[7] It is noteworthy that the patient's relations to women were, as in the case of the contrast between the two brothers, also of two types, molded after the extremes of aunt and governess. Indeed, it is possible that the division of the "mother imago" preceded the analogous split of the father imago. The aunt had spoiled the patient very much and preferred her to her siblings; once, she punished the younger brother for something the patient did, and so won her heart and burdened her conscience. When she left and her place was taken by the strict, hypermoralistic, and beating governess, the patient must have experienced severe conflicts and upheavals. At first it was difficult to understand how she nevertheless succeeded in turning her entire love toward this governess. Only in an advanced phase of the analysis did we succeed in exploring these vicissitudes of the homosexual libido and thereby solving as well the last riddles of the development of the patient's heterosexual love. The patient often told of a very excited time of her postpuberty, dominated by unlimited and un-understood affects, which set in soon after the governess had left them. This was obviously a manifestation of her cyclothymic mental constitution, a manic-depressively colored state. Strict ascetic ideals and devastating self-reproaches appeared simultaneously with a hypomanic urge to speak, vivacity, wit and humor. This condition corresponded to an identification with the neurotic aunt, in whom it appeared that depressive moods existed alongside of much social charm (she wrote poetry, sang, danced). In this excited time of postpuberty, the patient developed first a passionate, then a friendly love for one of her women teachers; she made efforts especially to praise and extol other classmates before this teacher, but when she succeeded in this, she was plagued by violent jealousy. Now, we know that the governess preferred her siblings to the patient, quite in contrast to the aunt. Her praise and jealousy of her classmates thus originated from her repetition-compulsion. Concerning the identification with the aunt, it should be remembered that it was she who scared the patient at night with her breast. The patient had also once observed her defecating. (This experience was also one of the sources of her excessive interest in the theater; the rising curtain corresponding to

easily demonstrable in the patient's character. Her neurotic shyness, her with-drawal, her inhibitions, were also manifest in her younger brother. Her anal traits, her defiant attitude, her sense of order, love for schedules and tabulations, for precise division of time, and so on, exactly copied the behavior of her governess.[8] A good many of her symptoms could, beyond doubt, be understood as "deferred obedience" to this governess. Her compulsive fear of having to take hold of a man's genitals unexpectedly and suddenly reminds us of the uncle who took hold of her genitals so suddenly and unexpectedly.

When the episode with her suitor was over, the patient could turn her libido toward her friend (the copy of her elder brother). Into the place now left free

---

the lifted-up chemise.) After all, this aunt was the permanent substitute for the patient's (dead) mother in the oedipus complex. Thus, the postpuberal period which began after the governess left was a regression to the time when once the aunt had gone away. This regression enabled us to re-construct the libidinal processes that were going on in the patient at that time. These were: identifi-cation with the abandoned homosexual object (aunt); object love toward the new one (governess).

The difference between the development of the patient's heterosexual and homosexual libido was, however, that in the former identification was reserved for the younger brother and object love for the older, while in the latter not only the aunt but the governess too was elevated to a superego by introjection. It is probably due to the extreme anal character of this governess that the patient reacted to every disappointment in love with a sort of periodic resuscitation of the identification with her which caused her to regress from the genital to the anal stage. At such times instead of the usual hysterical symptoms purely obsessional ones would suddenly come to the fore; she would issue a moral condemnation—even if not fully consciously—against all genital impulses, and would produce anal ceremonials which amounted to a deferred obedience to the governess and thus betrayed the identifi-cation. For instance, she would enjoy frightening a little nephew with a story about a lonely witch's house. The house was a street lavatory and the witch was the governess in the shape of the lavatory attendant who demanded money. Obviously the patient knew as a child that the governess, in con-trast with the unselfish love of the aunt, was paid for her labors by the father; a factor which played an important role in the later equation of governess and analyst. For this reason, the patient was also particularly afraid of every doorman, particularly since one called after her—exactly like the governess—that she ought to clean her boots better.

A period of identification with the governess could be particularly well observed at the time when the patient made an attempt to part with her friend. The described adaptation of her own person to this friend—i.e., the replacement of object-love by identification (devouring the friend, depression)—was completed by a regression to anality, in which the patient's hysteria changed temporarily into a compulsion neurosis, which displayed striking imitations of the governess.

While the patient's identification with her aunt (and with her friend) only *succeeded* her object love, her identification with her governess must have *coexisted* from the beginning *with* that love. The entrance of the governess into the family obviously occurred at a time when the patient's inclina-tion to repression was strong, probably following her bad experiences with her younger brother, which convinced her of the fact of her castration. The governess offered her a favorable opportunity to take the less dangerous path into homosexuality, and at the same time opened the way to anality, through her educational influence. The patient had reacted promptly in the sense of these possibilities, accepting obediently the governess's moral demands. Thus she acquired the governess's love and with it a lasting alteration of character. When then the governess too began her castration threats (compare the "jackass" episode), she reinforced the patient's identification with her at the price of her object love for her, just as the castration threats of her younger brother too had led to an analogous identification with him.

[8] This conception was neatly confirmed by the observation that these propensities appeared at various times with varying intensity. It could be seen that they were reinforced as soon as the patient had occasion to activate her identification with the governess.

by the younger brother she put the analyst, who, having pointed out her real femininity, and having against her will declared himself and the analysis as realities, could now readily take on the role of the castrator. This transference also made it possible to force the hunger symptom into the analytic hour. On one occasion when her penis envy was once again pointed out to her, she immediately wanted to get up and go to her older brother, who had promised to lend her Boccaccio to read. Thus she refused the analyst's realistic explanations, as she had refused the younger brother's, and once more sought after the poetic explanations of the elder brother. Now she could also attempt to identify herself with the analyst; for instance, she wrote to a doctor instead of "My dear doctor," "My dear patient."

The patient's relation to her friend took a decisive turn owing to his already mentioned aggression. Such a thing, he, the likeness of the *elder* brother, should not have done; that was the behavior of the *younger* brother. The equation with the younger brother which he thus provoked betrayed itself in the patient's subsequent reaction; she now essayed a depressive defense (which was easily resolved by analysis) in relation to him too. Indeed, one could even venture from this to come to the remarkable conclusion that her early infantile introjective procedure had left behind *a readiness to make a compulsory repetition of the loss of object*. The later lability of the corresponding object cathexes would accordingly be referable to this repetition compulsion.

This depressive defense was unsuccessful. Obviously the indestructible picture of the *older* brother opposed it. There followed a struggle between the two brother imagos, which betrayed itself in torturing restlessness, excitement, and other indications. Now, her analogous behavior in the transference to the analyst also became comprehensible; the same struggle raged around his person. We have already heard in what respects he became the younger brother; in his role as a friendly, well-behaved helping figure he was also the older brother. When the transference turned from the younger brother to the older one, the patient betrayed this by giving up the "swallowed" penis. She became nauseated in the analytic hour, she left her umbrella in the analyst's office, and finally brought back a book that he had lent her several months before, which she had "swallowed" and kept for so long. She dreamt of a doll-child, whose finger she broke off, whereupon, to her dismay, she found a bone in her mouth, which she spat out in disgust.[9]

---

[9] The person of the analyst, however, unlike that of the friend, combined in itself not only both types of heterosexual object but also both types of homosexual object as well, and this complicated the state of affairs extraordinarily. Thus, for instance, the patient repeatedly reproached analysis with being contradictory, since, while it wanted to make normal sexual life possible, it nevertheless demanded a renunciation of instinct. The former, *mutatis mutandis,* had been taught by the aunt, the latter by the governess. In a period of negative transference, when she regarded every word of the

Our insight into this *competition between the imagos* enabled us, in respect of the libidinal difficulties which it brought upon the patient, to assign to its proper place her observation of her father's penis—an event which had been too long neglected in the analysis. We could now assume that the mixed person who united the properties of both brothers was the *father*. The two object types corresponded to two contrary attitudes on the part of the patient toward her father, and her recent excitement was a repetition of her oedipus experiences in childhood, of whose probable course we now finally obtained some knowledge. We could assume that at an earlier time the patient had had a tender tie to the father, until she made the aforesaid observation of his penis. When this happened she must have recognized with horror his double nature: he was not only the loving and tender person she knew, but also a penis-bearing, castrating monster. Hate and envy rose high and her great ambivalency began. Probably her oral introjective attempts began then too. But she neither could nor would renounce the old tenderness, and those attempts failed. On the other hand, the repression of the traumatic scene must have been in some degree successful. It was probably supported by her view of the reversibility of sexual transformations, acquired at the stage performance (herself as Cupid). Further voyeuristic scenes must then have re-aroused the repressed; and the night scene with the aunt and the scenes with the brother in her fourth year finally created a painful certainty. But the same experiences also opened a way out of the ambivalent situation: she split her father-imago into two parts, creating the figure of a terrible penis-bearer and the figure of a tender and caring person. The former was represented by the younger brother, the latter by the elder one. Now in her unconscious she could devour the first and love the second. This assumption, continuing our previous discoveries, explains some hitherto not well understood features of the neurosis. The patient's enormous sense of guilt, which carried her whole neurosis, must have originated in a very early oedipal guilt. The *Sunday neurosis* from which she suffered could be traced back to the fact that the father, who was nearly invisible to the children throughout the week, was at home on Sunday. Her Sunday fluctuations of mood were related to her longing for the scene which, as we established with certitude, took place on a Sunday walk. Her fear of having to seize hold of men's genitals also corresponded, among other things, to a repetition of this scene. About her later relation to her father we discovered little, but one of the things we learned was that it was always difficult for her

---

analyst as a restrictive prohibition and expected to be punished by him, as she had been by the governess, the entire picture changed when, on an occasion when she had diarrhea, the analyst advised her not to take opium so that the spontaneous course of the diarrhea could be observed. In doing this, he, in contrast to the governess, granted her an extensive instinctual gratification, and thus became the all-permitting aunt.

to ask him for money; she always had the most severe feelings of guilt about it. The material showed that she experienced this as a castration of the father. The neatest expression of her doubt whether her father was a castrator or whether he could be castrated took the form of repeated mishearing of what he said. When he read *Struwelpeter,* she misheard his reading "Fie, calls *everybody,* nasty Struwelpeter" for "Fie, calls a *hunter* . . ." * because in another story in the same book a hunter is shot dead by a rabbit. When telling in her analysis about *The Merry Wives of Windsor* she began to doubt whether it reads there: "We two surely will catch *the wench*" or "We two surely will catch the *old gentleman.*" †

The patient encountered many difficulties in accepting this interpretation; but the later months of the analysis brought so many corroborating associations, dreams and symptomatic actions, that she could no longer doubt its correctness. I think it superfluous to report this corroborative material here. But I would like to discuss some details related to the Sunday scene, which were discovered very slowly and in the face of great difficulties.

We shall begin with a very remarkable symptom of the patient's which might be described as an expectation or wish of hers that every one of her experiences should have an "end." She could not herself quite say how this was to be understood; she needed some kind of formal conclusion to every occasion and was very dissatisfied when, for instance, she had to interrupt any activity, the end of which had not been announced in advance. This lack of gratification in all matters "without an end" corresponded to her lack of gratification on that Sunday morning. It was possible to discover, at first only hypothetically, later on with a sense of remembering, that the urinating father, startled by the little girl's curiosity, had quickly made his penis disappear once more into his trousers. This memory of the sudden unexpected disappearance of the penis, which had obviously been connected with an oral reproof of the questioning child, proved to be a nodal point in the patient's unconscious.

(1) This sudden disappearance of the penis demonstrated before the patient's eyes at once the possibility of castration and the certainty of the existence of the penis. Moreover, she herself caused this disappearance by betraying her curiosity; thus she had already castrated the father then—she, as the hare, had chased the hunter. From this came her tremendous feelings of guilt and probably also her deep fixation on the idea of revenge by castrating the man during the sexual act.

* In German the phrases are *"Pfui, ruft da ein jeder, garst'ger Struwelpeter,"* and *"Pfui, ruft da ein Jaeger . . .";* the mishearing is based on the similarity of the German words "everybody" and "hunter."—Trans. note.

† The German phrases are *"Wir beide kriegen sicherlich das Weibchen abzufangen"* and "alten Herrn *zu fangen."*—Trans. note.

(2) However, this retaliatory castration, which should have made the penis-possessing father like herself, brought no gratification. This scene remained "without an end," not only in the passive-feminine, but also in the sadistic-masculine sense, because, though the vanished penis was no more to be seen, it did not come into the patient's possession either. Its sudden disappearance withdrew the penis from the little girl's realm of power. Not only had she castrated the father; she had at the same time been castrated.

(3) This form of passive castration, in which the penis attached to the foreign body is suddenly withdrawn from the child who is reaching after it, immediately reminds us of the withdrawal of the mother's breast. Now we know that the patient's envy about the penis was built upon an older envy about the mother's milk. Already before that Sunday, in asking about the meaning of the breast, she had once obtained from her aunt the information that children are given drink from it. She also heard that she had been robbed of her rights there: while the siblings got the mother's breast, her mother died when she was two weeks old, and she had to be satisfied with the bottle. Just as she asked about the meaning of the breast, so did she on this later occasion ask her father about the meaning of the penis. In this way, the sudden disappearance of the penis was equated with the death of the mother.

(4) This equation corroborates our previous surmise that her attempts at oral introjection of the penis, or rather, of the penis-bearer, had already begun on that Sunday. Considering her high degree of oral fixation, this is not surprising. Had she not, as we have already heard, regarded the oral ceremonies of Passover also as a repetition of that Sunday scene?

(5) The patient's demand for an "ending" showed a meaningful detail, which may lead us a step further. She renounced this expectation if she retained as its equivalent "memories"; she liked to collect mementos of people, places, experiences, which were laden with memories. On the analyst's comment that these mementos were obviously the lost penis, an unexpected association followed: she had no memory of her mother. She thought that the best and safest memory would be if she could keep the mementos in her own body. If she had a piece of the mother in her body, then she herself would be the mother and could never be robbed of her. Now she remembered having the idea what a pity it was that she did not bite off her mother's breast in the first days of her life. Had she done that, her mother would never have died, for she herself would have become the mother. We know that her feeling of guilt arising from the oedipus complex took at times the conscious form that she had killed the mother, who died as a consequence of her birth.

(6) The oral introjection of the brother's penis, which the patient sought to execute as a revenge, had therefore a twofold prototype in each of which intro-

jection had been preceded by a real loss of object. Both times the object (mother's breast and father's penis) was shown to her, but then withdrawn again, before she could incorporate it; this was the great *deception by the adults.*

The later deceptions by adults, as for instance when she was dressed up as a boy though in reality she remained a girl, were only repetitions of those previous deceptions. In the transference, she experienced it as a deception that though the analyst held out the prospect of a gratifying sexual life after her analysis had been completed, he refused to give her this sexual gratification himself. A period of infantile pseudologia which she passed through was an attempt at revenge for this deception. The analysis succeeded in bringing to consciousness the patient's fantasies about a great day of revenge in the far future, of a "Last Judgment," which she perceived as a judgment day held by the "youngest" over the "adults." *

(7) Characteristically, her recognition that adults were not omnipotent but cheats was linked with the oral story of the fall of man in the Garden of Eden. She was told in joke that she must not eat one of the apples on a plate. She ate it secretly and nothing happened; neither the adults nor the Lord took any note of her sin. This experience was the strongest support of all her hopes about the Day of Judgment.[10]

(8) Her father's omnipotence, however, had already been impeached by the Sunday scene itself. When he made his penis disappear so suddenly, the child took it for an admission of guilt; thus, his sinfulness was unveiled, and her rebellion against him could begin.

These connections, established by detailed working through in the transference, yielded full proof for the surmised split of the father imago into those of the two brothers. Thus, in this case once more, the oedipus complex proved to be the nuclear complex of the neurosis.

## VII

Most of what seems to be theoretically significant in this case, and to justify its communication, has already been discussed in the course of presenting the case history. Thus the following comments are not so much intended to draw theoretical conclusions from our statements as to put together systematically all that has been suggested and thus to see what can be learned from this case history.

The analysis of the case seems to us to be particularly instructive in three respects. First—and this is the most easily settled—it brought a full confirmation of

---

* The German phrase for The Last Judgment is *"juengste Gericht."* The patient's association plays on the double meaning of *"juengste,"* which means "youngest" as well as "final."

[10] An attempt to execute this judgment was present in the fantasy idea, the memory of which was accompanied by severe feelings of guilt, that she had once shot her father dead with a toy gun.

Pfeifer's finding, which we took for our starting point. Like Pfeifer, we found that on two occasions after disappointments in love there followed a reaction of depressive mourning with introjection of the object (a reaction which, however, became more deeply understandable to us through the studies of Freud and Abraham, published since Pfeifer's communication). We found, furthermore, that a new search for objects began at the most primitive stages of libido development and passed through this development once again.

Secondly, we found that the disappointment in love which led to the introjection of the object was not determined from outside, but was the inevitable consequence of a *repetition compulsion,* which, based on and reinforced by early infantile vicissitudes of the libido, activated the mechanism of introjection in an altogether primary fashion. Perhaps we may allow ourselves the surmise here that in the *apparently spontaneous depressions* as well, a similar *acquired* preponderance of the oral introjective mechanism, coming from early infantile experiences, underlies the disposition that is decisive for these disorders.

To the assertion that the introjecting identification was not caused by an externally enforced object loss but that, on the contrary, it arose from internal causes and, as it were, enforced the loss of object—to this assertion let me add that I do not assume this to be by any means the case for the patient's first introjection of her father in childhood. At that time her object loss was obviously primary and enforced by reality. But the dominance of the oral components in her libidinal constitution made this process heavy with consequences. From then on, she retained a tendency on all later occasions to turn her erotic object trends into *oral-sadistic* relationships (cf. Abraham), which used the *executive mechanism of psychic incorporation* (introjection). This is the meaning of that state of affairs which we described above as introjection determined by repetition compulsion.

It will not surprise us also to meet in our patient most of the etiological prerequisites of depression described by Abraham.[11] Beyond the already stressed prevalence of the oral component, we have nothing further to say about the patient's constitution; the severe injury done to her infantile narcissism by coincident disappointments in love seem to be sufficiently explained by her observation of her father's threatening penis and his refusal to give an explanation of it, by the replacement of the tender aunt by the excessively strict governess, and by her brother's scorn. The first two of these disappointments certainly took place before her oedipus wishes were mastered, so that we are faced with the question why in this case there developed a hysteria and not a depression.

The approximation between these two disorders was presented by our patient

[11] K. Abraham, "A Short Study of the Development of the Libido, Viewed in the Light of Mental Disorders," *Selected Papers,* London, Hogarth, 1948.

in the idea—so well known to us and so common in hysterics—of biting off her partner's penis and swallowing it. Abraham has brought this oral castration into relation with the introjection of depressives, and speaks of a "partial incorporation of the object." The similarity between our case and the fragments of case histories with which he illustrates partial incorporation is striking. In this context I should like to call particular attention to the familiar equation of penis and breast, as well as to the compulsion symptom of having to look at men's genitals. It must not be forgotten either that if the man has his penis bitten off, he becomes penisless and thus fulfils the love conditions of hysteria. That this form of castration implies a genuine introjection is demonstrated clearly and beyond doubt by our case. Since for our patient's unconscious the penis represented what is most essential in men, there was no great distinction made between partial and total incorporation, between eating a penis and eating a body. But the incorporated object retains its separate existence, rages inside her against the sinful eater, becomes her superego; [12] the patient becomes similar to the object whose penis she has swallowed. Thanks to her excessively strong oral trends, the idea of oral castration was obviously more deeply meant in her case than in other hysterics, who react to it, for instance, with a *globus hystericus*. It was still the full original identification by devouring, to which after her disappointment in her object love, the patient regressed.

Let us attempt to give a schematic presentation of the libidinal development of our patient:

I. Disadvantaged by lacking a mother—I want to drink from the mother's breast—other children should not drink milk from the mother's breast—I want the breast for myself alone—I want to eat the whole breast—I want to eat the woman—incorporation of the governess into the superego.

II. I love my father, but I am guilty toward him—my father will castrate me —he has a penis to do this with—I will castrate him—ambivalence—splitting of the father imago.

III. The younger brother is the bad father—he robbed me of my penis, just as they robbed me once of my mother's breast—I want to eat his penis— I want to eat the man—in that way I shall myself become a man—the man in me kills me—incorporation of the younger brother into the superego.

IV. The elder brother is the good father—he has no genitals, he is a cripple, is sick, thus I may love him—but he disappoints me, because he prefers my older sister.

It is clear that this schematic survey cannot without further ado be brought into harmony with Abraham's scheme of the developmental history of the libido. The most striking contradiction appears to be that the *partial* incorporation

[12] S. Freud, *The Ego and the Id*, London, Hogarth, 1947.

which belongs to the first anal-sadistic stage here precedes the older oral *total* incorporation. But that is explained by the fact that the scheme which we have been able to trace here for our case describes a developmental path which is already distorted by regressions, and not the normal course of development. The apparent confusion of the developmental stages in the scheme is thus by no means accidental or irrelevant. Furthermore, it shows that our patient had fixation points at various levels of development, to which she regressed. According to her complaints, and also to the dynamics of her illness, she suffered from a hysteria with anxiety- and conversion-symptoms. But we have reported numerous compulsion symptoms, and we need not bring to mind in detail how many of her characteristics were of an obsessional-neurotic stamp. The similarities in her case to depression have frequently been mentioned, and mildly paranoid symptoms were also observed. Her symptoms thus undoubtedly made use of libido belonging to all the stages of its organization. The decision as to the choice of neurosis may well have been determined by the relative strength of these several portions of libido.

We must not be deceived by the overwhelming orality of the patient into overlooking the fact that all her symptoms were endowed with a good share of *genital libido;* her genital libido, however, was transferred, by a "displacement upward," to the *oral* zone, and used for its *genitalization.* The real motor of the patient's oral symptoms was, accordingly, her *castration complex,* that is to say, her wish to bring about by castration the necessary exclusion of the genital in the beloved (incestuous) object. She achieved this by identifying herself with the partner who was to be castrated and she thus brought to bear her orality which hid behind her genitality; this is like depression, but it is not depression. This behavior is fundamentally no different, though far more deep-going, from what —as Freud has so brilliantly observed in *The Ego and the Id*—every normal woman does, who, when she no longer loves, becomes like her abandoned love object. Identification is not only a means of regaining in the ego the lost object; it is also a means of *destroying in an oral-sadistic way* the object of an ambivalent attitude (the penis); but this intention is frustrated by a turning against the ego, which in our case was accomplished with the aid of "hunger" and "a sword of flame." Reactive tendencies appear and we observe the raging of the superego against the ego.

Thus the metapsychological difference between depression and oral hysteria, in so far as it can be decided from our case, seems to us to be a purely *economic* one. For it has so far not been possible to assess metapsychologically the different roles played here by *regression.* Genital and oral libido unite in a common symptom formation; in depression the latter, in oral hysteria the former, preponderates. The assumption which Reich expressed, in answering a question by Federn, that such oral hysterias turn into post-climacteric depressions through organic weakening of the genital libido in the climacteric appears to us altogether plausible.

Finally, I should like to point to a third factor. We are familiar with the division of a unitary love striving into two types, into the sensuous and the tender. We are also familiar with a duality of object relations: one object is loved, the other is only a model, an ideal. In our case these two divisions were combined. The object of sensuous strivings had, by introjection, always to become an ego-ideal. Of two series of love objects, no single one of which the patient could completely love, one had to remain incorporeal, and had to end up short in a disappointment; the other had to regress from object love to identification. In this, the first series corresponded to isolated tenderness, the second to isolated sensuousness. Their division was, however, as always, the work of the oedipus complex.

## *EIGHT*

# The Clinical Aspect of the Need for Punishment*

## I

Since Freud's work *The Ego and the Id* made profounder investigation of the psychology of the ego possible, this question has become the center of analytical interest. In particular the psychology of the sense of guilt has claimed special consideration, on account of its outstanding clinical and theoretical importance. Recognition of the importance of the sense of guilt is by no means confined to recent times. Apart from the part played by the conscious sense of guilt in manifestly neurotic forms of disease, Freud's doctrine of repression virtually implied that a sort of guilt feeling acted as a criterion for the decisions of the repressing faculty; in his description of the reaction formations of the obsessional neurotic, in his conception that every symptom complies with the repressing force as well as with the claims of the repressed instinct, the idea of self-punishment was already contained. What is novel is simply our insight into the importance of the *unconscious* elements of feelings of guilt, and of the resultant penalties. We know that this insight formed the starting point of those of Freud's investigations which revealed the differentiation of the superego from the ego, the creation of the former by introjection of the objects of the oedipus complex, and the genesis of the sense of guilt from the discrepancy between the superego and the ego. According to Freud's latest doctrine of instincts, the conscious and unconscious feelings of guilt owe their distinctive position to the circumstance that they are representatives of the destructive instincts; and these have lost some of their neutralizing, libidinal components as a result of the instinctual defusion that goes on *pari passu* with introjection.

* First published in *Int. Z. Psa.*, Vol. 11, 1925, pp. 469–487.

Once more it is only in extreme cases that the clinical significance of this fact becomes evident. Freud has at various times drawn attention to such cases; long before his latest works he described in "Those Wrecked by Success" and in "Criminality from a Sense of Guilt"[1] two neurotic types of person who become so enraged against themselves that they are driven either to self-destruction or, in order to avoid that, to the destruction of their surroundings. Even if the term "need for punishment" was first used only in his paper "The Economic Problem in Masochism,"[2] we know that Freud stated long before this that the most powerful resistances arise from a sense of guilt which finds discharge in the sufferings of a neurosis. He has, however, drawn attention to a special case in which the most obstinate resistances of this nature can be successfully dealt with. A footnote in *The Ego and the Id* deals with a "borrowed" sense of guilt, and runs as follows: "One has a special opportunity for influencing it when this Ucs. sense of guilt is a 'borrowed' one, i.e. when it is the product of an identification with some other person who was once the object of an erotic cathexis. When the sense of guilt has been adopted in this way it is often the sole remaining trace of the abandoned love relation, and not at all easy to recognize as such. (The likeness between this process and what happens in melancholia is unmistakable.) If one can unmask this former object cathexis behind the Ucs. sense of guilt, the therapeutic success is often brilliant, otherwise the outcome of one's efforts is by no means certain."[3]

Accordingly it is the libidinal element in the sense of guilt with which our therapeutics can deal successfully.[4]

Now in his paper on masochism Freud has contrasted the conscious "sadism of the superego" and unconscious "moral masochism," and has shown its close kinship with "erotogenic" and "feminine" masochism. Here, therefore, our therapeutic condition is fulfilled. We need only recall what he says about the "regression from morality to the oedipus complex," in order to understand the effect of this instinctual fusion. Its clinical application is immediately apparent. The masochism of the ego and the sadism of the superego certainly form a complemental series; but in practice it is important to discover which of the two trends predominates. Following Freud, in two cases, which it is instructive to compare with one another, I was able to observe in their origin the relation-

[1] S. Freud, "Some Character-Types Met with in Psycho-Analytic Work," II, III, *Coll. Pap.*, Vol. IV, London, Hogarth, 1948.

[2] S. Freud, "The Economic Problem in Masochism," *Coll. Pap.*, Vol. II, London, Hogarth, 1948, p. 263.

[3] S. Freud, *The Ego and the Id*, London, Hogarth, 1947, p. 72 footnote.

[4] In his lectures at the Berlin Psychoanalytic Institute in 1924, S. Rado suggested original ambivalence and instinctual defusion arising at a very early stage and there, to all appearances, irreversible, as constituting the limits of susceptibility to analytical treatment. In the face of destructive instinctual components which cannot be erotically bound our therapeutic efforts are as yet powerless.

ships (resulting from such instinctual fusions) between instinct and the need for punishment, and between the superego and the id (as well as the attitude taken up by the ego in regard to both). In part they exemplify clinically what has hitherto been only a matter of theory; i.e., they bring to completion our clinical observations,[5] and in part they fill in certain lacunae that have existed hitherto in our knowledge of this subject.

## II

In the case history of a young patient the manifestations of his acutely conscious sense of guilt played a conspicuous part. When he indulged in the slightest luxury or pleasure he immediately experienced an inner command to be wretched, exhausted, and thoroughly ill. He was unable to do any work; his illness had cost him several years that should have been devoted to study. Among other things that happened to him, a short time before the beginning of the analysis he had been run over by a motorcar and severely injured; after this, while still in the hospital, he felt quite well and was able to write reproachful letters to his parents, against whom he was otherwise never able to utter a single word.

The patient's father is a clergyman in a small town. He belongs to a religious sect that professes a strict moral code, and is narrow and bigoted in his beliefs, although in other respects he is peaceable and easy to get on with. So far as authority is concerned, he is quite subordinate to his wife. She belongs to the same religious body, is a hysteric, and fanatical and temperamental. Her prohibitions to her children concerned not only all that related to sex, but everything that was at all worldly. She beat her children without restraint for trivial misdemeanors, and then forthwith overwhelmed them with excessive demonstrations of affection. There were three other members of the family, all younger than he. He told me of two "attacks" of "nervous cardiac trouble" which he had had in his twelfth and sixteenth years. In a *pavor nocturnus* which was characterized by hallucinations and fantasies of the end of the world, he cried out for his mother to come to his bedside (his father was unable to quiet him); he was unwilling to allow her to leave him, but was suddenly overtaken by the anxious fear that she knew everything, that he was betrayed, that she was laughing at him, and that he would have to confess all his sins to her, although he knew that she was already aware of them. On one occasion he even wrote out a list of his sins—like a confessional certificate. The second attack of this kind ended in an illness of several years' duration, in the course of which he was either unable to move at all, or at other times was only able to walk with the aid of

[5] Cf. the competent researches of T. Reik, *Gestaendniszwang und Strafbeduerfnis*, Vienna, Int. Psa. Verlag, 1925; F. Alexander, "A Metapsychological Description of the Process of Cure," *Int. J. Psa.*, Vol. 6, 1925; and W. Reich, *Der triebhafte Charakter*, Vienna, Int. Psa. Verlag, 1925.

crutches, and was for months under medical treatment at a hospital. Both he and his parents, contrary to medical opinion, thought that death was approaching. The occasions of these attacks were easily discoverable. The first took place on the day when his father had confirmed one of his boy friends; previous to that the patient had eagerly read some books which his mother had prohibited. The second attack occurred when a youth joined his class at school against whom his mother had warned him on account of his conduct with girls, but with whom he had consequently fallen violently in love. As a result of his illness he ceased attendance at school. He felt bound to confess his fondness for this youth to his mother, but believed, nevertheless, that she knew about it without being told. This belief in the omniscience of his parents was transferred afterward to physicians. Whenever his pulse was being felt it rose to 200, because he was convinced that the physician knew everything and that he was doomed.

We see therefore, this his attacks were the expression of a sense of guilt that had reference to his sexual curiosity and to infantile sexual practices. There was no reason to question the patient's idea that his curiosity had been aroused by observations of his parents' sexual intercourse made by him in his childhood, and that these observations were not only punished, but even reproduced, in his attacks. A series of dreams disclosed the effects of such scenes; as, for example: *During a tremendous catastrophe a monstrous dog thrust a knife into the earth.—A catastrophic outburst of fire altered the whole face of the world; his mother then built a very tiny house out of straw.—A monster destroyed the house of his father's superintendent.*—In a similar dream, *he runs away after the catastrophe with two heads, one with hair on it, the other shaved.*

It turned out that the attacks represented, in particular, attempts to defend himself against the identification with his mother that had been acquired in this way, i.e. they were a defense against homosexual tendencies. We are reminded here of a sentence of Freud's: "In the history of homosexuals one often hears that the change in them took place after the mother had praised another boy and set him up as a model." [6]

This statement has to undergo a characteristic modification for the case with which we are concerned. The first attack took place after the *father* had *praised* (confirmed) another boy; while the manifest (though aim-inhibited) homosexuality succeeded in breaking out only after the *mother* had *found fault with* another boy; the repression and, along with it, the second attack only occurred when the boy with whom he had fallen in love entered the same class at school, and came into very close proximity to him. The patient's compulsion to confess his homosexual love to his mother corresponded to a convulsive attempt to

---

[6] S. Freud, "Certain Neurotic Mechanisms in Jealousy, Paranoia and Homosexuality," *Coll. Pap.,* Vol. II, p. 242.

defend himself against this inclination and to find a heterosexual object once more in his mother. We see now why his father was unable to quiet him.

Let us now return to our investigation of the sense of guilt. Even when he was shouting furiously in unconcealed resistance to his conscientious compulsions, "Why should I always torment myself, why must I thrash myself, why, why?" yet he had first of all to beat himself in the most violent fashion with clenched fist on forehead and breast. He even thought of killing himself in order to deliver himself from his pangs of conscience, i.e. going to the furthest limit of acquiescence in his conflict with his superego. He was himself aware that the palpitation he felt during the attack was an inner self-scourging, indeed, an attempted suicide. The attack which was based on the earlier reaction of the childish observer to overhearing sexual intercourse between his parents thus included, in addition to an aggressive impulse against his parents (hindrance of their *current* intercourse), an aggressive element against his own ego. The connection between deed and punishment turned out, however, to be very much more close and complicated still.

The patient developed the fantasy of being at home and pretending to be insane, either by storming and smashing everything up—then he would not need to be ill any longer; or by lying quietly, not replying to anything and getting taken to an asylum—in this way, too, he would evade his illness. These fantasied outbreaks of insanity, as he saw himself, were the equivalents of his attacks, and, in particular, of the "compulsion to confess" which accompanied them. He said quite definitely: "If I had smashed up everything, I shouldn't have had to confess anything." The compulsion to confess, the imagined simulation of insanity, and the real illness are thus psychological equivalents. Accordingly, we are able to agree with Reik in regarding a confession as a weakened action which at the same time has to give satisfaction to the claims of the repressing forces, i.e. which has to be a punishment.[7] The original repressed instinctual trends could also break through relatively undisguised into consciousness, if only provision had been made for a preceding self-punishment. If his mother were to rebuke him again, he intended to hurl her to the ground, violate her, and then shout to her, "You see now what your crazy upbringing has led to!" He invented a whole series of complicated schemes by which he might at the same time injure both his mother and himself—e.g., he broke a large mirror belonging to his mother and cut himself with it. He failed at the school inspection in order to cast blame both on himself and on his teacher.

The patient's conduct in regard to onanism showed a remarkable condensation of sin and punishment. He had been conscious of (heterosexual) onanism in his early childhood. At puberty a peculiar form of inhibition of masturba-

[7] T. Reik, *op. cit.*, p. 213.

tion had set in, conditioned by the accompanying homosexual fantasies. At the date of the analysis he had in the main substituted for masturbation gymnastic and athletic activities which, although they were entirely ego-syntonic, were still affected by the full strength of the prohibition against masturbation. Contrary to his conscious will, he felt that he ought not to do gymnastics; they would make him healthy, whereas he ought to be ill. When he experienced the need for punishment after gymnastics, he had to masturbate without enjoyment until he felt quite ill. In this way what had been forbidden was reproduced afresh in the punishment in a far less disguised form than it had assumed in the act that merited punishment.[8] The special vehemence of this compulsive masturbation confirms Reik's idea that *forced* instinctual satisfactions arise from the need for punishment.[9]

Frequently, however, the patient broke off masturbation before ejaculation. He did this consciously to exacerbate his punishment; the analysis showed that this stood for a latent safeguard against punishment, since the ejaculation was regarded by his unconscious as castration. If on occasion he carried the masturbation as far as ejaculation, he afterwards swallowed his own emission. This was, in the first place, a simultaneous satisfaction of his bisexual trends, which sprang from his twofold identification with the parents whom he had overheard in the sexual act; he had actually dreamed that he ran away from the "catastrophe" with two heads, one with hair, i.e. feminine, and the other shaven, i.e. masculine. But it was further an avoidance of castration, since he took back the lost emission into his body, although at the same time it was a repetition of the castration: the swallowing of the emission corresponded to the incorporation of his own penis (oral mother-identification).

The castration idea, which here, as so often, meant both a punishment and a feminine instinctual aim, was able at times in spite of deep repression to penetrate into consciousness in a gross and undisguised form; its penal significance was then intended to mask the wish fulfillment. Thus for some time during his illness he walked on crutches. Occasionally he tied up his testicles with the intention of cutting them off: "Then I shall at least be freed from these instincts." The whole significance of the inferiority felt by seven-month children, recently described by Hollós,[10] appeared as a rationalization of the inferiority due to the castration complex when he once exclaimed: "I wish I had been a seven-month child! I am certainly utterly worthless, *but in that case I should at least have known the reason for it!*" In the same way he occasionally recognizes quite con-

---

[8] Cf. G. Groddeck, "Wunscherfuellungen der irdischen und goettlichen Strafen," *Int. Z. Psa.*, Vol. 6, 1920.

[9] T. Reik, *op. cit.*, pp. 208–209.

[10] S. Hollós, "Die Psychoneurose eines Fruehgeborenen," *Int. Z. Psa.*, Vol. 10, 1924.

sciously the character of his neurosis as a simultaneous satisfaction of instinct and need for punishment; he scourges himself in order to suffer: "That will deliver me from my illness more quickly than the analysis will!" Just as naïvely he revealed the mechanism of criminality from a sense of guilt: "I will murder them all, and then at least I shall be put in prison, and shall not need a neurosis any longer." [11]

The conception that punishment also entails a license for the acts that follow it found confirmation in the relatively violent instinctual outbreaks that succeeded his self-chastisements without either a sense of guilt or a recognition of his morbidity. Reik has drawn attention to the fact that such outrageous and apparently guilt-free misdeeds, opposed to the patient's whole character but nevertheless permitted by the ego, are "crimes due to the sense of guilt." [12] Thus the patient seriously made up his mind to violate his sister or his mother (in doing so he was, it is true, also aiming at a denial of deeply repressed homosexual incest wishes); he perpetrated exhibitionistic actions without having the least notion that his conduct represented an instinctual gratification, just as he was entirely ignorant of the sexual nature of his self-scourging. He tortured animals and dolls horribly, had nihilistic fantasies, wanted to kill the whole of humanity and destroy the whole world. These sadistic fantasies of his had, however, never been realized on other human beings. They lead us to a very clear comprehension of the manifold relations between his conduct and his self-punishment. His instinct-ridden outbursts were (a) the cause of his self-punishment (the act that gave rise to his need for punishment), (b) its result (criminality from a sense of guilt), (c) its equivalent (repetition of the act in the punishment), and (d) an attempt to free himself from it (they did not involve a sense of guilt or recognition of being ill).

The prototype of the patient's sadistic fantasies was his mother, who was so furious when he or any of the other children got into any mischief. The adoption of his mother into the patient's superego thus developed its effects in both directions: the mother's corrections were continued on his own person by his self-chastisements, while his sadistic fantasies were evidence of his longing to imitate his mother in his external relationships. At the same time his mother was the object of his aggressive impulses; he wished to conduct himself with regard to her exactly as she, on her part, had acted toward him. He dreamed that his mother was lying in his lap like a child. This reversal of situations had in its time resulted in a narcissistic, homosexual object choice. When he reached

---

[11] The clear insight the patient had into his pyschic mechanisms will not astonish us, having regard to the nature of his symptoms.

[12] T. Reik, op. cit., p. 94.

maturity he assumed a friendly, condescending attitude toward his mother, but exhibited from time to time irrational outbreaks of wrath; he recalled from his childhood days a similar alternation of conduct on her part.

In the analysis he spoke insultingly of his mother for hours together with terrible vehemence and monotony, described with the utmost indignation her behavior, her bigotry, her preposterous educational maxims, and had fantasies of either killing or violating her out of revenge. There is no doubt that this over-determined hate against his mother served the purpose of concealing the normal oedipus attitude of hate against the weak father, as Boehm has shown with regard to homosexuals who hate their mothers.[13] Nevertheless, it was also very evident that the aggressions against his mother were the equivalents of aggressions against himself. He carried out in actual fact against himself the injury that he then said he wished to do to his mother. The mother whom he hated, who, he believed, demanded from him punishment, illness, death, proved to be a projection of his superego. In beating himself mercilessly, while reviling his conscience all the time, he was demonstrating in his own body how he would thrust a knife with delight into his mother's body. It was a kind of projection of his superego *backward* to the place in the external world from which it had come —a regressive projection. We recall the fact that Freud has already described [14] this decomposition of the function of conscience and its regressive projection into the external world in the case of paranoiac delusions of observation. The significance of such a projection is of an exquisitely *economic* character. This is immediately intelligible when we remember how Freud explains projection: "Towards the outer world there is a barrier against stimuli, and the mass of excitations coming up against it will take effect only on a reduced scale; towards what is within no protection against stimuli is possible. . . . There will be a tendency to treat them (such inner excitations as bring with them an overplus of pain) as though they were acting not from within but from without, in order for it to be possible to apply against them the defensive measures of the barrier against stimuli." [15]

The economic alleviation which projection affords was seen especially clearly in the occasional outcry of the patient, after he had been complaining about his rigorous conscious and had "resolved" never to punish himself again: "If anyone comes again to demand punishment from me, I will murder him in cold blood!" In his paranoid condition the transference, since it lay in a homosexual situation, furnished him with quite a special opportunity for projection. He had, for example, a "paranoid transference dream" of a kind similar to the one

[13] F. Boehm, "Beitraege zur Psychologie der Homosexualitaet, III. Homosexualitaet und Oedipus-komplex," *Int. Z. Psa.,* Vol. 12, 1926.

[14] S. Freud, "On Narcissism: An Introduction," *Coll. Pap.,* Vol. IV.

[15] S. Freud, *Beyond the Pleasure Principle,* London, Hogarth, 1948, p. 33.

Freud once communicated.[16] The analyst had put on a beard like his father in order to force a father-transference on him; occasionally he believed that the analyst had sexual intentions with regard to him.

He also employed purely paranoidal projections for the purpose of self-punishment in his complicated schemes for provoking quarrels with his father and with the analyst: e.g., indirectly through him his father received a document which contained numerous implicit accusations against him; then he exaggerated a really trifling piece of fault-finding on his father's part, stormed at his father's lack of understanding, and railed against him for hours at a time. He maneuvered everything in such a way that his father would have to blame him and thus furnish a reason for his insulting him. In this way, by a rationalized projection, he would liberate himself from the compulsion to revile himself. Should the provocation prove ineffectual, should his father not scold him sufficiently, he would thereupon alter reality in the manner of a delusion of persecution. His "conscience thus encounters him in regressive form as an external, hostile influence." [17]

In the analysis, when the analyst casually remarked that he ought not to spend twenty minutes in excusing himself for being five minutes late, he declared that the analyst had apparently unconsciously felt that his being late was an aggression directed against him; the analyst was afraid of it, and in order to divert him from the subject, he had given him so severe a rebuke, and treated him so badly. Thus not only is the aggression which he feels himself transformed into one which the analyst feels, but he suspects, once more delusionally, an aggression on the part of the analyst simply in order to be attacked *from without*. By his persistent lateness and his hour-long, monotonous talk about it, he was fighting, as the analysis proved, not only against his homosexual transference love, but also against the constant pressure of his own conscience. The sexual element in this paranoid mechanism is evident; what relates to punishment in it falls into the following scheme: (a) a predominant sense of guilt, (b) a provocation of punishment (criminality from the sense of guilt), (c) when punishment does not take place, a perception of punishment of the nature of a delusion of persecution, (d) abuse externally directed, representing a projection of the ego as the object of the superego's aggression. Freud has characterized the delusion of persecution in the following way: "I do not love him—indeed, I hate him—he hates (persecutes) me"; [18] in the case of our patient "I hate him" was intended to shout down not only "I love him" but "I hate myself." Ac-

---

16 S. Freud, "Certain Neurotic Mechanisms in Jealousy, Paranoia and Homosexuality," *Coll. Pap.*, Vol. II.

17 S. Freud, "On Narcissism: An Introduction," *Coll. Pap.*, Vol. IV, p. 53.

18 S. Freud, "Psycho-Analytic Notes upon an Autobiographical Account of a Case of Paranoia (Dementia Paranoides)," *Coll. Pap.*, Vol. III, London, Hogarth, 1948.

cording to Reich those parts of the superego that have remained isolated from the ego—i.e., those parts of the superego that have not effected any ego alteration—are particularly well suited for this regressive projection.[19]

The projection of the patient's conscience went with an excessively aggressive attitude to the casual agents his conscience employed. He wanted, for instance, to have the chauffeur by whom he had let himself be run down arrested, or else to give him a merciless thrashing.

These extensive processes of condensation were facilitated by the actual sadistic behavior of his mother. Behind his sadistic fantasies in which he imitated his mother, he concealed his passive libidinal wishes and his need for punishment. For several nights during a transitory phase of the transference, he ran the streets looking for a girl. He never managed to get one. It happened every time that some old gentleman, whom he roundly abused, would snatch the girls away from him just when he was on the point of accosting them. In this way he repeated his infantile disillusionment, not only in the sense that his mother preferred his father to him, but also that his father preferred his mother to him. It was this passive homosexual attitude that evoked the sense of guilt and afterward, in a regressive form, took its place. On seeing an old man urinating he felt that he heard the command: "Now you must die!"

The sexualizing of his self-chastisements certainly gave the impression of being secondary in character. The sadism of his superego seemed to outweigh the masochism of the ego, just as he had also been conscious of his self-reproaches. Undoubtedly he felt that *death* was the punishment that was really awaiting him; it was only by chance that the accident with the motorcar passed off so lightly. He had forbidden himself gymnastics because, according to his idea, they were calculated to restore him to health. In a narcissistic game he set a picture of the Apoxyomenos alongside his own reflection, in order to compare himself with it; there, bodily confronted with one another, stood his actual ego and his ego-ideal, the conflict between which consisted in his illness. He said to himself he did not dare to be as healthy as that; when this prohibition came to him from without, he felt it only as an alleviation. On that account he could not believe even that the analyst wanted to cure him; just when he wished to study a symptom it disappeared—what a villain he must be!

We append the following summary: The first thing to be taken into account in the clinical picture was the bisexual predisposition aroused by the primal scene (dream of the two heads). The introjection of his mother had a pathogenic result. This was followed: (a) in the ego, by its becoming the representative of homosexuality, warded off in paranoid fashion; (b) in the superego, by his accepting all his mother's prohibitions, and ratifying them by his self-chastise-

[19] W. Reich, *op. cit.*, p. 108.

ment. On the other hand, his mother appeared to him in his sadistic fantasies as his ideal. He wished to imitate his mother (stand in the same relation as she to his father).

These conditions are complicated by the fact that we have also to assume analogous processes going on in connection with the father-identification. Not only do the object trends compete with the identifications, but the different identifications compete with one another. The sexualizing of punishment appeared to be secondary; it had more essentially the character of an unrelenting aggression of the superego than that of an instinctual gratification of the id. A "borrowed" guilt from the mother was certainly in some degree probable, but it was not corroborated by the analysis.

### III

The second case furnishes a more distinct picture of "moral masochism." The patient's pangs of conscience were, as such, unconscious, and were manifested in the analysis as passive homosexual gratification. He came under analysis for impotence, but proved to be one of those patients about whom Freud has said: "We are usually able to make a confident promise of recovery to the psychically impotent, but, as long as we are ignorant of the dynamics of the disturbance, we ought to be more cautious in making this prognosis. An unpleasant surprise awaits us if the analysis discloses the cause of the 'purely psychical' impotence to be a typically masochistic attitude, perhaps embedded since infancy." [20]

At the root of the trouble there lay aggressive tendencies against the father, corresponding to the normal oedipus complex. These had led by reaction to a vast general inhibition of aggression, which had then been utilized for the satisfaction of a passive feminine attitude. The adoption of the mother into the ego which thus ensued was—in contrast to the earlier case—opposed by a *paternal* superego, to the influence of which one may ascribe the circumstance that the masochism originating in this way took a *moral* form. The identification with the father had miscarried in characteristic fashion, so that the borrowing of the sense of guilt from the father was quite impressive.

It was the trauma of an infantile observation of the maternal genitals that, as Freud has described,[21] activated the boy's castration anxiety and brought about a great mental revolution. In it he regressed from father- to mother-identification, and simultaneously from the phallic to the sadistic-anal stage. His neurosis could be recognized as a repetition of these early infantile libidinal vicissitudes, since his recent experience contained an exactly similar incident: he had been for

[20] S. Freud, "A Child is Being Beaten," *Coll. Pap.*, Vol. II, p. 193.
[21] S. Freud, "The Passing of the Oedipus-Complex," *Coll. Pap.*, Vol. II.

the first time having sexual relations with a woman (she had seduced him, and was twice his age); but the necessity for amputation of a finger had then demonstrated the reality of the danger of castration (just as once before the glimpse of the feminine genitalia had done) and his neurosis broke out with impotence and so-called "states of depression." The latter became recognizable afterward as self-punishments—suffering caused by an overpowering sense of guilt.

From the beginning of the analysis there came clearly into view both the complete oedipus complex and the castration complex. At a deeper level the castration which he feared was desired: since it combined both punishment and the passive feminine attitude, I shall add a few observations regarding it.

The obscurity surrounding the sadistic conception of the sexual act in the patient's mind had led to a condensation of the threatener and the threatened, of the castrator and the castrated. Thus it came about that circumcised Jews, who were despised in the *milieu* in which the patient lived, became dangerously sexual castrators, and women and their genitals became a power which menaced the penis. According to an infantile theory, he imagined that the penis crumbled away in the sexual act and that bits of it remained in the vagina. There could plainly be discerned in the patient's unconscious mind two opposing types of castration: the one masculine, consisting in cutting; the other feminine, consisting in biting. The latter type made use of a penis hidden within the feminine genitalia as its executive organ.[22] Behind the idea that the mother had robbed the father of his penis, which remained menacingly within her, like a shining jewel or a hidden sword, there lay the earlier one that the vagina was a hollow penis tucked in like a glove-finger. The return of the repressed from beneath repression showed that the purpose behind this supposition was to obliterate all traces of the possibility of castration which had been demonstrated *ad oculos* by the woman's lack of penis; the hollow penis eventually became a secreted penis which had been stolen from the father, and in this way what was originally meant for a denial of castration became a very dangerous castration instrument.

For a time the patient's impotence took the form of a premature recession of erection after it had set in promptly. He had the impression that his penis "withdrew inside him," became a hollow penis. His impotence thus represented his transformation into a woman. The change of the penis into a hollow penis—indeed the whole idea of a hollow penis—was a prophylactic measure against castration. *Transformation into a woman with an imagined hollow penis was, therefore, a means of avoiding castration.* Thus the form which the impotence took led to the discovery of the mechanism with which the patient sought to

[22] F. Boehm, "Beitraege zur Psychologie der Homosexualitaet, II. Ein Traum eines Homosexuellen," *Int. Z. Psa.*, Vol. 8, 1922.

protect himself from the menace to his virility, i.e. a secondary mother-identification.

His early sexual observations had left him with a prohibition which influenced all his later sexual activities and was especially directed against his excessive sadistic impulses, which had only been strengthened by regression. Frequent parental quarrels furnished an objective foundation for his rooted sadistic conception of the sexual act. In his fantasies and dreams he repeatedly saw symbols of the maternal and feminine genitals covered with blood. This aggression that was to be inhibited was, however, undoubtedly directed to a far greater degree against his own sex and originally against his father. There was a condensation here of inimical and sadistic impulses. Not only did he occasionally feel, to his extreme horror, murderous impulses against his father, but by mistake he had brought about two shooting accidents in which he had nearly killed his father in reality.

This compensating reactive inhibition dominated the patient's character. He was quiet and reserved, avoiding every kind of action that had in any way the appearance of aggression. Owing to his impotence he shunned all sexual aggressiveness, and had been potent only in the affair in which the woman took the active part. Otherwise he was afraid of his sadistic impulses because he expected castration by the woman as a revenge. He never protected himself against wrong, and allowed himself to be taken advantage of constantly. Even as a child he had always been "good" and quiet, and had never been able to refuse anyone a request. His slow progress in school and later on in his profession was because, it appeared, he might otherwise have outstripped his contemporaries and thus injured them. His masochism had therefore in typical fashion originated at first in the turning of his sadism against himself, in the transformation of activity into passivity. In this connection his tendency to self-destruction was by no means slight; the shooting accidents in which his father was nearly killed led, after a turning against himself, to his exposing himself recklessly in the direct line of enemy fire during the war; he was utterly unconscious of his own intention in so doing.

This transformation of sadism into masochism coincided with the reversion to the feminine attitude already mentioned. One had the impression that the compulsory inhibition of aggression due to the castration anxiety had been, so to speak, turned to advantage by the feminine attitude, with the view of extracting the maximum of pleasure from a situation of enforced deprivation. This outlet would not have been possible had a previous object love for the father not pointed the way to it. And of course the masochistic "depression" could also occasionally be used for the sadistic tormenting of other persons.

Analysis of the various repetitions in the transference of this all-important turning against the self showed that the *moral masochism,* the ceaseless self-punishments and self-restrictions, owed their origin to the same regressive transformation as the scanty feminine masochistic impulses. A single episode may be given as an example of many others similar to it:

While traveling to meet a woman friend he took part in a game of chance with some unknown men on the train and lost a sum of money which for a man in his circumstances was very large. As a result of this loss he could not pay the analyst his current fee, nor take the intended excursion with his friend. He was surprised that the analyst neither scolded nor punished him on this account; immediately on reaching the end of his journey he had said to his friend penitently that she ought to beat him. It occurred to him further that during the journey he had felt an urgent need to defecate, but had not paid any attention to this in the excitement of the game; it was not until later that he satisfied this need and soiled his fingers in doing so.

There are several points in this material that we are able to observe very clearly: (a) The strata-like structure of the feminine and infantile attitudes in masochism. (b) The eroticizing of the need for punishment. The repetition of the passive, feminine attitude evoked by the analysis leads to self-punishment in the form of loss of money. This loss, however, is at the same time a "crime due to a sense of guilt," as well as a sadistic injury of the father (analyst) and the mother (friend), and a repetition of the offense that needed punishment—a passive homosexual act. The punishment which he seeks for this, the request to be beaten, is again a satisfaction of a purely passive sexual trend. (c) The coincidence of regression to the feminine stage with regression to the anal. (d) The progressive building up in layers of feminine and moral masochism. *The regression from morality to the oedipus complex* is clearly evidenced in the need, following on self-punishment (itself also a crime), to be thrashed in punishment by his father or his mistress. The penalizing superego in this case is the surrogate of the actual father, from whom the patient seeks punishment as a form of regressive instinctual satisfaction. This falls into line with the fact that the patient grew more and more insistent in his requests to the analyst for *punishment* or—*hypnosis.* He had heard that Professor Forster was not particularly mild in his treatment of pathological patients, and he wished to go to him to be cured of his impotence. "He would make a thorough examination of my penis, and then give me a good scolding."

He also displayed unmistakably another unpleasant concomitant of moral masochism: the negative therapeutic reaction. As a result of the interpretation of his self-punishments his self-reproaches became gradually more conscious, and his "depressions" approximated more and more to pure melancholia.

The determining mother-identification was established in the ego totally unknown to the patient, who was constantly engaged in the endeavor to imitate his father. In vivid contrast to his supposed ideal, his conduct in life was like his mother's. His exhibitionistic and other instinctual characteristics could be traced to the behavior of his mother, while his father's abrupt temperament furnished him with the material and occasion for his fantasies.

This mother-identification was rendered possible by:

(a) *An early object-relation to the father,* which was continued in the adoption of the father into his superego; this had a further existence in the borrowed sense of guilt which will be discussed later on.

(b) *An anal eroticism of extraordinary strength,* which accompanied the sado-masochistic fantasies and was again regressively cathected at the same time as the genital inhibition of aggression took place. The copious anal symptoms of the patient showed clear traces of the mother-identification. Even his dread of castration was here regressively transferred to the anal zone. He had the impression that there was something behind in his body that was cut in two. He even realized an anal castration in his childhood by breaking a chamber pot under him and injuring himself on the seat, and later when he was grown up by undergoing an intestinal operation, of which he formed a similar conception.

(c) *Early visual sexual observations of his parents,* which activated the bisexual attitude, and found its issue in the sight of the maternal genitalia that had such important results. A whole series of screen memories and dreams suggested that an observation of this kind should be presumed. His skepticism, too, could be traced to the doubt whether he had seen correctly, whether there could really be anyone without a penis. In this way he often gave expression to the most grotesque doubts regarding psychoanalysis. In a *déjà vu* kind of reminiscence he recognized that during puberty he had cherished a similar doubt regarding the possibility of sexual intercourse between his parents. Occasionally even at the date of the analysis he expressed manifest scoptophilic desires.

A dream that brought into the transference the traumatic scoptophilic experience and its consequences is given in brief. It consists of two parts, and runs as follows:

(a) *He has to go to the elementary school and start from the very beginning.* (b) *A little girl is about to undergo an operation on the abdominal cavity or on the mouth. He asks a nurse: "Is the operation over? Ah! Has it already begun?" She says: "It is just over" or perhaps something else; she expresses herself very obscurely.*

The day's residues: A short time previously the patient's potency had been restored by the treatment; he took advantage of this by indulging to excess in sexual intercourse with his mistress. The day before it had been said that he might be right in suspecting that this was the cause of his feeling so worn out and "depressed." He therefore made up his mind not to have intercourse again; but, as a matter of fact, that same evening, in defiance of the supposed prohibition, he had intercourse again.

Associations: *For the first part:* When he was at school he always had to hurry in order not to be late. Anyone who was late in arriving at school was punished. When he was afraid he would not be on time his father used to give him roses out of their garden to take with him as a present to the teacher, and in that way he escaped being punished. That, however, should not have been allowed. When he was sixteen years old there had been on one occasion a scandal in the school. A youth had done something, he did not know what, to a little girl, and had been soundly thrashed for it. *"To start over again from the very beginning":* If he could begin the analysis over again from the start, he would be "nicer," would give better associations: i.e., he would bring roses with him for the analyst, so as not to be punished for the coitus of the previous evening.

*For the second part:* A woman friend of his had an operation for carcinoma in the tongue. The girl in the dream is her daughter. Something in her mouth was cut open, something that had been closed was opened: i.e., a vagina was formed, she was castrated. He now adds that in the dream he was perhaps to have been operated on himself. His intention in being there was to observe the operation. As an adult—it was shortly after the amputation of his finger—he had overheard a coitus through the thin walls of an hotel bedroom. At the operation in the dream everything was very obscure—the instruments and the apparatus were mysteriously large. Then he recalled that when he was about fourteen he had set a little girl of two on a chamber pot, and in so doing he had observed her genitals. Thus he had committed the same transgression as the youth at school—i.e., he replaced his recent misdemeanor in the matter of the coitus by the offense of scoptophilia; in the memory of the thrashing the youth had received as punishment, and in the repeated assertion that bringing the roses was a wrong action, he was therefore asking to be thrashed; he identified himself with a girl, and was castrated. Recently, when he had asked how long it would be before the analysis was finished, he had received just as "obscure" an answer as he had to the analogous question in the dream.

The coitus which preceded the dream had mobilized his sense of guilt in such a way that he desired the penalizing castration and forthwith sexualized it in a passive feminine attitude (identification with the woman). In doing so, however, he betrayed the fact that he considered his inspection of the feminine genitals to be the all-important guilty act.

In connection with his memories of sexual curiosity, it came to his mind that he had the idea he must infect himself with pathogenic bacteria in order to be ill and be made much of: i.e., a disguised idea of self-destruction, which represented self-punishment for the offense of scoptophilia. This was, however, again sexualized in the passive feminine sense; the infecting bacteria represented impregnating spermatozoa.

Once more then we will summarize the development of the mother-identification: The patient, warned as to the reality of castration by his observation of the mother's lack of a penis, first regressed from the genital to the sadistic-anal stage of organization. The reinforced sadism then gave way under castration anxiety into the reaction formation of inhibited aggression, and turned into masochism; this united with the newly cathected anal eroticism and wakened his former love for his father in such a way that a transition from father-identification to mother-identification was the result.

In order to gain a complete understanding of the moral masochism we must now continue to follow the vicissitudes of the older father-identification. Its libido flowed only in part back again to the old object relation. Part of the father-identification was retained in the superego; in the recognition that the self-punishments were made use of for satisfying homosexual trends there was implied an admission that the penalizing authority was a surrogate of the father. What further significance, however, was due to the father-identification only became manifest when it came to light with surprising clarity that the sense of guilt was *borrowed* from the father and that this borrowing—quite in the way Freud has described in the passage mentioned before—represented the residue of an old object love toward him.

A little episode, which occurred after repeated discussion of the conditions that have been already described here, may be mentioned. Heaping bitter reproaches on himself—as he now did frequently—the patient declared that he lived too extravagantly; he must discipline himself; he ought, for example, to sell his scarfpin. He informed me a week later in reference to this that his mother was complaining in her letters about his father's irresponsibility; for instance, the week before she had told him in a letter that his father had bought himself an expensive scarfpin.

By his proposal to sell his own scarfpin the patient was saying to his mother in the sense of the oedipus complex: "Just take me, I am better than Father." But he told her this in a peculiar fashion. The reference to his father's offense had mobilized his own sense of guilt; he had to atone for his father's sins.

Many details of the patient's behavior now became intelligible. For instance, he was ashamed when another person got into trouble. He felt that he himself was responsible when acts were censured of a kind for which he was really not at all to blame. The self-reproaches that were now becoming acute in his depression had the same significance as the latent reproaches against the analyst; "the likeness to melancholia" was "unmistakable."

The following facts have to be noticed: The patient had an extraordinary respect for his father, had set up for himself an ideal image of him, though the accounts he occasionally gave of his father's actual behavior did not at all fit in with this ideal. He was thereupon ashamed of his father, but made light of his feelings, and was patently engaged in endeavoring to close his eyes to the contradictions between the ideal father and the real.

But they continued, nevertheless, to exert their influence—to such an extent, indeed, that *it seemed as if he had committed his father's offenses himself, and was being called to account for it by the ideal father.*

For instance, it was remarkable that the patient's sense of guilt—first unconsciously, then consciously—should be aimed so particularly at his sexual life, as if he were a horrible debauchee. He quite groundlessly reproached himself with infidelity to his mistress and was oppressed after every occasion on which he had been in her company. The suspicion was now put to him that possibly his father had committed the offense of the (imagined) dissipation and infidelity, but it was indignantly thrust aside, although since he had been grown up he had already heard of two girls to whom his father had made sexual approaches. On his return, however, from a short visit to his parents, he related with amazement that he had only then noticed how his father would cast lascivious looks at any woman and frequently made offensive remarks about them; this had no doubt always been so, only he had never noticed it before. We could only express entire agreement with this supposition. Evidently as a child he had felt that similar behavior on his father's part was an *infidelity toward his mother,* but had refused to accept the knowledge implied in this observation, and by adopting ("borrowing") the guilt he turned the reproaches concerning excess and infidelity against himself. The father's infidelity gave him indeed access to his mother, made it possible for him to woo her—as we saw in the case of the scarfpin—and the oedipus guilt could also hide itself behind the borrowed sense of guilt that related to the "infidelity." This now furnished an explanation of what at first seemed so interesting and paradoxical—i.e., that the sense of guilt which the patient felt in connection with every other sexual action was lacking precisely in connection with that mother-figure with whom he had had happy relations: the sense of guilt borrowed from his father in relation to his *infidelity* of necessity made itself more noticeable in the case of persons unlike his mother than in that of persons like her.

The analysis was also able to discover the prototype—perhaps the original one —for the infidelity of his father; a sister of his father's had stayed with them for some time and frequent quarrels occurred, the aunt and the father taking sides against the mother. The child had a fantasy that the father had taken the aunt for his wife and forsaken the mother. This grievous accusation he then diverted from the ideal father-imago and turned against himself. Precisely the same took place here as in a case of moral masochism described by Lampl, where the guilt-borrowing took its origin in the father's adultery (in this case actual).[23]

The borrowing of guilt can only be explained by an original impulse to commit the same sin as the father. As a matter of fact, as a child the patient had tried to make a sexual attack on this aunt but had been repelled.

This wish to imitate the father was frustrated by castration anxiety. He may not do all that the father does, but he has to take on himself the penalties his father merited. "Thus the shadow of the object fell on the ego." [24] The paternal superego demands punishment, not only for all the actions of the ego disapproved by it, but also for those of the real father.[25] The adoption of the father into the ego had of course miscarried, but had nevertheless in some degree been effected, though certainly not in a manner approved by the ego. It was a compromise between the struggles of the id (to enjoy the father's sexual freedom) and of the superego (not to do the same as the father), and the ego had to suffer from it.

The father-ideal had thus become independent of the actual father. It had to be kept intact at all costs. In this way, however, there accrued very great libidinal gains in the direction of passive homosexuality, which became predominant after the regression: he could now overrate the beloved father without restraint, and the self-punishment which took the place of the original genital wish (to imitate the father) was enjoyed in a regressive fashion as a *passive feminine gratification through the father*.

When we recall that Freud has recently described [26] as a powerful motive, urging towards homosexual object choice, regard for the father or fear of him (the mechanism, namely, of "withdrawing from rivalry with him"), we can see now that "guilt-borrowing" is also such a form of withdrawal. By its means everything is permitted to the actual father; he is placed beyond criticism; while the ego with its inhibitions of aggression not only desists from all aggressiveness against the father but is even punished for his misdeeds. We know how great

---

[23] H. Lampl, "Contributions to Case History. A Case of Borrowed Sense of Guilt," *Int. J. Psa.,* Vol. 8, 1927.

[24] S. Freud, "Mourning and Melancholia," *Coll. Pap.,* Vol. IV, p. 159.

[25] Many traits of the borrowed sense of guilt could be explained by the idea, "What I do to myself my father should do to himself," and reminded us in this way of the "magic gestures" which Liebermann has described in his "Monosymptomatischen Neurosen" (lecture at the Salzburg Congress, 1924). We mentioned that the *anal* symptoms of our patient were based on the mother-identification. Now he had to defecate immediately after taking any food. That meant that the mother was not to become pregnant again. He also refused to eat fish, mushrooms, or asparagus. His mother, he said, was very fastidious about what she ate.

[26] S. Freud, "Certain Neurotic Mechanisms in Jealousy, Paranoia and Homosexuality," *Coll. Pap.,* Vol. II, p. 241.

an increase of (unconscious) homosexuality in our case went hand in hand with this withdrawal. The idea that is so fundamental in religion and ethics of *suffering for the guilt of others* may have its roots in a similar mechanism.

There was abundant material in the transference to confirm our hypothesis. This material consisted of an alternation between occasional attempts of the hitherto inhibited aggression to break out, and exacerbations of the depressions, which became more and more like pure melancholia. He cast the same reproaches alternately at the analyst and at himself. On the one hand he developed a quite extraordinary attentiveness to the "little sins" of the analyst, and on the other he declared that the analyst could do all that he himself could not do. While he lived a licentious life, the analyst certainly never had intercourse with women. He said this after he had seen a lady leaving the consulting-room and had spun fantasies about a relation between the analyst and her. He thus repeated directly his behavior in relation to his infantile sexual observations of his father. He does not wish to have seen anything, and feels that he is guilty himself. More and more memories gradually emerged of scenes in which his father had not conducted himself in accordance with his ideal of him. He had forgotten that he had once seen his father's penis, but had reproached himself on account of his exhibitionistic inclinations. Gradually the material of a normal oedipus complex came through, and the cure of his impotence ensued entirely in the form of a liberation of the aggression and a struggle against his homosexuality. He was potent for the first time, when in a sudden uprush of defiance, he kept his mistress with him all night against the expressed prohibition of his landlord. Later on erection took place after a castration ceremonial, the thought suddenly springing up in him like a revelation, "I am really alone with her!" It appeared that up till then he had always felt himself threatened from behind by a gigantic ghost on every occasion of the sexual act.

We know now the fate of the identifications with both parents which had begun in the primal scene: the identification with the father had partly undergone a regressive change into (repressed) homosexual object love, and partly had been idealized and established in the superego; there it raged against the ego, driving it to perpetual self-injuries, and affording by the sexualization of these self-injuries a homosexual gratification to the id. The identification with the mother had been effected chiefly in the ego; it dominated the actual character of the patient and was completely unconscious. He would prefer to be like his father and was—without knowing it—like his mother. The opposition between the two parental identifications was similar to the one which Reich has described as a type of masculine "mistaken sex-identity." [27] We might say that the perpetual

[27] W. Reich, "Mutteridentifizierung auf analer Basis," *Der triebhafte Charakter*, pp. 48 ff.

self-punishments signified an intrapsychic continuation of the abuse he had as a child heard his father giving his mother.

We reach the same result as so many other psychoanalytic writers do at the conclusion of their investigations. We find that a great part of what we have discovered has long ago been uttered in Freud's writings. The "adoption of guilt" turns out to be a new way of regarding a process which was described in *Group Psychology and the Analysis of the Ego* and even in *The Interpretation of Dreams* as "hysterical identification on the basis of the same etiological claim." [28] If all the girls in a class at school imitate the attacks of another girl, instead of, as they really wish, having a similar love affair to hers,[29] then in their case, too, the identification has been effected only in the negative form. In "A Child is Being Beaten," too, Freud has, in the first place, depicted the danger for the masculine character of a regressive homosexual fantasy of being beaten by the father, leading to perpetual self-injury being inflicted throughout life, and has further pointed out that the outcome of a feminine attitude without (manifest) homosexual object choice is "specially remarkable" in the development of the passive fantasy of being beaten.[30] Our patient had had the fantasy of being beaten by a woman only very seldom and with very slight affect. We believe we have shown why *moral* masochism with its strong ingredient of the death instinct was the particular form which the patient's masochism took. But that also made a "feminine attitude without a homosexual object choice" possible for him. His homosexuality, through his introjection of his father and his unconscious rage against himself, became a drama that was enacted within his personality, and hence required no real object.

## IV

We have little more to add. We hope we have succeeded in reproducing the impression received in the treatment of patients of this class. That impression may be regarded as an immediate clinical confirmation of the Freudian doctrine of the instincts, and the view that the sense of guilt is a unique, primitive, ruthless thing, which would not shrink from the destruction of the patient's own ego, and is not synonymous with passive sexual libido. It is the clinical representative of the mute death instincts. We have seen that in the neurotic clinical picture it appears always in instinctual fusion with the more noisy sexual impulses, that the proportion of both components in the fusion can be very different, and that this combination is extremely important for prognosis. We have

[28] S. Freud, "The Interpretation of Dreams," *The Basic Writings*, New York, Modern Library, 1938, p. 228.
[29] S. Freud, *Group Psychology and the Analysis of the Ego*, London, Hogarth, 1948, pp. 64–65.
[30] S. Freud, "A Child is Being Beaten," *Coll. Pap.*, Vol. II, p. 196.

further got to know a series of possible connections between the instinctual demands of the id and the demands of the superego for punishment. In the first case we see, particularly in the symptoms, the various condensations of deed and punishment, the quality of punishment attaching to deeds and that of wish fulfillment to punishments; the combination of "criminality from a sense of guilt," punishment as a license for further sins, and the part played by external projection of the superego in paranoid neurotics and probably also in criminals. In the second case we saw the genesis and constitution of moral masochism; the excessive sexualizing in it of all penalizing actions; the turning of the sadistic trends against the patient's self, and the change of the normal oedipus complex into the inverted form as a preliminary; further, the mechanism of guilt-borrowing as its most advantageous expression. Unfortunately, in regard to the therapeutic aspect, we cannot say anything more hopeful than Freud has already said in his footnote on the subject of the borrowed sense of guilt.

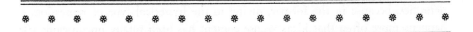

NINE

# Concerning Unconscious Communication *

FREUD has already described long ago—for the first time in *The Interpretation of Dreams*—how a person can react not only to parapraxes or other self-betrayals on the part of another person as though he understood them, but can respond without knowing it to even less clear indications of other people's unconscious intentions; and it occasionally even happens that two people unconsciously converse with each other without either of them being aware of it. There are two different ways of accounting for such events. Either minimal signals are perceived and intuitively understood by one's own similarly oriented unconscious, or there is an immediate communication—like what Loewenstein has called "induction of affect" [1]—except that here not only affects but ideas as well are communicated. We see an "induction" of this kind—where only the induced idea (but not its origin) became conscious to the receiving person—in certain cases which Freud recently described as telepathic; [2] and in which a subject perceived in this way the unconscious wishes of another person who was present. Freud noted there that ideas which are in the act of rising from the unconscious are particularly liable to such telepathic transfer. This is obviously also the reason why we can now and then suddenly and spontaneously guess in an analysis what unconscious ideas are operative in our patient at that moment. So far, I have only rarely experienced in a clear and unequivocal way such a sudden knowledge about an unconscious ideational content in the patient's mind; but every time I have, it has proved true and could be verified by the patient. Obviously, this is more frequent with hysterics than with obsessional

* First published in *Int. Z. Psa.*, Vol. 12, 1926, pp. 84–87.
[1] R. Loewenstein, "Ueber Affektinduktion," lecture at the Berlin Psychoanalytic Society, 1924.
[2] S. Freud, "Dream and Telepathy," *Coll. Pap.*, Vol. IV, London, Hogarth, 1948.

neurotics, because in the former, owing to the hysterical type of repression, it happens more often that ideas whose content has been totally unconscious rise into consciousness. Here is a small example to illustrate what I mean. The image of an egg and a glass of water appeared to a hysterical patient in the course of the analysis of her infantile sexual explorations. Though I did not remember ever having seen a magician manipulate such things, I suddenly got the association: "Those were the belongings of a conjurer." And so it was.

This phenomenon is very different from the unconscious perception of another person's unconscious by means of signals—a proceeding which is psychologically far more transparent. Let me give a rare example of such a—so to say—unconscious discourse. The "signals" involved were by no means "minimal," and what is noteworthy is not that they were perceived but that they remained unconscious to the two parties. Here something that at first sight appeared to be occult turned out to be amenable to complete rational understanding.

The patient, who came into analysis on account of characterological difficulties, had a relationship with a widow who was considerably older than he; he had made her acquaintance by "rescuing" her from financial difficulties. Consciously, he felt contempt for her, but could not break with her; and he came into the analysis with, among other things, the wish to be freed of this tie. That this widow represented his mother had not yet come up in the analysis. The woman herself was in her climacteric and obviously knew full well that were she to lose her lover, she would spend the rest of her life without gratification; she held onto him with all her might and occasionally made scenes of jealousy, but in general she anxiously overlooked—as far as was possible—all the indications he gave of his intention to break with her. She was a simple woman from whom neither subtlety nor lies could be expected. She lived in a suburb and rarely came to town, and my patient used to visit her in her home.

One morning, after lengthy internal struggles, the patient picked up a girl on the street, went walking with her, sat down in a small park—of the existence of which he had not known before—chatted and smoked some cigarettes with her, and then took her to a restaurant. After that, they agreed on a date and he went about his business. In the evening, as he was undressing, he saw that he had lost one of his cuff links. He remembered that while walking with the girl, he had noticed that a cuff link had come open, and he was angry with himself for not having put it to rights at once. The next day he visited his old friend. In her dining-room, on the table, there was a tray for visiting cards. As he entered the room, he saw a cuff link lying on the tray, as though it had been put there especially for him to notice. He picked it up and saw that it was a link of the same kind as his own and matched the one he was still wearing. He became very frightened; it at once occurred to him that the link was

there to convict him of his yesterday's adventure. He gave up this idea immediately, because he knew that his friend was unable to pretend and would
already have made a scene if she had known anything. He asked her: "What
is this cuff link?" "I found it yesterday." "Why is it here?" "It occurred to me
that one might need a cuff link like that on some occasion, so I brought it home
and put it down there for the time being." "Where did you find it?" "In such-
and-such a park." "How did you come to be there?" "Unusually enough, I had
to buy something in that neighborhood yesterday; I rested in the park, whose
existence I did not know of before, and there was the cuff link under the bench."
"About what time?" "About one o'clock." This was the time when he himself
had sat there. It was thus certain that she had sat down on the bench immediately after he had gone, found the link he had lost there, and taken it
home.

Two circumstances give one pause, one on the side of the patient, the other
on that of the woman. Throughout the time he spent in the park, the patient
had a bad conscience about his unfaithfulness, and thought of what his friend
would say if she saw him there; his whole psychological situation was such as
to lend itself to an unconscious self-betrayal. Furthermore, just before he sat
down on the bench he had noticed the open cuff link, and had thus offered his
unconscious, as it were, a convenient occasion for a self-betrayal. As for the
woman, it is striking, first that she should pick up the link and take it home,
and then that she should put it down in an unusual place so that her friend would
see it on entering and would be reminded of his misdemeanor. If she had seen
him with the girl and wanted to confront him with a *corpus delicti,* she could
not have done better. These circumstances admit of only one explanation. The
only part which chance [3] played in the business was that both of them had
come at the same time to the park which was unknown to them before. All the
rest was unconscious, purposive action at lightning speed. The man sitting on
the bench saw the woman nearing; without being in the least aware of it, he
was overcome by a storm of feeling in his doubt whether or not he should reveal
himself; he decided not to, and left the bench quickly with his companion,
but not without fulfilling his self-betraying tendency by shaking his arm so
that the loose cuff link dropped down. The woman must also have seen and
recognized the man. But she did not *want* to see anything; she did not go after
him, but sat down on the bench on which he had sat just before. She found the
link, took it home, and put it on the tray. Perhaps she did not recognize the
man for sure, and put him to the test with the link. It should be stressed once

[3] The temptation is great to deny to this peculiar event, too, the quality of chance, and to regard
it as psychologically determined—perhaps as being a telepathic phenomenon. But there was no
evidence for this in the analysis. Both partners' presence—each unknown to the other—in the neighborhood of the park was entirely well founded rationally.

more that she certainly did not lie, and even after my patient told her the story truthfully, she insisted that she had not seen him and had not recognized the link, and that she had brought it home and put it down without any intentions—and that, indeed, it did not even cross her mind that he could have been in that part of town.

The patient was at first very much astonished by this interpretation; but then a detail occurred to him which substantiated it beyond any doubt. He and the girl had wanted to go away five minutes earlier, but had then decided to stay for one more cigarette. Now he remembered that very suddenly, in the middle of the cigarette he had wanted to finish, he had jumped up, and said impatiently to his companion: "Now we really must go!" and made off with her as fast as he could. This must have been the instant at which he unconsciously caught sight of his woman friend.

Thus not only did the two parties, as though by agreement, immediately repress their having seen each other, since that would have been unpleasant for both; the woman also immediately understood the meaning of the loss of the cuff link and reacted accordingly. Indeed, she did exactly what the behavior of the man secretly challenged her to do. When he jumped up and ran away, but lost his link in so doing, he was saying to her: "You are not to *notice* that I have sat here with a girl; but you are to *know* it!" And that is what she did.

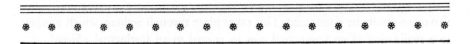

# *T E N*

# Identification*

## I

CHANGES in the ego, in which characteristics which were previously perceived in an object are acquired by the perceiver of them, have long since been familiar to psychoanalysis. They were named "identifications" and set over against "libidinal cathexes of objects" as another possible relationship of a subject to objects in the external world. Freud has given us a comprehensive survey of these processes in his *Group Psychology,* written in 1921.[1] Since the publication of this book, he has shown that the superego too arises from an act of identification. The consequent broadening of the concept of identification justifies an attempt, I think, to establish the common properties of, and differences between, identificatory processes, and to describe them metapsychologically even if such an attempt cannot as yet achieve that clear metapsychological representation of those processes which Freud calls for,[2] seeing that the gaps in our knowledge of the subject are still too numerous.

## II

We shall first consider identifications which occur in the adult, and we shall begin by investigating their dynamics.

The motive force of identifications is always supplied by *drives* (or instincts). These, originating in somatic sources and imposing demands upon the ego, which controls motility, strive for *gratification,* that is, for an adequate alteration of the external world by means of which the tension at the source of the

* First published in *Int. Z. Psa.,* Vol. 12, 1926, pp. 309–325.
[1] S. Freud, *Group Psychology and the Analysis of the Ego,* London, Hogarth, 1948, pp. 60–70.
[2] *Ibid.,* p. 63.

drive can finally be eliminated. This takes place through actions, which amount to a realization of an instinctual *aim* in regard to an instinctual *object*.[3]

Let us first consider normal object love in a schematic way. The object is first of all *perceived* by the subject and his percepts of it leave behind mnemic ideas in his mind. His primitive function of judgment recognizes that the object is capable of affording him gratifications; so now he cathects it with libido. How does this take place? All his ideas of the same object are integrated endopsychically into a unity, which may be labeled the "endopsychic representative of the object," [4] since, as a common expression of many single ideas, it stands for the object. It is on this, and not on the real object existing outside the subject, that the effective cathectic processes take place. By virtue of the cathexes, maintained by instincts in the id, this object representative acquires power over other ideas and object representatives, so that it can exert an "organizing, selective, and formative influence over a given range of psychic processes." [5] The ego has no other avenue to the objects of the external world than through these object representatives, since it is these alone which in the first instance permit of constant *objects* being picked out from the perceptual field. In all this the object representatives (the development of which in the mnemic systems has affinities with the construction of mental concepts) remain distinct from ego contents, thanks to the function of reality testing. The instinctual action demanded by the cathected representation is naturally real and is undertaken upon the external object; in "introversion" this orientation toward reality is missing from the instinctual action; it is replaced by imaginary experiences in regard to the object representative.[6] In object love, therefore, we have the following sequence of things: (1) percept, (2) formation of an object representative, (3) cathecting of the latter by the id, (4) instinctual demands, (5) real instinctual actions in regard to the object.

We know that this course of events may be disturbed in various ways by external or internal frustrations. The latter occur when the ego wards off an instinctual impulse and denies it access to motility; for the impulse, in order to obtain gratification, must now undergo changes. These changes—these vicissitudes of the instincts—may thus also be conceived of as "forms of *defense* against instincts," one form being repression.[7]

It is thus plausible to describe identification too as an instinctual vicissitude. A change is made both in the *object* and the *aim* of the original objectual in-

---

[3] S. Freud, "Instincts and Their Vicissitudes," *Coll. Pap.*, Vol. IV, London, Hogarth, 1948.

[4] S. Rado speaks in the same sense of an "ideational representative" of the object ("Das oekonomische Prinzip der Technik," *Int. Z. Psa.*, Vol. 12, 1926).

[5] *Ibid.*, p. 20.

[6] S. Freud, *A General Introduction to Psychoanalysis*, New York, Perma Giants, 1949, pp. 326–327.

[7] S. Freud, "Instincts and Their Vicissitudes," *Coll. Pap.*, Vol. IV, p. 69.

stinct which leads to the identificatory process. The subject no longer has any interest in the real object (or not nearly so much as before); his ego changes and becomes like an object and the libido concerned is desexualized.

Change of *object*: the place of the object is taken either in part or entirely by the ego. We are familiar with one vicissitude of an instinct in which a similar change takes place, namely its "turning toward the ego," and we explain this as a regression to narcissism.[8] In identification, however, it is not the ego as it has existed so far which becomes the object of an id impulse: the ego alters its form. It appears as if here the id had established its position more thoroughly than in a diffuse turning toward the ego; for even if it is forced by external and internal conditions to resign the object it is fixated on and to resort to its own ego, it finds a better object substitute in an ego which has become like the object than in one which has not. Thus the ego alteration which occurs in identification is done "for the sake of the id." The ego offers itself (as an object) to the id.[9] "Indeed, it is possible that such an identification is an indispensable condition for the giving up by the id of its objects."[10] The ego submits to the id, changes itself as a consequence of its dependence on the id, and thereby "spares itself repressions."[11] Identification seems thus to be a defense method of the ego, of the same order as repression, and is perhaps even more primitive than the latter. The "inconsistencies, eccentricities, and follies" which arise as consequences of the deformations which the ego must endure in its weakness relative to the id and superego [12] may for the most part rest on identifications too. We can also describe this process as a vicissitude of the object representative, for that psychic entity has extended its "formative influence" to the ego itself, has lent it both its form and cathexis, demolishing thereby the barrier between ego and the world of things, without there being any impairment of reality testing. (It is the *mnemic systems* and not the Pcpt. system which take part in the displacement of cathexes.) The ego has taken over the form, the cathexis, and the function of the object representative. In this interplay of ego and object representative either of the two may be considered as the active agent. In point of fact the operative energy arises from the instinctual demand of the id which endows both with cathexis in the first instance. The identifications are thus ego changes based on an instinctual demand of the id, which for internal or external reason is no longer (or not yet) directed toward the external world.

Alteration of aim: the alteration of aim in identification does not seem to subserve the substitutive gratification directly, but comes to the id as an un-

[8] *Ibid.*, pp. 74–75.
[9] S. Freud, *The Ego and the Id*, London, Hogarth, 1947, pp. 37–38.
[10] *Ibid.*, p. 36.
[11] S. Freud, "Neurosis and Psychosis," *Coll. Pap.*, Vol. II, London, Hogarth, 1948, p. 254.
[12] *Ibid.*, p. 254.

welcome consequence of the change of object. The substitution of the object by the ego enforces a deflection of aim from the unlimited sexual aim to an ego aim, that is, a *desexualization*.[13] The libido, bound secondarily to the ego, loses its specific sexual character and becomes thereby amenable to multifarious (intellectual) application. According to a conjecture of Freud's, *all* sublimation occurs by way of an identification.[14] Of great significance for this change in aim is the fact that every identification is accompanied by a defusion of instinct;[15] but we shall not be able to go into this point till later on.

## III

The most important features of identification as regards its topography are now clear. After the differentiation between ego and id has been completed, the identifications take place in the ego (at the bidding of the id). We know from Freud's discoveries that some parts of the ego which are thus changed set themselves up against the rest of the ego, obtain a separate status, and create a lasting change in the psychic structure. They constitute the superego.[16] In adults later identifications may perhaps take place in the superego also. We shall study these differences in detail later on. The close communication between the ego, the superego, and the id, which are the products of differentiations from a common source, makes an exact topographic description of the events concerned especially difficult. There are two cases in which ego changes due to identifications may be deeply rooted in the id: in the first place, when it is precisely the instinctual characteristics (id impulses) of an object which are taken up into the ego, as for instance in homosexuals who have identified themselves with the parent of the same sex;[17] and in the second place, when objects of the deepest impulses of the id find lodgment in the ego, for then they bring back into it a piece of archaic, undifferentiated id, as happens, for instance, in the formation of the superego.[18]

It is to be expected that identifications would not be conscious in their genesis, (this being a vicissitude of an id impulse), while they would be conscious in their result (this being the shape assumed by the ego). The first expectation is fulfilled. When we make an identification we know nothing about it and we

[13] S. Freud, *The Ego and the Id*, pp. 65–66.

[14] *Ibid.*, p. 38.

[15] *Ibid.*, pp. 79–81.

[16] *Ibid.*

[17] S. Freud, *Three Essays on the Theory of Sexuality*, London, Imago, 1949, p. 23 footnote; "The Psychogenesis of a Case of Homosexuality in a Woman," *Coll. Pap.*, Vol. II, p. 215–216; *Group Psychology and the Analysis of the Ego*, pp. 66–67; "Certain Neurotic Mechanisms in Jealousy, Paranoia and Homosexuality," *Coll. Pap.*, Vol. II, pp. 240 ff.

[18] S. Freud, *The Ego and the Id.*

resist any clarifying insight. The existence of conscious imitation does not contradict this view, for such imitation either rests on a deeper, unconscious basis,
or is unrelated to the process of identification proper which we are studying here
from a metapsychological standpoint. The second expectation is, however, not
altogether fulfilled. The close contact of ego and id often causes ego alterations
to pass unnoticed by consciousness. The weight of the repression which rested
upon the oedipus complex is extended to its heirs, so that the core of the superego—which is an identificatory product—is regularly unconscious. The fact that
many people know so little about their own manifest character may be due to a
similar origin of the formation of their ego from the id. Even the demands made
by an introjected object upon the rest of the ego may themselves become the
target of repression.[19]

All identifications bear an archaic character and exhibit the phenomena of the
primary process. That is the hallmark of their origin in the earliest epoch of
development. What we have so far called "identification" proves to be a regression to a primitive introductory stage of object love. This "primary identification" originates in a time when the ego was still very weak and its contradistinction to the id but little pronounced; and this may also explain why in the cases
mentioned the ego alteration due to identification appears to reach into the id.
Identifications themselves, moreover, contribute their share to giving the ego
its fixed differentiation from the id. Yet ego formation can by no means be explained by identifications alone. The notion that ego formation starts from the
system Pcpt.-Cs. as its core, is the basis of Freud's conception of the psychic
apparatus.[20] Thus Reik's view that "the ego is itself a precipitate of our earliest
and most significant identifications" [21] seems to me to be too sweeping.

## IV

We have already indicated that in the final analysis every identification is
motivated by an economic factor, namely, the striving to find a substitute for
lost gratification. The regular prerequisite for identification is a loss of object,
be it due to reality (as in mourning or character change after a disappointment
in love), or to the demand of repressive forces (as in homosexuality), or to
those of the repetition compulsion or deep ambivalence (as in melancholia).
"Primary identification," too, can be conceived of as a reaction to the disap-
pointing loss of the unity which embraced ego and external world. The fact
that even the superego, which is hostile to drives, arises from an attempt of this

[19] *Ibid.*, pp. 74–75.
[20] *Ibid.*, pp. 27 ff.
[21] T. Reik, *Gestaendniszwang und Strafbeduerfnis. Problem der Psychoanalyse und der Krimin-
ologie*, Vienna, Int. Psa. Verlag, 1925, p. 222.

sort to find a substitute for a gratification, shows that what is concerned here is not the obtaining of pleasure, but instinctual discharges on deeper levels of the mind and the maintenance there of psychic equilibrium in the sense of the Nirvana principle. But the "secret alliance" of superego and id [22] often makes the ultimate victory of the pleasure principle possible even here.

V

The preceding discussions impose on us two further problems: (1) If identification is an instinctual vicissitude, then we must ask ourselves which are the instincts that undergo the changes described. (2) Having recognized that the above-mentioned identifications are regressions, we should also like to know something about "primary identification," which was the predecessor of object love. These two questions are closely related.

Erotic and destructive impulses can never be observed in quite pure form. But their admixture is less complete on primitive than on higher levels of organization. In archaic identification the erotic and the destructive impulses act side by side, as yet unfused; and when object love is again replaced by an identification this event is always accompanied by defusion of instinct.[23]

Clinical investigation has shown that in all forms of identification an effective executive instrument is found in *oral incorporation*.[24] Abraham has divided the oral stage of libidinal organization into an objectless sucking stage and an ambivalent biting one. The narcissistic aim pertaining to the latter is a total incorporation of the object, and this aim coincides with primary identification; the succeeding aim of a partial incorporation (which in the main pertains to the early anal stage) coincides with partial identification.[25] That is why identification expresses tender and destructive wishes simultaneously,[26] is typically ambivalent (instinctual defusion), and is so closely related to narcissism.

It is thus first and foremost *oral* libido which, along with the *sadistic* impulses (in accordance with instinctual defusion) has a hand in identification. But in all regressions we must distinguish here between a genuine giving up of the genital position (as in compulsion neurosis and melancholia) and a backward flow of genital libido to pregenital zones, with a retention of its specific genital character (as in hysteria). Some identifications are real oral regressions, and then they are total and narcissistic (as in melancholia [27]). Others are oral expressions

---

[22] F. Alexander, "Neurosis and the Whole Personality," *Int. J. Psa.,* Vol. 7, 1926.

[23] S. Freud, *op. cit.,* pp. 57–58, 79–81.

[24] S. Freud, *ibid.,* pp. 36–37; *Three Essays on the Theory of Sexuality,* p. 75; K. Abraham, "The First Pregenital Stage of the Libido," and "A Short Study of the Development of the Libido, Viewed in the Light of Mental Disorders," *Selected Papers,* London, Hogarth, 1948.

[25] K. Abraham, "A Short Study of the Development of the Libido," pp. 484 ff.

[26] S. Freud, *Group Psychology and the Analysis of the Ego,* p. 61.

[27] S. Freud, "Mourning and Melancholia," *Coll. Pap.,* Vol. IV; K. Abraham, *op. cit.*

of a genital impulse; they are a means of creating substitutes for the genital object (as in mourning;[28] or character change after disappointment in love[29]), or even a means of bringing about the hysterical condition for love, that is, "the exclusion of genitality."[30] Here, for instance, is a typical hysterical fantasy: The patient swallows her partner's penis and thus becomes a man herself and can assume the male genital role; but she has made her object devoid of genitals.[31] As long as the genital cathexis is maintained, the object cathexis too remains. We are talking of a *partial* identification.

The assumption of a "primary identification" as the "earliest expression of an emotional tie with another person,"[32] at the time of the oral phase, is also supported by the following considerations. The distinction between the external world and the ego is learned by experience under the pressure of frustrations.[33] Although the primitive pleasure-ego is constrained to regard unpleasurable stimuli as coming from outside, it has not the same reasons for regarding pleasurable ones as doing so. Thus "it takes the objects which are sources of pleasure into itself, introjects them; on the other hand, it expels everything which becomes a source of unpleasure to the ego" (cf. the "purified pleasure-ego,"[34]). The acceptance into the ego of what is pleasurable and the referral to the external world of what is unpleasurable is also the beginning of the function of judgment.[35] Even later on, when reality testing is already developed, the endeavor to approach the pleasure-bringing stimulus as closely as possible still persists. Though the reality of the external pleasure object is already recognized, yet still the attempt is made to incorporate it in the ego. This endeavor constitutes primary identification. The purified pleasure-ego probably corresponds to the sucking period, and the succeeding stage to the oral-sadistic, biting period.

Phylogenetically, too, identification must be older than object love. Rado believes that he can recognize it in the mimicry which is so frequently found in lower animals.[36] The autoplastic processes which precede purposive alterations of reality are described by Ferenczi as being processes in which the subject seeks "imaginary substitutes on his own body for the lost object";[37] in that case, they, too, are one form in which identification is manifested.

[28] K. Abraham, *op. cit.*
[29] S. Freud, *The Ego and the Id.*
[30] K. Abraham, *op. cit.*
[31] O. Fenichel, "Introjection and the Castration Complex," No. 7 in this volume.
[32] S. Freud, *Group Psychology and the Analysis of the Ego,* p. 60.
[33] S. Ferenczi, "Stages in the Development of the Sense of Reality," *Sex in Psychoanalysis,* New York, Brunner, 1950; S. Freud, "Instincts and Their Vicissitudes," *Coll. Pap.,* Vol. IV.
[34] S. Freud, *op. cit.,* pp. 78–79.
[35] S. Freud, "Negation," *Coll. Pap.,* Vol. V, London, Hogarth, 1950.
[36] S. Rado, *op. cit.,* p. 21.
[37] S. Ferenczi, *Thalassa, A Theory of Genitality,* Albany, Psa. Quart. Press, 1938, pp. 23–24.

If it is a fact of psychological development that the more primitive form never altogether disappears but is only overlaid by the more differentiated form, then at the bottom of every object love there must be an identification. This is obvious where the choice of object is a narcissistic one.[38] Accordingly women, who are more narcissistic in their love than men, would identify themselves more extensively with their sexual partner than would the latter, whose object choice is more of the anaclitic type. Furthermore, the most general sexual aim of all, the striving of eros to ever greater unification,[39] is reflected in the mutual identification of the partners in the sexual act.[40] According to Helene Deutsch, we can speak of a regressive identification not only in disappointed love but also in the highest fulfillment of love. Moreover, it must not be forgotten that full realization of identificatory strivings to incorporate an external object bodily into the ego and to enable that object to carry on an independent existence there is afforded to the woman in the form of pregnancy.[41]

This is the place to remind oneself of the problem posed by Freud concerning the relationship of "empathy" to narcissistic identification.[42] Empathy—viz., the intuitive grasp of real psychic states of another person—is closely related to such identification, but is not identical with it. If we consider that in the final analysis it is only by empathy that we know of the existence of psychic life other than our own, then that agrees well with the fact that at the bottom of every object love we find identification. Other characteristics, too, which usually accompany this particular gift for intuitive empathy, accord with characteristics which fit in with a strong tendency to identification—such things as a high degree of narcissism or the passive sexual aim of being loved instead of loving. These conditions make it plausible that in general women are more emphatic than men. But the problem of what has to be added to identification to make it understanding empathy remains unsolved. Perhaps a more penetrating analysis of the phenomena of unconscious communication will one day provide the answer. If this is not a matter of a so far entirely inexplicable direct transmission of psychological contents,[43] but of an indirect one by means of signs, then the so-called "expressive movements" should be considered the most essential feature of those signs. The role of identification might then be to bring about

---

[38] S. Freud, "On Narcissism: An Introduction," *Coll. Pap.*, Vol. IV, pp. 47–48.

[39] S. Freud, *Beyond the Pleasure Principle*, London, Hogarth, 1948.

[40] S. Ferenczi, *op. cit.*, pp. 17, 25.

[41] H. Deutsch, *Psychoanalyse der weiblichen Sexualfunktionen*, Vienna, Int. Psa. Verlag, 1925, pp. 55 f., 72, 75.

[42] S. Freud, *Group Psychology and the Analysis of the Ego*, p. 70 footnote.

[43] S. Freud, "Some Additional Notes upon Dream-Interpretation as a Whole: (C) The Occult Significance of Dreams," *Coll. Pap.*, Vol. V; R. Loewenstein, "Ueber Affektinduktion," lecture at the Berlin Psychoanalytic Society, 1924.

the taking over by the subject of the object's expressive movements, which in turn would awaken the corresponding psychic state in him.[44]

Following the literature of the subject, we have uncritically adopted the label "introjection" for the oral incorporation which represents the pathway of identification. But for the sake of clarity it should be mentioned that originally Ferenczi meant something entirely different by "introjection." He had in mind the tendency to bring everything that was perceived into relation with the unconscious, to involve real happenings in repressed thought processes, as occurs, for instance, with the day's residues in the course of dream work.[45] Nevertheless, it might be worth investigating whether such processes too do not perhaps take place to the accompaniment of genuine identifications.

## VI

What kinds of identification are there, and how are they differentiated from one another?

As we know, Freud's first classification distinguished a *narcissistic* and a *hysterical* identification.[46] The narcissistic sort leads to a withdrawal of the libido into the ego, in the course of which the latter assumes the characteristics of the object; the hysterical sort, on the other hand, takes place on the basis of a common instinctual demand and retains the libidinal cathexis of the object. The difference "that in the former the object cathexis is given up, while in the latter it persists and exerts an effect which is as a rule limited to isolated actions and innervations" [47] complements the criterion of object relationship, in that according to it, narcissistic identification is a *total* one, while hysterical identification is only *partial*. It might also be said that narcissistic identification takes the place of object love, while hysterical identification occurs alongside it.

Freud's more recent investigations supersede this first classification. To begin with, the identifications which contribute to character formation and to the formation of the superego can also be partial, and yet they would have to be considered as "narcissistic."

As regards the rather rare *total* identifications, we have already heard that they differ from partial identifications in regard to the depth of the regression (the instinctual aim of total as against partial incorporation), and to the nature

---

[44] S. Freud, *Group Psychology and the Analysis of the Ego*, p. 70 footnote.

[45] S. Ferenczi, "Introjection and Transference," *Sex in Psychoanalysis;* "Zur Begriffsbestimmung der Introjektion," *Zentralb. f. Psa.*, Vol. 2, 1912.

[46] S. Freud, *A General Introduction to Psychoanalysis*, pp. 370–371; "Mourning and Melancholia," *Coll. Pap.*, Vol. IV, pp. 160–161.

[47] "Mourning and Melancholia," pp. 160–161.

of the drives involved (oral sadism in contrast to a backward flow of genitality).

These total identifications occur in two forms. One is pathognomonic for *melancholia*,[48] though it is occasionally also observed in schizophrenia.[49] The alterations described take place in full extent. The object loss, whether or not precipitated by a real event, is precipitated by the far-reaching ambivalence of the orally fixated patient, and the hostile component of his ambivalence continues to rage against the introjected object. It may be surmised that the diffuse narcissistic withdrawal of the libido to the ego, as seen in schizophrenia [50] and in sleep [51] differs from this total narcissistic identification in that in the former the regression is to the first, objectless phase, whereas in the latter it is to the second phase, with its aim of incorporation. This distinction, however, is a schematic one. It remains an open question whether identifications do not play a role somewhere in every narcissistic withdrawal of libido. If the condition under which the id will give up an object relationship is a change of the ego by which it becomes like the object, then the answer to Freud's question as to what the mechanism is by which the ego detaches itself from the external world [52] is that it must be a regression to the most primitive oral phase—an event which is always accompanied by identificatory phenomena. The final answer to this question, however, lies with clinical observation.

The other form of total identification faces us with unsolved problems which are metapsychologically of a much more difficult nature. These concern the normal process of superego formation, a process which according to Freud takes place in a more or less *total* fashion.[53] For the establishment of the superego supersedes the oedipus complex. The latter falls to pieces and the superego becomes its heir, while the wish for genital gratification is rejected at the behest of this newly acquired psychic institution. But the motive for this rejection is itself a *genital* one, at least in the case of the boy, for it comes from his castration anxiety.[54] Here, then, we see that state of affairs which is not understood as yet, namely, that object love can be totally replaced by identification without total regression to narcissism and orality taking place, even though the process must be described as narcissistic, in that object libido flows back into the ego.

---

[48] *Ibid.;* K. Abraham, "A Short Study of the Development of the Libido," "The First Pregenital Stage of the Libido," and "Notes on the Psycho-Analytical Investigation and Treatment of Manic-Depressive Insanity and Allied Conditions," all in *Selected Papers.*

[49] K. Landauer, "Spontanheilung einer Katatonie," *Int. Z. Psa.,* Vol. 2, 1914, p. 450.

[50] K. Abraham, "The Psycho-Sexual Differences Between Hysteria and Dementia Praecox," *Selected Papers;* S. Freud, "Psycho-Analytic Notes upon an Autobiographical Account of a Case of Paranoia (Dementia Paranoides)," *Coll. Pap.,* Vol. III, London, Hogarth, 1948.

[51] S. Freud, "Metaphysical Supplement to the Theory of Dreams," *Coll. Pap.,* Vol. IV.

[52] S. Freud, "Neurosis and Psychosis," *Coll. Pap.,* Vol. II, p. 254.

[53] S. Freud, "The Passing of the Oedipus-Complex," *Coll. Pap.,* Vol. II, p. 273.

[54] S. Freud, *ibid.,* "Some Psychological Consequences of the Anatomical Distinction Between the Sexes," *Coll. Pap.,* Vol. V.

Over against both these forms are the more frequent *partial* identifications.

*Hysterical* identification makes use of this process only for limited goals and to a limited extent.[55] Its meaning has been elucidated by the concept of "borrowed sense of guilt" introduced since by Freud.

If guilty feelings are in general the expression of a tension between the superego and the ego, then the "borrowed sense of guilt" [56] can be nothing else but an identification which has been altered by the influence of the anti-instinctual superego and which consequently has introduced into the ego, not the desired instinctual characteristics of the object, but only the guilty feelings connected with them.[57] The assumption by the subject of a sense of guilt is a sign of intended identification on his part in regard to an instinctual demand, and it brings him, besides a gratification of his need for punishment, a secondary libidinal gain.[58]

Partial identifications in normal persons are of common occurrence. They reveal with particular clearness their character as a substitute gratification, since they usually follow immediately upon a real object loss.[59] Furthermore, they are constant concomitants of every object love. They are particularly marked in mourning persons,[60] in sadists,[61] in the jealous,[62] and in masculine women and feminine men. In keeping with the "desexualization" with which they go along, the ego changes they give rise to manifest themselves mostly in character.[63] Contradictory character traits correspond to multiple identifications.[64] The adoption of the characteristics of former love objects, even if there is no crossover to homosexuality (male masochists) [65] leads to "faulty identifications in regard to sex." [66] The significance of identification for character formation is

[55] S. Freud, "The Interpretation of Dreams," *The Basic Writings*, New York, Modern Library, 1938; "Fragment of an Analysis of a Case of Hysteria," *Coll. Pap.*, Vol. III, pp. 41–47; "Hysterical Phantasies and Their Relation to Bisexuality," *Coll. Pap.*, Vol. II, pp. 57–58; "General Remarks on Hysterical Attacks," *Coll. Pap.*, Vol. II, p. 101.

[56] S. Freud, *The Ego and the Id*, p. 72 footnote.

[57] K. Abraham, "A Short Study of the Development of the Libido"; O. Fenichel, "The Clinical Aspect of the Need for Punishment," No. 8 in this volume.

[58] H. Lampl, "Contributions to Case History. A Case of Borrowed Sense of Guilt," *Int. J. Psa.*, Vol. 8, 1927, pp. 154–155; O. Fenichel, *op. cit.*

[59] S. Freud, *The Ego and the Id*, pp. 36–38; R. Markuszewicz, "Beitrag zum autistischen Denken bei Kindern," *Int. Z. Psa.*, Vol. 6, 1920, p. 249.

[60] K. Abraham, "A Short Study in the Development of the Libido," pp. 442 ff.

[61] S. Freud, "A Child Is Being Beaten," *Coll. Pap.*, Vol. II.

[62] S. Freud, "Certain Neurotic Mechanisms in Jealousy, Paranoia and Homosexuality," *Coll. Pap.*, Vol. II, pp. 232–233.

[63] S. Freud, *The Ego and the Id*, pp. 36–37 ff.; K. Abraham, "Character-Formation on the Genital Level of Libido-Development," *Selected Papers*, p. 415; O. Fenichel, "Introjection and the Castration Complex," No. 7 in this volume.

[64] S. Freud, *The Ego and the Id*, pp. 38–39.

[65] S. Freud, "A Child Is Being Beaten," *Coll. Pap.*, Vol. II, pp. 195–196.

[66] W. Reich, *Der triebhafte Charakter*, Vienna, Int. Psa. Verlag, 1925, pp. 43–55.

enhanced by the intervention of the superego, which is itself a product of identification. The first psychoanalytic insights into the genesis of character concerned reaction formations and sublimations of pregenital impulses.[67] These reaction formations were obviously enforced by the drive-negating superego. The factors which come into play in the shaping of character by the superego have been assessed by Reich.[68]

The identification with the parent of the opposite sex, which replaces the oedipal bond in homosexual persons, is also partial, being more or less limited to the manner and kind of their object choice.

According to Freud, a significant property in common—first and foremost, the same relationship to a third person—can also serve as a point of departure for a partial identification.[69] (Identification with the sexual partner of one's love object;[70] the identification with each other of the members of a group.[71]) Such an identification may develop further into object love.

Neurotics in whom the oedipus complex persists, even after the establishment of the superego, show a partial identification in their superego formation.[72] Theoretically one might assume that such people, who have preserved a part of their infantile genitality as such, should be healthier than others. Actually, the persistence of such impulses, which are unacceptable to the superego, brings with it a wealth of potential conflict between the ego, dependent as it is upon the superego, and the id; this provides a fertile soil for neuroses.

We thus distinguish the following kinds of identification:

    A. Primary identification.

    B. Regressive identification.

        1. Total identification.

            a. In melancholia (schizophrenia).

            b. In the superego formation of normals.

        2. Partial identification.

            a. Hysterical identification in cases of common etiological factors and in cases of borrowed guilt feeling.

            b. In normal persons after loss of object or alongside of object love.

---

[67] S. Freud, "Character and Anal Erotism," *Coll. Pap.*, Vol. II; "On the Transformation of Instincts with Special Reference to Anal Erotism," *Coll. Pap.*, Vol. II; J. Sadger, "Analerotik und Analcharakter," *Die Heilkunde*, Vol. 14, 1910; E. Jones, "Anal-Erotic Character Traits," *Papers on Psycho-Analysis*, 5th ed., Baltimore, Williams and Wilkins, 1948; E. Hitschmann, "Urethral Erotism and Obsessional Neurosis," *Int. J. Psa.*, Vol. 4, 1923; K. Abraham, "Contributions to the Theory of the Anal Character," "The Influence of Oral Erotism on Character-Formation," and "Character-Formation on the Genital Level of the Libido," all in *Selected Papers*.

[68] W. Reich, *op. cit.*, pp. 10–11.

[69] S. Freud, *Group Psychology and the Analysis of the Ego*, pp. 64–65.

[70] S. Freud, *ibid.*, p. 63, "Certain Neurotic Mechanisms in Jealousy, Paranoia and Homosexuality," *Coll. Pap.*, Vol. II, pp. 240 ff.

[71] S. Freud, *Group Psychology and the Analysis of the Ego*.

[72] S. Freud, "The Passing of the Oedipus-Complex," *Coll. Pap.*, Vol. II, p. 273.

c. In homosexuals.

d. On the basis of a recent common factor.

e. In the superego formation of neurotics.

## VII

The disadvantage of this classification is that, owing to the contrast it makes between total and partial identification, it creates a wide gulf between super-ego formation in normals and neurotics. Nevertheless, these formations have in common a special metapsychological position, and, from the topographic point of view, they are different from all other identifications.

We must now go on to discuss these topographic differences within the identifications.

It may be assumed that the identifications of early childhood already lead to ego changes which counterpose themselves to the rest of the ego and may be designated, with Reich,[73] as "pre-stages of the superego." The most essential feature about these is that with them the element of giving commands becomes included in the ego. According to M. Klein, such commands or prohibitions are already operative in the child at a quite early age,[74] and indeed they are expressed by its upbringers very soon in its life. But although the child complies with the merciless necessity of its first frustrations, it cannot in doing so acquire as yet a pre-stage of the superego. Though the pleasure-ego is constrained by reality to make renunciations, it is not induced by it to introject the unpleasurable stimuli and so to accept the frustration. This is conceivable only when the child already possesses objectual relations with reality in virtue of which the acceptance of frustrations brings some other hedonic advantage.

Rank distinguishes between "obedience" and "identification," which replaces the former when the object is given up.[75] It seems to me that "obedience" may already be regarded as a partial identification. Ferenczi too assumes that a fore-stage of the superego arises from training in cleanliness, and speaks of a "sphincter-morality." [76]

There is no doubt that this renunciation for the sake of object-libidinal compensations is the avenue by which the child achieves the inhibition of aim of his drives (their desexualization). Here, too, ambivalence is at the root of things. For not only gain of love, but defiance, too, can be the ground for accepting a prohibition. The child's hostile wish toward his parents to be grown up contributes its share to the identifications he makes with them.

[73] W. Reich, *op. cit.*

[74] M. Klein, "The Psychological Principles of Infant Analysis," *Int. J. Psa.,* Vol. 8, 1927.

[75] O. Rank, "Zur Genese der Genitalitaet," *Int. Z. Psa.,* Vol. 11, 1925, p. 422.

[76] S. Ferenczi, "Psycho-Analysis of Sexual Habits," *Further Contributions to the Theory and Technique of Psycho-Analysis,* London, Hogarth, 1950.

What characterizes all these "pre-stages" is that they exist together in a loose and independent way, rather like the partial drives before their integration into a single sexual organization. They lack the essential characteristics of the super-ego—its unity, its sternness, its opposition to the ego, its unconsciousness, and its power, all of which are proper to it as the heir of the oedipus complex. The actual formation of the superego is, as Freud has shown, a process by which the oedipus complex, which was shipwrecked on castration fears or disappointments, is replaced by an identification.

It follows from the nature of the ego and from that of the introduced object that the contrast which prevailed before between the weak ego and the great and omnipotent object, also finds an endopsychic prolongation.[77]

The "you shall" character of the superego's demands are explained by two circumstances. Firstly, those who brought up the child said to it "you shall"; secondly, the aggressiveness of the superego arises from the instinctual defusion which, as we know, accompanies every identification.[78]

Ferenczi already recognized years ago that identification with the frustrating parent was the precondition of obedience.[79] Abraham was able to discover behind the subject's self-reproaches not only reproaches against the introjected object, but, occasionally, reproaches leveled by the introjected object against the rest of the ego.[80] At times the self-reproaches represent a depreciatory judgment made by one parent who has been incorporated into the superego against the other parent who has been included in the ego.[81]

In the development of the superego we can find clinical support for Freud's surmise that drives are sediments of external stimuli.[82]

The passing away of the oedipus complex is phylogenetically so strongly indicated that we cannot believe in an absence of superego formation. It is probable that cases of a pathological lack of inhibition have to do with qualitative alterations of the superego and of its relations to the ego and the id,[83] not with a nonexistence of the superego.

To the double-sidedness of the subject's oedipus complex, which reflects his bisexuality, there corresponds the double-sidedness of his superego formation which takes both parents as prototypes.[84]

Freud considered the "relative strength of the two sexual dispositions" to be

[77] S. Freud, *The Ego and the Id*, pp. 68–69.

[78] *Ibid.*, pp. 79–82.

[79] S. Ferenczi, "Introjection and Transference," *Sex in Psychoanalysis*, p. 77.

[80] K. Abraham, "A Short Study of the Libido, Viewed in the Light of Mental Disorders," *Selected Papers*, p. 461.

[81] *Ibid.*, pp. 461–462; O. Fenichel, "The Clinical Aspect of the Need for Punishment," No. 8 in this volume.

[82] S. Freud, "Instincts and Their Vicissitudes," *Coll. Pap.*, Vol. IV; *Beyond the Pleasure Principle*.

[83] W. Reich, *op. cit.*

[84] S. Freud, *The Ego and the Id*, pp. 41–44.

responsible for the remarkable fact that superego formation based upon the parent of identical sex preponderates.[85] Reich calls attention to the fact that according to this, ambivalence would be decisive for the final outcome of the identifications.[86] This would be in harmony with the observation that "the disappearance of a strong father" favors the development of male homosexuality,[87] for the educational frustrations which in such cases come from the mother necessitate extensive identification with her.

If all "aim-inhibited" impulses may change back regressively into sensual ones,[88] so can the moral impulses arising from identifications. "Moral masochism" paves the way for regression from morality to the oedipus complex.[89]

### VIII

Whether in the course of later changes in ideal formations the prototypic persons (or ideas) are also "introjected into the superego" as were the objects of the oedipus complex earlier on, or whether the process is a different one is not at all certain. The significant facts with relevance to this have been pointed out by Freud. Often a real object takes over all functions of the superego.

In the state of being in love,[90] in hypnosis,[91] in psychoanalysis,[92] and in the choice of leader [93] a kind of "projection of the superego" takes place. Whereas in superego formation an object relation is abandoned and replaced by an ego alteration, here an object relation begins by an object taking over regressively the function of a part of the ego. This is particularly well seen in persecutory delusions [94] and in delusions of reference.[95] The more alien to the ego the superego has remained, the closer it is to the external world and the more easily it can undergo the vicissitude of projection.[96]

Some authors neglect these difficulties completely and proceed as if further introjections into the superego or the formation of new superegos would continue automatically throughout life.[97]

[85] Ibid., pp. 40–41.

[86] W. Reich, op. cit., p. 45.

[87] S. Freud, Three Essays on the Theory of Sexuality, p. 24 footnote.

[88] S. Freud, Group Psychology and the Analysis of the Ego, pp. 118–119.

[89] S. Freud, "The Economic Problem in Masochism," Coll. Pap., Vol. II, p. 266.

[90] S. Freud, "On Narcissism: An Introduction," Coll. Pap., Vol. IV, pp. 52–53; Group Psychology and the Analysis of the Ego, pp. 74–75.

[91] Ibid., pp. 77 ff.; S. Ferenczi, "Introjection and Transference," Sex in Psychoanalysis, pp. 91–93.

[92] F. Alexander, "Metapsychologische Darstellung des Heilungsvorganges," Int. Z. Psa., Vol. 11, 1925; pp. 170 ff.

[93] S. Freud, op. cit., p. 80.

[94] P. Schilder, "Zur Pathologie des Ichideals," Int. Z. Psa., Vol. 8, 1922; O. Fenichel, "The Clinical Aspect of the Need for Punishment," No. 8 in this volume.

[95] S. Freud, "On Narcissism: An Introduction," Coll. Pap., Vol. IV, pp. 53–54.

[96] W. Reich, op. cit., p. 108.

[97] F. Alexander, op. cit., particularly p. 176; W. Reich, op. cit., pp. 37 and 121.

Schilder assumes the existence of a number of "ideal egos" and disregards altogether the integration of the "pre-stages" into a unified superego which accompanies the fall of the oedipus complex.[98]

The neglected problem is this: Is what happens that the ego defends itself against undesirable object cathexes by regressive identifications, and is what then happens that an overpowerful incorporated object which clashes with the character of the ego sets itself up against the rest of the ego as a kind of "new superego"; and if so, what is the position of the older superego in regard to it? I cannot help feeling that to think one can simply disregard this question is to underestimate the deep phyletic roots of the superego (and of the oedipus complex). Rado, starting out from some thoughts of Freud,[99] has attempted to describe hypnosis metapsychologically. If the hypnotized person defends himself against a passive-feminine father-transference by the infantile method of regression to identification, the altered part of the ego arising from this is incompatible with the rest of the ego, which is masochistically oriented. "If the altered ego now succeeds in attracting to itself the topographically differentiated cathexes attached to the super-ego, then the functional sphere of the latter is handed over to a new power, and the elevation of the hypnotist from an object of the ego to a *parasitic* super-ego ensues." [100] The effectiveness of the oedipus complex, a weak superego which is ready to return its power to an external person, and a feminine-masochistic orientation of the ego—these are the prerequisites for the formation of such a "double" of the superego.[101]

The conditions of hypnosis cannot be extended without further ado to all situations in which later authoritative figures or even chosen models seem to occupy the place of the superego. It is possible that in some cases, for instance among fanatics, this is what happens. In other cases it may be—as Freud thought—that no introjection at all takes place.

In these topographic problems even more solutions must be left to future investigation than in the dynamic ones.

[98] P. Schilder, *Introduction to a Psychoanalytic Psychiatry*, New York, Nerv. & Ment. Dis. Pub. Co., 1928.
[99] S. Freud, "Four Prefaces: (A) Psycho-Analysis and War Neuroses," *Coll. Pap.*, Vol. V, p. 85.
[100] S. Rado, *op. cit.*, p. 20.
[101] *Ibid.*, p. 21 footnote.

*ELEVEN*

# The Economic Function
# of Screen Memories[*]

ACCORDING to Freud, as we know, the majority of spontaneous childhood memories owe their escape from general infantile amnesia to the fact that they are associatively connected with childhood experiences, laden with most important and vivid affects, that have themselves succumbed to repression. The emphasis has been *displaced* along associative pathways from those important experiences to scenes belonging to "screen" (or "cover") memories.[1] The latter remain in consciousness as the equivalents, so to say, of the former, and their emphasis has enabled the objective memory images to sink away. It is as if the pressure of the repressed material towards consciousness required some kind of safety valve, and as if it diminished (thus making repression possible) if a partial discharge is vouchsafed it through the consciousness of the screen memory. Thus the question of the nature of screen memories appears in the first place as an economic one. While in other cases everything connected with the repressed material becomes itself subject to repression—and the ego even succeeds, within certain limits, in blocking off percepts if these should recall what has been repressed—in this case the preservation from oblivion of psychic contents close to the repressed seems to alleviate the ego's work of repression. A similar problem seems to be presented in the phenomena of perversion, where repression of the oedipus complex is achieved in the same way by the retention in consciousness of prohibited pregenital impulses. In this case the contradiction was solved by Sachs, who showed that what the repressing ego achieved in giving free play

[*] First published in *Int. Z. Psa.*, Vol. 13, 1927, pp. 58–60.
[1] S. Freud, "Childhood and Concealing Memories," *The Psychopathology of Everyday Life*, New York, Macmillan, 1948.

to a relatively harmless part of the objectionable complex was to cause the greater part of the libido of the total complex to be displaced to this part, and thus to ally itself with the ego and help it to maintain the repression of the rest of the complexive content.[2] In screen memories the situation is analogous. In these, as Sachs puts it, "their apparent innocence, their indifferent character," [3] makes it much easier for the ego to exempt them from repression and thus use them to insure the success of the rest of the repression. Let us imagine a child who has to perform a difficult piece of repressive work. Let us say, for instance, that he is upset by having seen the female genitals. His ego, fearing castration, demands that what was seen be forgotten; but his percept was clear and vivid and cannot easily be made to vanish. Analysis has made us familiar with such struggles between percept and repressing ego, in which a disagreeable percept is now acknowledged, now denied. If in such a situation a substitute object, as it were, for the percept can be found which unites similarity to the objectionable percept with unobnoxiousness, then the struggle is decided in favor of repression. Thus in such struggles with perception the repressing ego must be searching for substitutive ideas of this kind, must have an outright "hunger for screen-experiences." Only by making such an assumption can we understand "retroactive screen-memories." [4] The ego searches its store of memories for images to present to consciousness until it finds a suitable one. Even the new perceptions made during the time of the struggle are also scanned by the ego to see whether they are suitable as substitutive images; the ego has a "free valence" for screen experiences and is economically eased when it finds them.

The screen memories of two patients illustrate these conditions with particular lucidity. Both patients remembered that while experiencing the innocent situation in question, they felt an inner injunction: *Pay attention! You must remember this scene as long as you live!* And they obeyed the injunction. There is no reason to doubt that they had this feeling at the time of the experience; on the contrary, the analysis of both experiences made it evident that the injunction corresponded to a direct endopsychic perception of the craving for screen experiences.

The first memory was this: in the first grade at school (at six years of age) "ladders" were discussed. The children were to make little ladders and bring them to school. Before the hour the patient's neighbor in the class played a game in which he made his finger represent a man ascending the ladder and said, "Here comes the little man." In this moment it flashed through the patient's mind: "You must remember this forever!" The analysis showed that observation

[2] H. Sachs, "Zur Genese der Perversionen," *Int. Z. Psa.*, Vol. 9, 1933, p. 180.
[3] *Ibid.*, p. 179.
[4] S. Freud, *op. cit.*

of parental intercourse by the patient at a relatively late date (at the age of four or five) had to be assumed, and that this observation became the cause of a definitive regression to the anal-sadistic stage. This observation was not remembered; the scene with the "little ladder-man" made its deep repression possible.

The second patient was peacefully playing with his brother, doing fret-saw work, when the idea came to him: "You must always remember this!" He had always been close friends with this brother; he had got along with him excellently save for minor squabbles and had felt all his successes as his own. The analysis showed that this identification with his brother, together with a mild homosexual attachment to him, had arisen in the manner described by Freud,[5] out of an original hatred from rivalry with him, of which no conscious memories were any longer extant. The screen memory of doing fret-saw work together stressed particularly the amicable character of their companionship. It had to be assumed that the patient's hostility had flared up once again as they were using the fret saw, and that a deep repression of this hostility was made possible by his noting this scene exactly but with a displaced emphasis: "Here we are, so peaceful together—I am sawing wood, not my brother." The peaceful character of the sawer meant on a deeper level a denial of the danger of castration.

Let me add two remarks on the craving for cover experiences. The first is that several years ago, Ferenczi, starting from a quite different point of approach, described a very similar phenomenon. In characterizing "introjection" as a striving to co-ordinate all experiences, however innocuous, with one's unconscious thought processes, and to perceive them as the representatives of the latter, he found that such "introjection" "molifies the free-floating affects" and makes it possible for the patient "to keep unconscious various affective connections with certain objects that concern him nearly. . . ."[6] The second is that a comparison with the phenomenon of "déjà vu" is also indicated.[7] The unconscious situation in "déjà vu" is the same as in the experience "You must remember this." In both cases a recent experience reminds the subject of a repressed one and by virtue of that takes its place. Indeed, in spite of the difference in the *content* of the experience "I have experienced this before" and "I will always remember this" there is a phenomenological similarity in the *manner* of it—in the peculiar feeling which accompanies the experience. It can also happen that a content attended by the feeling of "déjà vu" persists as a screen

[5] S. Freud, "Certain Neurotic Mechanisms in Jealousy, Paranoia and Homosexuality," *Coll. Pap.,* Vol. II, London, Hogarth, 1948.

[6] S. Ferenczi, "Introjection and Transference," *Sex in Psychoanalysis,* New York, Brunner, 1950, p. 50.

[7] S. Freud, "Fausse Reconnaissance ('Déjà Raconté') in Psycho-Analytic Treatment," *Coll. Pap.,* Vol. II, and *The Psychopathology of Everyday Life.*

memory. But the difference between the two phenomena is also easily found. In "déjà vu" the repression is deeper and more complete than in the experience of the "injunction to note": the ego does not want to be reminded of the material, and the "déjà vu" feeling is the compromise between memory and repression. In the "injunction to note" repression has not yet succeeded; it is still struggling with the perception, and the ego actively welcomes the recent experience in order with its assistance to be able finally to accomplish the repression.

# TWELVE

# Some Infantile Sexual Theories Not Hitherto Described*

In HIS paper on "infantile sexual theories"[1] Freud speaks of the difference between the theories formed at the stage of puberty and those of early childhood: The former are more rationalized, and are subjected to secondary elaboration. The latter have been long repressed by the time puberty has been reached; they are much more grotesque than the conceptions of a later period, and, as Freud says, always contain a fragment of truth in accordance with infantile pregenital sensations. Since actual bodily sensation points to a connection between the problems of child-getting and sex differentiation and impulses to cruelty and excretory functions, curiosity is bound to proceed along the same path. As is well known, the attempts that are made to give early and natural "explanations"—as Freud advises,[2] and so to avoid the hurtful results of premature sexual inquiries, which are doomed to frustration, often miscarry. There are children who will not accept any explanation, and either refuse to listen when one is given or quickly forget it again; they prefer their own theories to the truth. Reflection suggests that the child with its pregenital orientation is unable as yet to grasp genital reality. But that would not explain the affective refusal to listen. There must therefore already exist a repression, the ideational content of which approximates to the truth more closely than the theory the child clings to. Analysis teaches us that this points to a hostile attitude to the parents, which signifies: "You have up till now not told me the truth, and now I won't listen to you," or "If you do not give me complete sexual satisfaction, I do not want

* First published in *Int. Z. Psa.*, Vol. 13, 1927, pp. 166–170.
[1] S. Freud, "The Sexual Enlightenment of Children," *Coll. Pap.*, Vol. II, London, Hogarth, 1948.
[2] *Ibid.*

the surrogate of an 'explanation.'" (Patients who complain that their parents kept back sexual enlightenment from them mean, in their unconscious, the refusal of sexual satisfaction.) But we learn further that various unconscious motives can lead to the rejection of sexual truth. Alongside the apprehension due to the possible birth of further brothers and sisters there is undoubtedly another motive standing well in the foreground, namely, when the castration anxiety is so great that it clings convulsively to the belief in the female penis, then the truth must not be listened to, because it entails a recognition of the vagina, i.e. of the lack of a penis, and therefore a recognition of the reality of castration. We know that most boys cannot bring themselves to believe in the lack of a penis until they have had to convince themselves with their own eyes.

If the rejection of enlightenment is the result of castration anxiety, we know at once what are the fantasies that "approximate to the truth more closely," that are more deeply repressed than the pregenital theories, though these certainly spring from a still earlier time. They are, namely, the "castration theories" that regard castration as a phenomenon inevitably accompanying the sexual act. Their usual forms, as is well known, are the following: (1) The man in the act cuts off the woman's penis. (2) (In order to repress this theory) the woman has a penis which she retains all her life, only it is hidden. (3) (As a return of the repressed from repression) the woman in the act cuts off the man's penis with hers. (The common anxiety that castration will follow sexual relations as a punishment cannot be described as a sexual theory.) When a boy as the result of castration anxiety occasionally regresses completely from the phallic stage to the anal-sadistic, or when, indeed, he finally renounces even his oedipus wishes in order not to jeopardize his penis, he still clings at the same time to the older anal-sadistic theories in order to disown the more deeply repressed castration theories, which never were conscious, or were so for only a short time, accompanied by intense discharge of anxiety. Very infrequent are cases like that of a patient who consciously imagined at the age of ten that the penis crumbled to pieces during the sexual act and that fragments of it remained in the vagina; such cases are possible only when there is a strong feminine impress. It is otherwise in the case of girls; the castration theories bring them the hope of regaining their lost penis (aim of partial incorporation).

Accordingly, in the case of castration theories analysis will pay special attention to the discovery, through removing repressions, of fresh variants of infantile sexual theories. As may easily be conceived, there is a type of case which is inexhaustible in its production of theories and fantasies with reference to castration—male obsessional neurotics, who at the sight of the female genitalia have regressed under castration anxiety from an already strongly marked phallic position to the anal-sadistic level, who have become addicted to brooding, and who have taken traits of their higher stage back to that of the anal. All the three fantasies which we now give were produced by patients of this type: the first two from one who, for example, manifested the typical defecation abnormality of only being able to produce excrement in small pieces, as the result of his displacing the castration anxiety to the anal zone; in the main they represent attempts to explain the fact of the lack of a penis by making castration innocuous. Naturally they come to grief and are unable to prevent permanently the formation of anxiety.

One of the theories arose as a reaction to the sight of the father's penis combined with an already existing belief in castration. It had therefore the task of uniting the supposed fact of the patient's castration, and the inferiority of his own penis, with the hope of having at some later time just as large a penis himself. It ran as follows: *The small penis can in some mysterious fashion be unscrewed and be replaced by a larger one.* There exists accordingly the stage of lack of a penis as intermediate between the small and the large penis. Although his penis is small just now, he is able with the aid of this mechanism to be on equal terms with both his parents in succession, without at the same time forfeiting his own penis. A brief comment on this will suffice. The fantasy is strongly overdetermined; not only does the identification with both parents find expression, but also direct object love in relation to both as well as hatred of both, i.e. an active castration tendency towards both. It all seems so well fitted to give satisfaction that one is astonished that this fantasy does not occur more frequently in a similar constellation. A conjecture, which unfortunately was not verbally expressed in the analysis, would lead us to seek the real foundation for this fantasy in the experiences of the suckling when alternating between sucking the maternal breast (large penis) and his own finger (small penis). Large penis = breast; small penis = thumb.

The second fantasy comes from the same patient, and reflects the regression to the anal level from the phallus that is threatened with castration. It appeared manifestly in a dream occurring in a series of "corroborating dreams" that signified the acceptance of analytical results hitherto treated with suspicion, and reproduced in the manifest content theories formerly hypothetically inferred— e.g., women appeared with different kinds of penes. The dream ran as follows: *There exists a connection between my bowel and my childish penis. The gases from the bowel, instead of being voided in the air through the anus, flow into the penis so that it becomes erected.* There is no reason for doubting that this dream manifestly restores a sexual theory in which the patient at one time believed. The erection results from the intestinal gases, hence his inferior penis can become as large as his father's if only he can make wind as much as his father. We see here the "narcissistic over-estimation of the excretory functions" [3] serving that narcissistic pride in the penis which is intended to overcompensate for the castration anxiety.

The third fantasy reveals another characteristic, and does not seem to be so very infrequent. It combines castration anxiety with the fantasy of the mother's womb—that inhibited expression of bisexual incestuous wishes—with anxiety regarding the birth of other brothers and sisters, and with reminiscences of the primal scene. It was revealed in two cases and runs: *A girl makes her appearance; what had happened was that a boy had returned into the mother's womb, been rammed in, so to speak, and pressed back into the mother. There he is so treated by his father that he loses his penis. Then he is born again as a girl.*

The most important part of the material which made discovery of this fantasy possible will now be briefly related. Both patients were bisexual obsessional neurotics, who had regressed through castration anxiety, and who had had the real foundation of primal scenes for their two-sided identification with both parents. Both analyses were marked by "castration anxiety" and the "fantasy of the mother's womb." One of the patients suffered from a dread of bridges and heights; the deeps into which he was afraid he would fall corresponded to the mother's womb, the dread to castration anxiety accompanying his incestuous wishes, and the "hidden masochistic significance" of the dread of heights [4] to the hidden homosexual significance of the fantasy of the mother's womb.[5] The other patient produced similar fantasies of watery and fiery depths. Both had anxiety about the mother's womb in the most varied forms. As children they both had the dread of falling into the water-closet; both suffered from death- or burial-anxiety, in which they regarded death as a "return to the mother." One of them had lost his mother at the age of puberty and was afraid of her revenge. The dead, in hell, in their coffins, in fire or in water, tormented and tortured, tormenting and torturing, were constantly returning in dreams and fantasies. The man in the moon who had lived on earth, but had in punishment been transported to the moon, there to expiate his sins, was as much the subject of brooding speculation for one patient as hell—the anxiety-charged symbol of the mother's womb—was for the other.

Additional material left no doubt that a threat of castration lay within the mother's womb. The patient with the dread of heights was once as a punishment for "naughtiness" held out of the window in fun with the threat that he would be thrown down. In the case of the other the pains of hell left nothing to

[3] K. Abraham, "The Narcissistic Evaluation of Excretory Processes in Dreams and Neurosis," *Selected Papers*, London, Hogarth, 1948, p. 322.

[4] S. Freud, *The Problem of Anxiety*, New York, Psa. Quart. Press and Norton, 1936.

[5] S. Freud, "From the History of an Infantile Neurosis," *Coll. Pap.*, Vol. III, London, Hogarth, 1948.

be desired in the way of castration symbolism. When the former patient was made to persevere in the attempt to tolerate situations of anxiety, it appeared quite clearly that these were in reality pleasure states that had been eagerly desired. In them the patient, yielding to a sudden impulse, drew up his knees in the position of the fetal body; in them, too, he believed that men had deprived him of his right to instinctual satisfaction. The fantasy of the mother's womb was a condensation of all the oedipus wishes, and the repetition of the primal scene.

Further material showed the identity of the "intrauterine castration" with a mysterious "intrauterine transformation" (of sex). In the case of one patient an important part was played by the symbolism of mills! His anxiety concerned the invisible change of grain into flour. Max and Moritz were ground to pieces in a mill; in "Old Wives' Mills" old women were changed into young. The idea that he might be transformed into a beast, or wake out of sleep in altered form, was the subject of his childish anxieties. Once when he had a mask put on him as a child he reacted with an attack of anxiety. The idea that he would be changed into a girl was occasionally held consciously. He was continually imagining subterranean catastrophes with ever fresh variations.

Common to both cases was the fact—in correspondence with the regression—that the mother's womb was thought of as the inner bowel and the children in it as pieces of feces. In the case of one patient a train of thought led from mills to smearing with excrement, by the verbal bridge: *mahlen—malen* (grind—paint). In the unconscious were combined the ideas of a "devil's mill" in a fairy tale with the saying, "Don't paint the devil in the wall," the devil as an inhabitant of hell smeared with excrement, and the idea of transformation ("devil's work") with an inhibition in drawing. Both patients showed predominant anal traits in their character and in their sexual behavior.

The two cases seemed to differ in one point—and it was precisely here that the analysis proved complete agreement. In the one case it was easy to see that the anxiety, accompanying all the infantile symptoms, lest another sister should be born originated in the painful experience of the birth of a sister two and a half years younger. The birth of a cousin, which took place in his sixth year, gave him the opportunity of repeating his former psychical attitude. This revealed a twofold reaction. There was first the typical death wish against his little rival, that she would return to the place from which she came (fall from a window or into a chest). The mother's-womb anxiety (dread of falling from a window—falling from a height) showed itself in this fashion as a retributory anxiety on account of these wicked desires. "What you wished for your sister will happen to yourself. You will be thrust back into the mother and there suffer torment; your sister will remain behind." In the second place, however, there is the increase of castration anxiety caused by his sister's want of a penis, and linked inseparably with his ideas of "intrauterine torment" (perhaps the second circumstance was first occasioned by the arrival of his cousin in his sixth year, since in the meantime, in connection with bedwetting, he had had an opportunity of hearing threats of castration). The second patient had no younger brothers or sisters; in his case the facts seemed more complicated, and identification with an *elder* sister appeared to be the impelling motive. But ultimately the analysis of anxiety dreams was successful in eliciting the forgotten birth of a girl in their circle of near acquaintances; this had been connected with the fantasy of the "sacrificed boy," and from it there resulted the condensation of the elements of anxiety—the fear of being castrated and of getting a sister (characteristically he was never afraid of a brother).

It is evident that this fantasy is more condensed, more primitive, and less disguised than the other two. That is not difficult to explain. The first two fantasies were formed at a later period, when the denial of the lack of a penis by means of anal sexual theories could no longer be made—i.e., they are relatively superficial and hasty, and have the tendency to discount the importance of the more deeply repressed castration theories proper; while the third theory is itself such a profoundly repressed fantasy—a direct product of castration anxiety, with which the oedipus impulses were combined in the phallic stage. It was not necessary to assume that that anxiety expressed any supposititious pre-oedipal birth anxiety.

## THIRTEEN

# Examples of Dream Analysis*

### I. A CONDENSED DREAM

It is well known that there are very short dreams which contain in a most condensed form the entire neurosis or developmental history of a person. Recently I had the opportunity of analyzing such a dream which may be of some interest because it consists of a single word: *bees*. The dreamer did not even know whether he saw any bees or only heard the word "bees" in his dream.

The dreamer was a thirty-six-year-old man who had already reached an advanced stage of his analysis, which he had begun because of character difficulties. His manifest difficulties chiefly consisted in a marked moral masochism, and also in his living out, as it were, his oedipus complex. On the one hand, the main content of his life consisted of his conscious hatred of his tyrannical father and his continuous, but futile, struggle against him; on the other hand, he had lived for years with a woman much older than himself, to whom he remained tied, although consciously she did not mean much to him either spiritually or sexually.

The patient, in spite of his more than average intelligence and endowments, had no profession. The history of the failure of his attempts at choosing a profession showed clearly that this too expressed his hatred against his father ("It is your doing that I haven't learned anything!"); and at the same time it made the patient permanently dependent on his father, on whose support he principally lived. The patient had attempted again and again to liberate himself forcibly from his fixation on the parental house. He had traveled in other countries, kept company with people different in the extreme from his relatives (universal exogamy)—all in vain; for in his unconscious daydreams (and, in the course of

* First published in *Int. Z. Psa.*, Vol. 13, 1927, pp. 461–464.

analysis, in his conscious daydreams too) he was all the time in his parental house, trying to come to terms with his relatives.

It was easy to see that underneath the hatred against the father there lay an intense demanding, sadistic love, which had made it the patient's life task to take away from the father as much money as possible. (He went in for sweep-stakes and was waiting for the first prize, that is, for "father fate" to bring him at last the presents that were his due.) In accordance with this demand, he was jealous of his older brothers. He maintained that his father gave them every-thing and him nothing. A screen memory from his childhood was that a bishop had once kissed one of his brothers, but not him.

In the analysis, the oral wishes hidden behind his anal-sadistic love toward the father—the aim of which was to take from him money and presents (negative oedipus complex on the anal level)—had already become quite clear: he wanted to be maintained, that is, nourished, by the father. The unconscious idea of drinking from his father's penis represented the still more deeply repressed one of drinking from his mother's (his nurse's) breast. (The patient had been fed at the breast for more than a year, and though he had already been able to speak quite well by the end of that time, he did not speak for a whole year after he was weaned, so that he was considered to be dumb.)

A few days before this dream, the patient had received the news that his brother, the one who was kissed by the bishop, had become engaged. The pa-tient, who, with his pregenital fixation, was never fully potent, and who longed to get away from his aging woman friend to a young, loving woman, had thus every reason to reactivate his old envy. In addition, the patient maintained that this engagement was the doing of the father, who had sought out a woman for his beloved son. To the news of the engagement, the patient responded im-mediately with the following dream: *My photograph and that of my father are in a newspaper.* According to his associations, this was a wedding announcement, and the dream-thought was that the father should find a woman for him too—that is, he wanted to be connected with his father *via* a woman.

And now for the associations to the "bees." The first thing the patient thought of was a memory of how once, when he was somewhere between twelve and fifteen years of age, he was stung by a bee while taking a walk with his mother. Other than this, he had never had anything to do with bees. His associations already threatened to stop at this point. When I pointed out that apparently the essential thing about bees for him was that they stung, the patient's associations turned to this stinging. He remembered an earlier dream in which a man pierced him in the abdomen with a lance under peculiar circumstances. The lance of bees is their sting, only bees are numerous, they are many little animals. His complex about "little animals" was already familiar to us. It did not mean "siblings" to our patient, but something like "dangerous children, castrating germs, and spermatozoa," and this was because one of his brothers had gonorrhea at the time of the patient's latency period. This gave the patient's castration anxiety the content of being afraid of being eaten up alive by germs from within. Later on it turned out that the memory of the brother's gonorrhea covered an older memory of a gynecological illness of his mother's. She had been operated on for a myoma. The patient had heard something about cancer * and imagined that an actual crablike animal was in the genital, nipping off everything inside with its claws. These castrating germs, crayfish, bees, naturally come into the body as food through the mouth. According to the patient's unconscious idea, his mother's illness was due to his father's sexual brutality and his brother's illness to actual sexual intercourse. Thus, if one drinks what comes from the father's penis (the lance) and thus conceives a child—certain dreams which the patient had about baby crayfish and salamanders left no doubt as to the equation: little animals = embryo—one is punished by being destroyed from inside by bees (children, spermatozoa), by being eaten up by them, in accordance with the law of talion. Now the patient had to think about these things; and he also thought about the slaughter of the drones, and about the male bees' death after the sexual act.

To the slaughter of drones, the patient suddenly associated that he had entirely forgotten another time when he had had to do with bees. At one time, when he was a child, his father had kept bees on his estate; they got a lot of honey to eat in those days. But the whole thing had lasted only for a short while. His father was swindled, a bad beemaster ruined it all, and nothing came of the apiary which had been started with high hopes. "Everything that my father starts always fails," said the patient. I called his attention to the fact that now the father had started the brother's marriage and that he would have no objection if that failed, too. A few days later, the patient brought a striking confirmation of this interpretation; for when he received no immediate answer to his congratulatory telegram, he assumed at once that the engagement had been broken off. First, however, he had another association to it. He thought of the walk with his mother, in which he was stung. He remembered that his father was away on a trip at the time, and then that on this walk they met a certain idiot who always horrified him. Now this idiot had already come up in the analysis. Once—this, too, happened when the patient was between twelve and fifteen—this idiot had pursued the mother with his fly opened, so that she fled screaming into the house. This memory was so far the only one through which I had been able to

* The German for "cancer" is "Krebs"—that is, "crayfish" or "crab."—Trans. note.

make it plausible to the patient that his woman friend represented his mother, and that, in spite of his pregenital fixation, he had had phallic wishes towards the mother, which he had suppressed *in nuce* only because of his anxiety.

If we now attempt to interpret the patient's dream of "bees" we at once understand his most superficial latent dream-thought. It is, *"My brother's marriage shall come to naught,"* or more generally, *"My father's undertakings on behalf of my brothers shall come to naught";* or—one layer deeper—*"My brother, who gets presents from my father and enjoys his love, shall be stung and devoured."* It is easy, too, to see further that the anxiety about being stung naturally refers not only to the brother but also to the patient himself, so that we may formulate as further dream thoughts: *"My father shall get me married. He is to give me presents and love me."* In the final analysis: *"My father is to copulate with me per os"* (cf. the honey). Besides this, however, the dream also expresses clearly enough the defense against the drive, the castration anxiety, which was aroused by the wish-fulfilling character of the dream, as thus: *"If I have such wishes, I shall be stung, eaten up from inside, castrated; the 'little animals' coming from father's penis will eat me up within if I eat them up."* This fear is in a sense realized by the severity of the patient's superego. Underneath all this, however, the deepest layer makes itself noticeable. This is the patient's wish to drink not from his father's penis, but from his mother's breast. This in turn is a regressive expression of his wish to have sexual intercourse with his mother, which is made possible by his oral fixation. For the events of the walk with his mother when he was a boy can now be easily reconstructed. His father's absence and his walk alone with her had activated his repressed incestuous wishes, and his encounter with the idiot, which reminded him of the possibility of actual incest, had reinforced his tabooed wishes extraordinarily strongly. When now the bee stung him, he took this as a punishment, a castration, for his thought of incest with his mother. The deepest latent dream thought therefore was: *"Yes, I should like to get married like my brother; but if I am to give up my woman friend who is so much like my mother, then it ought to be my mother herself whom I marry."* But immediately comes the suppression: *"I must not wish for that, the bee has taught me that such wishes are immediately punished; therefore, I turn my love to my father."* And here, at last, we make connection with the dream-thoughts emanating from the negative oedipus complex which have been formulated above.

Let us note finally that bees are actually an apt metaphor for "dangerous pleasure." After all, what does a child know about bees? They make sweet honey and they sting.

## II. A SOMATIC STIMULATION DREAM WHICH PROLONGS SLEEP

A patient dreams: *There is a political meeting. Various speakers make speeches. The dream is very tedious, I have forgotten the details. Suddenly somebody comes running to the speaker's platform, pushes the speaker aside, and shouts to the audience something like this: "Everything that is being discussed here refers to unimportant future worries. There is only one thing that has to be settled right now: it must not happen any more that one has to get up in the middle of the night!"*—and the patient awakes with a strong urge to urinate.

## III. A UTERINE DREAM AS A EUPHEMISM FOR INCEST

In contrast to other psychoanalytic authors, Freud has attempted to conceive of uterine fantasies essentially as euphemisms for incestuous wishes, as incest fantasies of impotent people. The following dream substantiates this conception directly:

A thirty-year-old patient, with extraordinarily strong sexual repression, who had never had sexual intercourse, and who had masturbated only for a very short time, but who, in turn, clung to his mother in an absolutely infantile manner (the mother had forbidden him everything sexual), had as his only sexual gratification nightly seminal emissions, accompanied by the following repetitive dream:

*I go up an ever-narrowing spiral stairway in the tower of a church. On the top of the stairway there is a very narrow space, the ceiling is suffocatingly low, it is dark, one can only sit there in a crouching position. It is indescribably beautiful.*

To this dream were attached the most severe oedipal guilt feelings.

* * * * * * * * * * * * * * * * * * *

*FOURTEEN*

# Organ Libidinization Accompanying the Defense against Drives[*]

I

THE study of the organic phenomena accompanying instinctual conflicts of the psychic apparatus had a promising beginning in Ferenczi's "Pathoneuroses"; [1] this borderland between physiology and psychoanalysis, which can only indirectly be studied by psychoanalysis, has so far been little explored. In its discussion, certain conjectures still open to doubt are unavoidable; but if the heuristic value of the assumptions concerning organ libido, formulated mainly by Freud [2] and Ferenczi,[3] should be confirmed, they would certainly be justified as a first attempt at finding our way about in an obscure region.

Let us begin our investigation by noting the remarkable fact—and one which, as far as I know, has not yet been sufficiently explored by physiologists—that most healthy people, at least in our culture, display in greater or lesser degree a remarkable condition of muscle tonus. When in their everyday life they have not focused attention on the condition of their musculature, the latter exists in a state of hypertonus, the degree of which varies with the muscle group and with the individual, and which may occasionally reach complete rigidity. Movements may involve not only unnecessary muscle groups (associated movements), but innervations which are unsuitable and of unnecessary intensity. When in a state of rest we are sometimes inclined to let certain muscle groups become hypotonic, that is, to have an excessively lowered tension, so that their readiness

---

[*] First published in *Int. Z. Psa.*, Vol. 14, 1928, pp. 45–64.
[1] S. Ferenczi, *Hysterie und Pathoneurosen*, Vienna, Int. Psa. Verlag, 1919.
[2] S. Freud, *Three Essays on the Theory of Sexuality*, London, Imago, 1949; "On Narcissism: An Introduction," *Coll. Pap.*, Vol. IV, London, Hogarth, 1948.
[3] S. Ferenczi, *op. cit.*

to function is impeded or weakened. The whole phenomenon is better described as dystonic than as hypertonic. In brief, we are dealing here with a defect of varying degree of that "economization and rationalization" of the motor apparatus which is described by Homburger [4] as characteristic of adults.

It would require an exhaustive investigation, not relevant in its details to our purpose, to determine what is physiologically involved in the matter. Tonus is in fact a highly complex phenomenon. We know that a spinal—that is, extrapyramidal—rigidity which manifests itself in disorders of the pyramidal tract as a spastic paralysis is normally inhibited by pyramidal impulses, but that pyramidal impulses may also result in increase of tension, so that the concepts of "inhibition of movement" and "physiological inhibition" do not necessarily coincide. But this is not our concern here, since we know that the phenomenon we are considering in any case involves a *cortically* determined change of the cortical-subcortical tonus distribution. Besides the innervation of the musculature itself, the state of innervation of the blood vessels of the muscles is also decisive with regard to tonus; thus not only pyramidal and extrapyramidal spinal tracts, but the entire autonomic system, are involved in the phenomena under discussion.

The essential factor in all this is a functional impairment of voluntary movements through increased muscle tension, or through an alternation between increased and decreased muscle tension. Such alternations in tension are familiar to us, for example, in the gut (spastic and atonic constipation), and its occurrence in other organ systems has been particularly stressed by Heyer.[5] From the psychoanalytic point of view, then, we are dealing here with a restriction of ego function, with an "inhibition," according to Freud,[6] which can be manifold and does not usually reach such intensity as to be regarded as pathological. These motor inhibitions are similar to other psychic anomalies of inhibition which one would not term neuroses, in that they are attended by little or no subjective feeling of impairment.

What is the cause of inadequate motor behavior of this kind? Physiologists can only describe what takes place, but cannot explain it. The explanation of the nature of these slight somatic limitations of function cannot come from ordinary physiology, but rather from the "pleasure physiology" with which Ferenczi [7] proposed to supplement it.

Specific answers to the problem are to be expected only from specific psycho-

---

[4] A. Homburger, "Zur Gestaltung der normalen menschlichen Motorik und ihrer Beurteilung," *Z. Neurol. Psychiat.*, Vol. 85, 1923, p. 292.

[5] G. Heyer, *Das koerperlich-seelische Zusammenwirken in den Lebensvorgaengen*, Munich, Bergmann, 1925, p. 19.

[6] S. Freud, *The Problem of Anxiety*, New York, Psa. Quart. Press and Norton, 1936.

[7] S. Ferenczi, *op. cit.*

analytic—that is, psychoanalytic-physiological—investigations, which have not yet been carried out. Their results will probably not differ in principle from those obtained in the case of other, analogous ego inhibitions.[8] Our main interest here, however, lies in the general nature of these greater or smaller dysfunctions of the musculature.

Various observations and theoretical considerations make it probable that such "dystonic" phenomena are determined by the action of instinctual defenses, in especial the repressive activity of the ego—although, as we shall see, the converse does not hold good and not all repressions bring about chronic dystonic phenomena of any pronounced degree.

Repression consists in keeping given impulses from motor expression. (Excluding them from consciousness is a means of achieving this.) Thus in the last analysis repression is always a renunciation by the ego of certain movements. It is this inhibition of motor expression which the ego is at pains to apply to the substitute formations of the repressed instinctual impulses as well, so that even they are debarred from being translated into action.[9] From the inhibiting of motor expression of substitute formations there may in general develop a *partial limitation of the ego's command of motor expression*.

The actual purpose of repression is the prevention of instinctual actions. The ego of the child is continually forced to suppress motor impulses (of an auto-erotic, erotic, or aggressive sort). Landauer[10] has recently demonstrated that in certain conditions the motor inhibitions thus established are retained throughout life. The struggle of repression between the cathected instinctual impulse and the ego's anti-cathexes can therefore express itself physiologically—if at all—only in functional changes of the skeletal musculature. If now we learn that in certain suitable cases—primarily, of course, hysterical ones—persons when attempting to relax their spastically innervated musculature sometimes develop affective states which can only be compared to the states exhibited by patients in psycho-cathartic treatment when a significant "trauma" has been touched, whereby affects are brought to discharge, then we must recognize that the *dystonus was a means of keeping repressed material in repression,* and was a physical correlate of the expenditure of energy involved in repression.

Here we face a theoretical objection. This assumption contradicts Freud's well-founded observation concerning the controlling role played by the conscious system over motility. He remarks that this control is so firm that "it almost invariably withstands the onslaught of the neurosis and breaks down only in the psychosis."[11] Our assumption, in contrast, asserts that control of motility be-

---

[8] S. Freud, *op. cit.,* pp. 11–16.
[9] *Ibid.,* p. 22.
[10] K. Landauer, "Die kindliche Bewegungsunruhe," *Int. Z. Psa.,* Vol. 12, 1926, p. 388.
[11] S. Freud, "The Unconscious," *Coll. Pap.,* Vol. IV, pp. 111–112.

comes restricted in every neurosis, indeed even in the most common mild states of inhibition without a neurosis. The contradiction is resolved when one keeps in mind that Freud speaks of a "breakdown" of control over motility; in our case this term is not applicable, since what we are dealing with is only an undesirable consequence of the inexpedient application of this control, namely, the ego's refusal to carry out impulses to act, "in order to avoid a conflict with the id." [12] Furthermore, Freud refers to gross alterations of this control, while our assumption refers only to subtle limitations of it. That genuine limitations (that is, not mere uncertainties in the execution of willed movements) do occur outside of psychoses, is proven by the simple existence of somnambulism, symptomatic acts, and unconscious vasomotor reactions.

Often, too, we can observe in analytic treatment that if a person is engaged in an *acute* repressive struggle—as when, for instance, a patient can no longer escape the truth of an interpretation, yet attempts to do so—his whole skeletal musculature is clonically innervated, as though he were trying to create muscular safeguards against the emergence of repressed strivings concealed within him, as though he wanted to oppose an external muscular pressure to the internal pressure of the repressed.

A female patient, with speech inhibition, who at first could not speak at all in the analysis, used visibly to contract her body and clench her fists. Later on she described her condition as a feeling of emptiness of thought. She felt her inability to speak in a bodily way: her inside was so cramped, her breast and limbs so tense, that they "did not let anything come out." After a silent hour she was exhausted, as after great physical exertion. When she could again talk, it was like a sudden release. "I can't tell you how physical it all is," she would say. It is characteristic that the patient localized this cramp just below the ribs (diaphragm-cramp).

Ferenczi reports that many patients—who need not therefore be at once suspected of schizophrenia—exhibit, particularly when in a state of resistance, "an excessive stiffness in every limb, which, on their meeting with or leaving the analyst, may grow to a catatonic-like rigidity. With progress in the analysis, and a consequent resolution of psychic tensions, the somatic tensions may also vanish." [13]

Since thinking is "experimental action," inhibition of thought must manifest itself in changes in motility and tonus, just as inhibition of action does. In his short study "Thinking and Muscle-Innervation" [14] Ferenczi demonstrates that

---

[12] S. Freud, *The Problem of Anxiety*, p. 15.

[13] S. Ferenczi, "Psycho-Analysis of Sexual Habits," *Further Contributions to the Theory and Technique of Psycho-Analysis*, London, Hogarth, 1950, p. 281.

[14] S. Ferenczi, "Thinking and Muscle-Innervation," *Further Contributions to the Theory and Technique of Psycho-Analysis*.

this is indeed the case. The suspension of certain muscular abilities corresponds to quite analogous psychic inhibitions, to the suspension of certain qualities of experience. Finally, the fact that in narcosis, that is, when the conscious ego is eliminated, all hypertonus disappears, serves to show that the ego does in fact actively initiate the hypertonia.

Ferenczi and Deutsch have already expressed similar ideas. For instance, Ferenczi writes on one occasion: "Sometimes we find it necessary to call the patient's attention to his bearing (the tensions of his musculature) and through this to some extent to 'mobilize' him. As a result he usually begins to talk about something that was hitherto hidden or unconscious." [15] In another place, after he has discussed the recommendation to practice tension of the sphincters: "I have since found that it is at times well to advise *relaxation*-exercises and that this kind of relaxation facilitates the overcoming of psychic inhibitions as well as resistances to giving associations." [16] Deutsch maintains: *"Every* change in tonus, every movement and every rhythmic activity in the organism, as well as every increase and interruption of these, is an expression and effect of the current of instinctual impulses." [17] Naturally, the state of the muscles and the intensity of repression display a certain independence of each other. "Dystonia" is an inexact and too-inclusive concept which can only serve as a very elementary guide. There is great individual variability not only as to whether and to what extent psychic conflicts find somatic expression in muscular tension and function, but also as to the nature and localization of those expressions. The final result depends on a hardly surveyable manifold of physiological and psychological factors, the thorough understanding of which would require many specialized studies, and of which Kretschmer's catchword, "body-build and character" only depicts a small part.[18] One factor—certainly not the most important—is easy to recognize: in a person whose psychic conflicts are clearly reflected in the somatic sphere, the way in which they are reflected there depends also on what his characteristic manner of coping with conflicts is. For instance, of the mechanisms to be discussed below, "displacement of the sphincter-spasm" will play a considerable role in compulsion-neurotic types, and the blocking of internal perceptions in hysterical types. We have still to discover in which kind of people and situations neurotic symptoms and muscle dysfunctions go hand in hand and in which they diverge widely. We will again limit ourselves here to general is-

[15] S. Ferenczi, "Psycho-Analysis of Sexual Habits," *Further Contributions to the Theory and Technique of Psycho-Analysis*, p. 281.

[16] S. Ferenczi, "Contra-indications to the 'Active' Psycho-Analytical Technique," *Further Contributions to the Theory and Technique of Psycho-Analysis*, p. 226.

[17] F. Deutsch, "Psychoanalyse und Organkrankheiten," *Int. Z. Psa.*, Vol. 8, 1922, p. 291.

[18] E. Kretschmer, *Physique and Character*, New York, Harcourt, Brace, 1925.

sues. The fact that those phenomena can differ does not cancel the impression that they are closely connected. This impression is enhanced by the observation that the most extreme degrees of cramp occur in the musculature of the pelvis, both in that of the floor of the pelvis and in that of the hip-joints—an observation which is in agreement with the fact that what succumbs to repression is, in the main, the representatives of sexual drives.

Two examples will illustrate the point. As is well known, castration anxiety occupies an exceptional position among the motivations of repression. It would be surprising if this somatically oriented motivation of so much repression were not also to find a somatic expression. We know that under its influence the libidinal attitude toward one's own body changes fundamentally.[19] And we do in fact notice that strikingly unpurposeful innervations and an inability to attain natural tonus are often based upon anxiety. Spastic innervation and the putting out of action and functional paralysis of the skeletal musculature are signs of anxiety. Consider, for instance, the cessation of breathing in anxiety, or the fact that so-called anxiety paralysis is always spastic. Chronic anxiety, the equivalent of which is dystonus, is the fear of damage to one's body.

A patient reported that her gymnastics teacher continually called her attention to the intensity with which she kept her neck and throat musculature in a constant spastic tension. Attempts to loosen this tension only increased it, and made the patient feel sick. The analysis showed that as a child the patient saw a pigeon's head being torn off and the headless pigeon still moving its wings a few times. This experience lent her castration complex a lasting form: she had an unconscious fear of being beheaded, and this fear also manifested itself in numerous other symptoms, modes of behavior, and directions of interest.

Another example is even clearer. We know that many people have not overcome their anal eroticism. According to Abraham, there are two kinds of anal pleasure, the pleasure of expelling and that of retaining.[20] The former is the more archaic of the two. Now the child's environment forces him to relinquish this earlier pleasure. At first he experiences this as a restriction. Soon, however, he learns to appreciate as fresh possibilities of pleasure his new organ sensations of retention and the narcissistic power of self-control. Thus, in retention, what was originally a safeguard against forbidden pleasure becomes itself a pleasure gain. This safeguard and this pleasure gain are obtained in the sphincter spasm —that is, in muscular innervations which exceed what is physiologically adequate.

[19] J. Hárnik, "The Various Developments Undergone by Narcissism in Men and Women," *Int. J. Psa.*, Vol. 5, 1924.

[20] K. Abraham, "A Short Study of the Development of the Libido, Viewed in the Light of Mental Disorders," *Selected Papers*, London, Hogarth, 1948.

The patient mentioned above, who experienced her speech inhibition in such a bodily way and who, by means of her muscle spasm, would not "let out anything," proved—as was to be expected—strongly anal-erotic.

The hypertonus of such persons is the expression of their tendency to anal retention. Ferenczi was able to demonstrate that globus sensations, hysterical glottis spasms, and pylorospasms were displacements of sphincter spasms.[21]

The sphincter functions can be displaced to the whole skeletal musculature. People in whom this is the case have a constant unconscious fear of incontinence, and thus obtain a secondary pleasure gain. We must take in all seriousness the half-joking remark of Ferenczi, that the "manometry of sphincter-tension" is to be recommended as a measure of the intensity of affective fluctuations.[22] We must also keep in mind that not only anxiety but also defiance and suppressed rage manifest themselves somatically as muscular spasms, and that the suppression of the motor discharge of any affect leads to an increase of muscular tension.

These examples teach us one more thing. It would be premature to consider that "dystonia" stands only in the service of defense against drives, and to describe it as an equivalent of anti-cathexis. Retention pleasure is pleasure, and even the spastic-hypertonic expression of anxiety, that is, of instinctual defense, can—like the anxiety affect itself—be secondarily libidinized and placed in the service of instinctual discharge, as we are accustomed to see in compulsive symptoms. There is no doubt, for instance, that localized or generalized spasms of the body may mean erection. The original autoerotic libidinization of the musculature persists in all of us and can—as Freud has shown—be regressively revived.[23] "Unpurposive innervations" occur wherever the musculature refuses to yield its pleasure role to its physiological function. That rhythmical and continuous muscle spasms as well as all kinds of muscle play (such as tic or motor restlessness) may represent masturbation equivalents—the rhythmic ones in a direct, the continuous ones in an aim-inhibited fashion—and that the spasms in hysterical or occupational neuroses signify distorted sexual gratifications, all this has so often and so convincingly been described that we need not dwell on it at length. It is also clear that every possible partial drive may find distorted expression in muscular equivalents of masturbation no less than in genital masturbation. If an inhibition of instinctual actions can be extended to a partial inhibition of actions in general, this, too, is an indication that the musculature clings to its pleasure role, to its erotization; there would otherwise be no reason for the ego to inhibit its function. Thus the nonspecific significance of an instinctual defense presented by spastic conditions of the musculature may be overlaid by

---

[21] S. Ferenczi, "Psycho-Analysis of Sexual Habits," *Further Contributions to the Theory and Technique of Psycho-Analysis*, p. 268.

[22] *Ibid.*, p. 268.

[23] S. Freud, *Three Essays on the Theory of Sexuality*.

various specific meanings attached to instinctual discharge. One need only think of Ferenczi's "phenomena of hysterical materialization," which play a great role both in the spasms of hysterics and in the everyday innervations of normal persons.[24] There are all kinds of transitions between muscular tensions serving as a defense against drives, and muscular tensions serving as masturbatory equivalents. We give one example:

A patient was able to combat the setting in of anxiety after masturbation by a ceremonial action which consisted in spastically stiffening his legs. That here too the defense against an instinct later became a hidden repetition of the prohibited instinctual action was proven by the subsequent vicissitude of this muscular behavior; for it was later replaced by a rhythmic banging on the legs and in the end occasionally by a repetition of the masturbatory act.

Thus Vilma Kovacs said perfectly correctly about a patient of this sort (a woman suffering from tic) that the continuous spasm of her total skeletal musculature served the purpose of "maintaining and hiding sexual excitement." [25] When we consider the fact that orgasm consists of a *rhythmic* contraction of the skeletal musculature, we understand that its tonic continuous contraction on the one hand prevents the clonus and on the other makes it perpetual. Dystonia, just like a neurotic symptom, may be sustained from two sides.

Only this double role makes it understandable as a correlate of the repressive struggle. Just as the latter represents a dynamic struggle between instinctual excitation and anti-cathexis, so does the former represent a struggle between a motor impulse and the suppression of a movement.

## II

We shall now attempt to apply to these phenomena the Freudian concept of "narcissistic body libido." First we must make a preliminary remark. It is irrelevant for our purpose whether libidinal processes in regard to the body are to be considered as *directly* somatic and as occurring (chemically) in the organ concerned, as Ferenczi [26] thought, or whether they occur first psychically, upon the mental representations of the organ, and these in their turn bring about physiological changes in the organ itself. Freud assumed the former for actual neuroses.[27] If one wants to be cautious, one may content oneself with the second assumption. Just as object cathexes are in fact cathexes of the mental representation of the external object,[28] not cathexes of the object itself, so may the changes

24 S. Ferenczi, *Hysterie und Pathoneurosen*, p. 23.
25 V. Kovacs, "Analyse eines Falles von 'Tic convulsif,'" *Int. Z. Psa.*, Vol. 11, 1925, p. 322.
26 S. Ferenczi, *op. cit.*
27 S. Freud, "The Justification for Detaching from Neurasthenia a Particular Syndrome: The Anxiety-Neurosis," and "Sexuality in the Aetiology of the Neuroses," *Coll. Pap.*, Vol. I, London, Hogarth, 1948.
28 O. Fenichel, "Identification," No. 10 in this volume.

in organ libido occur endopsychically, in regard to the mental representations of the organ. Freud has assumed this recently in describing pain,[29] and he had already hinted at it in his "On Narcissism: An Introduction." ("Every change in the erotogenicity of the organs may run parallel with a change of libidinal cathexis in the ego [in the organ representation]." [30] When we simply speak in what follows of changes in, damming up, etc., of organ-libido, this issue is left open.

As we know, every repression requires a continuous cathectic expenditure. The ego cannot, or cannot always, manage to make headway against undesirable impulses merely by withdrawal of cathexis, but must erect an anti-cathexis the manifestations of which have been recently described by Freud in detail.[31] Thus, economically speaking, every repression (instinctual defense) amounts to an excess of bound libido and a lack of free libido.

It would seem that the organic counterpart of repression is nothing else than this. Owing to the fight between instinct and defense against instinct, a certain quantity of libido is unpurposively bound in the "dystonic" muscle.

We have seen that motor impulse and motor inhibition struggle with each other in the "dystonic" muscle. In accordance with the views of Ferenczi and Nunberg, who maintain that catatonia is a defensive struggle against local accumulations of organ libido and is a composite of single clonic defensive jerks,[32] and with the view of Hollos, who maintains that tonic discharge is a rhythmicity of high frequency,[33] we come to the conception that the hyper- and dystonus we are concerned with are also essentially hyper- and dysclonus; that is, they are the expression of a struggle between contradictory impulses, which, keeping each other in balance, fixate a quantity of organ libido in the locus of the struggle. While in catatonia, as a result of the preceding loss of object, it is purely narcissistic libido that is dammed up, in "normal dystonia" we are dealing with an inhibition of implementation of object libido. Thus normal dystonia relates to catatonia as the introversion of the neurotic relates to the object loss of the schizophrenic who has regressed to primary narcissism. We have also seen that the restriction of function of motility present in dystonia presupposes an erotization of the musculature. "Erotization," however, can only be conceived as a cathecting with libido quantities.

We must compare our assumption—that, owing to repression, cathecting and

[29] S. Freud, *The Problem of Anxiety*, pp. 120–121.

[30] S. Freud, "On Narcissism: An Introduction," *Coll. Pap.*, Vol. IV, p. 41.

[31] S. Freud, *The Problem of Anxiety*, pp. 102 ff.

[32] S. Ferenczi, "Psycho-Analytical Observations on Tic," *Further Contributions to the Theory and Technique of Psycho-Analysis;* H. Nunberg, "On the Catatonic Attack," *Practice and Theory of Psycho-analysis,* New York, Nerv. & Ment. Dis. Monograph, 1948.

[33] S. Hollos, "Ueber das Zeitgefuehl," *Int. Z. Psa.*, Vol. 8, 1922.

anti-cathecting libido quantities are unpurposively bound in the musculature—with a further theoretical assumption of Ferenczi. To explain certain forms of tic, he assumes that a trauma, the solution of which was unsuccessful, leaves a depot of stimuli in an ego memory system or somatic memory system (or as we would put it: in the endopsychic organ representations), and he believes that under certain conditions the stimuli that come from these depots which act like drives, attain direct outflow into motility.[34] But more frequently such an outflow fails to come about, being prevented by the ego, and the libido remains dammed up in the somatic memory system. Ferenczi describes this possibility as follows: "These are the neurotics who become conspicuous by the excessive caution, measuredness, and weightiness of their manner of walking and movements,"[35] in brief, those whose function of motility is encumbered. It is our opinion that even ordinary traumata bring about a certain depot of "stimulus," that is, of libido, in the organ (or rather in the organ representation) so that any defense against drives results in a damming up of libido—even if only a relatively mild degree of it—particularly in the musculature.

Freud has shown that when the pleasure principle is replaced by the reality principle, "innervations" that have up to now been "sent into the interior of the body" become replaced by "purposive alteration of reality" and that the motor discharge attains thereby a new function.[36] The dystonus is nothing but the sum of such innervations sent into the inside of the body, which as a consequence of the defense against instincts once more take the place of instinctual actions directed to the external world. The instinctual defense prevents muscular innervations from leading to action, and replaces them by innervations not externally manifest (or at least not useful). That such an introversion must lead to a damming up of libido was shown by Freud.[37] This damming up of it corresponds to the dystonia.

F. Deutsch has suggested that "somatic health means—in the psychoanalytic sense—freedom from pathologically bound organ-libido."[38] It would follow from the above discussion that this also holds for psychic health, though with a grain of salt.

Originally the musculature subserves only the pleasure principle, or more correctly, the Nirvana principle, in that it discharges stimulations into motility

---

[34] S. Ferenczi, "Psycho-Analytical Observations on Tic," *Further Contributions to the Theory and Technique of Psycho-Analysis*, p. 158.

[35] *Ibid.*, pp. 161–162.

[36] S. Freud, "Formulations regarding the Two Principles in Mental Functioning," *Coll. Pap.*, Vol. IV, p. 16.

[37] S. Freud, "On Narcissism: An Introduction," *Coll. Pap.*, Vol. IV, pp. 42–43.

[38] F. Deutsch, "Der gesunde und der kranke Koerper in psychoanalytischer Betrachtung," *Int. Z. Psa.*, Vol. 12, 1926.

in an unco-ordinated fashion (the period of magic-hallucinatory omnipotence, according to Ferenczi [39]). Residues of this pure discharging function, however, always persist.[40] Only with the advent of the reality principle do the unco-ordinated movements change into actions.[41] Subsequent damming up of organ libido in the musculature amounts to a partial rescinding of this reality function —in that every defense against drives is ultimately a defense against actions— and thereby to a partial regression to the original pleasure function of the musculature. More exactly: just as a defensive operation directed against a re-pressed instinctual demand may itself become the expression of that demand, so may the musculature mobilized against objectionable instinctual impulses again subserve the pleasure principle (admittedly an inhibited one) on this very point.

## III

Organ-libidinal phenomena accompanying defense against drives are also present, however, in the sensory sphere. The data of deep sensibility—of the interior muscles of the joints and viscera—reach the ego in the form of internal perceptions in the same way as do feelings and sensations.

Freud has shown us how bodily sensations become conscious.[42] From the un-derlying multi-located changes in the depth of the organism, excitations arise which must then be relayed to the perceptual system, if a sensation—that is, a conscious inner perception—is to occur. Freud refers to these changes cautiously as "something qualitatively-quantitatively different in psychic life." [43] For our present point, it is of extraordinary significance that this "something different" can, under certain conditions, behave like a repressed impulse, that is, that its being relayed to consciousness may be hampered or blocked by the intervention of the ego; for then all these qualitative-quantitative different "somethings" have the same dynamic background as do sensations, though no sensations actually arise from them. "When the process of relaying them [to consciousness] is blocked, these (excitations) do not lead to sensations, even though that 'some-thing different' in the process is present. In a not quite correct shorthand, we speak then of *unconscious sensations*." [44] Such unconscious sensations can be conceived of either—with Freud—as the discharge reaction succeeding in over-whelming the ego before a sensation can come about, or as the discharge reaction

---

[39] S. Ferenczi, "Stages in the Development of the Sense of Reality," *Sex in Psychoanalysis*, New York, Brunner, 1950.

[40] K. Landauer, *op. cit.*

[41] S. Freud, "Formulations regarding the two Principles in Mental Functioning," *Coll. Pap.*, Vol. IV.

[42] S. Freud, *The Ego and the Id*, London, Hogarth, 1947, pp. 24–26.

[43] *Ibid.*, p. 25.

[44] *Ibid.*, pp. 25–26.

not taking place at all. The point is that the ego successfully shuts itself off from forbidden internal perceptions, just as it does under certain circumstances against external perceptions.[45] To cite a few examples: A female patient with strong repressed exhibitionistic inclinations overcompensated by an excessive sense of modesty had to be examined by a doctor near her genitals. She long resisted this, and feared that she would not be able to survive the situation. When she finally had to submit, something remarkable happened: she suddenly lost the feeling of her body; the lower half of her body was "strange" to her, did not belong to her any more—and she could allow herself to be examined.

In another patient—a man with anxiety hysteria—the anxiety attacks began with the remarkable sensation that his legs were being pulled off him, or were running away from him. Then he lost the feeling of his legs, he no longer had legs, he was no longer himself, and with this feeling of depersonalization the anxiety set in. The analysis brought out a mass of material related to "leg eroticism"; let us say—not quite correctly, but for the sake of briefness—that owing to specific infantile experiences his legs represented the penis for him. The anxiety-arousing situations were always those which for the Ucs. were conducive to sexual feelings. Before the ego made a defense against the temptation by a full mobilization of castration anxiety, it attempted to make it by inhibiting the seductive organ sensations, as if to say: "It is not true that I am sexually excited; for I have no legs—no penis—that could get excited." In this way, to be sure, it prophylactically anticipated the dreaded castration.

A woman patient exhibited the connection between spasm and estrangement. At the time that her castration anxiety had reached its peak through the analytic uncovering of her infantile masturbation, she had to be given an anesthetic [for medical reasons] and she awoke from it with "stiff" arms and the feeling that her hands were not her own. This condition lasted for a day and recurred repeatedly when her associations approached the subject of infantile masturbation.

These alienations of body sensations and body organs in the service of instinctual defense exist not only in a localized form but in a generalized one. The altered bodily feelings of depersonalized people are well-known phenomena. But there are similar ones—outright blockings of bodily sensations—present in much less severe conditions. Compulsion neurotics and compulsive characters, in whom all conflicts are completely "internalized," often show, along with their defense against their sexual wishes, an inhibition of the total body feeling, which occasionally assumes enormous proportions. Disturbances of sensibility belong to the hysterical stigmata. Our understanding is that the defects in the ego's control of motility, discussed in the preceding sections, are intimately related to the corresponding defects in muscular feeling.

[45] S. Freud, *The Problem of Anxiety*, p. 104.

Thus repression may manifest itself somatically not only in changes of motility (hyper- and dystonia), but also in alterations of sensibility (estrangement of certain body feelings and kinesthetic sensations). Not only does somatic ego feeling lose intensity and extent in states of tiredness and depression; the great "differences in, and limitations of, ego-feelings in normal people during the waking state" which Federn speaks of,[46] are also greatly dependent on the repressive, or rather defensive, activity of the ego. Just as the ego defends itself against ideas which, as derivatives of repressed instinctual representations, seek their way toward consciousness, so does it defend itself to a certain extent against corresponding internal perceptions too. This is nothing new. It is what Freud had already assumed to be the basis of hysterical disturbances of sensibility.[47] Just as vaginismus as a defense against intercourse presents the simplest example of muscular spasm used for the purpose of instinctual defense, so is the simplest example of organ estrangement used for that purpose to be found in the extreme forms of frigidity which often accompany vaginismus and in which the sexual region is not felt at all during intercourse. The latter mechanism, manifest in gross form in hysteria, is widespread in its milder forms.

Admittedly, Ferenczi also emphasizes that occasionally hysterical symptoms require not only a lack but also at times an excess of capacity for innervations and body feeling.[48] He is correct when he maintains that the progress of evolution makes for retrogression of somatic abilities, that "the child's organism has, even in its autoerotic and organ-erotic plays, avenues of excitation open to it which adults do not have at their disposal," and that "education consists not only in the learning of new but, to a considerable part, in an unlearning of such 'super-normal abilities.'"[49] But this unlearning, which Ferenczi himself describes as a "repression" of somatic abilities, can be explained only by assuming that the repression directed at the autoerotic activity also affects the somatic ability by means of which that activity was achieved. The result would then be a *limitation* of the expanse of the body-ego, a *restriction* of ego activity. Here we see what Bernfeld means by saying that we are always inclined "to exclude a disobedient organ from the body."[50]

The practical significance of such mechanisms becomes clear only if we remember the fundamental significance of the subject's perceptions of his body in the formation and maturation of his ego. The idea of one's own body, that is, the co-ordination of the data of external perceptions (touch)

---

[46] P. Federn, "Some Variations in Ego-Feeling," *Int. J. Psa.*, Vol. 7, 1926, p. 441.

[47] S. Freud, "Some Points in a Comparative Study of Organic and Hysterical Paralysis," *Coll. Pap.*, Vol. I.

[48] S. Ferenczi, *Hysterie und Pathoneurosen*, p. 17.

[49] S. Ferenczi, "Psycho-Analysis of Sexual Habits," *Further Contributions to the Theory and Technique of Psycho-Analysis*, p. 283.

[50] S. Bernfeld, *Psychologie des Saeuglings*, Vienna, Springer, 1925, p. 238.

and internal perceptions (sensation) which constitutes the idea of one's own body, as Freud has shown [51]—and as, according to Bernfeld,[52] Preyer had already concluded from direct observations of infants [53]—is fundamental for the formation of ego feeling. This has only recently been emphatically restated by Federn.[54] It was, moreover, well known to pre-analytic psychology. For example, according to Schilder, Scheler speaks of a somatic consciousness ("*Leibbewusstsein*") which is a composite of body-sensations, external body build, and knowledge of the mastery over one's own body, and is fundamental to all psychic life.[55] It is thus understandable that secondary encroachments on this body consciousness will secondarily affect psychic experience in many ways.

Reik—in contrast to Freud—has recently attempted to conceive of internal perception not as a function of the ego, but as a function of the superego.[56] Though fully appreciating the fact that internal perception and critical self-observation are intimately related, we believe, particularly on the basis of the ideas developed here, that it is necessary to hold on to the Freudian conception of the activity on two fronts of the perceptual apparatus, which forms the kernel of the ego. It is probable that the situation is not very different here from what it is in defense against drives, which also can be carried out only by the ego even though it is in practice subject to the superego. In the same way, the ego also remains that region of inner perception which is influenced by the superego.

### IV

How is the estrangement of body sensations or bodily organs related to organ libido? The simple conception that the ego has withdrawn its cathexis from the estranged organs does not always do justice to the complications of reality. To begin with, it is probable that the "estranged muscle" will not, in regard to its libidinal cathexis, be very different from the "dystonic muscle."

Let us remember an observation Tausk made on schizophrenics. In his patients a hypochondriacal phase, that is, a local damming up of libido, was often followed by a phase of "alienation" of the organs in question, by a disappearance of the sensations originating in them.[57] We cannot assume, however, that the accumulation of libido had disappeared, but only that the ego had managed to fend off the unpleasant sensations. The latter no longer become conscious, the organ is alienated, but the cathectic investment remains bound to the estranged

---

51 S. Freud, *The Ego and the Id*, p. 31.
52 S. Bernfeld, *op. cit.*, p. 252.
53 W. Preyer, *The Mind of the Child*, New York, Appleton, 1896.
54 P. Federn, *op. cit.*
55 P. Schilder, *Medizinische Psychologie*, Berlin, Springer, 1924, p. 252.
56 T. Reik, *Wie man Psychologe wird*, Vienna, Int. Psa. Verlag, 1928.
57 V. Tausk, "On the Origin of the 'Influencing Machine' in Schizophrenia," *Psa. Quart.*, Vol. 2, 1933, pp. 549–550.

organ. The damming up of libido is not removed but is prevented from manifesting itself, by means of an appropriate amount of anti-cathexis. Just as in repression, so in the blocking of internal perceptions the simpler mechanism of withdrawal of cathexis usually yields to the more complicated one in which a high cathexis is neutralized by an approximately equally high anti-cathexis.[58] Thus, Federn's finding that libidinally cathected parts of the body tend to retain their body feelings more than averagely [59] must be amended by stating that under certain conditions of instinctual defense it is the very organs that have a particularly high libidinal cathexis which disappear from the field of body feeling. Schilder had already recognized this in the case of a singer, in whom precisely the vocal organ succumbed to depersonalization.[60] Not only an excess but also a lack of somatic self-observation can express a damming up of organ libido, just as not only the most emphasized but also the most affectless parts of a manifest dream may correspond to the greatest amounts of repressed libido. Localized "estrangements" (expulsion of "disobedient organs" from the body feeling) probably bespeak a simple withdrawal of libido, while the more general alienation of the body in "internalized" compulsive characters corresponds rather to heaped-up libido kept in check by anti-cathexis. When self-observation obviously increases, that is, when total or partial body alienation is realized with horror or some other feeling—as in our example of the patient's "loss" of his legs—then the self-observation itself may come to represent a part of the anti-cathexis—as in the compulsion neurotic who, constantly on the watch against himself, cannot associate freely. Where there is no such self-observation, and the person does not know that he has anesthetized parts of his body, we may be dealing with a simple withdrawal of the libido; as is the case in some hysterical disorders of the sensorium, and in many "normal" people who do not even know that one can feel one's organs, or in what way. But even in such cases there may be an unconscious struggle with anti-cathexes erected by the ego, which is not directly indicated to consciousness. It is the same as in repression, where the two mechanisms cannot in practice be separated. Reich, who has occasionally touched on such trains of thought,[61] would probably also attempt to localize these libido displacements somatically, and assert, say, that the organ libido regresses from the phylogenetically younger sensorimotor system to the phylogenetically older vegetative one, which is not, or not as easily, accessible to internal perception. An alienation of which one knows nothing (which, descriptively, is a pure inhibition, and metapsychologically, a withdrawal of cathexis) would correspond to a

[58] S. Freud, "Repression," Coll. Pap., Vol. IV.

[59] P. Federn, op. cit., p. 439.

[60] P. Schilder, Introduction to a Psychoanalytic Psychiatry, New York, Nerv. Ment. Dis. Pub. Co., 1928, pp. 36–38.

[61] W. Reich, Die Funktion des Orgasmus, Vienna, Int. Psa. Verlag, 1927.

successful repression; an alienation of which one is painfully conscious (descriptively a neurotic condition and metapsychologically an anti-cathexis) would correspond to an unsuccessful repression.

If such a damming up is undone, the ego experiences new body sensations, repeats in part the original "discovery of the body," [62] and recognizes something new as part of the "ego."

The analogy between this process and identification is regarded by Mueller-Braunschweig as a relation of identity.[63] He believes that not only object libido, but also autoerotic libido can be desexualized by identifications. By identifications with organs or excitatory processes, autoerotic libido becomes desexualized-narcissistic libido. The "acquired narcissism" of Tausk [64] comes about not only by a detour through the objects to the already existing ego,[65] but also through autoeroticism to the ego, whose very differentiation is effected by this means in the first instance. The desexualization therewith increases the physiological function of the libidinally cathected organ, in contrast to autoeroticism, which disturbs the physiological function. (Freud writes: "We have found in general that the ego-function of an organ is hampered when its erotogenicity, its sexual significance, increases." [66]) The masturbator and the painter have both "libidinized" their hand. The former thereby weakens the ego function of the hand, the latter has desexualized the libido of the hand, so that the cathexis of his hand is no longer primitive-autoerotic but desexualized-narcissistic. Hermann has elaborated this contrast and speaks—not entirely correctly—in the one case of "genitalization," in the other of "erotization progressing toward sublimation." [67]

The transition from alienation to depersonalization is fluid. In the former the "bodily ego feeling," and in the latter the "psychic ego feeling" too, are disturbed by the blocking of internal perception. That there is such a thing as blocking of psychic sensations was shown by Freud in *The Ego and the Id,* and was demonstrated by him in the example of the repression of feelings of guilt emanating from the superego in hysteria.[68] There are people with "cold natures" who prevent the development of finely differentiated feelings by active inhibition. In depersonalization other "feelings" and "sensations" are analogously "repressed." The "missing" of the sensations in question by the self-observant patient corresponds to the missing of a lost name on the tip of one's tongue. In regard to the significance of the body feelings for the coming into being of the ego, de-

[62] V. Tausk, *op. cit.*
[63] C. Mueller-Braunschweig, "Beitraege zur Metapsychologie," *Imago,* Vol. 12, 1926.
[64] V. Tausk, *op. cit.*
[65] S. Freud, *The Ego and the Id,* p. 65.
[66] S. Freud, *The Problem of Anxiety,* pp. 14–15.
[67] I. Hermann, "Organlibido und Begabung," *Int. Z. Psa.,* Vol. 9, 1923, p. 297.
[68] S. Freud, *The Ego and the Id,* pp. 74–75.

personalization and alienation cannot be sharply separated. It is therefore all the more reassuring that Reik should have advanced considerations concerning depersonalization which are similar to ours concerning alienation. He too—correctly, as we think—has described depersonalization as a defense against drives.[69] We believe that a point left unclear by both Schilder [70] and Nunberg [71] can now be clarified. Nunberg left open the question of whether in depersonalization there is a lack of narcissistic libido (libido loss) or an excess of it (loss of gratification, that is, damming up of libido). Schilder stressed that in depersonalized cases the feelings are not lacking objectively, that the patients "only raise from within an objection to their own experiences," [72] that "self-observation" represents the "inner objection," so that "we have in depersonalization two mutually contradictory tendencies," [73] that, indeed, "it is the narcissistically cathected organ which succumbs most strongly to depersonalization"; [74] nevertheless metapsychologically he maintains only that "the patients *withdraw* libido from their own experiences." [75] Presumably, just as in repression and "alienation," both events occur in depersonalization: a withdrawal of cathexis, but also a damming up of it through the erecting of an anti-cathexis.

It is the latter event that is described in detail by Reik.[76] Reik asserts that the increased self-observation which has so frequently been described in connection with depersonalization does not primarily belong to it, but attaches itself in a secondary way as an attempt at putting the situation right. We would like to conceive of this as follows: the defense against drives in depersonalization, as in repression, is *first* attempted by the withdrawal of cathexis; if this proves unsuccessful, an anti-cathexis is *then* erected, which—as Freud has described in compulsion neuroses [77]—becomes manifest as self-observation. This cathectic energy may originate precisely in the cathectic energy which the ego has previously withdrawn from the psychic material it is fending off. Thus the analogy between depersonalization and other instinctual defense would be complete. The constitutive characteristic of depersonalization would be only that what the ego defends itself against here are not impulses toward instinctual action in general, but specifically data of feelings and sensations obtained from internal perception.

---

[69] T. Reik, *op. cit.*

[70] P. Schilder, *Introduction to a Psychoanalytic Psychiatry.*

[71] H. Nunberg, "States of Depersonalization in the Light of the Libido Theory," *Practice and Theory of Psychoanalysis.*

[72] P. Schilder, *op. cit.,* p. 32.

[73] *Ibid.,* p. 33.

[74] *Ibid.,* p. 38.

[75] *Ibid.,* p. 33.

[76] T. Reik, *op. cit.*

[77] S. Freud, *The Problem of Anxiety,* p. 56.

Ideas that are being remembered, also, are cathectic changes going on in the depth of the psychic apparatus which are being noted by internal perception. From this point of view repression proper, too, is a specific partial putting out of action of internal perception. Depersonalization and repression differ only in the matter of what data of internal perception are put out of action. This being so, it is understandable that, as Nunberg has pointed out,[78] nearly all repressions are accompanied, to begin with, by mild phenomena of partial depersonalization.[79]

## V

Like all the phenomena subserving instinctual defense—as we have specially stressed for dystonia—the described changes in body feeling may also be secondarily libidinized and used in masturbatory activities, and this by no means

[78] H. Nunberg, op. cit.

[79] We can conceive of this defense against internal perceptions being quantitatively increased. Just as it is possible to exclude certain internal perceptions (such as ideas representing drives, guilt feelings, or localized bodily sensations) from becoming conscious, so is it conceivable that the whole realm of internal perceptions may become blocked for reasons of defense. This seems to be the case in syncope, where the data not only of external, but also of internal perception are completely in abeyance; that is, the total function of the perceptual apparatus—including that of consciousness itself —is suspended (K. Landauer, "Die Bewusstseinsstoerungen," Das psychoanalytische Volksbuch, Hippokrates-Verlag, Stuttgart, 1926). But this extreme case presents us with new metapsychological difficulties: can the ego suspend itself, its own differentiation, and submerge itself again in the id?

In sleep there is no such problem, since sleep does not subserve defense against drives. True, sleep, too, must be considered as a similar sort of phenomenon, as a removal of the differentiation of the ego by means of a cessation of all perceptual functions. The narcissism of sleep (S. Freud, "Metapsychological Supplement to the Theory of Dreams," Coll. Pap., Vol. IV) does not reinforce the cathexis of the ego, but rather withdraws it into the id; the diagnostic faculty of the dream is not due to an increased ego cathexis, in the narrower sense, but rather to the circumstance that the internal aspect of perception, resisting the wish to sleep, retains its cathexes longer than does the external aspect. But the occurrence of sleep can also be conceived of as due to an automatic compulsion to achieve periodic suspension of differentiation. Freud's formulation, that in sleep external world and ego again merge periodically (S. Freud, Group Psychology and the Analysis of the Ego, London, Hogarth, 1948, p. 104) must be complemented from the structural point of view: in sleep the ego, which, in the narrower sense, represents the external world too, merges once more with the id.

But how about syncope, where this merging is purposive and subserves defense, and can originate only from the ego? The problem is the same as with unconscious resistance: to explain the latter Freud introduced the concept of the "id" (S. Freud, The Ego and the Id, pp. 15 ff.), but he was nevertheless constrained later to attribute most forms of unconscious resistance to the ego rather than the id (S. Freud, The Problem of Anxiety, p. 106). It must never be forgotten that the ego is but the product of a differentiation from the id; only where the barriers of repression are erected are ego and id sharply divided from each other; otherwise they flow easily into each other (ibid., p. 18). There are deep layers of the ego which are close to the id. To these presumably pertains the instinctual defense by means of loss of consciousness, the most archaic form of defense ("flight"), residues of which are still recognizable in the higher forms of defense of depersonalization and repression. It is in good agreement with this that the defensive loss of consciousness either appears to correspond to the most archaic Nirvana principle—syncope from intense pain could, for example, be considered as an economically necessary withdrawal of ego-cathexis in order to erect a pain-binding anti-cathexis—or else is a trait of psychotic or infantile people. Thus, depersonalization, organ estrangement, and repression too may be regarded as highly differentiated partial syncopes.

solely in a masochistic fashion, though such a gain, as Reik has particularly emphasized,[80] may be extremely frequent. The patient who "lost" his feet before having anxiety attacks, used to stand naked before the mirror to watch himself, until the feeling What is I? Am I I? arose, which then gave him pleasure. Less conscious is the sexualization of the changes in ego feeling which take place in states of half-sleep, changes which may originally also have been used as a defense against drives. Infantile masturbation before sleep becomes associated with changes in body feelings, and these are woven into fantasies (fantasies about the ego before it was an ego, about birth, intrauterine life and conception, together with the progressive loss of body feelings in association with the sensations of flying and falling dreams, and the like) which often serve as covers for the recollection of a primal scene. Occasionally the feelings of depersonalization and estrangement stand later on for these repressed fantasies in consciousness. Sometimes it is only by such accompanying sensations that hypnagogic fantasies betray their masturbatory (or masturbation-suppressing) meaning. In the same way, too, the feeling that a word has lost its meaning, that a verbal image has lost its factual image—a feeling which is similar to depersonalization and which was originally equivalent to a repression—can be utilized for masturbatory activity.

[80] T. Reik, *op. cit.*

## FIFTEEN

# On "Isolation"*

IN HIS *The Problem of Anxiety* Freud makes a theoretical distinction between repression in the obsessional neurotic and in the hysteric, by which he calls only the latter phenomenon "repression" while in the former he sees the combined activity of various defense mechanisms of the ego against unacceptable instinctual demands. This is another example of those Freudian formulations which, once made, appear self-evident. At first it may seem merely a matter of nomenclature whether one prefers to distinguish two kinds of repression or to speak of different forms of defense, of which one is repression. The essence of the difference was known before. Freud had described long ago the regression of obsessional neurotics to the anal-sadistic level of libido organization, their diphasic symptoms, the second part of which is opposite in content to the first and is meant to cancel it, their keeping apart groups of ideas which belong together or a group of ideas and the affective quality which belongs to it, while nothing loses access to consciousness. (As Freud stated in his *Introductory Lectures,* it is not the traumatic memory, but its connection with the symptom, which is unconscious.) Yet the view which co-ordinates all these mechanisms and contrasts them with repression does bring something really new. It alone enables us, by means of conceptual clarification, to understand properly some things that are actually obvious and observable in the ordinary psychoanalytic treatment of obsessional neurotics.

In spite of the abundance of opportunities for observing the phenomenon of isolation, we present the following examples of it because they show it in an unusually marked degree. Just as a hysteric who cannot remember certain days of his life lends himself particularly well to the demonstration of repression, even though all hysterics repress, so there are especially "isolating" obsessional neurotics, though all obsessional neurotics isolate.

* First published in *Int. Z. Psa.*, Vol. 14, 1928, pp. 243–248.

A young man of seventeen fell ill as a result of his struggle to wean himself of masturbation. After a brief period of guilt-free masturbatory gratification, which he always practiced alone, though he frequently observed the mutual masturbation of his friends without participating in it, he heard his pastor preach a sermon against masturbation in which he advised his flock not to have anything to do with young persons who practiced it. The genitality of our patient had been inhibited in his childhood by an excessive castration anxiety, and a passive-anal fixation facilitated later regression. He took his pastor's words very much to heart, and decided to follow his advice and not to talk any more with one boy who was particularly bad in this respect. For a while he succeeded. Then, however, the danger of temptation demanded stronger defenses; the avoidance of social intercourse with the boy took on phobic forms and had to be secured by obsessional mechanisms: when he met him, he had to spit. He had a number ritual pertaining to the compulsive determination of the number of necessary spittings, which could not, however, be sufficiently elucidated in the course of his brief analysis. His phobia increased in extent. Social intercourse with the relatives and friends of the "shunned one" (as the patient called the boy, being prohibited from uttering his name) had to be stopped; then—since the "shunned one" was the son of a barber—he stopped visiting this particular barbershop, then visiting any barbershop, then intercourse with all people who went to barbershops for a shave, and then visiting that part of town in which the barbershop was located.

The further course of this phobia, which was from the beginning shot through with compulsive symptoms, led—*sit venia verbo*—to an "isolation neurosis." Thus far the symptoms had revealed nothing about the causes of the inhibition encountered by the patient's puberal genitality. But now the patient demanded that the relatives with whom he lived, particularly the womenfolk—his mother, grandmother, and sister—should not enter the prohibited part of the town either. He suffered severely from the fact that his relatives would not accept such limitations of their freedom of movement. While he himself abided by the prohibition and avoided the tabooed neighborhoods, he had, instead, an increasing compulsion to *think* about them. That he suffered under this was understandable. But his explanation of his suffering was unexpected. This was that at home he saw his mother and grandmother and *that* was why he must not think of "antipathetic" people or localities! Although the patient knew of the connection between his illness and his struggle against masturbation, he ignored it; to all appearances his masturbation had ceased easily and the need for it did not continue; but its place was taken ever more distinctly by the neurotic striving to keep apart, to *isolate*, the ideas "members of the family" and "antipathetic people and localities."

Isolation now became the main content of the neurosis and the phobia receded into the background. The patient could again think of antipathetic things, but not at the same time as "sympathetic" people. Thus he disclosed the fact that the oedipus complex was the objectionable factor in his masturbation. The elaboration of this attempt at isolation on the part of the ego, as a defense against the oedipus complex which had been activated in puberty, gave rise within a few months to an obsessional neurosis of the most severe sort.

The patient fared like the man in Wedekind who was forbidden to think of bears: when he thought of a barbershop, his grandmother immediately came to his mind. This most torturing symptom he called "connecting." Against this there was only one remedy: defense by "undoing." In this case this was the so-called process of "disconnecting." If, after thinking simultaneously of a tabooed place and a sympathetic person, he was able to see in a totally isolated way the *pure* picture of the antipathetic thing, free from all sympathetic admixture, then everything was made right again and the patient was calmed. Very soon he was exclusively occupied all day long with "disconnecting."

At this point two new phenomena which usually aggravate a developing obsessional neurosis were added: an enormous extension of the field of symptoms and the break-through in the symptom itself of the impulse that was being warded off.

First of all, the division of objects into "sympathetic" and "antipathetic" came to embrace all people and places. Not only were all schoolmates antipathetic and all relatives sympathetic, but all other persons were also subsumed according to superficial associations in one or other of these categories, and thus became subject to "connecting" and "disconnecting." Thus, for example, the friends and colleagues of people whom he saw going toward the forbidden neighborhoods became antipathetic, and nearly all women, provided that he had nothing specific against them, sympathetic. The same happened with all localities. In this way there came about numerous varieties of "connecting"—viz., sympathetic person with antipathetic place, and antipathetic person with sympathetic place; also sympathetic person with antipathetic person and sympathetic place with antipathetic place. There were further "mixed persons," that is, those uniting features of antipathetic and sympathetic persons, as, for instance, his grandmother, who had the facial features of the mother of the "shunned" youth; and there were "mixed localities." All these were subject to corresponding "disconnections." Furthermore, all concrete things now fell within the scope of his symptoms. For example, mirrors, which reminded him of the barbershop, became antipathetic, so that such a phenomenon as his sister's image in a looking-glass was a torturing "connection." Later on this happened to abstract things too. For example, a few words which he heard said by antipathetic people became antipathetic to him, so that he could not use them in sentences in which there were sympathetic words.

The obnoxious "connections" (the prohibited oedipal impulses) were constantly entering the patient's consciousness, and had constantly to be defended against by means of "disconnecting," that is by "undoing," which in this case coincided with "isolating"; otherwise they gave rise to anxiety and painful feelings of tension. All this was further exacerbated by the stipulation that before he succeeded in "disconnecting," he was not to leave the place he was in when the "connecting" occurred, nor was he to interrupt the activity he was engaged in at the time. This stipulation was socially the most damaging of all: since "disconnecting" would occasionally take hours, the patient would have to stand in the same place or continue a senseless activity for hours on end. Thus it was always questionable whether he would succeed in leaving the couch when his analytic hour was over, and his anxiety lest it might end in a period between connecting and disconnecting tormented him throughout his sessions. Moreover, if the process of disconnecting differed in even a minor detail from that of connecting, it was ineffective. This is apparently characteristic for the mechanism of undoing.

Finally the symptoms themselves became the expression of the prohibited instinctual impulses which they were meant to ward off. The patient's compulsion to disconnect made it necessary for him always to have a sufficiency of antipathetic people, places, things, and qualities on hand. His craving to end the torturing tensions quickly triumphed over his phobia and brought about a return of the repressed. He visited antipathetic places and observed antipathetic people as closely as possible, so as to have them in readiness should the need arise! It is true that he did not accomplish this with everything that was antipathetic. The "shunned" one, for instance, continued to be shunned. Finally a graduated series of differences came into being: there were entirely antipathetic things which be phobically avoided; less antipathetic ones, which he sought out in order to be able to disconnect quickly when something sympathetic appeared; a few indifferent things; then mildly sympathetic ones, and finally what was entirely sympathetic. In the end he thought consciously and hard almost solely of antipathetic things, in the hope of being the more quickly able to disconnect. If we remember that thinking of what was antipathetic meant essentially masturbation, we see that he now masturbated continuously. Indeed, when the tension reached its maximum and he could not succeed in disconnecting, in spite of his greatest efforts, pollution would, to his surprise, occasionally occur.

Even the very act of connecting, that is, the bringing together of sympathetic people and antipathetic words, now occurred, unnoticed by the patient, in defiance of the isolating ego. One of the many secondary gains of his illness was that he had himself dressed by others like a little child, because otherwise dressing would take hours, owing to the many intervening disconnectings. When he was being dressed by his grandmother he would burst out with the wildest words of abuse. They were not, however, aimed at her, but at the antipathetic people, whose images came into his mind in the course of this activity, thus forming a connection.

Just a few more words concerning the unfavorable outcome of the analysis. It was very difficult to make contact with the patient, who was entirely introverted and for long stretches of time busy with disconnecting, during which he was not allowed to talk. It took several months to bring to light the developmental history of the neurosis described above. Interpretations, even of quite obviously related things, as for example that the "shunned one" was shunned because of masturbation, met no understanding. The patient's deeper transference, too, was ushered in in an unfavorable way: an apparently trifling matter made the house in which I lived, and with it myself, the treatment, and everything connected with it, antipathetic. Thus uttering anything sympathetic in the analysis became impossible to him, and the demand of his analyst that he should speak was a constant torment. In reality that trifle was only a pretext; the analysis had to become antipathetic because masturbation was discussed in it. Therefore, the patient—who had previously already admitted that he was coming to the analysis very unwillingly—used the occasion of the summer vacation to terminate the treatment against the wish of his understanding relatives.

In the case before us we can see clearly how, when a simple phobia has failed to master an instinctual demand ensuing from the oedipus complex, an attempt is made to do so by the mechanism of isolation (undoing). The symptom of disconnecting is the direct expression of this attempt; but in the further course of the neurosis it itself becomes the representative of the forbidden oedipal impulse.

I was able to make a similar observation in a second case. A patient who was suffering from severe compulsive speculation and doubting, and with whom analytic work was hardly feasible because of the gravity of his illness, protested against the fundamental rule. It turned out eventually that he was anxious to conceal the existence of a girl friend—not because he did not want to talk about the matter at all, nor yet because he did not want to expose her, but because he had already spoken of masturbation in the analysis and had to keep all crude sexuality isolated from his friend. Nevertheless he felt that he might want to talk about her if he could only be sure that nothing crudely sexual would come into his mind afterward during the same hour. The confirmation of the idea that in this case too the "disconnecting" was a reaction to a compulsive "connecting," a defense against oedipal impulses, came only much later. The symptom which the patient most anxiously guarded, and most elaborately tried to conceal, was that whenever he saw this girl friend or heard her name mentioned, he had the obsessive idea, "little whore." This symptom also corresponded to the desires of his oedipal impulses against which his ego was putting up a defense by means of isolation. We are here reminded that the splitting of a person's sexuality into sensuality and tenderness, which Freud described as characteristic of our culture and particularly of puberty, is maintained by measures of "isolation" put into effect by the ego in order to prevent the break-through of his sensuality which was originally directed to the object of his tenderness as well— viz., his incestuous object. It was interesting too, to see how this patient, who was prone to use paranoid mechanisms, combined instinctual defense by means of isolation with defense by projection. I elicited a resistance from him which it was subsequently difficult to overcome through the following piece of carelessness. On one occasion, in an effort to reduce analysis to an absurdity, the patient argued that only what one wants comes into one's mind; I answered that "little whore" came to his mind though he did not want it to. For days after that he persisted in reproaching me with being so vulgar and sensual as to call his girl friend a whore and to take advantage of what he had once admitted to accuse him of obscenity in relation to her; as he had all along known, she did not belong in the analysis.

Another patient of mine created "isolation" on a grand scale by his marriage. His life with his wife was to have no relation to his infantile history. At those points where his infantile sexual strivings obtruded themselves into the marriage in defiance of the intention to isolate them, severe defensive symptoms of a compulsive kind had arisen. As a result of this isolation, a thoroughgoing analysis of his childhood remained therapeutically ineffective until its full relationship with his married life had been worked through in the face of the resistances which maintained the isolation.

I should like to mention a fourth case in which the isolation subserved resistance. When this patient's associations came close to "repressed material," that is, to contents which were being warded off by the ego, he would interrupt them ten minutes before the end of the hour and bring up only unimportant material. The transition from the important to the unimportant occurred suddenly and abruptly. The unconscious purpose of this technique was to prevent the analytic material from influencing reality. The unimportant material at the end of the hour was an isolating layer which prevented the material brought out in analysis from having any contact with everyday life, by interposing itself between them.

The intention of this brief communication is simply to present examples showing how isolation as a mechanism of defense dominates the manifest picture of some obsessional neuroses.

## SIXTEEN

# The Inner Injunction to "Make a Mental Note" *

IN A former paper [1] I discussed the economic meaning of "screen memories" in connection with a phenomenon which I called the inner injunction to "make a mental note." We know that the function of screen memories is to facilitate tendentious forgetting by noting in a special intense fashion material associated with that which is to be repressed. When children are struggling to effect repressions they have a kind of "hunger for screen experiences"; that is, when they experience anything which they can use as a screen memory they sometimes feel a kind of inner injunction: "You must make a note of that!" They obey this injunction, and this enables them to forget something else. I gave two examples of this, and I can now add a third, which is particularly clear.

A certain patient recollected that one day, when he was a child, he determined to "test his memory" by resolving "forever to remember" something. The idea occurred to him suddenly as he was out walking and saw an advertisement of a kind of margarine called "Palmona" or "Palmin." He made up his mind that he would never forget this advertisement.

Margarine is a substitute for butter. In association to this the patient thought of a song which he used to sing as a child, though he thought it was not a "nice" song. The words were, "My mother always smears the butter on the wall." At home they always ate butter—never margarine, and it was always impressed on his mind as a child that they had only the very best butter. His mother also laid great stress on the fact that she had always been "genteel"; she never used margarine, nor would she ever allow a song like the one the patient recalled.

* First published in *Int. Z. Psa.*, Vol. 14, 1928, pp. 402–403.
1 "The Economic Function of Screen Memories," No. 11 in this volume.

This "proper" mother, therefore, was a contrast to an "improper mother" in fantasy, who would tolerate margarine and allusions to anal habits. But a mother like that would not be a real mother, but a mother substitute, just as margarine was a substitute for butter. A real mother seemed to go with real butter, and a bad mother with margarine.

I must now tell you that the patient's own mother had died when he was a baby. He had a stepmother, whom he professed to have believed to be his real mother, learning the truth only when he grew up. Analysis showed that actually he had known it unconsciously throughout his childhood and had repressed the knowledge at a heavy psychic cost. Thus the antithesis butter–margarine signified mother–stepmother, and the stressing of his stepmother's "genteel" nature helped him to repudiate his unconscious knowledge.

After this interpretation it occurred to the patient that the incident of the advertisement had happened just as he was on his way to a class for remedial exercises. At that time this lesson was the very embodiment of horror to him because all his castration anxiety had attached itself to the orthopedic apparatus used. His mind rebelled against his mother for sending him to this inferno, and so he had looked up at the Palmona advertisement as the goose-girl in the fairy story looked up at the horse's head, and had said to himself, "O Palmona hanging there, if my mother knew it her heart would break." The little boy's thoughts can be reconstructed as follows, "I have only a wicked stepmother, who sends me to the exercises. Oh, if only my mother were alive!" But this thought was objectionable, and he had to subdue it with other thoughts of the opposite kind, "But yet she is so good and gives us only the best butter (i.e., is the best mother to us)" and perhaps "I must never think like that again." But the conscious thought was, "I must always remember that."

156   COLLECTED WORKS OF OTTO FENICHEL, FIRST SERIES

# *SEVENTEEN*

# The "Long Nose"*

THE scornful gesture of making a "long nose" was the topic of a small discussion, some time ago, in the German Psychoanalytic Society. In this discussion the gesture was regarded as being mainly an exhibitionistic demonstration by the subject of his own penis, and the greater preference for it shown by girls as compared to boys was put down to its being a wish fulfillment: boys, who have a real penis, have no need to demonstrate an illusory one.

This view leaves the meaning of the gesture as a gesture of *scorn* entirely unexplained. The meaning: "See my penis!" could, as the case may be, arouse pleasure or anxiety, but never shame, unless it were to go on, "You haven't got one," to which nothing in the gesture points. These considerations also hold good for the sticking out of the tongue, which is an analogous gesture to making a long nose.

Let us note that the object of scorn is always the *scorned* person and his attributes, while the attributes of the subject-person are objects only of showing off, wanting to impress, but not of derision. Moreover, the meaning of the scorn would be familiar to us and psychologically understandable at once if the scorner were to hold up another person's *weaknesses* to him. There would be no problem if the "I have it and you haven't got it" were expressed in the gesture by a representation of the *lack* of the thing—thus, for instance, by making a *"short nose."* Most of the gestures of scorn in folklore and among children are to be taken as imitations of the weaknesses of the object-person. That aping another is apprehended as scorn is a commonplace both in psychoanalysis and in everyday life, particularly when the weaknesses are represented in isolation (as in caricature).

Is it possible to maintain the absurdity that the "long nose" and the stuck-out

* First published in *Imago*, Vol. 14, 1928, pp. 502–504.

tongue are a demonstration of the penis of the *object*-person and mean: "Look, this is how long *your* penis is!" when otherwise the possession of a long penis is perceived in the unconscious as a sign of strength?

This question leads us to the same problem which Marie Bonaparte has attempted to solve in connection with the phrase "horned husband" (i.e., cuckold), in which, once again, the attribution of a penis symbol to a person is meant to make him an object of scorn and mockery.[1] Her answer, which seeks support in Freud, was that this was a "representation by the opposite." "The representation by the opposite is the most essential mechanism of *irony*, of that social phenomenon by which one ascribes in conversation certain extraordinary qualities to precisely the person who has least of them, instigating thereby the listener or listeners to take away from him in thought what has just been given to him in words."

There is no doubt that this is so, and that this explanation holds for the "long nose" and the put-out tongue as well. These gestures, too, are made by preference before an audience, and the scorner has presumably the wish that the audience should again deprive the scorned person of the exceptional penis which was attributed to him by the gestures. A minor observation on a woman patient, however, gave me an opportunity to see *how* this occurs, under what circumstances it is possible to use this "representation by the opposite," and to express sexual impotency through the symbol of a big penis.

The case was one of a woman who was close to her climacteric, whose whole life stood under the rule of the castration complex. An early identification with her father had made her ignore her femininity to a far-reaching extent, and her menses meant to her the most severe humiliation and shame. In her earlier days she had led a very lively sexual life, which consisted in her getting herself courted in a quite narcissistic way, only in the end to disappoint the man in one way or another. She gave herself to the man only when she was the "stronger," for instance, when the man had broken out in tears. Active castration tendencies were in the foreground, and it was a triumph for her if a man ejaculated prematurely and was then "helpless." Her aim was to shame men as sexual creatures, not to let them get to her, and then to say, "If they were so weak that they could not seduce me, then it serves them right." Naturally, in her transference the analysis was also a constant competition for dominance, and she continually tried to create occasions for humiliating the analyst. The men who did not prove equal to her became the object of her scorn. But not only men; the penis, in particular, too. She found it grotesque, she had to laugh when she saw it and when she thought that men were proud of *that!* This woman when making fun of her husband would call out to him: "What a long thing!" This is to be

[1] M. Bonaparte, "Ueber die Symbolik der Kopftrophaen," *Imago*, Vol. 14, 1928.

completed as follows: "You've got a penis and still you can't get me!" It will be readily believed after this brief sketch that as a child she had continually—in the literal and figurative sense—made long noses at the grown-ups.

Now, it seems, we have found the addition which the meaning of making a long nose must be given. To "What a long penis you have!" is added "and you are still powerless!" The scorner does indeed demonstrate not his own, but the object's penis; and he does this in order to show the *incongruity* between it and the object's actions. "Get at me with that long penis of yours, if you can!" calls the mocker to his victim, in the conviction that he won't be able to do it. The long penis thus is a sign of weakness and not of strength, if it is only morphologically big, but functionally small.

This condition seems to our mind to be fulfilled by the phrase "horned husband" also. The betrayed husband too has been unable, in spite of his penis, to keep sole dominion over his wife.

The scorner imitates a characteristic of the scorned person. He thus uses identification. Just as identification is in general probably only employed in regard to objects toward whom one is ambivalent, so the characteristics of an object also become targets of scorn only if one is ambivalent toward them. But another person's penis is the target of the highest degree of ambivalence. In our patient, the scorn hid *anxiety*. She mocked the penis to overcompensate her envy. She behaved toward it as did the fox toward the sour grapes. She denied her wish to possess a penis by making the whole penis ludicrous and by scorning the bearer of it. Circumcised people, too, scorn all uncircumcised people. The "long nose" is scorn rooted in resentment.

## EIGHTEEN

# The Dread of Being Eaten *

Not long ago I reported an infantile sexual theory which I had come across in two male patients.[1] It was as follows: In order that a girl may be born a boy must first go back into the mother's womb—be "stamped in" or eaten up by the mother. When inside the mother he is robbed of his penis and then reborn as a girl. In both patients this theory had been evolved as a result of a girl-baby's birth in the child's home, and it was the more readily adopted because the boy had a passive-feminine disposition, so that the rebirth was at the same time dreaded and longed for. The idea of "intrauterine castration" seems to be widespread in a vague and undefined form; the whole material cited by Rank in support of his theory of "birth-anxiety" is probably connected with it. Apparently this theory occurs in all those patients whose castration anxiety has been verified, not by the sight of female genitals (or at any rate not only by this), but by observations of a pregnancy or birth. This is especially so when the birth was that of a female baby and the patient's psychic attitude at the moment admitted of an identification with the newborn child (or the fetus), rather than with the mother. Such children react to the discovery that a child is in the mother's abdomen with the anxious dread: if this is possible, could I myself get into my mother's body again or be eaten up by her? To the child who dreads being eaten, pregnancy signifies what the female genital does to the child who dreads castration. We can easily realize that fears of this sort regressively express in terms of anxiety the boy's incestuous wishes. We then find that the figures of "the terrible mother," of the witch who eats up Hansel and so forth, appear in the patient's associations. In general, the dread of being eaten by the mother, with this determination, is found in psychoanalyses more frequently

* First published in *Int. Z. Psa.*, Vol. 14, 1928, pp. 404–405.
[1] "Some Infantile Sexual Theories Not Hitherto Described," No. 12 in this volume.

than the dread of being eaten by the father, which Freud calls "the primeval property of the child."

For obvious reasons the dread of being eaten is in practice indissolubly connected with the idea of being castrated. We cannot say offhand which dread is the older, and what are the genetic and economic relations of the one to the other. Probably it is generally the case that the dread of castration is the deeper, repressed *motif*, and that of being eaten is its regressive distortion. We can understand this when we remember that Freud has called the fantasy of being in the mother's womb "the incest-fantasy of the inhibited." As castration anxiety corresponds to the incest fantasy, so the longing for the mother's womb corresponds to the inhibited incest fantasy, and inhibited castration anxiety to dread of being eaten.

There is no contradiction in the fact that in our cases the dread of castration and that of being eaten existed side by side in the form of the fantasy of "intrauterine castration." We have the same phenomenon when the obsessional neurotic, in spite of his repudiation of incestuous fantasies, still has through regression the dread of castration, e.g. is afraid of monsters in the water-closet, etc.

There is no need to quote analytical material in proof of the existence of the dread of "intrauterine castration." I will merely point out what abundant proof we have of it in folklore. Here we have not only the figures of "terrible mothers" who eat their children, but, above all, we have myths and fairy tales telling of punishments and perils of castration which have to be faced in caves or other symbols of the womb—for instance, the underworld, and especially hell. But there is one fairy tale which reproduces in an almost undistorted form the fantasy upon which I have based my researches—the tale of the Nose Dwarf. The associations of one of the two patients whom I mentioned in my last paper [2] showed me the meaning of this story.

The Nose Dwarf has to accompany an old woman home from market. He comes to an enchanted castle and there, by eating a magic meal, he is turned into a porpoise and has to serve for a number of years in this guise, being finally released with a long nose. When we recollect that in the one patient the dread of being turned into an animal played the chief part, and that we were able to interpret it analytically thus: animal = embryo = girl, and moreover, that the monstrous nose ( = monstrous penis) is an overcompensation for thoughts about the lack of the penis, we can interpret the fairy tale as follows: the Nose Dwarf is enticed into the mother's womb, is there changed into a girl and born again, this time without a penis.

[2] *Ibid.*

## NINETEEN

# Analysis of a Dream*

IN OUR everyday practice it does not very frequently happen that an analysis of a dream, carried through to the end, throws a sudden light on the whole picture of a case. It is therefore perhaps permissible to report an instance of this here. The dreamer was a twenty-nine-year-old girl, who came into analysis because of homosexuality and frigidity. She had had a difficult childhood, with severely neurotic parents. When she was about twenty, she left her home and moved into a strange city, where she broke off all relationships with her parents and began a new life. Her unconscious fixation on the anxieties of her childhood still betrayed itself, however, in severe disturbances of her affective life. For her frigidity was not limited to the sexual field; all her differentiated feeling-relations to other people were constantly in danger of ending in a sudden cooling off. Only after a longish time in analysis did the patient confess the true conscious core of her anxieties. Between the twelfth and fifteenth years of her life, her father, who was a very sick man, had repeatedly visited her in bed and had put her hand on his penis, and so got her to masturbate him. Several screen memories suggest that he had done the same thing to her when she was only in her fifth or sixth year. The patient herself remembered these nights only with anxiety and horror, and she had always pretended to be asleep. She could not believe that she too had been sexually aroused. Nevertheless, some details suggested this. For not only had she never betrayed her father, she had let excellent occasions for doing so go. Her present conditions for love only in part took the form: "It must not be as it was with my father" (which was the formula of her homo-sexuality); in part they took the form: "It must be just exactly as it was with my father." At the time of the dream the patient was friendly with a young man; in intercourse she was still completely frigid, and she was struggling with the idea

* First published in *Int. Z. Psa.*, Vol. 15, 1929, pp. 502–507.

of breaking up this relationship—as she had often done previously in similar cases—if it should become serious. The dream was:

*"On the façade of a house hangs a giant woman, whose body reaches from the roof to the ground. She hangs there like an advertisement. She holds onto the rooftop with both hands, the head and the trunk hang down perpendicularly, but the legs are pulled up so that body and legs form a right angle and the legs are horizontal. Suddenly the woman falls down, and crawls through a door into the house, which is very difficult for her, because she is so big and the door so small. Then I am selling vases. One of the women buyers has brought along with her the flowers that are to go in. They look like red may-bells. When the woman puts the flowers into the vase, they turn out to be too small for the big vase; they fall in and 'swim,' as it were, in the vase, which is far too big."*

To the "giant woman" the patient at first associated volubly about the repulsion she felt toward giants, dwarfs, and other monstrosities. Years ago she had been to a summer festival where a giant woman walked around, for the amusement of the public; the patient had felt great pity for her. Incidentally, she was shortly going with her friend to a summer festival and did not feel like it. The atmosphere at such festivals was usually so forced and unnatural, she did not want to go, there might again be such a giant woman there. (The real reason for her unwillingness was no doubt her fear of being with her friend.) Even as a child she had never wanted to go to the panopticum because she had felt disgust and pity at the monstrosities exhibited there. And now an episode from the previous day occurred to her. As she was eating cherries, she found a double-malformation among them, was disgusted by it, and put it aside; her girl friend wanted to eat it, but the patient knocked it out of her hand and cried, "Ugh, one doesn't eat that!" The idea of "Siamese twins" was unspeakably disgusting to her. As a child, she once saw two June bugs flying, which were grown together, and ran away in anxiety and disgust. I threw in the question whether those June bugs were really grown together. It occurred to her for the first time now that the bugs might have been copulating; she had never thought of this, had always believed that it was a malformation. In connection with this fear of malformations, the patient remembered various animal phobias of her childhood, particularly a fear of mice, whose sexual meaning had already been discussed in the analysis. This permitted me to give the first hint here to the patient that the associations "summer festival," "June bugs," "mice," indicated that the theme of the dream was "fear of sexuality."

*"The house on which the woman hangs."* The patient recognized it as a certain house, and in her next association she remembered that there really was a giant advertisement on it; it was not of a woman, however, but an inscription which ran, "The biggest bar in the world." I then commented that giant

women are often advertised with the formula "the biggest woman in the world," and asked why she substituted the word "bar" for "woman." She answered immediately: because the text of the inscription continued, "fifty bar-women." * Therefore, the text of the dream "the biggest bar in the world—fifty bar-women," was condensed into "the biggest woman in the world." The patient related that she was once in this bar with a large company, and went through the rooms. The *milieu* was disagreeable, the barmaids looked like elderly prostitutes, and the patient felt pity for them, just as she had for the giant woman. Thus the *motif* is again pity on account of sexuality. Now she knew: the tables in the bar were arranged in a right angle, just in the way that the woman in the dream was hanging on the front of the house. There was music in the bar. She now remembered that on the preceding day she had had a conversation about the senselessness of the words of hit-songs. Most hits contained smutty allusions, but in some the sexual hint, which must be in them, was not discoverable. She had been wondering where the joke and the allusion was in the song "Meyer on the Himalaya." It says: "Go up, he could—but how will he get down?" The main point was the image of the little Meyer on the big Himalaya. (Thus we have the disproportion between big and small, which seems to occupy a prominent place in the dream thoughts, as we see in the big woman in the small door, and the small flowers in the big vase.) There were yet other songs with the theme "small man and big woman."

At this point I said that she had already answered her question about the secret sexual meaning of the song: it is an allusion to masculine masochism. Yes, the patient said, this disproportion certainly had a sexual meaning: in sexual intercourse, she often had the feeling that the penis was much too small; she didn't feel it at all, it was swimming in her vagina like the flowers in the vase. I commented that the flower and the vase were sexual symbols, and that this part of the dream simply expressed her feeling in symbolic form. But at times she had had the opposite feeling too; the penis seemed huge, it could not penetrate into her at all without damaging her. I said that in dreams opposites could mean the same thing, and that both feelings were very likely concerned with the same unconscious ideas. Which idea, I asked, did she consider to be the original, the older, of the two—the idea about the penis that was too big, or the penis that was too small? The answer was, the penis that was too big. This could only refer to her father's penis, which, for the little girl, was huge. The erection must really have appeared to her as a "malformation." The equation malformation = cripple had already occurred to her before. I told her that since her father was actually a cripple, the giant woman could only represent

---

* I.e., "barmaids." The German word here is *"Bar-Damen"* = *"bar-ladies."* The German equivalent for "the biggest *woman* in the world" is "the biggest *lady* in the world."—Trans. note.

him, or rather, his penis, and the words "the biggest woman in the world" should be changed into "the biggest man in the world." At this the patient was taken aback by her next association: her father used to lie all day long on the couch exactly as the woman hung in the dream—with his trunk upright and his legs horizontal. Only one thing did not fit in: the woman was holding onto the top of the roof with her hands, so that her arms were stretched up; her father's arms, however, hung down. Thus, in the dream, the motif "hands down" is distorted by a "representation through opposites"; therefore the idea "hands down" must imply an objectionable motive. "Hands down" must mean "hands on the penis" and must be a reference to her father's nightly visits, in which she put her hands on his penis.

There is no doubt, therefore, that the giant woman represents the father. But why is the man changed into a woman in the dream? The patient could answer this question, too, since the main features of her homosexuality had already been analyzed. In her fear of the man (of the penis), she took flight to the woman. She changed the man into a woman, just as she displaced the hands from below upwards. She must have been afraid of a particular danger from the man and from the penis.

Her homosexual relationships had begun with a small episode about which she had incomparably greater feelings of guilt than she had about the incest with her father. This was that when she was about fifteen years old, she had seduced her younger sister: one night when the father was absent and thus could not come to her, she had got into her sister's bed, taken her hand, and put it on her own clitoris. This form of gratification remained the method of all her later homosexual gratifications, and the content of her masturbation fantasies. Thus she had identified herself with her father; in her sister she had chosen an object similar to herself, and she behaved toward her sister as her father did toward herself. Thus her homosexuality had come about through the same mechanisms as, according to Freud, does the homosexuality of most men. All that remained unclear was what had occasioned her turning away from her father, that is, her replacement of object love by identification. We know that the patient was afraid of her father's visits, and we emphasize this anxiety even before we can state clearly to what in her unconscious it referred. Since the theme of her dream is "the dangers of sexuality," we may hope that it will give us the answer to this question also. For the moment it suffices to say that the giant woman represented not only the father and his penis, but obviously the dreamer and her penis as well after she had identified herself with her father. The giant woman was a malformation—her father was a cripple; but over and above the symbolic equation, malformation = cripple, the giant woman of the dream obviously also has as its content an anxiety idea, which might be formulated as follows: "If I

want to be like my father"—or also, "If I want to have sexual relations with him—
I must become a cripple like him." This was supported by much material already
obtained before the dream, all of which derived from a particular fear of *con-
tamination*. This was also the reason of the patient's *pity* for the monstrosities.
Thus the giant woman also expressed the ideas: (a) "I should like to be as big
as my father," and (b) "I am afraid I might become a cripple like my father."

If now the flowers in the vase represent the penis in the vagina, then the idea
"I should like to be as big as my father" may be supplemented by: "and he shall
be as small as I was." Thus we are dealing with a fantasy of revenge which
reversed the relationships and which admitted only of the interpretation that
the point of departure of the anxiety ideas was solely the disproportion between
the little girl's hand and the father's erect penis. The patient objected that at the
time she did not know anything about the vagina. I replied that I did not know
about that one way or another, but that it seemed she knew that the penis was
meant to penetrate into the body, and it was precisely this which she was afraid
of, perhaps just *because* she knew nothing about the vagina.

Then I reminded her that a proper dream always stood on two feet—on repressed infantile material and on current events. In this instance the current
precipitants of the dream were not yet sufficiently transparent. And now the
patient had an answer to this also: On the preceding day she had met, after a
long time, an old friend about whom the analysis had already demonstrated
that he was a father-substitute, and who had proved impotent. Just because
of that, the patient had been particularly attached to him for a long time. The
erect penis was antipathetic to her, and so an impotent man was welcome as a
love object just as a woman was. She had met this friend, then, and had wondered why she did not have intercourse with him any more. She had thought:
"I do not see why I should not deceive my present friend with the old one." Now
we can understand that the whole dream is an answer to these thoughts. It
expresses her longing to replace her present-day friend (and his dangerous
penis) with her old friend (who, it is true, has no penis because he is impotent,
but who represents her father): but it also tells us why she is afraid of the erect
penis, and why she must not yield to this longing, which would tempt her to her
father: intercourse with the father, or rather, with the erect penis, brings with it
great dangers, which are the consequence of the disproportion between the
small girl and the big father. The dream attempts furthermore to banish these
dangers by means of the reversal fantasy.

Now the patient recognized in the giant woman's falling down the flaccid
fall of the old friend's penis. Her problem about the erect penis was thus: "Go
up he could—but how will he get down?" Her desire to castrate her father's penis

is recognizable here. Upon this interpretation, the patient remembered an epileptiform seizure which her father had had and which she, a girl in her puberty, appalled and helpless, had been witness of. Her father had fallen down suddenly, exactly as the giant woman of the dream had fallen down all at once. In her fear of the penis, the patient must therefore have had the idea of somehow robbing her father of his penis. Now she remembered that the worst about the nightly visits of the father was her fear that she might *damage* her father in taking hold of his thighs; but she thought that much stronger and older even was her fear that she might be *contaminated* by touching him, and might become a *cripple,* just like him. It is perhaps permissible to reverse this sequence, and say that the patient had the idea she might make the father into a cripple, just like herself, namely, into a penisless creature. Yet we readily believe that the patient is right, and that the fear of *being* damaged is deeper-seated than the fear of *doing* damage. (That the fear of being damaged also meant the fear of getting a child was discussed as well, but it did not turn out to be very significant in this particular dream.) The giant woman's crawling through the door is a duplication of the vase and flower *motif,* only here the state of affairs is reversed: the *big* body must go through the *small* opening. The dream distortion was least successful in this place; for this was actually the patient's greatest fear: the big penis might want to penetrate into her small body.

The sale of the vases covered prostitution fantasies, and corresponded to the day's residues to the effect that the patient wanted to renew her relationship with her old friend.

Concerning the bouquet of flowers, the red may-bells meant menstruation. If the flowers are the penis, then we have here the dream-thought that the penis should be as bloody as the patient is in her menses. The patient also had a great fear of this blood. Thus her thoughts ran: "If the penis were to penetrate into me, I should bleed." And: "Let the penetrating penis get damaged and bleed!"— The flowers themselves, however, were very remarkable. They were not regular may-bells, but flowers every blossom of which was double; there were always two blossoms very close together. The patient associated to this that a few days ago she saw a picture of gonococci (gonorrhea is the *real* sexual danger and as such is a suitable screen for *irrational* sexual danger). And the gonococci appear in pairs. The bouquet also reminded her of the malformed cherry and of Siamese twins. These double-malformations were thus gonococci. In other words, the unconscious sexual anxiety which was screened by the idea of gonococci reads: if the too-big penis penetrates into me, a split double-malformation might come about. And now we suddenly understand what kind of a double-malformation this is. these are the labia, the feminine genitals. We have come upon the trail of the patient's castration anxiety: it is the fear of being split by the father's too-big penis. The reaction formation against this anxiety consisted in active castration tendencies, and the reaction formation against these was the condition of love for the patient, namely, lack of a penis in her object, or complete inability in herself to love.

# TWENTY

# The Psychology of Transvestitism*

## I

ALL authors who have dealt with the subject of transvestitism are agreed that the mysterious behavior of the victims of this perversion has points of contact with various other perverse practices. It was not until 1910 that this manifestation of *psychopathia sexualis* was, rightly, described by Hirschfeld as a specific form of perversion.[1] Earlier authors had classified cases of the sort on the basis of their points of contact with other perversions. This affinity leads us to hope that the psychoanalytic elucidation of transvestitism may contribute something of importance to the explanation of the psychology of perversions in general. Again, in so far as the allied perversions have already been exhaustively studied by analytical methods, the fact that it is akin to them will enable us to understand the phenomenon of transvestitism.

The behavior of many transvestites gives an entirely masochistic impression: we call to mind, for instance, the figure which is the ideal of many such perverts—Hercules clothed in woman's garments and serving his mistress, Omphale. We know, too, that many who practice this perversion obtain gratification only when they are seen in the clothes of the opposite sex, i.e. strictly speaking, they are exhibitionists. But there are other, far more obvious, points in which transvestitism is related to fetishism and homosexuality, and these points have already been the subject of scientific controversy. I refer to the overestimation of clothing and body linen, and to many purely fetishistic traits in cases of the sort, e.g. a particular preference for shoes or earrings. These characteristics have led writers on the subject to conceive of transvestitism as a specific type of fetishism. Hirsch-

---

* First published in *Int. Z. Psa.*, Vol. 16, 1930, pp. 21–34.
1 M. Hirschfeld, *Die Transvestiten*, Berlin, Pulvermacher, 1910.

feld [2] and Ellis,[3] on the contrary, rightly emphasize the fact that the transvestite has one characteristic which is foreign to fetishism proper. To him the fetish becomes a fetish only when brought into relation with the person of the patient, not (or at any rate only in a very modified degree) as an object in itself. But transvestites want not only to wear women's clothes but to live altogether like women; that is to say, they are effeminate. This fact afforded sufficient reason for their being frequently grouped with passive homosexuals, a view energetically controverted by Hirschfeld, who demonstrated that transvestites in general are erotically attracted exclusively to persons of the opposite sex. Later, he [4] and Näcke [5] classified transvestites according to their sexual aim as the heterosexual, homosexual, narcissistic, and asexual types. To psychoanalysts there is no meaning in such a classification, because it is based solely on the manifest expressions of instinct and completely disregards the unconscious instinctual processes. In this connection Stekel [6] is of the opinion that transvestitism should be construed simply as a mask for homosexuality. But the problem which then confronts us is to find out under what conditions this mask in particular is selected.

To sum up: the point which the transvestite has in common with the fetishist is the overestimation of feminine clothes and body linen, while he shares with the passive homosexual (and the feminine masochist) the feminine psychic attitude. The point of difference between him and both these other types of perverts lies in his specific sexual wish to assume the dress of the opposite sex. Psychoanalysts will suspect that where there is this manifest agreement, there will be a corresponding resemblance in the fundamental unconscious mechanisms. And the analysis of transvestites entirely confirms this suspicion.

Fetishism and passive homosexuality in men have been so exhaustively studied analytically that the results of the investigation can be reduced to certain short formulas. According to Freud [7] castration anxiety prevents the fetishist from accepting the fact of the lack of the penis in women, and he can love only when he has supplied his female love object with an illusory penis. The cause of the feminine homosexual's abnormality is, likewise, castration anxiety. He is incapable of loving a being who lacks the penis; castration anxiety (and, of course, also constitutional factors) have led him to solve his oedipus complex

---

[2] *Ibid.*

[3] H. Ellis, *Studies in the Psychology of Sex, Vol. VII. Eonism and Other Supplementary Studies,* Philadelphia, Davis, 1928.

[4] M. Hirschfeld, "Die intersexuelle Konstitution, *Jahrb. f. sex. Zwisehenst.,* Vol. 23, 1923.

[5] P. Naecke, "Kriminologische und Sexologische Studien. I. Zum Kapitel der Transvestiten nebst Bemerkungen zur Weiblichen Homosexualitaet," *Arch. f. Krim. Anthrop.,* Vol. 47, 1912.

[6] Cf. W. Stekel, *Sexual Aberrations; the Phenomena of Fetishism in Relation to Sex,* New York, Liveright, 1930; *Onanie und Homosexualitaet,* Berlin, Urban and Schwarzenburg, 1917.

[7] S. Freud, "Fetishism," *Coll. Pap.,* Vol. V, London, Hogarth, 1950.

by substituting identification with his mother for his love of her. He is now himself the mother, the woman, and in this role he seeks for new objects, whether it be the father or a representative of his own self.[8] The transvestite, who is akin to both these types of pervert, seems to be the one to whom both formulas simultaneously apply: he has not been able to give up his belief in the phallic nature of women and, in addition, he has identified himself with the woman with the penis. Identification with the woman, as a substitute for, or side by side with, love for her, is so plain in the manifest clinical picture that Ellis, as we shall hear presently, regarded it as the essence of transvestitism.[9] But the woman with whom the transvestist identifies himself is conceived of by him as phallic, and *this* is the essential feature in the situation—a feature which, since it is unconscious, could not have been discovered but for psychoanalysis.

In the act of transvestitism both object love and identification are present, the forms in which each manifests itself being modified by the castration complex and the patient's obstinate retention of his belief in the woman's possession of the phallus. The act has a twofold significance: (1) object-erotic (fetishistic), and (2) narcissistic (homosexual). (1) Instead of coitus with the mother or her substitute the patient enters into fetishistic relations with her clothes, which he brings into as close contact as he can with his own person, and particularly with his genital organs. This is the explanation of the "condition of love," frequently met with, that the garments or body linen in question should have been used and, if possible, should still retain something of the warmth and odor of the woman's body. This intercourse is conceived of in typically sadistic terms. (2) The patient himself represents a woman with a penis. A woman: he shouts that abroad. A woman *with a penis:* that is revealed by analysis. Here we have a twofold representation of the penis: (*a*) in the patient's genitals, actually present under the woman's clothes (one transvestite had recurrent fantasies of the amazement of a lover who, approaching him under the impression that he was a woman, discovered the penis when the woman's clothes were removed); (*b*) in the garment, which is a symbolic substitute for the penis and which the transvestite (even if he indulges his passion only secretly and onanistically) always wants to display—a form of displaced exhibitionism which, like true exhibitionism, is designed to refute the idea of castration. In order to make the clinical picture of transvestitism intelligible in terms of psychoanalysis we must expand these formulas by a description of the way in which the transvestist, like the homosexual, proceeds to fresh object choices, having completed his identification with the woman. In these choices we shall again find an element

[8] Cf., for instance, S. Freud, *Three Essays on the Theory of Sexuality,* London, Imago, 1949, p. 23 footnote.
[9] *Ibid.*

both of narcissism and of object erotism. With regard to the former we must note that only in a subject of a peculiarly narcissistic disposition is it possible for object love to be so extensively replaced by identification. It is a fact that the narcissistic regression manifested in this identification goes far beyond that which we are accustomed to observe in homosexuals. Love for the subject's own self—fantasies that the masculine element in his nature can have intercourse with the feminine (i.e., with himself) are not uncommon. Love for the phallic mother is often transformed into love for the ego in which a change has been wrought by identification with her. This is a feature in the psychic picture which has struck even non-analytical writers, who have described a narcissistic type of transvestite besides the heterosexual and homosexual types.

On the other hand, patients are influenced by their feminine identification in their choice even of real objects; they want to be looked upon and loved as women or, alternatively, where the primal sadism has been turned against the ego, to suffer masochistic tortures. (Here again we note in the passive sexual aim, which, in spite of the phallic character of the illusory woman, dominates the picture, the introduction of the narcissistic factor.) Analysis demonstrates that this object tendency of the transvestite is directed (1) in the deeper mental strata toward the *father*. In this point the transvestite resembles the passive homosexual, but the former is seldom conscious of the homosexual character of this object choice. He says in effect to the father: "Love me, I am just as beautiful (in the phallic sense) as my mother." Or, more correctly: "Love me as you love my mother; it is not true that this wish of mine places my penis in jeopardy!" But the tendency of which we are speaking is also directed (2) toward the mother. This is the more superficial and obvious relation, and it was this which justified Hirschfeld, who did not include the unconscious in his purview, in denying the homosexuality of the transvestist. Perverts of this type consciously take a special interest in feminine homosexuality; they want to be loved as women by women, to be in the relation of the slave to her mistress. The analytical explanation is to be found in the most important accidental factor in transvestitism, namely, that, as a rule, contemporaneously with the identification with the mother, there exists in another, more superficial, psychic-stratum, a similar identification with *a little girl*. This is designed to secure for the subject all the advantages of a regression into early childhood. (For example, a patient of this type who had handled a female infant during the day dreamt the following night that he put on women's clothes, and during the dream he wetted his bed.) This second process of identification may occur when, as seems often to be the case, a sister has at an early period to a great extent become a mother-substitute. Then the transvestite not only addresses the father as we have already described, but at the same time says to the mother: "Love me, I am just as beautiful (in the phallic sense) as my sister." Or, more correctly: "Love me as you love my sister! It is not true that this wish of mine places my penis in jeopardy."

## II

I think it now behooves me to cite some analytical material in proof of these propositions. I will confine myself to putting before you the most important points in a case which was subjected to a thorough analysis, and I hope that they will illustrate the meaning of transvestitism as I have tried to present it to you.

The patient was a married man forty years old, who, in spite of his neurosis, was successful in his professional life and was the father of several children. He suffered from obsessional neurosis and hypochondria with certain paranoid symptoms. He loved his wife deeply and was very considerate and affectionate to her, but sexual intercourse with her left him unsatisfied. He could obtain gratification only in onanism; this he practiced with the accompaniment either of transvestite fantasies, or, more often, of actual transvestite behavior—dressing himself in his wife's clothes. The content of the accompanying fantasy was simply: "I am a woman." Of the details which he communicated in analysis I may mention the following: he indulged in an additional important fantasy, whose content was: "And I am seen to be a woman," and, further, gratification was conditional upon the wearing of women's clothes being a matter of every-day occurrence—i.e., he experienced the most lively excitation when he imagined that he was putting on women's clothes not for the purpose of stimulation but because it was natural for him to be dressed so. He had, in addition, various masochistic fantasies of the type in which the female slave serves her mistress, and he entertained the desire to be a woman, quite apart from any actual sexual situation.

From the history of the patient's childhood I may communicate the following facts. His mother died early and his father soon married again. His father was a man of a petty, fault-finding, anal character, while the stepmother was domineering, quarrelsome, and very strict with the children. Evidently there must have existed a very strong sensual (probably passive-anal) bond between the father and the stepmother, but at the same time the former kept up a kind of cult of the memory of his first wife. In everything the stepmother ruled the house (here we have the type of "the feeble father"), so that the patient had plenty of opportunity to believe in her phallic nature. His attitude to her was ambivalent throughout, but both in his hatred (fear) and in his love he remained entirely passive. There emanated from her a strong atmosphere of prohibition; the castrating figures in his dreams proved to be screen figures standing for her. When the patient was a little boy, she had forced him to wear gloves and had bound his hands to prevent his practicing masturbation (or possibly to prevent his scratching himself at a time when he was being treated for worms). (This binding gave rise later to masochistic fantasies.) Moreover, as a little boy he suffered from prolapse of the rectum, and every time he defecated she pressed back the rectum with her finger. In analysis the patient could still recall the tremendously pleasurable feeling which this gave him.

His principal sexual object in childhood was a sister three years older than himself, with whom he indulged in all manner of sexual games, mutual masturbation, etc. Probably this elder sister originally played the part of seducer, and this seduction caused a similar disturbance in his sexual development as is recorded in that of the Wolf-man.[10] There certainly was a period in which he assumed the active role in their mutual relations; for example, he remembered that on one occasion he had purposely wetted her with urine. This relation, like his relation with his stepmother, was highly ambivalent. He not only loved his sister, but hated her as a rival. This hatred combined with the sensual element to produce a markedly sadistic attitude (possibly to cancel the seduction). One day this attitude vanished, and the patient became purely passive in his relation to his sister. We shall return to the question of this later passive attitude, and discuss when it developed and why. During analysis it was still recognizable in a certain apprehensiveness of an obsessional nature and, further, in an important screen memory in which the patient professed to have pulled one of his sister's arms from its socket. Otherwise, the passive attitude was repressed, and the underlying tendency, having been diverted toward the subject's ego, had been converted into masochism.

It was from his relation to his sister that the patient developed his transvestitism. His sister used to play at "dressing dolls," and she would dress up the living doll—her little brother—putting clothes of her own on him. This used to happen when the patient was about four years old, and at first he disliked it, because it degraded him into a doll. After some repetitions, however, he began to enjoy the game, because he derived sexual pleasure from the smell of his sister, which clung to things she wore, especially to her hair-ribbon and pinafore. In his eighth and tenth years the children used to act little plays, in which they changed clothes with one another. They went on doing this in their games, and the patient, when he imagined he was a girl and especially that others regarded him as a girl, experienced pleasure which was unquestionably sexual, and was accompanied by sensations resembling orgasm. Presently his sister became bored with the game, and he had to be more and more artful in persuading her to play it. Finally he took to putting on her clothes in secret, when he was

[10] S. Freud, "From the History of an Infantile Neurosis," *Coll. Pap.*, Vol. III, London, Hogarth, 1948.

alone, and the pleasure this gave him roused a lively sense of guilt. At the age of about thirteen he forgot this game, but in his seventeenth year he recollected it and began it again with unmistakable sexual excitation. From that time on, dressing up in women's clothes became associated with manual masturbation, and the beginning of the perversion dates from this. It is noteworthy that for a long time the patient made use of his *sister's* clothes and, later, those of sister-substitutes. The idea of putting on garments belonging to his stepmother or to women resembling her did not stimulate his imagination in the least.

What, then, is the meaning of this perversion? The object-erotic factor is the easier and simpler to understand from the case history. The pleasure which the patient derived proceeded in the first instance from the smell of the clothes: a hair-ribbon and, above all, a pinafore, represented parts of the body of his sister, with whom he was in the habit of masturbating. This practice sometimes took the form of his sister's sitting on his knee and sliding backward and forward. When he wore her pinafore he used to move it about in a similar way. The pinafore represented his sister's body. Later, when he made use of her clothes instead of her person, he had the advantage of ceasing to be dependent, for his sexual enjoyment, on the caprices of his sister, who was not always inclined to gratify him. Another circumstance was that, originally, using the same bed or the same bathwater as she had the same significance as wearing her clothes. How came it about that the sister herself gradually lost her sexual significance for him, while "symbols" (her clothes) were substituted for her? Analysis revealed the answer unmistakably. It was because the brother discovered that she had no penis. We mentioned the remarkable screen memory of his pulling his sister's arm from its socket. This memory "screened" their mutual onanism and especially the patient's sadism. Once, when he and his sister were having a bath together in the bathroom, he caught sight of her genitals, and this reactivated a still earlier, repressed recollection of his stepmother's genitals. It happened that at the same period his sister was having electric treatment for enuresis (the patient himself used for a time to wet his bed) and used to scream dreadfully when the treatment was in process. There could then, he reasoned, be only two possibilities: either the electric treatment was the punishment by castration for sexual naughtiness; in that case he was threatened with it, after his sister. Or it was a medical remedy for the lack of the penis, which had fallen a victim to his own sadism. In that case it was but just that the talion punishment of castration should await him. In this anxiety he desisted altogether from his sadistic behavior and turned the tendency against himself. He wanted to have nothing more to do with his sister, who reminded him of the mischief he had done, and he substituted for her her clothes, which did away with the dreadful nakedness. The bath (and, later, water in general) remained a situation of terror. We shall have to discuss the fact that his anxiety took the form that the water in running out might carry off one of his fingers or his whole body and that the dread became displaced to the water-closet, where the flush might wash away the whole child as well as his motion. So far, the patient's mental processes followed the scheme which Freud has worked out for fetishism.

The patient, however, became a transvestite because his retention of the idea of the female penis was reinforced by his identification with the woman. In later years it became transparently clear that he himself was enacting the role of the sister, whom he desired to *be*. In imagination he lived her life, and in the same way, after his marriage, he would feel unwell during his wife's period of menstruation. This has a significance in connection with the question of punishment. It meant: I harbored the wish to do my sister an injury, so now I am forced to become like her, so as to submit to suffering. From the point of view of his instinctual life he had sufficient reason to envy his sister. She was the elder, and both parents evidently made a favorite of her. He was especially jealous of her relation to their stepmother, who talked "feminine secrets" with her. Later he developed a neurosis, when his parents were about to arrange a marriage for his sister. Analysis revealed the jealous thought: "Why do they arrange for her to marry and not for me?" The patient had also a recollection, important in connection with the deeper mental strata, of a fit of envy which overtook him one Christmas, when his mother with much ceremony presented his sister with a particularly beautiful doll. Such ambivalent feelings indicated that, in obedience to the inner prohibition by which his castration anxiety prevented his entering into an object relation with his sister, he had regressed to identification.

Now this identification with the girl was bound to come into direct opposition to the most intense castration anxiety. The influence of this made itself felt in the aim which the patient set before him: "I want to be my sister and yet to retain my penis." When indulging in his perverse practices, it was his custom, as soon as ejaculation had taken place, to tear the borrowed clothes off as quickly as possible. In connection with this he had the association that he had been warned that, if one made faces and the clock struck, one's face would stay so. Thus he was afraid that he might actually "remain stuck" in his feminine role, and this would involve his forfeiting his penis. His transvestite behavior was designed to counter his castration anxiety. We have evidence of this in a recollection that, when on one occasion he caught sight of a crippled boy, he felt an impulse to change clothes with him. The implication was a denial that the boy really was a cripple. The patient combined his femininity with a naïve, narcissistic love for his own penis, upon which he bestowed a number of pet names, as though it were a child. Moreover, the girl's name which he chose to be known by when enacting the role of a girl had a striking resemblance to one pet name for the penis. The first time he had sexual intercourse with a woman, he did not know where to find the vagina and looked for it on the upper part of her thigh. Even at the time when I knew him, he always had a feeling during coitus that he must look for something which he could not find. At one of the dramatic performances in which he acted the part of a girl, he represented an Easter Rabbit. He recollected being troubled because he thought the rabbit's ears and tail were not stiff enough. Here we have a proof of the phallic nature of the woman whose role he assumed—a matter which becomes more intelligible to us when we picture the overwhelming castration anxiety under which the patient labored. We have mentioned that his stepmother represented to his mind the person who castrates. From the innumerable screen memories connected with the idea of castration I will quote a single example. An obsessive action of the patient's was that of clutching at his penis (analytically interpreted: to see if it was still there) and of counting his toes (to see that none were missing). Analysis revealed that he had dreaded that his mother, in pressing back the prolapsed rectum, might rob him of the intestine, and at that time he was haunted by the fear that it might fall into the lavatory-pan. The uncanny thing about the water-closet and the bath was that the feces and the water simply disappeared— were no longer there—just so, he feared, had his sister's penis vanished. Further, this idea of being "gone" was his conception of death. And in his mind the whole terrifying mystery of castration was intertwined with the terrifying mystery of his mother's death. The content of his unconscious anxiety was not simply: "My sister's penis vanished because of some sexual act," but also, "My own mother died because of some sexual act." Accordingly, particularly during the period of his subsequent hypochondria, the patient suffered from the most intense dread of death (and especially the dread of infection, as I will show later). Detailed analysis of this anxiety led us first of all to ideas about the color "black" and of "hair." (As a child he himself had long hair and dreaded its being cut. He treasured the locks which were cut off. His stepmother wore false hair, i.e., hair which could be taken off. The hair of the head stood for pubic hair.) These ideas led back to dreams of the primal scene and to occasions, long before his experiences with his sister, when, with anxiety and a feeling of protest, he became aware of the nature of his mother's genitals.[11]

Thus, the patient's transvestitism was evidently an attempt to allay these various anxieties. The content of the perversion was: "Phallic girls do exist; I myself am one."

[11] The female genital, when thus caught sight of, becomes an object of fear not simply because of the lack of the penis but because it is regarded as a menacing weapon. (The waste pipes of the water-closet and the bath are thought of as devouring mouths.) Cf. my article "The Dread of Being Eaten" [No. 18 in this volume].

Let us now examine his search for fresh love objects, when once the identification had been completed, and let us consider the relation to the mother which underlay that to the sister.

The factor of narcissism was transparently clear. Not only did he love himself in the role of a girl (acting a woman in plays, posturings before the looking-glass, a preference for a girl's long hair), but this love took an *active* form, such as he longed for from his sister. Thus he dreamt that he was embracing a little boy, saying to him tenderly: "My little brother!" In passing on to consider his actual choice of new love objects, we will again begin with a dream. This was as follows: "My wife had a disease of the lungs. A stout woman stabbed her in the back from behind. Thereupon I found myself in a theater, with the upper part of my body naked." The exhibition-situation at the end prepares us for the fact that the dream relates to transvestitism. Actually the patient, who was a hypochondriac, suffered from a dread of lung affections. In the dream, he is the woman whom another woman stabs from the rear. His associations to this stab were as follows: the uvula, fantasies of poisoning by way of the anus, and, finally, enemas which his stepmother had given him as a child. Before going to sleep on the night of this dream, the patient had indulged in his perverse practices. Hence we arrive at the interpretation: "When I am in women's clothes I should like my stepmother to stick something into my 'behind,' but at the same time I dread it." The passive-anal desires implied in the patient's femininity had become abundantly clear: the recollections of enemas and the prolapsed rectum showed that these wishes had reference to the mother whom he conceived of as phallic. This is where the fantasies of the female slaves come in, the meaning being: "I want my stepmother to treat me like a little girl, but there is no need for me to fear castration." In correspondence with this wish the patient cherished in his mind two types of female imagos between which he strictly differentiated: the "little girl" and the "Amazon," i.e. the sister and the stepmother. The women whose clothes he desired to put on belonged to the first type only; on the other hand, he wished to enter into masochistic relations only with women of the second, masculine type.

Having discovered this anal dependence on women, it seemed obvious to reason as follows: The patient's oedipus complex was normal in so far as he, like other males, wished to take his father's place with his mother. Only, the real father's attitude to his second wife was of a passive-anal nature; similarly, the patient wished to enter into a passive-anal relation to the phallic mother. In actual fact the stepmother tended the father in connection with his anal functions and this did really rouse in the patient the wish that his father would die.

But the child had not always seen his father in such a helpless and passive guise. Once he too had been strong and active, and it was to him that in the deepest mental strata the patient's feminine attitude had reference.

Analysis of his social inhibitions revealed that his passivity and anxiety related, fundamentally, not to women but to men. Again, his exhibitionist tendency— the craving to be admired as a woman by people in general—had reference to men. When we were investigating this subject of the father of his infantile days, the first thing that emerged in his memory was a long-forgotten figure which was a "screen figure" for his father: a carpenter, who had done some work in the patient's home and whose admiration he had solicited. Next, he felt an urgent impulse to change into women's clothes in front of his father's portrait. Finally, there came recollections of excitation, obviously sexual and accompanied by anxiety, which he experienced when lying in bed with his father. But the most striking thing about this part of the analysis was the way in which the patient suddenly grasped the meaning of many inhibitions from which he suffered in his real relations with men! The picture was then blurred once more by a recollection of his later childhood: "I wanted to thrust something into my father's 'behind.'" We found that this implied: "I want to love you, Father, in just the same way as my stepmother does." But we were obliged to conjecture that, before he felt the desire to stick something into his father, he must have wished his father to stick something into *him*. Quite in accordance with this interpretation was the fact that he had *not* identified himself with his stepmother; on the contrary, behind the identification with his sister lay the first identification of all—that with his own mother. His heart cried out to his father: "Do not put away the memory of your first wife. Remember her; she lives still, in me. Love me, your first wife, more than my stepmother!" And the content of the fearful anxiety which came into conflict with these wishes was this: "Did not death overtake my mother because she let my father love her? Then I, too, shall have to die." It now becomes clear that the overwhelming castration anxiety, which the transvestitism was designed to eliminate, was at bottom a dread of impregnation by the father. This was the meaning of the dread of infection, poison, and water and also of a number of screen memories in which the patient envied the act of parturition. As a child he must have fantasied that his mother perished through pregnancy and must have evolved the theory that having children meant losing the penis. In his transvestitism he was trying to repudiate this dread also, saying to himself: "I may wish to be a woman and capable of bearing children—and yet keep my penis!" [12]

### III

We have adduced analytical material in proof of all the hypotheses we put forward in Section I. If, now, we are in search of a pathognomonic etiology of the patient's transvestitism, we are obliged to admit that we have not discovered one.

---

[12] Deeper analysis of the narcissistic mental strata finally revealed that the identification with his dead mother (her "spirit") was performed by means of introjection (inhaling) and that in the un-

We must in any case assume that he had a special bisexual disposition, for otherwise the desire to bear children, for example, could never have acquired such importance. But we do not know whether, if life had brought him different experiences, his strong sadism might not have enabled his masculine side to develop satisfactorily. But this mental make-up is common to homosexual and transvestite alike. Again, the series of experiences, the primal scene—castration anxiety—flight into femininity, based on narcissism, occurs in other clinical pictures, and we do not know what circumstances cause the belief in the phallic woman to be retained with the specific perversion of transvestitism, since the above series is present in other forms of nervous disease as well. It is true that we frequently find transvestitism combined with precisely these diseases: narcissistic neuroses, hypochondria (cf. the case quoted by Alexander [13]), and other perversions. Over and above all this, the case we are examining seems to have been determined by specific environmental factors: the characters of his father, mother, and sister, and their interplay, seem to have thrust the patient's role upon him. But, again, similar specific environmental conditions appear by no means rare, for all writers on the subject tell us of transvestites whose mothers had a very great desire for a daughter! Ellis goes so far as to cite this circumstance as a proof of the purely hereditary etiology of transvestitism, but in this he is in error.

Such communications about this perversion as are to be found in analytical literature bear a remarkable resemblance to our own conclusions. It is only thanks to the writings of Freud which have appeared since Sadger [14] and Boehm [15] discussed the question that it has been possible for me to give a greater coherence to my account. Sadger evolved the following formula as summing up the transvestite's train of thought: "As a female I should be loved more by my mother and, indeed, by everyone. When I put on my mother's dress I feel as if I were she herself and so could arouse sexual feeling in my father and possibly supplant her with him. And, finally, a third person derives as much pleasure from a woman's clothes as from herself and looks on the putting on of her frock as a sexual act." This formula is correct, but in my opinion it leaves out the phallic factor, which is so important and which Sadger does mention accidentally elsewhere, though there are yet other passages in which he contradicts this by asserting that it is the vulva which is the fetish. Boehm, again, lays stress in isolated

conscious the introjected mother was equated with his own penis. Thus we arrived at the following symbolic equation: patient in women's clothes = the mother with a penis = the penis in general. We recollect the similarity between the girl's name by which he so much wished to be called and his pet name for the penis.

[13] F. Alexander, "Instinct Fusions—A Case of Masochistic Transvestitism," Lecture 7 in *The Psychoanalysis of the Total Personality*, New York, Nerv. Ment. Dis. Pub. Co., 1930.

[14] J. Sadger, *Die Lehre von den Geschlechtsverirrungen (Psychopathia Sexualis) auf psychoanalytischer Grundlage*, Leipzig, Deuticke, 1921.

[15] F. Boehm, "Bemerkungen ueber Transvestitismus," *Int. Z. Psa.*, Vol. 9, 1923.

instances on precisely this phallic character of the transvestite's perversion ("In the clothes which they put on they represent the mother with the penis"),[16] and on the sadistic nature of the wishes which originally related to the mother. Stekel contents himself with the incomplete statement that transvestitism is based on homosexuality and mother-fixation. Pre-analytic literature gives but a meager account of the matter to analysts; nevertheless, even the manifest material of such cases as are described in it contains all sorts of data which go to prove our hypothesis. We note, side by side with the transvestitism, fetishistic, masochistic, and exhibitionistic tendencies, narcissism, fantasies of the mistress and the female slave, identification with the mother, histories of seduction by elder sisters, aversion from physical sexuality and especially from nakedness, the naked female body, and homosexuality, the *retour à l'enfance* (Ellis), but also a passion for women of a masculine type (Hirschfeld). One of Hirschfeld's cases gave rein to his transvestite tendencies by joining in a display of trick shooting in the guise of a woman, thus publicly courting admiration as an "armed woman." [17] Ellis quotes one case which seems to contradict our view, because the patient's sexual aim was quite obviously castration, but this same man used to put on women's shoes and earrings, which indicates that, although he wished for castration, he was always impelled to cancel it again.[18] Cases of actual self-castration by transvestites or of disgust felt by them for the male genital and longing for that of the female would have to be examined analytically before we could make any pronouncement about them. Ellis's theory is as follows: All normal love contains an element of identification; in the perversion of transvestitism this element is hypertrophied: "He has put too much of 'me' into the 'you' that attracts him." [19] This theory is, in our view, correct but incomplete. We think that we have been able to predicate something about the nature and causes of this identification. Just as correct and just as incomplete is Ellis's formula about the relation of transvestitism to homosexuality; they are, he says, "two allotropic modifications of bisexuality." But it is possible to differentiate the characteristics of these modifications.

## IV

We have recognized that the specific factor in the perversion of transvestitism is its relation to the castration complex. It remains for us to ask whether this conclusion contributes anything to our understanding of the psychology of the

---

16 Dr. Boehm has been kind enough to tell me that further analyses of transvestists have confirmed this view. He had one patient who used to turn a bottle upside down on his penis and then to put on women's clothes and dance in front of a looking-glass and so, finally, to masturbate.

17 M. Hirschfeld, *Die Transvestiten*, Case V.

18 *Ibid.*, pp. 63 ff.

19 *Ibid.*, p. 108.

perversions in general. Sachs, in an article in which he examines the latter question, demonstrates that what characterizes the pervert is his capacity to transfer part of his infantile sexuality over to the ego, to permit himself to indulge it, and by this very means to hold in repression those infantile sexual impulses which still remain (i.e., the oedipus complex).[20] The riddle we have to solve is how this process is possible, under what conditions perverse component instincts can retain or acquire the capacity to produce orgasm. As we now know that *all* perversions, including transvestitism, are so intimately connected with the castration complex, we can at least reply with the following hypothesis: Normally, what conditions the disappearance of infantile sexuality (the passing of the oedipus complex) is the dread of castration.[21] Now the homosexual has no regard for any human being who lacks the penis, the fetishist denies that such beings exist, while the exhibitionist, the scoptophiliac, and the transvestite try incessantly to refute the fact. Thus we see that these perverts are endeavoring to master their anxiety by denying its cause. In so far as they succeed in maintaining the illusion that there is no such thing as a lack of the penis, they save themselves anxiety and can indulge in infantile sexual practices *because,* just in proportion as they can effectively deny the grounds for it, their castration anxiety, which otherwise would act as a check on such sexual behavior, is diminished. We must, however, qualify this statement by saying that this process succeeds only up to a certain point. That is to say, such infantile activities are bound up with a simultaneous, incessantly renewed denial of the reason for anxiety, and it is this denial which is represented in the perverse practice. The behavior of the pervert implies: "You have no need to be afraid" and, so long as he believes himself, his infantile sexual activities can produce orgasm, which signifies the gratification of his oedipus wishes.

It is true that this hypothesis makes the feminine perversions and the whole subject of the castration complex in women all the more problematic. Indeed, one does receive the impression that they are to some extent different in character from, though akin to, perversions in men. This strikes us, for instance, when we think of female exhibitionists and recall Hárnik's work on the differences between masculine and feminine narcissism.[22] Female fetishists are extremely rare, and female transvestites seem to be simply women who covet the penis and, out of desire to possess it, have identified themselves with men.

[20] H. Sachs, "Zur Genese der Perversionen," *Int. Z. Psa.,* Vol. 9, 1923.

[21] S. Freud, "The Passing of the Oedipus-Complex," *Coll. Pap.,* Vol. II, London, Hogarth, 1948.

[22] J. Hárnik, "The Various Developments Undergone by Narcissism in Men and in Women," *Int. J. Psa.,* Vol. 5, 1924.

# TWENTY-ONE

# The Pregenital Antecedents of the Oedipus Complex*

## I

THE oedipus complex has been called by Freud "the nuclear complex" of the neuroses, and we may go further and say that it is the nuclear complex of the unconscious of mankind in general. Every single analysis provides fresh evidence of this fact, if we except those cases of extreme malformation of character which resemble a lifelong psychosis and in which a true oedipus complex has never become crystallized, either because the subject's object relations were destroyed root and branch at an earlier period, or because such relations never existed at all. However strong may be one's theoretical convictions on the point, it comes as a fresh surprise every time when we find that final solution and cure in an analysis which has remained obscure depend invariably on the deepening of our knowledge of the oedipus complex.

Freud holds that it is in the fourth or fifth year of life that the oedipus complex reaches its zenith, that is, that this coincides with the attainment of the *phallic* level of organization.[1] We know that (as is in accordance with this hypothesis) the content of the complex is the wish for *genital* union with the parent of the opposite sex, together with a jealous hatred of the parent of the subject's own sex. Melanie Klein[2] states that she has found in the analyses of children that the complete oedipus complex is already established at a far earlier period. This view contradicts our experience of the analyses of adults. It is undoubtedly true that at a far earlier period the child is attached to the

* First published in *Int. Z. Psa.*, Vol. 16, 1930, pp. 319–342.
[1] S. Freud, "The Passing of the Oedipus-Complex," *Coll. Pap.*, Vol. II, London, Hogarth, 1948.
[2] M. Klein, "Early Stages in the Oedipus Conflict," *Int. J. Psa.*, Vol. 9, 1928.

parent of the opposite sex, and feels jealousy and hatred toward the other parent. But these preliminary phases differ in certain fundamental points from the oedipus complex at the time of its zenith. (We have an exact analogy in the difference between the preliminary phases of the superego—not sufficiently differentiated by M. Klein—and the consolidated superego established after the passing of the oedipus complex.[3]) These preliminary phases have contents (not genital) other than those of the true oedipus complex; they are still competing with autoerotic tendencies; the jealous hatred still exists without conflict side by side with love for the parent of the subject's own sex. Moreover, these preliminary phases are by no means always comprised in one single "complex." Thus it is certain that pregenital object relations exist, and it would be a fundamental error to imagine that "pregenital" and "autoerotic" are synonymous terms. Similarly, the *objects* of these pregenital relations will be pre-eminently the parents. The *content* of these relations was first described by Freud [4] and later by Abraham,[5] who, as the result of his close study of persons with pregenital fixations, gave an exact and systematic description in the "Origins and Growth of Object-Love." Let me recall this to your minds by quoting his main headings: Total incorporation, partial incorporation, partial love without incorporation, post-ambivalent love.

Abraham [6] also established the fundamental facts about the causes and mechanisms of the advance from one stage of object relationship to that immediately above it. The question now before us is a more special one. How is the true oedipus complex evolved from the pregenital preliminary phases? Or—to take the descriptive standpoint first—where and how are its pregenital antecedents reflected in the oedipus complex? In answer to this question, psychoanalysis can begin by producing an abundance of one special kind of material, namely, the results of regression. They are illuminating but also very confusing. All neurotics suffer from having fended off the oedipus complex by some inappropriate method, and so having failed to master it. But, in contrast to hysterics, persons suffering from obsessional neurosis and other mental diseases are characterized by the fact that they try to evade that complex by reverting to earlier modes of gratification and regressively substituting for it something pregenital. They may do this so completely that their later acquirements seem wholly to disappear, and to judge by his instinctual behavior, the patient seems to be altogether at a pre-oedipus stage (as in many psychoses). Or the regression may be less complete

---

[3] Cf. M. Klein, "Symposium on Child-Analysis," *Int. J. Psa.,* Vol. 8, 1927.

[4] In various passages.

[5] K. Abraham, "A Short Study of the Development of the Libido, Viewed in the Light of Mental Disorders, Part II: Origins and Growth of Object-Love," *Selected Papers,* London, Hogarth, 1948.

[6] *Ibid.*

and behind the pregenital façade it may be possible to reveal the presence of the forbidden oedipus wishes. This mode of defense is facilitated by two factors: (a) the subject's constitution, (b) some experience which causes fixation during the pregenital period. It is true that persons who have regressed produce an abundance of material by means of which they amalgamate the oedipus complex with the pregenital object relations, and it would be carrying coals to Newcastle if we cited particular examples. But we also called this material "confusing" because it is only with the greatest difficulty that we can recognize which of the numerous "pregenital" traits in the oedipus wishes of these patients is a subsequent, regressive distortion and which represents the residue of their real, original, pregenital experience, and so gave a characteristic tinge to their oedipus wishes when first these arose in childhood. Naturally, if a man suffers from obsessive impulses to kill his mother and cut off his own penis, we have no difficulty in recognizing in the first impulse the regressive distortion of the wish to have sexual intercourse with the mother, and in the second, the superego's demand that this wish be punished. Or, again, if a woman is afraid that a snake may come up out of the water-closet, analysis can show that the anxiety once took another form, namely, that the snake might be hidden in her bed, and that it signifies the father's penis, the idea of which has been connected with anal erotism by a process of defensive regression. Neither phenomenon would be possible had not the male patient at some time had sadistic impulses and the female had sexual sensations in the water-closet. But at first they still give us no hint as to how long *before* the shattering of the oedipus complex its own pregenital antecedents were reflected in that complex itself. For *every* oedipus complex has such antecedents. Little indications, vestiges of these antecedents, characteristics of the complex may prove its origin from the pregenital material, like the trade mark "Made in Germany," which Freud uses as a metaphor in another context. If so, we may conclude that precisely these traits will probably be of great importance in the formation of the subject's character (pregenital tingeing of the superego). But perhaps we shall acquire more reliable material in this connection from just the types which are not regressive, i.e. normal people and hysterics, but also—in a far more pronounced form—from persons with faulty development of character and from psychopaths, whose oedipus complex, owing to the specially strong pregenital fixation, had from the very beginning a pregenital tinge.

In women the transition from the pregenital relations to the oedipus complex involves not only the change of aim, which we have so far considered, but a change of object. The first pregenital object—the mother—has to be exchanged for the father. As we know, this change of object has been made the subject of a lively discussion, in which very different and sometimes contradictory views have been expressed.[7]

These questions are further complicated by the fact of bisexuality which sometimes causes men to change their object, like women, and women to fail to change it. We learn from Freud that with every human being we have to reckon on the presence of the *complete* oedipus complex, i.e. not only that of the subject's own sex but that of the opposite sex.[8] The normal solution is that the relation of the subject to the parent of his or her own sex passes into an identification, while the relation to the other parent passes into object love. We know that this normal solution often breaks down wholly or in part and that total or partial "errors of sexual identification"[9] take place. It is very common to meet with isolated features of such erroneous identifications. They may cause the oedipus complex to betray from the very beginning characteristics of an original ambivalence, which will be marked in proportion as a person is sadistic (i.e., suffering from pregenital fixation), ambivalent, and bisexual.

It may be asked: What is the typical way in which the object relations of the pregenital period are reflected in the oedipus complex? The answer is that it will vary greatly in normal and in pathological cases; we know something, but of much we are ignorant. Supposing that we make a dogmatic statement of the points on which all psychoanalytical writers are agreed. They hold that the following features of the oedipus complex are influenced by pregenital factors: (1) the oedipus prohibitions by the earlier prohibitions of autoerotism; (2) the dread of castration by the dread of the loss of the mother's breast and of feces; (3) the little girl's love for her father by her pregenital relations with her father; (4) the idea of the penis by that of the mother's breast and of feces; (5) the wish for a child by the desire for a penis and, hence, for feces; (6) the conception of coitus by that of total oral incorporation. The following points are disputed: (1) the causes and mechanisms of the change of love object in women; (2) the relation of oral to genital sexuality;[10] (3) the relation between receiving and surrendering (cf. Abraham's subdivision of the oral and anal levels of organization[11] and Ferenczi's view on the "amphimixis" of pregenital instinctual impulses[12]).

---

[7] S. Freud, "Some Psychological Consequences of the Anatomical Distinction between the Sexes," *Coll. Pap.*, Vol. V, London, Hogarth, 1950; K. Horney, "The Flight from Womanhood," *Int. J. Psa.*, Vol. 7, 1926; A. Lampl de Groot, "The Evolution of the Oedipus Complex in Women," *Int. J. Psa.*, Vol. 9, 1928; E. Jones, "The Early Development of Female Sexuality," *Papers on Psycho-Analysis*, 5th ed., Baltimore, Williams and Wilkins, 1948.

[8] S. Freud, *The Ego and the Id*, London, Hogarth, 1947.

[9] W. Reich, *Der triebhafte Charakter*, Vienna, Int. Psa. Verlag, 1925.

[10] Cf. B. Rank, "Zur Genese der Genitalitaet," *Int. Z. Psa.*, Vol. 11, 1925; W. Reich, *op. cit.*; O. Fenichel, "Introjection and the Castration Complex," No. 7 in this volume.

[11] K. Abraham, *op. cit.*

[12] S. Ferenczi, *Thalassa, A Theory of Genitality*, Albany, Psa. Quart. Press, 1938.

Satisfactory answers to all these questions can be given only after exhaustive analysis of very many instances, which must exclude the regressive factor as far as possible in order to bring to light the true genesis. Perhaps the analyses of children may throw some light on the subject. In adults the most important material is very hard to come by and can be understood only after very long and deep analyses.

In the following article I want simply to make a modest contribution to the collection of such material. I will give an account of three cases, all of which were under analytic treatment for two or three years. Naturally it is neither possible nor necessary to communicate the whole of the case histories. In each case I will quote exclusively the historical material relevant to our problems. The first case is not a typical one: it is that of a faulty character development, peculiarly bisexual, ambivalent, and sadistic (manifestly masochistic). But on the other hand it affords a remarkable mass of material. A strongly developed oedipus complex proves to be essentially based on pregenital factors (whereas a markedly anal-sadistic attitude is found in obsessional neurotics to have its main basis in the oedipus complex). The two other instances I shall quote are cases of hysteria and will show us what part of the material contributed by the first case can be utilized in normal psychology as well.

## II

In a short communication about the interpretation of a dream which consisted solely of the word "bees," I have already given some account [13] of the form and structure of the symptoms of the first patient, a man thirty-six years old. He suffered from various difficulties of character, the most important of which were marked moral masochism and a neurotic inability to take up a profession. His oedipus complex was very clearly developed and, manifestly, it dominated his life. For years he had lived with a woman considerably older than himself, and he remained attached to her in the most irrational fashion. He had come to know her through "rescuing" her from financial straits. In accordance with the principle of exogamy he appeared to have selected a woman as unlike his mother as possible, but nevertheless, in spite of their totally different environments, the two women had many traits in common and also the same name. During the analysis, the figure of this woman was at times indistinguishable in dreams and fantasies from that of the mother, but all the same, before analysis, the patient was quite unconscious that she was a mother-substitute, as he was unconscious of any affective attachment to his real mother. On the other hand, conscious hatred of his tyrannical father and the perpetually fruitless struggle with him formed the main content of the patient's life. The

[13] O. Fenichel, "Examples of Dream Analysis," No. 13 in this volume.

vehemence and fury of the death wishes against the father, which broke out during the analysis, were almost beyond description. Moreover, the patient's inability to take up a profession proved at the outset to be due to his violent hatred of his father. "He must give me his money" was the *leitmotif* of this life. His lack of a profession and his whole mode of life, which at times was very like that of a swindler, he justified by the expectation (amounting almost to a delusion) that before long he would draw a winning lottery ticket. He was a passionate devotee of lotteries and behaved as if "luck" were a father on whom he had a claim: "You *must* give me all the money." (The form his demand took was derived from an incident during puberty, when his father once won in a lottery.) The first stratum which the analysis of his hate revealed was that of an unconscious love of his father, concealed under the hate. It manifested itself in "fits of remorse" in contrast to his rebellious attitude (which invariably occurred when his father had *really* sent him money), in a disguised form in various daydreams and, above all, in the transference to the analyst, which, although completely positive, was a pure father-transference. (I will discuss later why hate did not enter into the transference, or at least only to a relatively small extent.) As the patient was constantly requiring money and his mode of life kept him dependent on his father, his love was naturally of a demanding, sadistic character, its aim being to extort money and presents from his father. In the unconscious, corresponding to this love there was the full negative oedipus complex—his jealousy of his brothers (one of his childhood recollections was that a bishop had once kissed one of the brothers but not the patient himself), dreams in which men pierced him with spears or locomotives ran over him, etc.; and, finally, the form taken by his castration anxiety left no doubt of the interpretation that he wished to have coitus with his father and have a child by him. The main content of his anxiety was that he was being eaten up from inside by little animals in his body and being robbed of his penis. Experiences in connection with gonorrhea (bacteria) and morbid growths ("cancer" = the animal "crab" *) had determined the form of this anxiety, the unconscious content of which followed the lines of the oral theory of conception: "When one conceives a child in the sexual act" (thought of in terms of the oral theory) "one is devoured from within by little animals" (children, spermatozoa, embryos) "which, when birth takes place, eat their way out through the penis."

The image the patient had in mind of the animals living inside the body was that of oxyuria (anal), and these he pictured like macaroni, which had been his favorite food when he was a very young child. Let me give a few examples of his excessive anal and oral fixations: (a) (*anal*) His whole life was dominated by his completely irrational libidinal relation to money. Even as an adult he

---

* In German the same word, *"Krebs,"* is used for both.—Trans. note.

occasionally failed to retain his stools. During puberty he had once evacuated onto a piece of newspaper and kept it for months. (b) (*oral*) He displayed a large number of the character traits which Abraham [14] described as "oral": in matters of "getting" and "giving" he was quite undisciplined. He attached particular importance to good food. He was markedly interested in words. "To take money from one's father" meant also "to be nourished by one's father." He conceived of passive homosexual intercourse orally, as consisting either of sucking or biting off the penis. At the same time there were various traits which indicated identification with his father. For instance, he lived with a woman who was a mother-substitute (when this was interpreted to him, it had actually the effect of a trauma); he wanted to draw a winning ticket like his father, and he was exceedingly fond of traveling, which was traceable to the desire to elope with his mother. An unusually intense love for his home and his part of the country proved to represent his love for his mother, or, as could be inferred from relatively early associations, his grandmother.

Now let me give the most essential historical facts in this case and, first of all, those concerned with the period of puberty. The strong, diffused sexual excitation (for, from the beginning, genitality was weak) had for its object a servant whose name was the same as that of the patient's mother. Later on he learned that his father had had relations with this girl and that she had a child by him. There, then, was the whole constellation of the oedipus complex: the father had "taken away" the woman from the patient. The *motif* of "taking away" governed his whole erotic life. His childhood was characterized by his ambivalent attitude toward his father, who was severe and used to beat him and forbid things he wanted, and by the failure of his attempts at a father-identification and, further, by his completely repressed, pregenital love for his mother. The idea of sucking the penis concealed the more deeply repressed idea of sucking at the breast. (The dream of the bees.) In his dreams and fantasies his grandmother kept appearing with increasing frequency and with the suggestion that her authority was equal to his mother's. Finally we discovered the fundamental, primal history of the case. On account of his mother's illness the boy had been separated from her soon after his birth and sent to his grandmother's, where he was fed by a wet-nurse. At first the patient said that he was there for the first six months of his life. He said, too, that he was very much spoiled there and was given such quantities of macaroni to eat that his stomach was all puffed out and when he went home the doctor put him on a strict diet. He then did not speak for a whole year, so that he was supposed to be dumb, till at the end of a year he astonished the whole family by suddenly uttering a complete sentence (a complaint against his brothers). Now this seemed quite

[14] K. Abraham, "Psycho-Analytical Studies on Character-formation," *Selected Papers*.

incredible. No child of six months could eat so much macaroni or lose, out of defiance, the power of speech, once acquired. By means of further analysis and objective information we were finally able to correct the patient's account. He had stayed with his grandmother not for six months but for eighteen months, and during that whole period he was fed at the nurse's breast. During the second half of the time his grandmother spoiled him greatly in other oral ways (macaroni). When he went back to his parents this paradise of spoiling was left behind, and there followed a sudden and radical frustration. The breast which gave him milk so lavishly suddenly vanished, and so did the macaroni and the women who fulfilled the child's every wish. To *this* frustration the patient, who could already speak a little, responded by going on strike and refusing to speak for a year. The character of this sudden frustration is shown most clearly in a remark of his father's, when the patient during his analysis asked him about his recollections of this time. "You did nothing but scream 'Macaroni, macaroni,' but I soon broke you of that! I used to give you a whipping every day!" The memories which came up in analysis and, above all, the patient's dreams testified to the correctness of the father's recollection.

The fact that the child was first spoiled—by women (mother-equivalents)—and then suddenly made to undergo frustration—by his father—on the oral (and, as we may add, the anal) level, caused the pregenital fixation which colored his whole life. The result where the oedipus complex was concerned was that his wish for his mother remained essentially oral. We have an illustration of this in a dream which occurred when the analysis was already well advanced. "I was walking along with a parcel under each arm. I knew that my father was dead. The parcels opened and I saw that they were full of macaroni." Thus the longed-for death of the father gave him the opportunity of oral gratification, as it might give another the opportunity for sexual intercourse with the mother. In close relation to this dream there occurred others, which gave the patient a great shock: in these he was having coitus with his mother. The effect of his early experiences upon the negative oedipus complex was that he demanded of his father, though the latter forbade the things the child desired, that the father himself should restore what he had taken away—namely, oral or anal gratification. The instinctual impulse originally directed toward the mother was transferred to the father, and the frustration which had meanwhile been inflicted imparted to it a sadistic, rebellious character, so that the love of the negative oedipus complex expressed itself as follows: "You took it away from me and you must give it back!" The instinctual aim was still that of partial incorporation: the parts incorporated were represented by the "little animals" and had a different significance in the different mental strata: milk, money (feces), semen, and also the penis. (During an illness of his father's the patient had the following dream, arising from an actual experience of his own impotence: "One of my teeth was loose." The tooth represented in the first place the father—its shakiness his illness and the death wish against him. But, further, it stood for the father's penis, incorporated orally by the patient, the latent dream thought being: "Give me your penis, so that I can satisfy the woman with it, if I cannot with my own.")

Now it became plain why the transference to the analyst was always so positive. The analyst was the good father who fulfilled these demands of the negative oedipus complex. The *interpretations* given, the *words* spoken during the analytic hour, represented to the patient the oral gratification he longed for.

While the central point in the patient's life appeared to be the inward coming to terms with his father (the moral masochism corresponded to the sadism whose real object was the father but had been turned against the subject's own ego), the deeper, original heterosexual attitude betrayed itself in two ways. First, it enabled the patient to make himself in some sense independent of his tyrannical father by going abroad and placing himself in an environment the very reverse of that at home, while both his brothers remained in their father's business, continuing to react in unison, in a neurotic fashion, not only to their father-imago but to the father in person. My patient, in contrast to them, had made the inalienable discovery of the existence of another world, independent of his father. But he had a false idea of his world. He anticipated with complete confidence that it would be a paradise, where the ideal woman and the winning ticket alike would be his. Since reality was no such paradise, his neurotic reaction was to turn away from it and once more to make his father responsible for the fact that his life abroad did not resemble his life with his grandmother in his early infancy. He was in despair when all he wanted did not drop into his mouth of its own accord and, at the same time, he held the unwavering belief that it *must* do so. His real attitude toward women was almost entirely pregenital. During the analysis his father died, and the patient's reaction was a very considerable regression to narcissism which manifested itself chiefly in organic neurotic symptoms. These demonstrated his helplessness—a sick man cannot look after himself; he *must* have a father or (still further back in the subject's mind) a nursing mother. But the symptoms signified, besides, a continuation on narcissistic ground of the ambivalent conflict of which his father was the object. His attitude to the diseased organs of his body, which represented the introjected father, was in detail identical with his earlier attitude to his father. The analysis of these symptoms revealed that he had practiced phallic onanism in his early childhood and that the habit was interrupted by a threat of castration. Owing to the marked pregenital fixation this threat was construed as a repetition of the oral traumas. The threatened loss of the penis was not merely regressively *represented* by the loss of the grandmother ( = home) and of fostering care; it was from the beginning only a special case of this general frustration.

To sum up, the history is as follows: pregenital fixation to the mother (nurse, grandmother); bitter disappointment by the father followed by a twofold reaction—(a) fixation of the heterosexual object relation and hence of the subsequently established oedipus complex on the pregenital level, (b) a rebellious turning toward the father, characterized by features of the previous heterosexual relation, which were now displaced onto the father; the development, by reaction, of a marked sadism; all this resulting in a most radically pregenital fixation of the negative oedipus complex as well as the positive.

### III

A woman patient of thirty-six came to be analyzed on account of various neurotic symptoms which were serious but did not handicap her too badly in her work. This was hard work, a "man's job," for she held a responsible post as a manager. Prominent in her case also was the influence of a strong, unsolved oedipus complex. This was specially evident in her erotic relationships, in which typical "conditions for a love-relation" mentioned by Freud were clearly present: namely, the prerequisite of an "injured third party," the series of similar figures, the love for superiors.[15] When she grew up, her relation to her old father was one of specially warm friendship; its unconscious erotic sources soon came to light in analysis. There was no open hostility between her and her mother, but the fact that, deep down, she passionately detested many things in the latter was not far from consciousness. Analysis revealed in a most striking manner her infantile wish to get a child from her father (longings at Christmastime, acts of losing other "substitutes" and gifts, and much besides). Her case, then, seemed to fit into the scheme of hysteria, where the patient comes to grief over the oedipus complex, but without regression. Her behavior in the transference represented in typical fashion the wrecking of her oedipus wishes and her reactions to the frustrations of that period. On the idea "If I can't have my father, I will take whoever comes first" she had built up a strong harlot complex, in accordance with which she experienced from time to time a violent eruption of erotic excitement, which she relieved principally by onanism and which was in complete contrast to her usually calm and self-controlled nature. Onanism had been practiced by her without interruption during the latency period and was accompanied by manifestly masochistic fantasies (of being beaten). Here analysis was able relatively early to show that there was a "reversal," an underlying powerful unconscious sadism: she identified herself in fantasy with the

[15] S. Freud, "Contributions to the Psychology of Love: A Special Type of Choice of Object Made by Men," *Coll. Pap.*, Vol. IV, London, Hogarth, 1948.

person doing the beating—her masturbation took an active-masculine form (pulling at the labia)—she developed a strong hate-attachment to lovers who had disappointed her, and fantasies of revenge evoked the outbursts of erotic excitement of which I have spoken. She had also a perverse inclination—a special pleasure in cunnilingus—which seemed to spring from a tendency to abase men. In order to make her case clearer I will quote some of the material from her childhood. Her ideal of a calm, self-controlled person she derived from her father, an official of upright character. Affectionate and conscientious but of an obsessional type, he not merely preached but practiced extreme self-control and calm reasonableness. The sudden outbursts of sensuality were such as she had seen in little girls she played with, but she could never get rid of the feeling that her own mother was a very sensual person. Thus sensual wishes relating to her father had to be repressed with special force, and the more so because once he had found her masturbating and had beaten her, which was quite un-like him. Her tender attachment to him, then, caused her to reject all sensuality. The repressed sensual feelings joined forces with the hostile attitude which was her reaction to them: there were vehement reproaches of her father for his "cold reasonableness," his lack of understanding of behavior actuated by elemen-tary instinctual forces. During and after puberty this latter reproach took the sublimated form that he had no sympathy with her literary ambitions. An enormous transference-resistance when her compositions were for the first time to be subjected to analysis—the determination "not to be robbed" of them—was the first clear indication of castration anxiety. The sensuality characterized by hostility to her father soon took a homosexual direction. Once, shortly after puberty, she had actually performed a homosexual act with a friend and it had roused a deep disgust in her. It turned out that, as a child, she had played sexual games with this friend and, especially, that the two little girls had always gone to the water-closet together. Her subsequent homosexual inclinations and her attraction to the "injured" wives of men she loved seemed, like the harlot fan-tasies whose volcanic character they shared, to be the reactions of revenge to disappointments at the hands of men. At last there emerged a repressed memory of a nurse who was dismissed because she always took the patient into bed with her, and we thought that the prominence of the homosexual attitude was con-nected with the reality of these childhood experiences as contrasted with the fantastic nature of the sexual wishes relating to the father. It seemed that, as in the case of homosexuality in a woman of which Freud [16] gives an account, the homosexual attitude meant a declaration to the father: "If you are not willing, I don't want you!" Finally, I must mention that a masochistic trait in the patient's character fortified itself principally with self-reproaches (cer-

[16] S. Freud, "The Psychogenesis of a Case of Homosexuality in a Woman," *Coll. Pap.*, Vol. II.

tainly exaggerated) on the ground that she had harmed her father with advice on money matters during the period of inflation of the currency.

For a long time nothing was said about the mother. There were only hints that the patient disliked her more than she knew; in dreams she sometimes appeared as the "bad mother," a witch or castrator. We did not get any further in this direction till the analysis reached the pregenital period. And here I must first say something about the patient's penis envy.

In many respects her behavior was masculine and her work was that of a man. In the structure of her character, penis envy had been displaced upward; she took every opportunity of competing with men in the field of intellect. We discovered that the father-identification underlying this attitude was still being utilized in *wooing* her father. She wanted to prove to him by it that she was equal or superior to her only brother, who was older than she. It seemed at first as though her real penis envy had reference to this brother, as was indicated by numbers of memories which gradually emerged and which we traced to the comparison between his powers of urination and her own. We succeeded, too, in bringing to light fantasies of a hidden penis of her own, or one which might perhaps appear again; finally, a daydream, in which she lived with a child which was born by parthenogenesis, showed that she fantasied herself not only the mother but the father of the child and the latter itself as her penis. She could not urinate so well as her brother and was not allowed, as he was, to do it when out walking? Very well: she would concentrate her ambition on another bodily power—she could retain her urine longer. This retention—"self-control"— was in accordance with her father's ego-ideal, or the ego-ideal based on her father's character, which required above all things "self-command." The outbreaks of sensuality and the masturbation were the psychic equivalent of incontinence. The inclination to masturbate had to be suppressed like the desire to pass urine or evacuate feces at an inconvenient time. Later, the patient still tried to suppress the habit, at least in part, endeavoring, when masturbating, at any rate to prevent herself from breathing in gasps. This gave rise to various symptoms and forms of anxiety (dread of suffocation). We then discovered that, whereas we had long supposed that her brother must have put her to shame by his possession of a penis while she had none, the humiliating episode had really taken place in another connection and referred to the equivalent power of continence. She had once been given an enema and, midway between her bed and the chamber, evacuation had taken place and her brother, who was standing by, had laughed at her. This proof of incontinence was felt by her as the deepest humiliation and taken as evidence that she had been castrated. In the history of her childhood it appeared that a change occurred in her character in connection with an intestinal illness which she had at the age of three: she had been a quiet and docile child, but now became peevish and tiresome. This had various determinants, and among them was the fact that she regarded the illness as a humiliation, on account of the incontinence of feces associated with it. Here is a symbolic equation: to be ill = to be incontinent = to be castrated, and to this experience she responded with the change in her character. The reason why the episode of incontinence shamed her so profoundly was that she had been trained in habits of cleanliness at a remarkably early age—ostensibly without any difficulty and by her mother alone. One significance of cunnilingus was the canceling of the humiliation inflicted on her by her brother: it meant that he recognized the value of the dirty and incontinent anus—the genital which has no penis.

In connection with this material, memories of her third year at last emerged, from which we learned something of the methods employed by her mother in training her in cleanliness and also how long that training had lasted. Up till the time of the patient's illness her mother had always gone with her to the water-closet (the games with the friend were screen memories). She used to urge her daughter with much talk to defecate and used to praise her when she did her business well, and especially when the stool was well formed. It was all done in such a way that the child understood clearly that her mother took a libidinal interest in these acts. Undoubtedly she herself also derived pleasure from them and in this way she formed what may be called an anal-erotic association with her mother. The repression of these scenes had as its counterpart the feeling that her mother, in contrast to her father, was very sensual. Actually, she was never allowed to say a word in his presence about these anal concerns, and he himself was most particular that the children should never notice his going to the water-closet. Thus the child probably very soon had the feeling that he disapproved of the closet-association with her mother. The pregenital fixation to the latter was inhibited by two experiences. The first, which reappeared in a dream, was that she noticed in the water-closet that blood was flowing from her mother, and this made the little girl think of a bloody punishment for the delights of the closet. The second experience was the illness I have mentioned. We discovered that not only her incontinence but also the nature of the stool, which was unformed on account of diarrhea, wounded her narcissism severely. ("I am not creating anything—no child.") It happened that her father reproached her mother, saying "Whatever did you give the child to eat?" or some such words, whereupon the little girl came to the conclusion that her mother had made her ill—i.e., sensual enjoyment with the mother made her ill, incontinent, castrated her: "It would have been better to obey my father, who always disapproved of it." The mother was the witch who seduced one and gave pleasure, but the pleasure was fatal. The idea that her mother had given her something bad to eat brought us to the analysis of the oral attachment to the mother which existed before the anal period. A screen memory from the time before the illness was that she was drinking milk out of a bottle. It turned out that this was the last occasion on which she drank any milk before her illness and her father suspected it of being the cause of the trouble. She thought then: "Mother has poisoned me with milk." In connection with the memory of cows' udders and the confusion between udder and penis, the idea then emerged: "She has given me urine to drink." It turned out that once, when the child was at the same age of three, her mother let her fall in the bath, i.e., nearly killed her (to drown [*ertraenken*] = to give a noxious drink to [*schlecht traenken*]; it was to this incident that her fear of suffocation could be traced). From the idea of poisoning a succession of transitory oral symptoms led back to the idea of drinking purulent fluid, and this was finally linked up with the objective information that the mother had had to wean the child because she herself developed mastitis. Thus, the pregenital attachment to the mother ended with the verdict: "What we did was wrong. Father never did anything like that." She was doubtful as to whether the disastrous result would be a punishment by the father (as was indicated by the earliest memories of him, dating from before her illness—how he intervened when the little girl was "hurt") or whether it would happen automatically—i.e., through her mother's fault—in which case he would be the rescuer rather than the avenger.

Now there was another point to be cleared up about the idea "mother = witch." The patient had an increasingly strong feeling that her mother was a *vampire* and meant to suck her dry for her own pleasure. The only thing which could give rise to this idea of "sucking out what was inside" was the mother's encouraging words when the child's stool was well formed. The mother, then, had robbed her daughter of the well-formed stool—i.e., by a familiar equation, of the penis. Material derived from dreams and symptoms did in fact suggest the hypothesis that, immediately before she fell ill, the child had happened to see an erect penis. "Sucking dry" was the form in which the mother performed the act of castration. The harlot fantasies—so closely related to homosexuality—corresponded among other things to the idea that the harlot, forced into coitus to the point of exhaustion, was "sucked dry" by the men. In a second screen memory from the time immediately preceding her illness (a memory which we evoked at the same time as we discussed that of the scene about the milk) she was walking between two boys and shouldering a shovel. This meant: "Before my illness I still had my penis."

Now for the first time we were able to understand the deeper strata of her oedipus complex. In her dread of her mother she turned to her father for help—her attitude being ambivalent from the outset, for she feared her father would punish her. But unconsciously she could imagine only one form of help: he must give back what she had lost through her mother's fault. For a time the patient changed her method of masturbation, and this gave her a deep sense of guilt, so that she refused to speak of it in analysis. Finally, however, she admitted that she was practicing vaginal masturbation, by means of objects, and that these were always made of glass. Analysis showed that this referred to the enemas given to her by her father, and so the infantile wish was reconstructed that he should put the whole apparatus into her rectum. In the anal sense this meant: "He ought to give me a *formed* stool (penis, child) not a motion like diarrhea (fluid injection)." This meant: "He ought to give me back the stool—the penis—which my mother has stolen from me." In the patient's mental history this idea came to her in connection with the motion of the hand. She remembered playing that her father's hand was a "child," and she recounted a fantasy of being raped by five men—who were the five fingers. The prototype of this "rape" by the hand was undoubtedly the enema syringe. Her demands that what she had lost should be replaced by the father's body were met with refusal on his part. Thereupon her oral-anal sadism was turned against him: just like the patient in the first case I quoted, she demanded of the father partial incorporation. In accordance with her experiences she constructed the sexual theory that her mother sucked her father dry, and she began to wish that she could do exactly the same. *This* was the root of her active behavior and her sadism. The oedipus complex was built up on an unconscious partial love, together with the idea of incorporation; the mouth and the anus gave place to the vagina, while the child was substituted for feces and penis. The break-up of the oedipus complex followed the lines of that of the pregenital mother-fixation: just as, then, the patient had reached the conclusion that her mother "sucked her dry," so, now, she felt that her father's intellectual type of character, with its aloofness from instinctual behavior, implied a "theft of the finest capabilities," a kind of "drying up." The periodic, nymphomanic obsessional masturbation in which she indulged was *mainly* determined by *these* pregenital components of the oedipus complex. The unconscious fantasy accompanying the act was as follows: "I am biting off—or sucking out—my father's penis, so that I shall have a penis and a child, and *he* will die." This oral-sadistic trait was the cause of the patient's deep sense of guilt: her masochism represented the same tendency directed against her own ego. Her sadism she directed not only against her father but also against the child stolen from him. As a child she had feared being poisoned or sucked dry by her mother (i.e. orally castrated and destroyed): so, unconsciously and in identification with the vampire-mother, did she wish, by biting off and sucking out, to destroy the child which she would steal from the father's body. The deepest strata in her oedipus complex were represented in the following fantasies: (a) that of biting off a penis and so killing it—eating something "dead"—having something "dead" inside her and so perishing (the principal fantasy about her intestinal illness in childhood); (b) that of having something "half-dead" inside her, which could be saved by medical intervention (this was the principal fantasy of the unconscious wish for cure: that the analyst should draw forth and make manifest the penis which was inside her and excited her to masturbation).

To sum up: The mental history of this patient was as follows—pregenital fixation to the mother, first of an oral and then of an anal character; bitter disappointment by the mother (prototype: mastitis; later, illness conceived of as castration); turning toward the father; substitutes demanded from him, with a transferring to him of tendencies and ambivalent feelings originally relating to the mother; formation of the oedipus complex, colored by this sequence. In this case, as in the first quoted, sadism was called forth by frustration, and the castration anxiety, originally having reference to the mother, was displaced onto the father.

## IV

I shall be able to give a somewhat shorter account of the third case. The patient was a woman of forty-four, with a neurotic character formation and symptoms which were mainly those of anxiety hysteria. Her character was dominated by a castration complex of excessive strength. An early identification with her father, of which I shall presently speak in greater detail, caused her largely to ignore her femininity: she regarded her menstrual periods as the most profound humiliation and shame. She had formerly had a very active sexual life, the principal feature of which was that she led men on in a wholly narcissistic fashion to make love to her, in order somehow to disappoint them in the end. She yielded herself only when she was the "stronger," when for instance the man had burst into tears. Active castration fantasies played a prominent role; she counted it a triumph when a man had a premature ejaculation and was therefore "helpless." What she aimed at was to put men as sexual beings to shame, to refuse them and then to say: "If they were so feeble that they could not seduce me, it serves them right." Naturally, in the transference her analysis also became a ceaseless contest for the mastery and she was constantly on the lookout for opportunities to make a fool of the analyst. Men who were no match for her were the objects of her derision. But not only the men—she mocked specially at the penis itself. It struck her as grotesque and made her laugh when she caught sight of it. Of course, this mockery had its origin in resentment and masked a vehement penis envy.[17]

---

[17] Cf. O. Fenichel, "The 'Long Nose,'" No. 17 in this volume.

This behavior becomes immediately more comprehensible when we learn that in this woman the whole oedipus complex was nothing but an object of fantasy in a different sense from that in which this is true of other people. She had never known her father. He died the day she was born. And so no man was the right one. The only right one would be the father of her fantasy, the fairy prince coming from the beyond. She had endless fantasies of "salvation," and anxiety about her Christianity constituted the most powerful resistance in her analysis.

Her father died the day she was born. Here was reason enough for her identifying herself with him early and very widely. The mystical union with him, representing at one and the same time sexual intercourse and identification, was conceived of as oral union, as communion. She had an abundance of dreams and fantasies about devouring fragments of corpses, about fruit trees growing on graves, about oral impregnation, eating feces, etc. The hysterical symptoms were mainly oral. She suffered from cravings of hunger and from loss of appetite, and she felt obliged to avoid various kinds of food: must not eat any meat or, above all, any fish and so on. (Fish had a "soul" and therefore represented her father.) She had pains in the region of the diaphragm, and it turned out that, as a child, she had thought that the word *Zwerchfell* (diaphragm) was the same as *Zwergfell* (literally, "dwarf's skin") and had pictured a little dwarf sitting inside and making a noise. She suffered from a dread of poisoning which, just as Weiss [18] has maintained, turned out to be dread of the introjected object. A further account of these symptoms would be interesting but is irrelevant to our present subject. To sum up: The purely fantastic oedipus complex was characterized at all levels of libidinal development by total or partial incorporation, and the object introjected had to be interpreted, according to the stage of the analysis, as father, child, feces, or penis.

The two principal real sexual experiences of her childhood corresponded to these ideas. On one occasion she had performed fellatio with a little boy and with another boy she had often played at "slaughter" and experienced sexual excitement.

The manifest anxiety was the most prominent feature in the clinical picture. In accordance with her real attitude toward men this anxiety proved to be, first, a dread of being the "under dog," secondly, the expression of inhibited aggressive impulses against men, and, at bottom, an overpowering dread of the loss of love. Her behavior gave cause enough for the fear that all men would desert her. On the other hand, she was aggressive toward men because they were disposed to leave her in the lurch.

[18] E. Weiss, "Der Vergiftungswahn im Lichte der Introjektions- und Projektionsvorgaenge," *Int. Z. Psa.*, Vol. 12, 1926.

The further the analysis advanced, and the more completely the infantile amnesias were dispelled, the clearer did it become that her real experiences with men were relatively unimportant and that the chief object which influenced her real character formation was the one parent whom she knew—her mother. She was a "posthumous child," and her brothers and sisters were many years older than she. In her enormous craving for tenderness the only person to whom she could turn was her mother. But here, from the very outset, she had every reason for her great fear of "loss of love," for the mother's attitude toward this posthumous child, all that her husband had left her, was from the beginning highly ambivalent. The father had died of a mental disorder. The child often heard that she had been by no means a welcome arrival. She also heard her mother deplore her little daughter's ugliness and say, "We thought that the child would turn out an idiot." So she could not help hating her mother, and the fiercest ambivalent conflicts were inevitable. Her aggressive tendencies manifested themselves in the way in which she caused her mother anxiety: the talion law decreed that she herself should suffer anxiety because of this, all her life long.

During analysis she remembered a forgotten Aunt Ottilie, and we were able to see that her transference behavior really had reference to a woman—ultimately to her mother—and that all real men were only screen figures for the latter. It was to her mother that her longing for tenderness, and also her hatred, her aggressive impulses, and her active castration tendency were directed.

The great traumas of her life, which led to her neurotic illness, were the birth of her own daughter and that of a daughter to her lover by a strange woman. She always felt that her own daughter was ugly, all wrong—it was not the child of her own fantasy father. Above all she feared retribution: "My child will actually do to me what I wished to do to my mother." A second cause of her neurosis was the feeling of injury: "The other woman has the child, not I." This led us to the discovery that the principal wrongs from which she had felt she suffered in her childhood were: "Other children have a father and I haven't. Other children have a penis and I haven't." It is certain that she held her mother responsible for both these disadvantages. We are accustomed to find the oedipus complex in normal women taking the following form: "My mother has taken my father away from me." In this case there was a special meaning: "My mother let my father die." The main content of the ideas which caused her anxiety was that when someone dies, the other people are unmoved and just let him die. We had reason to assume that, even as a child, she suspected that her father's mental illness was the result of venereal disease; it followed that her mother had killed the father. In the "mystic union" she received into herself the father whom her mother had slain. Her anxiety attacks had also an exhibitionistic meaning—

a reproach leveled at her mother: "Look, this is how my mother is the death of me!" The mother was guilty, too, of the child's lack of the penis; the "mystic union" restored the father and therewith the penis (obsessional thoughts about Christ's penis, etc.). When she demonstrated her helplessness, in an anxiety attack, she was disclosing her lack of the penis, with an implicit reproach against her mother; on real occasions of exhibition she repeatedly had such attacks, in order to demonstrate her helplessness—the fact that she had been castrated—and to accuse her mother.

Certain obsessional symptoms concealed under the patient's anxiety hysteria led to the conclusion that behind the thoughts of castration there were older, hidden, anal thoughts. It is true that at this point regressive factors obscured the picture. Later, she gave greater prominence to anal than to urethral functions, because in the former she could compete with boys. At the same time thorough analysis of her very complicated anal erotism showed beyond any doubt that she also made quite primitive accusation against her mother of bothering too much about her daughter's anal concerns and destroying all pleasure in them. As in the case quoted earlier, the idea of the mother as castrator had, as substructure, the idea of her as the person who stole the child's feces. But here again there was ambivalence: even when she was grown up, she could imagine no greater proof of love than that her lover should empty the bed-pan when she was ill. The symptom picture which I have described makes it abundantly clear that an oral phase preceded this anal ambivalence, but I am not able to give exact particulars about the time when she was an infant at the breast.

To sum up—the patient's mental history is as follows: Pregenital (first oral and then anal) love for the mother; from the outset disappointments by the mother; aggressive reactions against her and an increased anxiety relating to loss of love; repression of aggressive impulses; anxiety still further increased; the turning to the father is possible only in fantasies—real men are, in fact, a screen for the figure of the mother. Sadism is once more a reaction to frustrations. The castration anxiety originally having reference to the mother was subsequently displaced onto men.

## V

Supposing that we now attempt to draw some theoretical conclusions from the material that we have amassed. The first point which strikes us after our discussion of the two last, female, cases is what may be learned from them on the disputed question of "the change of object in women." Let us try to sum up briefly the principal points in the views held on this subject by various authors. Freud found that the little girl's discovery that she lacks a penis is felt as a purely narcissistic injury, for which she holds her mother responsible, and that it causes her to go over to the father, by way of the symbolic equation: penis = child. Freud urged analysts to investigate whether this were so in every case. K. Horney laid special stress on precisely the opposite situation, holding that little girls and women in whom there is manifestly a very marked penis envy utilize that envy and their "masculinity" in general *secondarily* as a defense against an already developed oedipus complex. This is a finding which does not necessarily contradict Freud's. A. Lampl de Groot, starting from Freud's view, supplements it with a suggestion which, if it could be substantiated, would be of the utmost importance. She holds that the penis envy of the period prior to the oedipus complex is not narcissistic at all but is in the fullest sense masculine and phallic: the little girl really begins as a little boy and desires a penis in order to be able to have coitus with the mother. According to this view, the positive oedipus complex in little girls would regularly be preceded by the negative.

The view which our two female cases obviously confirm first of all is that of Freud. Both patients were in the first instance attached to the mother (but *pregenitally* attached), both went over to the father and to the desire for a child, as a reaction to disappointments by the mother. In both the discovery of the lack of a penis played an important part, and both undoubtedly held the mother responsible for it. But, we must hasten to add, the idea "My mother has castrated me" seemed to be co-ordinated with other frustrations—to be only one factor among many. In one case, side by side with the reproach that the patient had been castrated by the mother were the further reproaches that the mother had poisoned her (oral), robbed her of her strength (anal). In the other, the idea that the mother had robbed the father existed from the outset side by side with that of castration, and besides, here again, we came upon important oral and anal frustrations. It chanced that all three patients were the youngest members of their families; otherwise we should certainly have found that the birth of younger brothers or sisters was a crucial instance of disillusionment. We can see immediately from our material that, among the disappointments emanating from the mother, the lack of a penis must play, economically, the most important part. This is very probable even when we only consider the matter theoretically. Of the co-ordinated disappointments which come through the mother those which are oral and anal affect both sexes equally. But the experience of "castration" is one which affects the female sex only. If, then, females are impelled by these disappointments to change their love object, while males are not so impelled (for the male case quoted is exceptional in this respect), the crucial instance of disappointment must be that connected with the lack of the penis, and it must be this which operates, in conjunction with constitutional biological factors. At all events our cases go to prove that, in

females, the act of castration is originally attributed to the mother and that female sexuality is built up on a basis of partial incorporation, on the idea "My
mother has stolen it; my father must give it back."

Of course, the view put forward by K. Horney, that a more superficial penis
envy may act as a screen and defense for deeper oedipus wishes, is not to be
called in question, for it expresses a situation met with every day in our analytical
experience. For instance, in our last case, the "masculinity" symptoms, so os-
tentatiously presented, were a screen for fantasies of mystic union with the
father. But these facts tell us nothing of the possibility of a primitive narcissistic
penis envy, prior to and beyond all oedipus wishes. Jones is right when he speaks
of a pre- and a post-oedipus penis envy. But nothing in our material bore out
the suppositions of A. Lampl de Groot. The original mother attachments were,
most markedly, exclusively pregenital. The fact that in one case this attachment
was not, or not altogether, feminine and receptive but had for its aim the idea
of giving the mother something or letting her take it away does not make it
possible to call it a masculine, genital attachment. It is true that in the other case
also there were masculine-genital wishes, having reference to the mother—e.g.,
the patient wished to place her own leg between her mother's thighs—but they
arose at a much later, "post-oedipus" period, long after a secondary identification
with the father had taken place. So the cases quoted by A. Lampl de Groot do
not appear to be typical.

Actually, then, the oedipus complex is influenced by the pregenital attachment
to the mother, and its break-up by the earlier break-up of that object relation.

Let us once more sum up and compare our findings in the three cases schematically:

Case I. Pregenital attachment to the mother—disappointment by the father—
(a) fixation of heterosexuality (of the oedipus complex), (b) turning toward
the father: pregenital tendencies having reference to the mother are carried over
to the father and there is a sadistic reaction.

Case II. Pregenital attachment to the mother—disappointment by the mother
—turning to the father: pregenital tendencies having reference to the mother
are carried over to the father and there is a sadistic reaction.

Case III. Pregenital attachment to the mother—chronic disappointment by
the father: since he is no longer actually in existence (a) introversion takes place,
(b) many pregenital tendencies having reference to the mother are carried over
to real men and there is a sadistic reaction.

The second and third cases are doubtless more typical than the first. To judge
by what I have recounted of them they seem characteristic instances of the
development of the oedipus complex in women. The subject's bisexuality manifests itself in the varying degrees in which the relation with the father is clouded

by the importation of hate-tendencies really relating to the mother. The first case is more complicated. If it had taken a typically masculine course, the boy would probably have reacted to the disappointment by his father by turning to his mother with redoubled vehemence. Instead, however, it developed along the feminine line: that of turning to the father, after the disappointment, and transferring to him tendencies relating to the mother. We must suppose that this happened because the mother of his earliest days was replaced by his nurse and grandmother and then, later, these two were no longer present. There was also, no doubt, a special constitutional bisexual factor.

In conclusion, let us consider in the light of the material at our disposal the problems of the pregenital antecedents of the oedipus complex, referred to at the beginning of this paper. The points upon which, as we said, all analysts are unanimous have certainly received fresh confirmation.

(1) The oedipus prohibition reflects the pregenital prohibition: in Case I, the loss of the environment associated with the grandmother remained, throughout the patient's life, the principal disaster with which he felt himself threatened; in Case II, beneath the father's commands of self-control ("being dried up") was the basic pregenital idea of "being sucked dry"; in Case III, the overpowering dread of loss of love—originally, of the mother's love, conceived of in pregenital terms—was throughout life the chief content of the patient's anxiety. In the main we have dealt only with the material of the pregenital *object relations* and have disregarded the question of autoerotism, from which we might have learned still more on these points.

(2) In Case I, the castration anxiety really always remained oral, while in Cases II and III it was built up out of the dread of losing feces and the mother's breast.

(3) In all three cases there was originally a pregenital attachment to the mother, and characteristics of this attachment were imported into the relation with the father.

(4) In all three cases the introjected object in the unconscious ideas of "partial incorporation" could represent equally the penis, feces, and the mother's breast.

(5) In the cases of the two female patients it was particularly clear that the desire for a child was built up out of penis envy and the longing for a well-formed stool.

(6) In the "eruptions" of sensuality in Case II it was easy to recognize the longing for oral incorporation as the basis of the wish for coitus.

Now, as regards the points which we said were "disputed": With the first, the question of the change of love object in women, we have already dealt at length. As regards the relation of oral to genital sexuality we were able in all three cases to demonstrate the feminine, *direct* transition of the incorporation wishes from the oral to the vaginal level by way of the anal. This is a notion which Helene Deutsch [19] also puts forward. Obviously the three hollow organs simply succeed one another, as for example in Case II, where the coitus wish was the direct successor of an anal incorporation wish (enema syringe). In this sense Jones speaks of an "equivalent series" of female organs. It is plain that the active-phallic libido, about which we could say nothing directly, is evolved from the active excretion components of anal sexuality, just as feminine libido is evolved from the receptive-retention components. This brings us to the third and last point: the relation between retention and excretion. Our own findings would seem to testify to these tendencies' alternating with, or possibly succeeding, one another in *every* erotogenic zone (in Abraham's [20] sense of the term) rather than to the localization in the urethra of all pleasure in excretion and in the anus of all pleasure in retention as postulated by Ferenczi in his theory of amphimixis.[21] Pure genitality seems to exist as independently as urethral and anal erotism. Only because it flowers later does it retain so many of those traces of pregenital origin which are derived from an earlier period. The object relations were begun in that period, and therefore at their genital zenith they still bear vestiges of their origin.

[19] H. Deutsch, *Psychoanalyse der weiblichen Sexualfunktionen*, Vienna, Int. Psa. Verlag, 1925.
[20] K. Abraham, "A Short Study of the Development of the Libido, Viewed in the Light of Mental Disorders," *Selected Papers.*
[21] S. Ferenczi, *op. cit.*

# *TWENTY-TWO*

# Specific Forms of the Oedipus Complex*

THE "oedipus complex" is the term used by Freud to denote the medley of strivings, feelings, and unconscious ideas grouped round the individual's wishes to possess sexually the parent of the opposite sex and to get rid of the parent of the same sex. When we speak of the "complete oedipus complex" we imply the co-existence of the converse situation, in which the parent of the same sex is desired sexually, while the parent of the opposite sex is the one whose removal is wished for. Anyone who has come to recognize the fundamental importance of the oedipus complex, whether through discovery in himself or others, or because he accepts the statements of psychoanalysts without being more deeply conversant with psychoanalysis, will find that there are two problems—or perhaps it would be more correct to say two apparent problems—which demand a solution.

In the first place he will say: "I now understand that this oedipus complex is to be regarded as the 'nuclear complex' in neurosis. If, unconsciously, a man's sole love object is his mother, he will see her in every woman he meets and therefore he will have to repress his sexuality; the return of the repressed sexuality constitutes neurosis. And if, unconsciously, a man desires to kill his father, he will scent parricide in every action and this will inhibit his initiative; the return of this drive, again, is neurosis. But how are we to reconcile these facts with the statement that the oedipus complex is *normal* and that its presence in every individual is as much a matter of course as, for example, his nose?"

And secondly: "It was precisely psychoanalysis, as opposed to schematic medicine, which proclaimed that the personal destiny of each one of us is entirely in-

* First published in *Int. Z. Psa.,* Vol. 17, 1931, pp. 37–54.

dividual and unique and that the causes of neurosis are forgotten experiences, traumas, which the person in question has at some time actually lived through. The task of recovering these facts in the patient's personal history is what makes psychoanalysis necessarily so long a process. This was all quite comprehensible. But now we are told that the oedipus complex is the nuclear complex of the neuroses. All neurotics at bottom suffer from the same unconscious constellation, which know of beforehand. Why then should we not inform the patient of it, as soon as he has got far enough to listen and understand? What is the object of delving into his history in analysis?"

I said that both these problems were only apparent problems. They are easily solved, and yet the whole purpose of this paper is to comment on this self-evident solution.

Let us take the first question. The oedipus complex is not normal in the way in which the nose is normal. Rather it is like the thymus gland—i.e., it is normal at a certain period but abnormal if it persists unchanged beyond that period. Everybody has it between the ages of about four and six; later, in normal people, it seems to vanish. We see then that neurosis, regarded as a diseased oedipus complex, is an *inhibition of development,* the persistence of an early phase of development. For *the adult neurotic has retained his oedipus complex.* He knows nothing about it, but nevertheless we can show it to be operative, and this is what we mean when we say it is "unconscious." But all this cannot after all be quite correct. It will be objected that Freud has told us that the analysis of the works of poets or the dreams of normal people shows that the oedipus complex is still active in these adult persons, who are not neurotics. The last point, it must be said, is not in itself a valid objection, for dreams are *regressive* and reactivate old infantile attitudes which need not therefore be in evidence in the daytime. Nevertheless, we must admit that our first statement was not quite correct, and that even normal adults have an oedipus complex. The difference in this respect between the normal person and the neurotic is *quantitative.* Freud shows that it is characteristic of psychic development that, when an advance is made to higher levels, the former phases never wholly vanish, but continue in some degree to exist and can in certain circumstances be revived. He compares this development with the advance of an army which leaves troops to occupy all the places it passes through on its forward march. If it has to fall back, the main body of the army retires to the place where it left the strongest troops in occupation. If the garrisons thus left behind are very large, the vanguard will be correspondingly weak and more easily forced to retreat. The normal person has indeed also left forces in occupation of the situation which we call the "oedipus complex," but the main body of the army, the whole personality, has advanced. Under *very adverse* conditions, however, it may fall back too, and so become neurotic. The person who is neurotically disposed, of whom we were thinking in speaking of neurotics so far, has left almost all his forces at the point of the "oedipus complex." Only a small body has advanced; quite trivial difficulties suffice to force him to retreat and to reanimate his oedipus complex. Thus the characteristic feature in the *neurotic disposition* is not the existence of the oedipus complex but the failure to overcome it. The interest of the general etiology is shifted from the existence of the complex to the conditions under which it may be overcome.

The antecedents of the oedipus complex and its subsequent history are complicated, and at the moment I will only outline them as far as we shall need them for the present discussion. This complex is the point of function, in the child, of two lines of development, both of which again may have suffered disturbance at any point: (a) We have first the development of the principal physical zones which are the source of the instinctual drives—i.e., the libidinal development characterized by the stages known as oral, anal, and phallic. The oedipus complex proper belongs to the phallic stage, but is being prepared for earlier and so contains to a greater or lesser extent oral and anal elements: (b) we have next the development of object relations—the individual's attitude to external objects—i.e., the libidinal development characterized by what we know as narcissism (absence of any external object), by archaic, ambivalent object relations with the idea of wholly devouring the love object (total incorporation) or of biting off a part of it (partial incorporation); and, finally, by love and hate. The oedipus complex proper belongs to the love-hate period, but it begins to develop earlier and so contains to a greater or lesser extent elements of the "incorporation" phase. The mastering of this complex becomes necessary when the child acquires the conviction that the gratification of the desires bound up with it is highly dangerous. It is mastered by the complicated mechanisms which we comprise in the term "superego formation," through the child's learning to identify himself with his parents' requirements. Those who later on become neurotic succeed only imperfectly in this. To simplify matters we will on this occasion consider only one aspect of their failure. Identification with the parents, by means of which the oedipus complex is mastered, is in fact a decisive step in the formation of human character. We will not now attempt to study the possible defects in this process, although it offers complicated problems which are today the focus of scientific interest. Instead, we will turn our attention to the *libidinal oedipus complex* which persists to a considerable degree in neurotics, so providing the opportunity for subsequent regression. We said that the idea that gratification of the wishes belonging to the complex was fraught with danger was the reason why the oedipus complex passes. The danger so deeply feared unconsciously and thought to be bound up with the gratification of instinct is, first, that of the loss of the parents' love, and secondly—singularly enough—of physical injury to the genitals, i.e. of "castration." [1] It is the dread of loss of love and castration which opposes the instincts. If either this anxiety or the instinctual wish which it relates to is unusually strong or premature, there will be an unusually strong or premature *defense,* and what has thus been fended off prematurely or with special intensity can obviously no longer be dealt with by identification later on; it therefore persists unchanged in the unconscious.

It seems that the first of the two apparent problems is now satisfactorily explained. But the second has become all the more difficult. All that we have said goes to show that psychoanalysis today professes to know in advance what is the matter with *every* neurotic. There is a *general theory of the neuroses,* which is as follows: Neurosis occurs when an individual reacts to the disappointments of life by regressing to the oedipus complex and then trying to defend himself against it. This can happen only when part of that complex, fundamentally unchanged, has persisted in the unconscious from childhood. This, again, can be the case only if the subject's love for the parent of the opposite sex and hatred for the parent of the same sex have been peculiarly strong or premature, and if he develops anxiety lest, because of this, he should be left alone or have his genital organ violently injured. And further, there is also a *specific theory of the neuroses* which adds: Supposing that the pregenital development has been correct, there will be repression of the oedipus complex; what will develop later will be *hysteria.* Or if, either by constitution or experience, the child has early, pregenital points of fixation, he will defend himself against the premature or overstrong oedipus complex by falling back to these points. Anal-sadistic wishes will then surge up, and if he makes various further attempts at defense but they nevertheless break through, the result is an *obsessional neurosis,* etc. So the diagnosis in itself enables us to say beforehand with some degree of approximation what must have been the patient's typical experiences in childhood. If, then, all these etiologically important experiences are *typical,* why should we spend time and labor on the *atypical,* unique, traumatic features of personal history?

The answer to this question, though a commonplace, cannot be sufficiently emphasized. All that we know of these typical experiences is their *form,* not their *content.* "Oedipus complex" and "castration-anxiety" are words: the psychic realities which they represent are infinitely various. The analytical theory of the neuroses is the *frame* into which may be inserted a thousand different pictures. What are "love," "hate," and "anxiety"? Affects, bound up with a hundred *in-*

---

[1] The dread of genital injury manifests itself in the mental life of boys almost exclusively as dread of losing the penis—the organ from which pleasure is derived; the testicles play an astonishingly small part. Psychoanalytical terminology recognizes this fact, for in the *psychological* sense (as distinct from the accepted biological usage, which implies by "castration" the removal of the seminal glands) the term "castration" is used primarily with reference to injury or destruction of the penis. In girls the "castration complex" takes the form of "envy of the penis" of the other sex: this is associated with the fantasy of having lost a similar organ (by castration).

*dividual memories,* each of which is unique. When a man says, "I love a woman," it tells us very little about his mental life, and children's love is no more uniform than that of their elders. We may draw a parallel with the concepts of the theory of heredity. There are *determining* factors which ensure the development of the oedipus complex and of castration anxiety; their occurrence is predestined. But the mode in which they occur—that is, the factors which *realize* them—depends on the actual events of the individual's life and his reaction to them; and this, again, depends on his constitution and his whole previous experience. It is important to lay stress on this. *The work which has to be done by psychoanalysis on the histories of individuals and the difficulties arising out of this stand just where they did.* Quite recently Ferenczi [2] has very rightly emphasized how much of the old theory of traumas still holds good. In this he opposes the view of certain other authors who have erroneously held that children's constantly recurring phantasies of oral, anal, and genital gratifications and anxieties, of castration and oedipus complex, were more important than their real life. Not only does the character and behavior of the mother whom a little boy loves make the most vital difference, but also the child's idea of "love" and the way in which such love fits into his whole mental structure will vary for every individual. Each case is unique.

It is impossible to lay down a law as to why the oedipus complex is, in practice, mastered in one case and not in another. But we can understand how, in certain individuals, through particular experiences, or experiences reacted to with their particular constitution, the oedipus complex and castration anxiety were prematurely aroused or exceptionally powerfully stimulated. And the comparative analysis of many individuals enables us to distinguish up to a point certain typical forms of the complex which depend on the subject's experience, unique as each case is. There are relatively typical responses to relatively typical experiences, and by these the *specific forms of the oedipus complex* are governed.

This is at once clear in the case of the different ways of *mastery of oedipus complex.* When this is achieved by identification, the resulting superego will vary as much as the possible educational influences brought to bear may vary. We do, in fact, find these manifold variations in human character. But we are not considering the conscious mind or the ego, which is closer to consciousness, but the unconscious, which, paradoxically, is much better known to us. Yet the same situation holds good of the unconscious oedipus complex and the castration anxiety which threatens it.

Let us pass on without delay to examples which illustrate this variety.

We said that everyone suffers from the dread of his genital organ being mutilated. But the anxiety takes a different form in each person. And it is not only

[2] S. Ferenczi, "The Principle of Relaxation and Neocatharsis," *Int. J. Psa.,* Vol. 11, 1930.

the secondary forms of anxiety—those products of displacement which are to serve as substitutes for the more deeply repressed genital anxiety—which depend on specific experiences in childhood. (For instance, one child, after the shock of a tonsil operation, displaces his anxiety to the throat, while another, who is forced against his will to see a pigeon's head cut off, will retain throughout life a dread of decapitation as a substitute for the idea of castration. Again, conscious or unconscious dread of injury to the eyes indicates particular experiences in connection with sexual scoptophilia, while the localization of anxiety in the thumbs shows that it has been acquired in connection with sucking for pleasure, in infancy.) Apart from these displacements, the form taken by the imagined menace to the genital itself varies greatly. In males the most truly "genital" form of castration pictured is that in which the father cuts off the penis as a punishment for the phallic wishes relating to the mother. There is a special form of anxiety, in which we have already an admixture of feminine tendencies, which regards just the father's penis as the menacing weapon. The penis may be thought of, according to circumstances, as exposed to what we may call a male threat, i.e. by a penetrating pointed object, or a female threat, by some sort of snapping instrument, according to which of his parents the boy fears more and what ideas his experience has led him to form about sexual intercourse. An individual who has an oral fixation will show anxiety lest his genital organ should be bitten off, and will develop a tendency in his turn to bite off other people's. This may give rise to curious composite anxieties: the dread of being eaten fused with the dread of castration, in the shape, perhaps, of the dread of being robbed of the penis when it is inside a woman's body. This is the meaning of the fairy-tale of the Nose Dwarf, who gets into an enchanted castle (symbolizing the inside of the body) and leaves it with a long nose (as a compensation for the idea "without a nose").

Often, however, castration anxiety takes quite grotesque forms, sometimes shaping the whole course of the subject's life, which can be explained only by some unique experience. For instance, a patient of marked oral tendencies, who unconsciously equated sexual gratification with devouring, and who, besides, had come to adopt the feminine attitude and made his father his chief love object, had heard that his mother was threatened with *"Krebs"* * and later on had learned about bacteria. When he discovered that females had no penis, he constructed the following remarkable fantasy-theme: his oedipus wishes had taken the form of the desire to eat the father's penis or what came out of it. His castration anxiety, acting as a defense mechanism, took the form: "But if I eat these little creatures and they grow into children inside me, when they are being born they will eat away my penis from inside." With girls the content of their anxiety varies according to the sexual theories which their predisposition and their experience have caused them

---

* *"Krebs"* = "cancer." The same word in German means "crab."—Trans. note.

to form. A girl who clings to the belief that she has a penis and that it is only small and will grow larger has the true dread of its being cut off, just as a boy has. If, on the other hand, she thinks that there is a penis hidden inside her body, she has a dread of operations (and a longing to be operated on so that the penis may emerge), whereas if her attitude is the feminine one but she happens, for example, to see the penis of a grown man, she is terrified by its size and fears that she may be torn and rent asunder by it. We can understand that these specific forms of anxiety are very important for neurosis and life in general.

Just as the anxiety ideas vary, so do those about love and killing. Genital love has very many components, and they may be very variously stressed. Apart from this, the genital wish may have a more or less strong pregenital tinge. (The sadistic oedipus complex with a marked substructure of oral tendencies is met with in many forms of neurosis and is specially important.)

Death also may be conceived of in every imaginable way and is even sometimes sexualized into sadistic love, thus giving simultaneous expression to the inverted oedipus complex.

Upon what experiences do the special forms of the oedipus complex depend? Upon all experience. There is no perception which does not immediately enter into the instinctual nexus. All the child's experiences at the period of the oedipus complex, but also everything that has ever happened to him before, exercise an influence; the experience of the earlier period will do so mainly in the sense that if it has taken a pathological form it will from the outset give a pathological, i.e. excessively pregenital, coloring to the formation of the oedipus complex itself. Indeed, children whose earliest phases of development have been seriously disturbed will never achieve an oedipus complex at all: in their object relations they remain throughout life fixated on "pre-oedipus" levels. Such cases, however, no longer come under the heading of neuroses; they involve most serious malformations of character and anomalies in development and approximate to psychosis.

What are the specially influential experiences which we must consider? They are of two kinds: (a) single traumatic events; and (b) chronic influences.

To the former psychoanalysis has always attached special importance. They often supply the sufficient reason why the oedipus complex or castration anxiety has become operative so strongly or so early that the former cannot be mastered in the normal way. Now what has this traumatic effect? Special forms of gratification or frustration, or experiences in which the two are combined, especially if they occur suddenly and unexpectedly. As we are speaking of the genital oedipus complex, let us consider first of all the genital factor. *Children who have been seduced* are specially strongly "genitalized": they are unable to effect the normal inhibition of their instinctual aims and therefore are forced to repress them; but this, of course, means that their anxieties are peculiarly intensified. In general, everything which causes anxiety, especially genital anxiety, may be classed as a "trauma." This includes all threats and real experiences which act as threats, such as accidents, injuries, and deaths, which seem to reinforce the belief in castration; or the *sudden* sight of the genitals of an adult, which, in the case of male and female alike, tends to produce an intensification of castration anxiety. And castration anxiety, when specially intensified, produces repressions and therefore disturbances in the mastery of the oedipus complex. Experiences in "aim-inhibited" fields may, by displacement, have the same effect as genital experiences. Of special importance in this connection are survivals from the pre-genital period, "fixations," as we call them, due to some special experiences during the oral or anal phases of libidinal development, particularly during the periods of weaning and training in habits of cleanliness. It is not necessary, indeed, for the content of these experiences to be itself of an oral or anal character; it is enough that they take place at that particular period. Of special importance for the oedipus complex is all that the child learns or puts together in its own mind about the sexuality of its parents; here again, the effect is specially strong if the knowledge comes suddenly, as a surprise. Often the child combines real experiences with erroneous perceptions. We have an example of this in the whole field of *sadistic conceptions of sexuality*. The most important factor in this connection is the so-called *primal scene*—the observation of parental coitus. An experience of this sort acts as a most powerful sexual excitation (the content varying greatly, according to the age of the child) and at the same time convinces him of the danger of sexual gratification, either because he misinterprets what he observes, taking it to be a sadistic act, or because he catches sight of the "castrated" female genital. The content and intensity of the effect of such an experience and the moment at which it makes itself felt naturally vary according to its details: what the child perceives, what he is able to guess, and in what mental context perception and guesses are set, whether they are elaborated and assigned to their place in the mental scheme at once or later—all this depends on individual factors. It is certain that the primal scene does influence the oedipus complex, but in different ways, according to circumstances. Invariably, however, the concepts "sexual gratification" and "danger" are coupled in a special way, and this must increase the tendency to repression. Observations of the coitus of animals or the sight of the genitals of human adults, or even of animals, can take the place of an actual primal scene as psychically equivalent to it, especially if other, objectively harmless situations assist the transference of such experiences to the parents. Freud has pointed out that the idea of overhearing the primal scene is included among what we call "primal fantasies" and that, where no such experience has taken place, fantasies are substituted for it; nevertheless the impression remains that the actual experience acts with quite another traumatic force than a fantasy. The second most important factor is the birth of younger brothers and sisters, not only because this produces a traumatic disturbance of the oedipus gratification (because the parents cannot give the child so much attention as before), but also because his sexual anxiety is increased by his perceptions or speculations with reference to the act of birth and because of the impetus given to his own tendency to regress to the pregenital delights of the suckling period.

Now to turn to the consideration of chronic experience—a child's reaction to his parents and the demands he makes on them will depend on who and what these parents are and how they behave toward him. Where the parents or their behavior are unusual, the reaction will be unusual. That this is really so is already made clear by the first broad family history recovered from neurotics. Neurotic parents have in their turn neurotic children, and the child's oedipus complex reflects that of his parents. For this complex in children is in part stimulated also by the corresponding attitude in their parents: the father loves the daughter and the mother the son. This unconscious sexual attachment to the children becomes specially strong wherever the parents' real sexual gratification leaves them unsatisfied, whether from external or internal reasons (e.g., owing to their own neuroses). This attachment then proves a fatal thing for the children, for they on their side inevitably develop a corresponding excessive oedipus complex.

The ideal oedipus complex requires a threefold relation. Only children have, typically, a particularly strong oedipus complex, because there is no one to whom they can transfer their feelings from the parents. "Special forms" of the complex arise when there are too few or too many persons involved. Thus from the point of view of the oedipus complex the child brought up in modern family life feels its *brothers and sisters* to be superfluous. They are, above all, objects of jealousy, and, according to the individual circumstances, they may either increase the hatred directed in the oedipus complex against one parent or they may deflect it and so diminish it. But the brothers and sisters may also be love objects and so serve for the transference of love. This is specially the case with those who are older or not more than a year younger than the child himself, so that he has never known what the world is like without them. Often, when there are several elder brothers or sisters, we find a "double" of the oedipus complex, and then there occur processes analogous to those which have reference to the parents, sometimes forming a useful outlet but sometimes giving rise to new conflicts. Younger brothers and sisters are generally viewed principally as rivals, but, in certain circumstances, especially if the difference in age is considerable, the child may regard them as his own children. It will then depend on the rest of the oedipus situation whether the complex receives additional stimulation or whether its intensity is decreased by its imaginary gratification. We find the opposite side of the picture—the oedipus complex with too few protagonists—where children grow up without parents or with only a father or a mother. We will consider later the case of children not brought up in a family. Here we will deal rather with the cases in which one parent has died early or left the family circle. Of course, it makes the greatest possible difference here whether the children have or have not known the missing parent, whether there are step-parents, when these appear on the scene, and how they behave. But even when a child has never known the missing parent, he does know that that parent once existed and that other children grow up differently, that is, with both a father and a mother. He then tends to regard himself as an "exception," to whom fate owes some special compensations, and this in itself may act as a reinforcement of the oedipus complex. In general one may say that when the parent of the child's own sex dies, this is perceived as a fulfillment of the oedipus wish and specially strong feelings of guilt are therefore aroused. If the other parent dies, the oedipus longing which remains unsatisfied leads to the fantastic idealization of the dead parent and to an increase of the longing. The rest depends upon when and how the parent's death becomes known to the child. There are two points which I think are very fateful in this connection. First, we find a very close and almost indissoluble connection between the ideas of "sexuality" and "death," for they are found together through their common sphere, that of the "grown-ups' secret." The result is a strengthening of the masochistic tendencies, for, if sexual gratification is thought of as associated with dying, death itself becomes a thing longed for. Or, on the other hand, most intense sexual anxiety may be aroused, for in the unconscious the subject has the conviction that gratification involves death. This anxiety then produces a repression of sexuality, which has most far-reaching effects. Secondly, in his grief for the dead, man commonly regresses in some measure to the oral level of libidinal organization and identifies himself with the dead love object as a form of consolation for the loss. If this happens at an early age, fixations will result which will be profoundly significant for the oedipus complex and the subject's whole life. In this way the child acquires not only an oral fixation but also the tendency to mingle a considerable amount of identification with all his subsequent object relations, including the oedipus complex. Thus, for instance, a patient who had lived happily with a man for years refused to marry him, though she could give no reason for the refusal. Analysis revealed that "marriage" signified to her "having children," and that she had a strong unconscious dread of pregnancy and parturition. Her mother had died when the patient was four years old; the child had at that time developed the fantasy that her mother's death was connected with sexuality or birth and now, as a punishment for the gratification of her oedipus wishes which she had experienced on her mother's death, she anticipated that she herself would have to die in a similar fashion. Something very analogous was observable in the case of a male patient whose castration anxiety had prematurely driven him over to the feminine attitude. On his mother's death he developed the most intense dread of castration and death, which manifested itself later in hypochondriacal ideas. The unconscious content of his hypochondria was as follows: "I must die like my mother because I have put myself in her place. If my father gratified my wishes and made me pregnant, as he did my mother, I should have to die." Here the analysis showed very clearly the marked condensation of the sexual mystery and the mystery of death, which imparted a special tinge to the castration anxiety, leading to a dread of "being gone" and to the unconscious equating of all that may vanish away—corpses, feces, the penis.

To this must be added that the death of the parents represents a peculiar fulfillment of the oedipus complex: directly, if it is the hated parent who dies; indirectly, through idealization, if it is the loved parent. This enhances the intensity of the oedipus complex and reinforces the subject's defense (his feelings of guilt). Thus one of my patients, who had also, when she was five years old, lost her mother, told me that, though she was usually a subdued child, inclined to depression, there was one summer when she had been really happy. It was only analysis which, to her great surprise, revealed to her the fact that it was the summer immediately following her mother's death: for that period she had felt that her wishes were fulfilled and that she was succeeding to her mother's place. These expectations were doomed to disappointment, when she perceived that the grown-ups, and especially her father, continued after all to treat her as a child. Her reaction to this disappointment was inevitably an oral-sadistic one, for it was precisely this mode of reaction which had also been activated by her mother's death.

A boy who has lost his father (or whose father is a cipher in the family) easily becomes homosexual or feminine in his attitude. This is because he identifies himself more with the parent at whose hands he experiences the chief frustrations in his life. One patient, who had never known her father, was sadistic in all her relations with men, her behavior conforming to the extreme "revenge" type of the feminine castration complex. Her fantastic oedipus complex, never corrected by any actuality, impelled her in the first place to hate all men, because none of them was as her father, whose death had made him godlike; and, secondly, over and above this, the impossibility of satisfying one half of the oedipus complex caused the other half to develop to all the more grotesque proportions. Unconsciously she hated her mother fiercely for having enjoyed the father's love and yet having let him die, and so depriving her both of her father himself and of the penis. This very intense hatred meant for her mother she had likewise transferred to all men. Another patient who suffered from acute depression and general inhibitions had the following early history: When she was only about a year old, her parents had separated and she had never seen her father again. She thereupon developed the following oedipus fantasy: "My father could not endure life with my mother: she was not worthy of him, but one day he will come and take me away with him." He did not come. This gave rise to a tremendous reactive hatred which, in her state of depression, the patient turned against herself with the following unconscious rationalization: "I too am entirely worthless and unworthy of him. That is why he does not come."

It is obvious that conflicts between the parents and their temporary or permanent separation must have a similar effect on a child to that of their death. If the children themselves are the bone of contention and each parent tries to win them over, the result is likely to be a special accentuation of the complete oedipus complex and a fixation at the infantile narcissistic level, which causes them to believe that the whole world will woo them as their parents have done. Expectations of this sort inevitably lead to disappointment.

We have said that, if the parent's character or behavior is unusual, the child's reaction will be unusual. "Unusual behavior" is to be interpreted as spoiling a child, or frustrating its desires, or a combination of the two. Spoiling and frustration are in one sense complementary, for it is just the spoiled children who are bound to be traumatically affected by those indispensable frustrations which are otherwise easy to endure. We are least concerned here with deliberately adopted methods of discipline and most with the involuntary, everyday, real behavior of the parents. Two points should be noted as specially important. The first is the parents' attitude towards the child's sex: very often a mother only desires a son and lets her daughter feel it, and so forth. And the second is the parents' attitude to one another, for this is the source of the child's ideas of sexuality. We have only to think of unhappy marriages and their effect on the instinctual life of the child.

The whole "moral code" of the house, then, influences the form of the oedipus complex. The extent to which a child regards his instincts as permissible or as something fatally "bad" depends not only on whether, when, and how he is forbidden, for example, to practice onanism, but ever more on the type and force of the *general standard of sexual morality* which prevails in his home. Knowingly or unknowingly, on principle or by chance, his parents in all that they say and do testify to his standard. The idea thus inculcated that "instincts are bad" has the same effect as the continual prohibition of onanism, and, since infantile onanism is the active expression of the oedipus complex, the result is to intensify the tendency to repress that complex. The most important combination of spoiling and frustration—one which is very common—is an enhancement of excitation in children by excessive tenderness on the parent's part, with simultaneous prevention of gratification, i.e., the appropriate discharge of this excitation, by prohibitions. I have already said that in such cases the parents' own unconscious oedipus complex is the determining factor in what takes place. Very often mothers say to their sons and fathers to their daughters, "in fun," that they do not want them to marry, because they want to be always with them, etc., etc. In the anamnesia of psychoses we sometimes meet with the most extreme forms of the "parents' oedipus complex."

These observations do not apply to the genital field only. We have seen that there is a pregenital foreshadowing of the oedipus complex and that the methods by which children are weaned and trained in habits of cleanliness leave their mark and help to determine from the outset the form which that complex will take. This is a very difficult matter to elucidate in analysis because everything which is the result of regressive distortion has to be eliminated from the blend of oedipus complex and pregenital impulses presented by the material which comes to the surface. I have tried to sum up a few contributions to this topic in a short paper, "Pregenital Antecedents of the Oedipus Complex." [3] From the point of view of clinical practice and the study of character I think that the "oral-sadistic" form of the oedipus complex is of special importance. Here the demand for gratification from the parent of the opposite sex may be expressed as follows: "You *must* give it to me or else I will take it by force." By "it" is understood (in the different strata of the unconscious): gratification, a child, the penis, feces, milk. Whether this form of the oedipus complex will develop depends on the child's experiences during his training in cleanliness and when he is at the mother's breast. In my paper I was able to give a detailed account of the case of a man who, as an infant, had had eighteen months of complete oral indulgence and then suddenly underwent the most drastic frustration. The result was a negative oedipus complex, characterized by sadistic demands. The patient had no profession but lived the life of a passionate gambler, unconsciously governed by the one idea directed toward his father: "You must give me all your money." In another case a girl had to be weaned because her mother contracted mastitis and this experience acted on her traumatically. Subsequently her mother evinced much libidinal interest in the child's training in cleanliness. At the age of three she fell ill with an intestinal trouble. She reacted with the fantasy that her mother had made her ill by taking "it" (i.e., feces—the penis) away from her. Later, in the oedipus complex, the fantasy went on that her father must give back what had been taken away. In the face of the ascetic character of the father, whose ideal was, above all things, self-control, she maintained her unconscious

[3] O. Fenichel, "The Pregenital Antecedents of the Oedipus Complex," No. 21 in this volume.

demands with an unbridled passionateness, which, for example, expressed itself at times in a kind of pseudo-nymphomania.

The character of the parents is, however, also regularly reflected in the children's oedipus complex in forms less obvious than those I have mentioned. To take a simple example, the father of one of my women patients had a contempt for all women and frequently reiterated his feeling. He laid great stress on "modesty" and demanded that all anal impulses should be repressed. He showed a marked preference for the patient's elder sister. The patient was then as a child confronted with the following tasks: She loved her father, but she had to eliminate loving the penis, for it marked the difference in sex which made him despise women. She also had to suppress her constitutionally strong anal erotism. She wanted to do her sister an injury and she had to endure her father's severity and contempt. She solved the problem by becoming a masochist, whose sexual aim (of course, unconscious) in accordance with the oedipus complex, was to be beaten and despised by her father. Thus the contempt which jeopardized her father's love for her actually became a condition of that love; the offensive penis was replaced by the hand which struck the blows and the offensive anus by the buttocks. Moreover, her hatred of her sister thus found a vent also, for, at bottom, the imaginary whippings were destined for her and had only later been turned against the subject's own ego (herself). With many people we are struck by the fact that their love relations always have the remarkable characteristic of "dread of the community" focused in the love object. What such persons want above anything else from those whom they love is judgment, forgiveness, and, in some circumstances, also criticism, condemnation, and punishment. Analysis then shows that this curious, narcissistic kind of love has had its origin in the oedipus complex which has assumed this pathological form owing to pathological behavior on the parents' part. That is to say, the parents brought the child up very strictly, in a way which fixated him upon the ideas of guilt, punishment, and forgiveness, which were continually being thrust into the foreground, while at the same time forbidding all direct expression of instinct. Nothing was thus left for the trammelled impulse to do but to effect cathexis of the only sphere left open to it. At the same time the training in question, by its inconsistencies, brought the child to the point of forming no independent judgment of what was good or bad but allowing the love objects of the period to decide this as a mode of sexual gratification. Let me quote as a last illustration of this point an example which is trivial indeed, but all the more obvious. The father of a patient with a very strong father-fixation one day sent the following telegram to his forty-year-old son, then more than 400 km. away and recovering from an attack of angina: "In view uncertainty weather, don't go out today."

It will have been noted that we have as yet said nothing about the significance for special forms of the oedipus complex of what is probably the most important feature in the child's real experience in the world of today, viz. the *social status of the parents*. We must now repair this omission. Analysis of the most common fantasies of children on the subject of social position shows that in the unconscious the socially humble is equated with the instinctual, the socially superior with the inhibited or sublimated. Recently Helene Deutsch has demonstrated this fact anew and very clearly in her analysis of the so-called "family romance." [4] When a member of a family of high social standing feels himself especially attracted to the lower classes, analysis generally reveals a tendency towards the purely instinctual, as, for instance, in the preference of a prostitute in contrast to a love object of good position. The mechanism is that of idealization: "I help my fellows; I am not so unjust as my father; I sublimate my sexuality into love of humanity." But all such reflections on these or similar unconscious equivalents of class distinctions as revealed by analysis do not help *in the least* to answer our question: what is the effect of real social status on the real oedipus complex? We are not considering unconscious *fantasies* about social position but the influence of that position *in reality*. This influence is incessantly brought to bear upon the child and must therefore prove significant for the shaping of the oedipus complex just as much as the character of the parents. That this happens was shown by Freud in his famous example: "On the Ground-Floor and in the Mansion" in his *A General Introduction to Psychoanalysis*.[5] We have only to think of the bearing of the housing shortage on the "primal scene" to realize instantly how important this factor is. Bernfeld [6] has shown that certain modes of mental development can occur only under the conditions provided in a given social stratum. For instance, it is only in a certain "social region" that it is possible to escape from depressive states or the dangers of loss of love by simply running away. Yet, having said all this, we must admit that according to analytic experience the part which this important circumstance of the family's social status plays in giving to the oedipus complex its specific form is less than might be anticipated. What is the explanation? Is it perhaps that, so far, psychoanalysts have drawn their material too much from one social stratum only? Or is it not rather that in our modern society middle-class morality and middle-class principles or the training of children prevail as much in the homes of the proletariat as in those of the middle classes themselves? In my opinion this fact renders it impossible in the society of today to make any pronouncement as to what would be the relation between training and instinctual development in the absence of

---

[4] H. Deutsch, "Zur Genese des 'Familienromans,'" *Int. Z. Psa.*, Vol. 16, 1930.

[5] S. Freud, *A General Introduction to Psychoanalysis*, New York, Liveright, 1935, 1948, p. 305.

[6] S. Bernfeld, "Der soziale Ort und seine Bedeutung fuer Neurose, Verwahrlosung und Paedagogik," *Imago*, Vol. 15, 1929.

the middle-class code of morality which dominates the former, even if we select for our investigations persons belonging exclusively to the proletariat.

The position is somewhat analogous when we turn to the problem of the oedipus complex in children who are not brought up in any family. For none of these children really live entirely without any family influence. Sooner or later they learn that the institution of the family exists and wherein it consists: that other children have a father and mother, and that they themselves are the inferior exceptions. They too have their oedipus complex, i.e. not only instinctual attachments of love and hate to those who bring them up and to all grown-up people with whom they come into contact, but also fantasies about father and mother—fantasies which closely resemble the oedipus complex of other children, only drawing a special form from their fantastic character. Their oedipus complex is characterized by the discrepancy between fantasy and reality, though of course the fantasies draw sustenance from real experiences. In so far as they have been analyzed, we may say of them that the same applies to them, in a double way, as we found true in the case of children who have not known one parent. If they do not grow up in a situation, e.g. within a community, which still allows of their forming firm attachments, but are constantly moving from place to place and being exposed every year to fresh influences and brought into contact with new people, two results will follow. First, their characters will become full of contradictions (asocial types with superego aberrations always present this sort of anamnesis) but to go into this aspect of the question would take us too far. Secondly, they have never rightly learned to love and to hate: their oedipus complex is fantasy and the reality is an infantile-narcissistic form of object relations, which is governed by identifications and their accompanying conflicts and dread of the community instead of by love and hate. In a permanent community, on the other hand, there is always somebody to play the part of father or mother, but of course, even so, the difference between being brought up in such a community and being brought up by the child's own father and mother will be reflected in the oedipus complex.

There is, then, no doubt that the specific forms which that complex assumes depend on individual experience. But what of the frame of the picture? Is the oedipus complex itself—the fact of love and jealous hatred of the parents—a biological datum, as a physical organ like the nose or the thymus gland is a biological datum? Or is it not ultimately also a product of experience, arising out of the institution of family upbringing, and, as such, changeable? Put thus, the question is intrinsically absurd; for, if we believe in the theory of evolution, it follows that the complex *must* be variable, since then the nose too, like all characteristics of species, is changeable. It is true that according to the theory of evolution it is not individual but phylogenetic experience which counts. There are many points about the oedipus complex, in especial its close connection with archaic modes of thought and with the idea of castration, which indicate that it too has its phylogenetic roots. Freud supposes that it was acquired at the period when all human society took the form of the horde, the precursor of the family. We may join in Freud's suppositions without committing ourselves to an opinion whether this patriarchal horde must be regarded as the first or as a later form of human organization. In any case, to assume that the oedipus complex has this phylogenetic root is by no means to contradict the notion that the complex itself is bound to change when the institution of the family disappears or changes. This is really quite obvious and what we have found as regards the specific forms of the complex forces such a view upon us. If there are no parents to bring children up they will indeed still feel love and hate for the adults round them and conflicts will still result. But this phenomenon can only be called the oedipus complex so long as it is accompanied by the parent fantasy and so long as love and jealous hatred are combined as they inevitably are in the family situation. That a different *milieu* calls for the different reactions and that all the phenomena of life are in flux is an obvious inference from the Darwinian theory, but of course we must not suppose that such modifications are very rapid.

## TWENTY-THREE

# Respiratory Introjection*

FREUD has demonstrated that identification with an object of the external world, which plays an essential role not only in the pathogenesis of depression, but also in the character formation of normal people, particularly in the establishment of the superego, is conceived of as an oral incorporation.[1] This finding has since been confirmed in various clinical and ethnological studies. The pregenital basis of identification, the circumstance that unconsciously it is actually thought of as a devouring of the object—a view which sounds so unbelievable to those unfamiliar with psychoanalysis—has been proved with certitude in depth-analysis. Before man could love, he wanted to "incorporate" objects either "totally" or "partially." [2] Identifications are the traces of this just as his castration anxiety too rests on a pregenital foundation. But Abraham [3] has demonstrated that there exist other ideas of incorporation besides oral ones, though certainly these are of much less general importance, being of a more passing character, and less evidenced in fantasies and identifications. There is an anal one, which manifests itself, for instance, in the paranoid's equating of persecutor and feces, the infantile prototype of which is the enema; [4] there is an epidermal one, which corresponds to infantile smearing of feces; finally a respiratory one is suggested by an episode in the history of the Wolf Man: [5] the patient, whenever he saw a cripple, had to exhale forcibly, in order not to become like him.[6] Since

---

* First published in *Int. Z. Psa.*, Vol. 17, 1931, pp. 234–255.

[1] S. Freud, "Mourning and Melancholia," *Coll. Pap.*, Vol. IV, London, Hogarth, 1948; *The Ego and the Id*, London, Hogarth, 1947.

[2] K. Abraham, "A Short Study of the Development of the Libido, Viewed in the Light of Mental Disorders," *Selected Papers*, London, Hogarth, 1948.

[3] *Ibid.*

[4] J. H. Ophuijsen, "On the Origin of the Feeling of Persecution," *Int. J. Psa.*, Vol. 1, 1920; A. Staercke, "The Reversal of the Libido Sign in Delusions of Persecution," *Int. J. Psa.*, Vol. 1, 1920.

[5] S. Freud, "From the History of an Infantile Neurosis," *Coll. Pap.*, Vol. III, London, Hogarth, 1948.

[6] *Ibid.*, p. 542.

he thus exhaled objects, he must have previously incorporated them by inhaling.

It is a commonplace in psychoanalysis that one must not immediately tackle the oedipus complex in interpreting a symptom. The intermediary material which is interpolated between the oedipus complex and the symptom is indispensable for actually penetrating to the oedipus complex. What holds for analytic procedure holds in a certain sense for analytic theory also. An example of this is, for instance, the studies of Daly.[7] Fear of menstruation is certainly something intermediary in relation to fear of castration; but the theoretical importance of emphasizing this intermediary factor is clear. Similarly, respiratory introjection is an intermediary factor in comparison to oral introjection; nevertheless, it will be worth while to make it for once the subject matter of a special study.

The various introjective fantasies become eminently understandable if we consider that identifications are but residues of, or regressions to, pregenital object relations. Incorporation is the object relation of pregenitality. *All* pregenital erotogenic zones, therefore—in so far as the sensations arising from them are not merely autoerotic, but are directed to objects—must be a point of departure for fantasies of incorporation. For this reason, oral, anal, and epidermal erotism has its counterpart in oral, anal, and epidermal introjection. According to Freud, even *perceptions* are, to begin with, related to introjection. The pleasure-ego's tendency to perceive only what is pleasant, and to hallucinate negatively what is unpleasant, also corresponds to a selective incorporation of the external world.[8] Eyes and ears too are known to be fantasied as sexual organs which take in objects; but they are obviously less suitable than the *nose* for the idea of permanent introjection which underlies identifications. We have to keep in mind that with the olfactory sense an incorporation of the world of objects occurs materially too. Nasal introjection corresponds to respiratory erotism, as does oral introjection to oral erotism.

Is there such a thing as a respiratory erotism? Certainly. The function of breathing has heretofore been treated by psychoanalysis in a rather stepmotherly way, and this is due to the fact that its erotogenicity appears in such close connection with oral and anal erotism, which immediately attract attention to themselves in the analysis, for instance, of bronchial asthma, or breathing compulsion. But indications are not wanting that the respiratory tract too has an autonomous erotogenicity, and no unimportant one at that. We shall have to enter into a further discussion of this later on, but we will in the main limit ourselves to the problem of introjection. The treatment of this question, how-

---

[7] C. D. Daly, "Hindu-Mythologie und Kastrationskomplex," *Imago*, Vol. 13, 1927; "Der Menstruationskomplex," *Imago*, Vol. 14, 1928.

[8] S. Freud, "Instincts and Their Vicissitudes," *Coll. Pap.*, Vol. IV.

ever, will bring to light its intimate confluence with other pregenital erotisms—of orality, anality, and epidermality.

I have not been able to confirm—perhaps for lack of appropriate cases—Abraham's surmise that *oral* introjection always corresponds to *total* incorporation, while other introjections correspond to *partial* incorporation.[9] In such obscure strata of the mind my material scarcely permitted of a clear differentiation between total and partial incorporation. No distinction was made between the whole object and its penis as instinctual objects. Theoretically, however, Abraham's view is plausible: the anal stage of libido organization is a later formation than the oral one, and similarly partial incorporation is later than total incorporation; thus they fit together better temporally. Respiratory introjection stands between the two. The upper respiratory pathways are naturally closely related to the mouth, but the idea of olfactory reception ties it closely to anal erotism. Olfactory reception and inhaling are not distinguished in the unconscious.

I should now like to put off any further discussion of theory till the end, and present some clinical material. This material comes from two cases. The first was very thoroughly analyzed. A study of it will give the second, less deeply analyzed case evidential value as well.

The first case is the one I described in detail in my study "The Psychology of Transvestitism." [10] There I wrote in a footnote: "Deeper analysis of the narcissistic mental strata finally revealed that the identification with his dead mother (her 'spirit') was performed by means of introjection (inhaling) and that in the unconscious the introjected mother was equated with his own penis. Thus we arrived at the following symbolic equation: patient in women's clothes = the mother with a penis = the penis in general. We recollect the similarity between the girl's name by which he so much wished to be called and his pet name for the penis." * Now I want to document this footnote and to comment on it.

I will first recall in brief the salient material of this case history. The patient had originally a very sadistic, attacking attitude toward an older sister by whom he was sexually seduced at an early age. This attitude disappeared after he discovered that she had no penis, for which he felt responsible because of his unconscious wishes. His object relation to her was replaced by an identification in which, in order to lessen his feelings of guilt, he enacted the part of the penis-possessing sister, amid extreme castration anxiety, and sought to be loved in this role by his stepmother. On a deeper level of the mind, however,

[9] K. Abraham, *op. cit.*
[10] O. Fenichel, "The Psychology of Transvestitism," No. 20 in this volume.
* See pp. 174–175.—Trans. note.

he was not only the phallic sister, but also the phallic mother, and his object was not only the stepmother but the father. His own mother had died early. He reproached his father for his having taken as her substitute not himself (the patient) but the stepmother. Unconsciously, he was at war with his stepmother over whether the "mana" of his dead mother had passed on to her or to him.

Now I must add that the patient suffered mainly from hypochondria and came into analysis because of that. After every sexual experience he had to go to a doctor to obtain absolution by being declared well. He was particularly afraid of sepsis, apoplexy, and infectious diseases. Sepsis and apoplexy proved to be castration symbols; for his father had warned him against these just as strongly as he had against the dangerousness of his attacks upon his sister. His fear of infection was a fear of poisoning, which he equated to impregnation by his father and which would have to be fatal since he assumed unconsciously that his mother had died from a pregnancy.

Now, it had long been noticeable that the infection which the patient feared was always an inflammation of the throat or pneumonia; and he expected the sepsis to start at these points. He frequently went to specialists to have his throat and lungs examined. He also managed to acquire a chronic pharyngitis through clearing his throat in a special way, and this constantly brought him to the throat specialist. It was easy to demonstrate in the analysis that the throat and the feminine genitals were equated. The infantile prototype for his throat-anxiety was a severe attack of diphtheria which he had had as a child at about the same time at which he discovered in the bathtub that his sister had no penis; thus he was easily able to displace his castration anxiety to the throat. Yet this did not suffice to explain the outstanding role played by the respiratory tract in his symptoms, and one began to think of a somatic compliance—until the analytic picture changed, and in the worst part of his treatment there arose an immense *anxiety centered around the nose.* He began to behave exactly as the Wolf Man did in his second illness, as described by Mack-Brunswick.[11] Throughout the day he was concerned exclusively with worrying about his nose; he looked continuously in the mirror to see whether sepsis of the nose had already declared itself; he had all kinds of painful sensations inside the nose, which incited him to bore in it continuously, for which in turn he reproached himself violently. When he thought he had damaged himself by boring in his nose, he smeared immense amounts of vaseline into it, or washed it out with alcohol, so that his defense against the supposed damage really did endanger the nose. Then, filled with anxiety lest he had actually damaged it with his attempts at cure, he began

[11] R. Mack Brunswick, "A Supplement to Freud's 'History of an Infantile Neurosis,' " *Int. J. Psa.,* Vol. 9, 1928.

again to bore into it so as to eliminate the vaseline and alcohol, thus creating a vicious circle of boring and smearing. Or else he tried to powder his nose and inhaled some powder, and then he began seriously to worry about pneumonia; and so on.

The exclusiveness with which the patient at this time lived solely for his nose-hypochondria left no doubt of its narcissistic nature. The way he concerned himself with his nose and talked about it was exactly like the way he concerned himself with his wife and children and talked about them under the influence of his neurotic reaction formations. Thus the suspicion arose that his relation to his nose was a narcissistic-regressive expression of an old object relation. It had already become clear that the anxiety about the nose was a displaced castration anxiety, for his symptoms were very unambiguous in this respect, and in this it became evident that, as being an organ with a cavity, the nose, which is generally known as a penis symbol, also had a female significance.

Before our suspicion that the nose represented an external object could be confirmed, we succeeded in substantiating further its genital symbolic meaning. Childhood memories showed that the infantile predecessor of the nose-hypochondria was a *penis*-hypochondria. The patient remembered that he had been anxiously and tenderly concerned about his penis, and the pet name already mentioned which he had for it spoke for this also. A screen memory that he was pulling a hair out of his penis could be transformed into the meaning that he had a bandage on his genital region and was pulling at that. This pointed to a particular castration experience, for which the diphtheria was only a cover. Thus there was no doubt about the equation nose = penis; but both were treated by him like ambivalently cathected objects about whom one is concerned (wife and children), which are not a part of the self. Besides the hypochondria, the main symptom of his neurosis was excessive worry about his wife. The continuation of the equation nose = penis by nose = penis = wife seemed improbable, but was nevertheless confirmed by two circumstances: [12]

(1) By his deep-reaching identification with his wife. Not only did he put on her clothes in his transvestite doings: he always felt unwell when she menstruated.

(2) His pet name for the penis was similar not only to the feminine name which he longed for, but also to the name of his dead mother, as later analysis showed. Thus the equation: nose = penis = introjected mother was proved.

[12] The unconscious equating of a hypochondriacally afflicted or somatically diseased organ with an introjected object has been described by Simmel in various places. Thus he wrote: "The introjected parent-substitute became the substance which caused disease and which must be ejected in order that the patient might recover," and he speaks also of the possibility that a single organ may represent this substance—E. Simmel, "The 'Doctor-Game,' Illness and the Profession of Medicine," *Int. J. Psa.,* Vol. 7, 1926, p. 477.

This equation was the basis of his transvestitism, in which he acted the part of both mother and penis simultaneously.

But how did the dead mother get into his body, into the penis, and why was the penis replaced precisely by the nose? At the time of his hypochondria, the patient's wife called his attention to the fact that the wallpaper beside his bed was always smeared with vaseline in the morning. While asleep the patient bored into his nose, into which he had put the grease, and then smeared the grease onto the wall. In this symbolic activity, the anal and feminine meaning of the nose became clear. We interpreted this as follows: at the present day the patient first smears something into his nose, then while he is asleep he puts his finger to his nose once more to get that something out again, and then touches the wall; as a child, he first put his finger into his anus, then carried it to his nose to smell, and then onto the wall. His symptom disappeared, and we gained the impression that the *introjection of the mother must have had something to do with smelling and smearing of feces.*

About this we already had some material. The characteristic form of the patient's castration anxiety was that of "being gone." He was afraid that when his wife left the house she might not return, that she might simply disappear, be gone. When she went on a trip, he fantasied how the friends who came to fetch her at the train did not find her. Thus what he imagined was always only her mysteriously "being gone," never that something might happen to her. This was due to the indivisible condensation that had occurred in his childhood between the secret of his mother's death and that of sexuality. His fear was that his penis might be gone one day, just as his dead mother was. Since it was in the bath that he discovered his sister's lack of a penis, that place naturally became a place of anxiety for him. He was afraid that he might be carried down with the water from the bathtub into the underworld, and be gone. This idea was naturally influenced by his observation of the feces being flushed away by the water in the toilet. Gradually a lot of material came up about how, as a child at the seaside, he had watched with horror the beetles that seemed to disappear in the sand, and, finally, how he had observed girls urinating there and had been amazed that the urine should disappear into the sand and then simply be gone. All this pointed to the equation: corpse = feces = penis = things which disappear. Thus the idea "feces" was the mediating link between the ideas "dead mother" and "penis." The unconscious idea "my mother is inside me" appeared thus to be condensed with "I have taken feces into myself." [13] ("My mother is

---

[13] The unconscious equation of introjected object = feces has been repeatedly proved in psychoses as well as in ethnological material. See K. Abraham, *op. cit.;* also E. Simmel, *op. cit.;* and G. Roheim, "Nach dem Tode des Urvaters," *Imago,* Vol. 9, 1923.

inside me" was, by the way, condensed with "I am inside my mother"; and numerous uterine fantasies ran through the whole neurosis.)

The interpretation was therefore made that an idea approximately of this sort must be active in the patient: "I have smelled feces and thereby my mother has got into my nose." The first corroborations of this were ideas which the patient had about his mother's soul or spirit, conceived of as breath, which he had inhaled = smelled.

That identification with the mother is *dangerous,* threatening death and castration, has already been discussed in my study of transvestitism. Thus fantasies about "fatal smells or breath" should corroborate our interpretation. I may therefore begin the series of dreams which I now want to present, with one about dangerous anal aggressions, pointing to smell and breath:

*I am filling a cannon from above with jam. In doing so I dirty the rim. This brings danger of explosion or from gas. Then a lid is screwed on.*

Three residues of the day make this dream comprehensible. First, a discussion about a special cooking pot,* the lid of which could be screwed on, and which was considered as carrying with it the danger of explosion; next, the patient's having accidentally dirtied the toilet and his anxiety and shame about it lest he should be detected as the author of the deed; and lastly, his compulsive uncertainty before going to sleep whether or not the gas jet was shut off, and his fear of being gassed to death in his sleep.

According to his latent dream thought, then, feces could kill by developing gases. Since he had thought of buying this dangerous cooking pot for his wife, it is she who is the object of his anal desire to kill. Conversely, he was afraid that his wife would kill him for this. The screwing on and off reveal that ideas of castration are once more added to and condensed with his ideas of death. The main thought of the dream thus is: "I would like to kill my sister or mother, and I am afraid that I will be killed or castrated for it." What is important for us, however, is the manner of execution of this killing. He who inhales the gases of another person, or smells his feces, dies of it. Various symptoms spoke of the same fear of killing somebody by means of feces, or of being killed by somebody (by his father who cohabits with him as a woman) by means of them (as, for example, through infection).

In a second dream, the same *motif* is linked to that of identification, so that the symbolic equation: woman = nose = feces = penis = child becomes very clear. The dream is this:

*I see a child who is squashed flat.*

On the preceding day, the patient had lain down on the couch beside one of

* A pressure cooker.

his children, and had been told jokingly that he would squash it to death. I had called his attention in the same way to the instinctual roots of his pedagogical measures, and thus I too had warned him that he might harm his children. He recognized in the object which was squashed flat the dry scabs he had scratched out of his nose on the previous day and which had scared him very much because he considered them a sign of severe illness. Thus, the thoughts "I have damaged my child" and "I have damaged my nose" are condensed. An association about the story of Max and Moritz who were baked flat in the baker's oven, showed the castration idea that lay behind this. The following castration memory out of his childhood fits in with this. He had an anxiety attack when children touched the screen at a magic-lantern performance; he was afraid that their fingers might march away with the soldiers that were being projected onto the screen—that the children might be too severely punished for their thoughtless grasping. Already, then, it was a problem for him to distinguish, in what he saw, between what was corporeal (the fingers) and what was only picture, that is, "squashed flat" (the soldiers). The antecedent cause of this anxiety was his discovery, which had occurred shortly before, that his sister, on whose lap he was sitting during this performance just as he used to do in his sexual games with her, had no penis. Thus the meaning of the dream is: "I want to castrate my sister with my sexual attacks, and I am afraid that I myself will be castrated for that." In this, however, his sister is condensed not only with his own children, but also with his penis (the touching and disappearing finger) and his nose, which he had damaged by boring in it, and furthermore with his feces = the scabs out of his nose. The thing which is squashed flat is sister, feces, nose, and penis in one. It was no accident that after this dream it occurred to the patient that during his diphtheria an inhaling apparatus was used and that this was both pleasurable and anxiety-arousing, because the inhaling apparatus reminded him too much of the magic lantern, which could thus not only make fingers flat but also send out gases.

This kind of material again centered attention upon the patient's enormous pleasure in smelling. Not only had he as a child sniffed everything, distinguishing things by their odor; his whole transvestitism had begun with his perceiving on his sister's clothing the exciting smell of her body. After the analysis had shaken the unconscious foundations of his transvestitism, he regressed to the origins of this symptom: he no longer put on feminine underclothes, but held them to his nose to smell at them and masturbated while doing so. Smelling and inhaling feminine odors thus replaced dressing in feminine clothes. Just as the latter had proved to be a condensation of an object-libidinal act (clothes = woman) with an identificatory act, so was the smell-masturbation both a sexual act with the feminine smell and an identification—a becoming a woman by taking in the feminine smell. In this we found that the idea of the fecal smell (feces = corpse) was more superficial than that of the vaginal and particularly the menstrual smell.

One dream ran as follows:

*Somebody has died. There is a smell of corpses.*

Before going to sleep, the patient masturbated in the described way, with a piece of lingerie of his wife's. Thus, it is his wife who has died. Through smelling he kills the corpse magically and takes it into himself. The counterpart of this fantasy is again the fear of being poisoned by smells. A phobia of rancid butter which he had belongs to this. He could eat only the freshest butter, bought in the best store. If we now remember how after transvestite acts he had to tear off the clothes as fast as he could, in order "that they shouldn't stick," then we understand here that if by smelling the woman he kills her and breathes her in, then the talion punishment awaiting him is that he himself, having become a woman, will die of a smell- and gas-poisoning. By inhaling, he takes into himself the feminine "mana" and becomes himself a woman. That the terrible danger which threatens him as a woman is once again castration is shown by the fact that he thinks of femaleness as blood, and female smells as menstrual smell. The patient, who cannot bear to see blood, admitted that he very much liked to smell it, indeed that he was always glad when he had scratched the inside of his nose till it bled, because then there was such a fine smell of blood. This confirms our conception of the bisexual nature of the nose, which represents not only the penis, but also the bleeding female genital, deprived of the penis. The patient's nose-hypochondria was a real castration anxiety—was a fear that his smelling and masturbating might make his penis a bleeding organ. Clearly, the smell of feces was in part already a regressive substitute for the smell of blood which he had certainly perceived with sexual excitement when sleeping in his step-mother's bed, but which, noticing her lack of penis, he had repressed and re-placed by the smell of feces. This might have been what occasioned him, *via* the equation feces = penis, to substitute for the real stepmother the dead mother, and with it to replace object love by identification and heterosexuality by homo-sexuality. This, however, did not become clear. What was certain was that incorporation of the woman by smell was a dangerous business which might result in one's becoming a woman and thus losing one's penis like one's step-mother or sister, or dying like one's mother.

A dream which followed later on reads:

*My youngest child is endangered by an inhaling apparatus.*

Day residue: That night, as an exception, the patient had slept in the same room with this child. The previous day he had been afraid that his children might be infected by a strange child with a cough. We know already that as a child he had both loved and feared the inhalation apparatus. An aunt, his father's sister, had died of tuberculosis when the patient was a small child, and when the patient's sister coughed, his father would say, "Oh, she will die, like my sister." Thus, once again, we have death wishes against his children and sister, talion anxiety about himself, danger of death represented by inhaling, and the cause of death as a respiratory illness.

Thus we find side by side, or rather layered over each other, the following ideas:

(1) I want to castrate and kill my wife (sister) by gas (doubtless to take her place) and therefore she will kill me, by means of smell;

(2) smelling of the female odor is a sexual pleasure, but it is attended by the danger of castration, for it makes one into a woman;

(3) to smell the female odor is to incorporate the female corpse, and is the prerequisite for the sexual pleasure which my father is to give to me as a woman—and that brings with it the danger of castration.

This third stratum—without doubt the deepest—becomes particularly clear in a series of dreams which may be entitled "the struggle with the stepmother over the succession to the dead mother." The death of his father, which occurred shortly before the analysis began, gave the patient occasion to reactivate his childhood fantasies pertaining to his mother's death.

Dream: *I left a box belonging to my stepmother somewhere.*

Day residue: His stepmother had left his wife's umbrella somewhere. He now accordingly takes revenge by losing an object that belongs to her. Why a box? His first association was the grave of Frederick the Great in Potsdam; then a joke, in which a coffin is mistaken for a case of cheese and the smell of the corpse with the smell of cheese. Then he thought of quarrels with his stepmother about the inheritance. We may interpret this to mean, "I want to take from my stepmother the corpse, the 'smell,' of my father; it is not she who is his rightful successor, but I." This covers a corresponding train of thought of his childhood: "Not she but I was my mother's successor at that time." In these thoughts rightful succession is represented by the possession of the odor, that is, the spirit, of the dead. But why does the dream replace a real umbrella by a box? This might be due to active castration ideas against the father: he had no penis (umbrella), but a vagina (box); but it certainly belongs more to ideas concerning the death of the mother, whose spirit, as we know, he conceived of as vaginal smell, that is, a smell coming out of a box.

To this is connected a somewhat complicated dream, consideration of which, however, is worth our while.

*A woman is sick in bed with swellings. She reproaches my sister for stealing furs. I myself have a swelling under the eye.*

Both the woman and he have swellings; thus he again equates himself with a woman. To the eye he associates a poster of *Fromm's Act* * and says that during these days, too, he has had particular fear of syphilis. The latent dream thought, then, is: "I and the woman have a primary lesion, are castrated." Why "swellings"? He once saw a woman with uremia who had edema under her eyes. He did not know what uremia is, but he thought "something connected with urine." As a child he smelled at the urine of his sister. Thus his thought is: "I (that is, a woman) have been castrated through the smell of urine." Concerning the sick woman, he associates that he read about the island of Finkenwerder, where the women early become widows, because the men are fishermen and die at sea. To fishermen he associates a joking remark made by his wife that when in eructating he put his hand before his mouth, he was fishing for his stomach gases. The widows of Finkenwerder naturally stand for his stepmother after his father's death. "My stepmother and I became ill owing to smells or gases."

Why furs? He had inherited a fur coat from his father; in the dream, his stepmother contests his ownership of the fur coat, as in reality he contested with her about the inheritance. This means, then, "My stepmother and I have become ill through having introjected my dead father by breathing him in." But why did the sister and not he steal the furs? For two reasons: first, as repetition of the unrightful seizure of the dead man by a woman; second, the sister had actually once stolen some china. But there was still some china in the house which was a memento of the first mother. Thus, in deeper strata of the mind, once more, it was not the father but the mother about whom he was thinking, and we may interpret thus: "Why do these women, my stepmother and my sister, take the place of my dead mother, which should be mine? I want to rob them of this place, by inhaling their spirit; but I am afraid that I shall be castrated in so doing and die." Now we also understand his aggressive attitudes and active castration wishes against women, particularly his sister. One component of their psychogenesis (among others) is: "I would like to tear out the penis of these women, inhale away their smell, so as to get possession of my mother's insignia which they have stolen; but as a retaliatory punishment for these thoughts my own respiratory organs and penis become sick."

Before leaving this case material I should like once more to lay emphasis upon the already-mentioned condensation of respiratory introjection with other kinds of introjection. *Epidermal* introjection is indicated in this dream by the fur coat, which, worn on the surface of the body, lets the poison of the father's corpse penetrate through the skin. I should add here that in the patient's unconscious, homosexual intercourse was always perceived as a mutual smearing with feces,

* The trade mark of a well-known make of condom in Germany.—Trans. note.

and the feared infection as a fecal infection transmitted by the skin. Oral intro-jection, too, was pronounced in this case, in spite of the particular emphasis on the respiratory apparatus (for I have expressly brought together only the respira-tory material and neglected the rest). I might add that the oral factor came to expression, for instance, in the patient's idea of having become infected by kissing his dead father, and we have already seen it in his constant longing for fresh butter. Let me give one example of this in one more short dream.

*My sister gave me something bad to eat.*

His sister had actually done so. The tomato soup she had prepared for dinner was wretched, and afterwards she locked herself in her room and would not let him come in. As a child, she was a bed wetter. When the parents spoke about this, he was sent from the room. He had smelled her urine. Thus, in the dream she gave him her urine not only to smell but also to eat. However, it was tomato soup, so it was not only urine, but blood—menstrual blood. Thus in this dream the feminine "mana" was incorporated orally.

In this connection, let me cite from another case the analysis of a single symp-tom. Fear of asphyxiation and breathing ceremonials had already played a great role in the first phase of a young man's complicated compulsion neurosis. The analysis had quickly revealed these symptoms as expressions of castration anxiety, directed against homosexual fantasies, without, however, giving any inkling of a connection with identifications. One day, for instance, the patient had a fantasy that the analyst might "cut off the air" with a pair of scissors, that is to say, might stop an imaginary supply pipe of air, such as divers have, and so let him suffo-cate. This went back to an anxiety originating in his latency, that he might be as-phyxiated under the blankets while asleep. (At that time he used to hide under the blankets when fantasying.) The fantasies, mostly about huge monsters of cosmic dimensions devouring whole worlds, were derivatives of old masturba-tion fantasies, and the hiding under the blankets was a continuation of the pro-hibited early infantile putting-the-hand-under-the-blankets. Thus hidden away, he enjoyed the smell of his own flatus, and this made it possible for him to give his old castration anxiety the form of fear of asphyxiation. The analysis of the symptom which I want to discuss here brought us closer to an understanding of this. The patient began to have a compulsion to imitate the tooting of cars, and when he heard them, to say "toot toot" himself. After a fairly prolonged analy-sis, he finally had the association that the car was a huge monster and he could do just the same as it. Gradually we learned that this imitation served to banish the monster, just as, according to Anna Freud, children can banish their fear of an animal by imitating it.[14] The idea was: "If I can make the same loud noise

---

[14] A. Freud, "Ein Gegenstueck zur Tierphobie der Kinder," paper given at the 11th International Psychoanalytical Congress. Author's abstract in *Int. Z. Psa.,* Vol. 15, 1929.

as the monster, it cannot devour me." That is, the anxiety is overcome by identification with the object. That the monster represented the father in this case also was indicated by the patient's having already as a child always been impressed by the loud noises which his father made. He admired his passing of flatus, his snoring, and above all, his loud, slurping eating. The patient's first compulsion symptom was that he had to open his mouth wide; and we now understand that this symptom already meant the same as the later "toot toot." It means, "I can gobble just like father, so I need not be afraid to be gobbled up by him." It was an identification with the father for the purpose of warding off fear of him, which in turn warded off a feminine longing for him. This identification appeared, to begin with, to have oral roots, since it referred to gobbling and making loud noises. But after the analysis of the symptom got to this point, the symptom changed: he still had to imitate cars, but the "toot toot" had to be followed by a forced exhaling, by a blowing out. We could see that his symptom had thus become diphasic, and that the second part, the exhaling, was intended to undo the first, the "toot toot." In the deepest stratum, all his obsessional symptoms gave expression to the conflict: "Shall I identify myself with men, or shall I give myself to them passively?" In the "toot toot" he identified himself with the car; in exhaling, he got rid of it again. If, however, this getting-rid-of occurred by breathing, then the preceding introjection of the object must also have been thought of as breathing. But what was it that he had breathed in? His own flatus under the blanket, also that of his father—and cars are wont to smell too.

Just as in our first case the patient's mother had died, so in this case had an older brother of the patient died. His feelings of guilt about this were the main content of his neurosis. He had later transferred his entire ambivalence toward his father onto this brother. Numerous symptoms and dreams left no doubt that the object with which he identified himself on the one hand, and to which he wanted to subject himself on the other, was also this dead brother, whose spirit he inhaled with the "toot toot" and then forcibly exhaled again. (The fantasied monsters were all cosmic creatures who inhabited the universe, just as his dead brother lived in heaven.) The patient, too, had fear of gas and a remarkable fear of kitchens: kitchen smells might penetrate into his bedroom and kill him. This is a condensation of his warded-off oral and respiratory introjections. This patient also had particular smoking ceremonials, the unconscious content of which was the doubt whether he should behave like his father, or exactly the opposite; and this suggests that in smoking in general respiratory erotism and introjection may play a greater role than oral erotism, which has so far been the only one to be observed.

This material clearly demonstrates that there is a pregenital tendency to incorporate the object totally or partially by inhaling or smelling, that this tendency appears condensed with oral incorporation, that anxieties can oppose themselves to it and conflicts rage around it and that it can be prolonged into the genital phase in special forms of persisting identifications. I should like to justify the emphasis I have put on these findings in two further ways: firstly, by linking them to the previous literature of the subject; secondly, by discussing the role of respiratory erotism and identification in social life.

Oberndorf has published a case,[15] without, however, sufficiently exploiting its material from a theoretical point of view, which has some similarity to our first case. A very narcissistic, pregenitally fixated, polymorphously perverse patient had, among other things, a sniffling tic which commanded his entire attention when he was with a woman and so interfered with his erection; furthermore, he had a nose-hypochondria. His entire life was oriented around his nose and smells. Concerning his pleasure in smelling, one of his oldest memories was that he once had occasion to sniff his mother's anus through her clothes. From this was derived a game which became the basis of his later perversions, the "praying game" (the patient suffered later on under compulsive religious scruples). A chair on which his mother had just sat was the altar, and the child knelt down and pressed his face to the seat, and drew in her smell. That an identificatory tendency was involved in this was not directly obvious, but it could be inferred from his femininity, and from the reverse fantasy which played a great role. He imagined that he was penetrating more and more deeply into the rectum of a woman with his nose until he finally crawled into it entirely. In my patient, too, uterine fantasies were frequent. "To become one with mother" is a regressive expression, through ideas of incorporation, of hetero- and homosexual incestuous wishes.[16] The tendency to incorporate the mother has not been noticed by Oberndorf, though he treats at length the pregnancy fantasies of the patient. But he does explicitly say that the nose-hypochondria is concerned with ideas of castration (hence the title of his paper), and he mentions the bisexual nature of the nose, the significance of these things for the addiction to smoking, and the affinity of sniffing up through the nose with oral sucking.

Another study which must be mentioned appeared simultaneously with my "The Psychology of Transvestitism," namely, Bertram D. Lewin's "Kotschmieren, Menses und weibliches Ueber-Ich." [17] Without entering upon the leading idea of this paper, namely the relation of these things to the superego, I would like to bring out some of its agreements with my findings: (1) Epidermal introjection is described by Lewin as an equivalent of oral introjection, in regard to the

[15] C. P. Oberndorf, "Submucous Resection as a Castration Symbol," *Int. J. Psa.*, Vol. 10, 1929.

[16] S. Freud, "From the History of an Infantile Neurosis," *Coll. Pap.*, Vol. III.

[17] B. D. Lewin, "Kotschmieren, Menses und weibliches Ueber-Ich," *Int. Z. Psa.*, Vol. 16, 1930.

purpose of regaining lost objects by smearing. Our patient's smearing of vaseline in his nose and on the wall confirms this completely. We have only added that besides this epidermal introjection a respiratory one must also be assumed. (2) Lewin, also, stresses the relationship of these introjections to anal erotism by way of the symbolic equation: introjected object = corpse = feces. (3) Lewin points out the equivalence of menstrual blood and feces in women. We have been able to demonstrate the same in relation to introjection in men.

Menstrual blood as the feminine principle, which attracts but is also contagiously dangerous, reminds us of the works of Daly,[18] whose general cultural-historical conception we have been able to confirm as regards the unconscious of our patient. His heterosexuality was borne by the idea: "I would like to come near to the woman (that is, to the menstrual smell), but the blood (that is, the danger that I myself will become a woman) scares me away." But it is true that our material has also shown us what Daly overlooked, that such anxieties are regressive substitutes for castration anxiety.

Daly's material reminds us that instructive material about these problems is to be found in ethnology. The ethnological field of data already contains much more preparatory work concerning "respiratory introjection" than does the clinical field.

The familiar fact of the general magic significance of breath is certainly not to be explained solely by the circumstance that breathing is the only function in which man can influence his vegetative system at will. There is no narcissistic-animistic view of the world in which the breath is not narcissistically cathected as being life itself. The Latin word *anima* means at once breath, life, soul, wind, and smell. In German, the word which corresponds to it most closely is "Odem" ["breath"]. Breath magic in connection with introjection, too, is widespread, as for instance, when the medicine man inhales the patient's sickness out of him and then gets rid of it by subsequent exhaling. Indeed, the concept of mana, which we were compelled to use in order to represent the unconscious trains of thought of our patient, means nothing but "introjected infectious breath or smell of a thing." Roheim has systematically summarized all the magic narcissistic actions which pertain to one's own ego; and in this breathing plays no small part.[19] True enough, he, too, is inclined to underestimate the autonomy of breath magic and to consider it as only a particular aspect of oral magic, as when he describes "breathing-out magic" as a "reduced, less obvious, half-symbolic form of spitting" (and therefore one, he thinks, which is more prone to sublimation);[20] but he too cites that medicine men blow out "demons." More important

[18] C. D. Daly, *op. cit.*

[19] G. Roheim, "Das Selbst," *Imago*, Vol. 7, 1921.

[20] *Ibid.*, p. 5.

for us are his discussions of the "soul stuff," in which he studies the universal distribution of the so-called "breath-soul." His general conclusion that "in our sense, the breath-soul implies the assumption of the oral erotogenicity of the breather, and of the epidermal erotogenicity of the one breathed on" [21] again disregards the respiratory nature of breathing, though it shows its close relatedness to oral and epidermal erotism. His material concerning the equating of the dead with the soul and of the soul with feces on the one hand, and air or breath on the other, covers many pages, and corresponds to the unconscious thinking of our patient, for whom the dead mother became feces and thereby also the content of breath. The belief in insemination by the wind is closely related to this; and in this context we must cite Jones' study of the conception of the Virgin Mary.[22] Though ideas about breath are but a *part* of magic-animistic thinking, they are not an inconsiderable part, and a special survey of this material, scattered as it is in all the relevant studies—as, for instance, in Rank's "Doppelgaenger" [23]—would be worth while making, particularly if it is compared with clinical data.

But we are drawn to turn once more to the clinical material. We intended to limit ourselves to discussing introjection, but this could not become comprehensible, were not a more general view of respiratory erotism also to be considered. The idea of incorporating an object by breathing or smelling it is the expression of a particular sexualization of the respiratory and olfactory function. The desire to smell has been often accounted to anal erotism in accord with its most outstanding object; but not quite rightly, because its excitations reside not in the rectum but in the nose. Analysis has demonstrated that whenever breathing is sexualized, quantities of anal and oral libido are displaced to the function of breathing, just as happens in the sexualization of the function of thinking. But breathing is more primitive than thinking, and it is to be assumed that there is an autonomous respiratory erotism, which, though not intense in itself, gains importance through the displacement of quantities of oral and anal energy onto it. This respiratory erotism has an archaic pregenital character. Respiratory introjection is the expression of those of its components which are directed to objects. It is not dominant in any phase of libido development, but is only co-ordinated with other erotisms—and not first and foremost with anal but with oral erotism. Sniffing up does not appear to us as "an equivalent of sucking," as Oberndorf suggested,[24] but as something which *also* happens during the act of sucking. Certainly it attracts the suckling's interest less than

---

[21] *Ibid.*, p. 145.

[22] E. Jones, "The Madonna's Conception through the Ear," *Essays in Applied Psycho-Analysis*, Vol. II, London, Hogarth, 1951.

[23] O. Rank, "Der Doppelgaenger," *Imago*, Vol. 3, 1914.

[24] C. P. Oberndorf, *op. cit.*

does his oral intake. But one must keep in mind the physiological observation that much that is called "taste" perception is in reality olfactory perception.

The existence of a respiratory erotism is fundamentally self-evident. It proceeds from Freud's theory of the erotogenic zones.[25] It becomes important when it produces pathological phenomena; and it would become important, too, if it could be proved that respiratory introjection as well as oral introjection plays a role in the identifications made by the normal person. It produces pathological phenomena at two places: where the sexualized function of breathing breaks through in neurotic symptoms, in organ neuroses of respiratory organs (bronchial asthma) and in the breathing rituals of some obsessional neurotics; and where the defense against such impulses manifests itself in the form of nose- or lung-hypochondria (as in our case) or in fears of asphyxiation. These are the places, too, where cases in point have already been studied psychoanalytically.[26]

In the literature of asthma there is much material concerning respiratory introjection, but it is nowhere brought out in this light, but—correctly enough—referred for the greater part to anal erotism. All the authors agree on one point, namely that asthma is not a conversion *hysteria*. The sufferer from asthma behaves like a compulsion neurotic or even like a case of narcissistic neurosis. Between the most basic content of infantile sexuality which breaks through in the symptom—that is, the oedipus complex—and the conversion symptom a *regression* intervenes. This regression appears often to extend to narcissism, so that the conflict which obtained originally between the patient and his objects is now represented by a conflict between him and his lung; but the regression always extends at least to the anal-sadistic stage. Abraham once called the tic an "anal-sadistic conversion."[27] We ought to add to the tics various other hysteri-form illnesses, such as some genuine organ-neuroses, stuttering, and above all, bronchial asthma, and put them in a group of "pregenital conversion neuroses," separating them from hysterias. That respiratory neuroses differ thus from hysteria, that breathing symptoms are often found lodged in a compulsion neurosis as a single conversion symptom together with some intestinal phenomenon or other, clearly indicates the archaic, pregenital nature of respiratory erotism. In this connection, I should also like to call attention to the subject of narcosis. The disintegration of the ego, artificially elicited by pharmacological means, is certainly the cause of the re-emergence of archaic forms of experience

25 S. Freud, *Three Essays on the Theory of Sexuality*, London, Imago, 1949.

26 See, for instance, H. Deutsch, "Zur Psychogenese eines Ticfalles," *Int. Z. Psa.*, Vol. 11, 1925; J. Sadger, "Ist das Asthma bronchiale eine Sexualneurose?," *Zentralbl. f. Psa.*, Vol. 1, 1911; E. Weiss, "Psychoanalyse eines Falles von nervoesem Asthma," *Int. Z. Psa.*, Vol. 8, 1922; M. Wulff, "Zur Psychogenitaet des Asthmas Bronchiale," *Zentralbl. f. Psa.*, Vol. 3, 1913.

27 K. Abraham, "Contribution to a Discussion on Tic," *Selected Papers*.

in narcosis; but possibly it is not without importance that narcosis is induced through respiratory paths.

*Fear of breathing* has recently been thoroughly studied by Hárnik.[28] I should like to bring out two points in his work which appear relevant in our present context. If, in analysis, we discover behind a manifest fear of suffocation a repressed castration idea (as, for instance, in the idea of "cutting off air"), we must consider the fear of suffocation to be a distorted expression of castration anxiety; but this does not prevent the distortion having taken a *regressive* path. The idea of suffocation may already have been cathected with anxiety at a time when there were no castration ideas as yet. The same holds, for instance, for the oral fear of being devoured.[29] Hárnik's finding, therefore, that the fear of asphyxiation underlies every fear of death and is actually the most archaic anxiety-content of all does not mean that when an expected danger connected with the gratification of infantile sexuality is perceived as the danger of suffocation, this sexuality itself need have a respiratory character. Anxiety to do with breathing need not always be a defense against respiratory erotism; the factor of breathing may have been added subsequently, owing to the quality of the anxiety. But in nose- and lung-hypochondria and in cases where the idea of asphyxiation plays a quite particular role, this is probably not so. Such an *outstanding* emphasis of anxiety on the factor of breathing has to be taken as a pointer to a special sexualization of breathing. Hárnik has also shown how often the infant and small child must have had experiences of suffocation, so that in the deepest strata of its mind every dangerous experience remains connected with the idea of asphyxiation. A closer consideration of Freud's theory of anxiety [30] makes it clear that this must be so on theoretical grounds. For respiratory innervations belong to the very essence of anxiety. They were present in the archetype of every traumatic situation, namely, the act of birth, and every later anxiety is a partial re-experience of this situation. This connection of anxiety and breathing is so essential and close that one has even to consider whether, conversely, a special sexualization of the respiratory function is not frequently derived from a primary sexualization of anxiety. At any rate, it is advisable, in dealing with pathological manifestations in the realm of the respiratory function, to have an eye on the role of anxiety, and therefore I would like to supplement Hárnik's fine study by bringing an all-too-little-considered symptom, which is within the field of normality, into relation with the fear of asphyxiation.

Breathing is like other muscular functions: the average person does not carry them out optimally, but exhibits remarkable phenomena of an inhibitory char-

---

[28] J. Hárnik, "One Component of the Fear of Death in Early Infancy," *Int. J. Psa.,* Vol. 11, 1930.
[29] See, for instance, O. Fenichel, "The Dread of Being Eaten," No. 18 in this volume.
[30] S. Freud, *The Problem of Anxiety,* New York, Psa. Quart. Press and Norton, 1936.

acter, which I have called "dystonus." [31] The continuous minor psychic changes exert their inexpedient dystonic influence on the respiratory function by changes in the rhythm of respiration, mostly in a passing stoppage of breathing, in variable, uneven participation of the parts of the thorax in breathing, etc. This influence becomes particularly striking when a new action is intended, indeed, in every movement, and in every change in direction of attention. Self-observation will readily convince us of the extent of these disturbances. Their relation to attention is particularly clear. Hollos assumed that such disturbances of breathing correspond to disturbances in the rhythmic alteration of direction of attention from outside to within. [32] According to Heyer, [33] this has been demonstrated experimentally also. I shall not dwell on this at any length, but shall only quote Suter, who goes as far as to say that "complete inhibition of breathing" is "the theoretical optimum of achievement in attention." [34]

But these disturbances prove corrigible by exercise; and it is easy to convince oneself that they are set in motion by the ego—that part of the personality which is close to consciousness and defends against drives—for they can to a great degree be stopped if one sets oneself to it. Thus, we are dealing here with the inhibition of an ego-function. The close relationship between anxiety and breathing makes it probable that the continuous fluctuations of breathing are based upon a continuous unconscious anxiety-readiness. Analysts can daily observe passing stoppages of breathing going along with an increase in castration anxiety in their patients; and spasms of the diaphragm are considered by non-analysts, too, as signs of anxiety. The breathing symptoms would be "anxiety signals" of minor extent. The impression is given that, in inhibiting breathing at an intended new action, at a perception, at a change of attention, the ego tests out whether or not it needs to be afraid. True, not every experience is a danger, to be indicated by an anxiety signal; but it *could* become one, so that a kind of "pre-signal" in the form of inhibition of respiration seems indicated to the ego.

We have strayed away from introjection, but perhaps we shall find our way back to it. Our examples of the effects of respiratory identification were narcissistic and pathological. Now we still want to ask: do respiratory introjections play any role in the identifications of everyday social life as well? There is one circumstance which makes this probable. The readiness to make changes in

[31] O. Fenichel, "Organ Libidinization Accompanying the Defense against Drives," No. 14 in this volume.

[32] S. Hollos, "Die Phasen des Selbstbewusstseinsaktes," *Int. Z. Psa.*, Vol. 5, 1919.

[33] G. Heyer, *Das koerperlich-seelische Zusammenwirken in den Lebensvorgaengen*, Munich, Bergmann, 1925.

[34] J. Suter, "Die Beziehung zwischen Aufmerksamkeit und Atmung," *Arch. ges. Psych.*, Vol. 25, 1912.

breathing at every new event, which we have just discussed, the readiness to test reality with the help of breathing precautions, brings it about that in our daily intercourse with people, too, we continuously alter our respiratory activity in various ways. In this, however, we depend on the real quality of the objects and their breathing activity. It has often been said that in social life we continually identify with others by taking over their expressive movements—indeed, that such a taking over of expressive movements is the first act in every process of empathy.[35] It appears that in this the taking over of the rhythm and kind of breathing play a considerable role. Taking over the breathing activity of the other does not yet mean that we have, unconsciously as it were, inhaled them. But if we keep before our eyes the pathological material which we have discussed, this becomes to some extent probable. When we identify ourselves with someone this shows itself in our imitating him. Perhaps we do this in large measure by following his breathing with ours.

[35] S. Freud, *Group Psychology and the Analysis of the Ego*, London, Hogarth, 1948, p. 70, footnote. Cf. also O. Fenichel, "Identification," No. 10 in this volume.

※ ※ ※ ※ ※ ※ ※ ※ ※ ※ ※ ※ ※ ※ ※ ※ ※ ※

## TWENTY-FOUR

# Further Light upon the Pre-oedipal Phase in Girls*

### I

THE present paper does not profess to put forward any new discoveries: it merely aims at making a somewhat more detailed clinical contribution to the discussion of Freud's study of female sexuality.[1]

In recent times views have quite often been voiced to the effect that the discoveries of Freud and his pupils have now in all essentials elucidated the contents and mechanisms of the unconscious mental life that originates in childhood, and particularly of infantile sexuality and its vicissitudes. It is suggested that there is nothing much more to be found out about the problems of psychogenesis: the time has now come for psychoanalytic research to shift its main interest in some other direction—onto the task of shortening analytic treatment, for instance, or onto a more accurate study of the details of the patient's characterological and conscious behavior.

To me views of this sort seem completely mistaken. It is no doubt true that the fundamental contents and mechanisms of the unconscious have been established and no longer require any fresh proof—such matters, I mean, as the development of infantile sexuality through the various stages of libidinal organization or the development of object relations through a period when the aim is incorporation up to the time of the oedipus complex, or again the history of that complex and the establishment of the superego. But if we seek to carry things further and describe every detail of these developmental processes, we

---

* First published in *Int. Z. Psa.*, Vol. 20, 1934, pp. 151–190.

[1] S. Freud, "Female Sexuality," *Coll. Pap.*, Vol. V, London, Hogarth, 1950. See also Chapter 33 (on the psychology of women) in *New Introductory Lectures on Psycho-Analysis*, New York, Norton, 1933.

soon discover what gaps there still are in our knowledge and what an immense amount still remains to be investigated. And, for an analyst, what can the "study of the details of characterological and conscious behavior" mean but the understanding of these details *in their genesis* as well? The only concession that might be made to the views I have mentioned would be what Freud has expressed in these words: "Everything that is to be seen upon the surface has already been exhausted; what remains has to be slowly and laboriously dragged up from the depths." [2] But many problems remain to be "slowly and laboriously" solved. In order to master them it will be necessary to make a comparative study of a great number of analyses to which more time and trouble have been devoted than to average analytic treatments.

I will begin by stating what seem to me to be the two factors which put the greatest difficulties in the way of a scientific investigation of the deepest levels of the apparatus of the mind and so too of the earliest period of life.

One of these factors is that the world of thought at those levels is quite alien to our own, so that it is quite impossible to reproduce them in words as one seems to perceive them in analysis. Let us consider, for instance, what a demand we are making on anyone who has not been able to convince himself of the fact in an analysis, if we ask him to believe that a small child becomes like his mother because he thinks he has eaten her up, and that, if he thinks he is being tormented or "poisoned" by this internal mother, he can in some circumstances spit her out again. The details of this kind of "body-thinking" of which we have a glimpse in analysis and which is bound up with ideas of incorporation must perpetually evade any exact comprehension, especially when we are faced in addition with the characteristics of an ego which is only just in the process of development (which, for instance, makes only an imperfect distinction between ego and non-ego). It seems to me that, in an effort to represent this kind of thought, so remote from words, into which we are led by deep analysis, some authors, and in particular some of our English colleagues, have been too ready to make use of words derived from adult life, which are far too little integral and far too exact.

The second difficulty arises from the familiar mechanism of regression. When in an analysis we have penetrated to the deep levels of which we are in search, we never find them in a pure form but always obscured with admixtures from a later time. Thus, an oedipus complex of a particularly strong oral construction may throw no light on the question of what part of its structure arose from the oral period and set its impress from the very first upon the oedipus complex as it was in the process of formation, and what part of it arose later, when the

[2] S. Freud, "Some Psychological Consequences of the Anatomical Distinction Between the Sexes," *Coll. Pap.*, Vol. V, p. 187.

oedipus relation came up against obstacles and was consequently warded off by means of a resumption of oral mechanism. We know that fixation and regression—that is, original persistence and subsequent harking back—are explanations which form a complemental series. But it remains the task of anyone who sets out to explore the pregenital prehistory of the oedipus complex to separate these two factors from each other. I have already had occasion to indicate why this is so difficult and what criteria can and must be employed in the process.[3]

In his last paper [4] Freud has shown us once again in an exemplary fashion that these difficulties can be overcome. He has examined in particular the prehistory of the oedipus complex of the female sex, which has hitherto always been more obscure to us than that of the male, and has shown that the "pre-oedipal period" lasts much longer than we had supposed—as far as into the fourth and fifth years—and that it by no means coincides with the primal periods when there is no object and when there is only "partial love." He has shown that, on the contrary, the mother—the first love object of every human being—is recognized as a whole personality by little girls as well as by little boys and loved and hated by them before the father becomes their preferred object, and further that this relationship exercises important influences over the whole of their later life. These findings raise a further set of problems for analytic research. Their solution is already adumbrated in part by Freud himself in this same paper; but a record of experiences obtained from any sufficiently deep-going analysis of a female patient is likely to contribute to their elucidation.

If I hesitate before the task of putting in order my own experiences in this field, incomplete as they are, of giving a comprehensive view of them and of making use of them in the service of theory, I find some comfort in Freud's complaint that everything in the sphere of the earliest attachment to the mother seemed to him "in analysis . . . so elusive, lost in a past so dim and shadowy, so hard to resuscitate," and that he too had "not succeeded in completely unraveling any of the cases in point." [4] Clearly it cannot be otherwise. It is due not only to the weight of repression but to the difficulties I have already discussed of verbal disparity and of regression.

Let us begin by considering what the essential problems are with which we are here concerned. They are the points at which the development of the female sex diverges from that of the male and leads to a more complicated configuration: namely, the greater part played by bisexuality in the life of a girl and the task of making a change in object (that is, of passing from an attachment to her mother to one to her father) which is absent in the case of the male sex. The

---

[3] O. Fenichel, "The Pregenital Antecedents of the Oedipus Complex," No. 21 in this volume.
[4] S. Freud, "Female Sexuality," *Coll. Pap.*, Vol. V, p. 254.

two points are of course intimately connected. Though the fantasy of being a woman occurs widely among men, there can be no doubt that the analogous desire among women to be a man, resting as it does upon penis envy, has a far more general significance. It may be argued that an envy of child-bearing among men is analogous to the envy of the penis among women. But the comparison fails at once, since the desire for child-bearing is doomed to the same disappointment in both sexes. A little girl can no more have children than a little boy and she must console herself with future hopes, whereas a little boy really has his penis and experiences pleasurable sensations in it. Following Freud, I attribute the universal character and the importance of penis envy to the circumstance that little girls too possess a "phallic" sexuality, which is concentrated in the clitoris, and that in this respect they are in actual fact at a disadvantage as compared with little boys. It is true that the analysis of women suffering from penis envy very often shows that they took up that position as a defense against a powerful repressed feminine oedipus attachment. But this fact, which has been emphasized by Karen Horney [5] and which has certainly not been overlooked by Freud, is no argument against the existence of an original narcissistic penis envy. In the same way, the fact that the anal-sadistic instinctual impulses of obsessional neurotics serve as a defense against their oedipus complexes does not contradict the existence of a pregenital anal-sadistic stage of organization, but on the contrary is what first makes such an assumption really probable. Very closely linked to these problems are those of the relation between clitoridal and vaginal erotism and of the existence of an infantile vaginal sexuality. While other writings dealing with the early phases of female sexual development are mainly concerned with these problems,[6] Freud considers far more important—and as his paper itself seems to show, with justice—the problems surrounding the feminine change in object. It has always been known that a girl's first love object was her mother. What is new is the stress laid upon that period, the evidence of its long duration, and the investigation of its aims and of the causes of its coming to an end.

We had become accustomed to regarding the oedipus complex as the essential content of the genital period of infantile sexual life in both sexes. Before that period—so it seemed to us—the pregenital stages of the organization of the libido were developed. These were in part autoerotic; in part they had, in both sexes, the mother as their object, and, still earlier, portions of the mother which had not yet been united into a single whole. The pregenital object relations seemed to be in the highest degree ambivalent, their aims to be characterized

[5] K. Horney, "The Flight from Womanhood," *Int. J. Psa.,* Vol. 5, 1926.

[6] See, for instance, K. Horney, *ibid.;* also C. Mueller-Braunschweig, "The Genesis of the Feminine Super-Ego," *Int. Z. Psa.,* Vol. 12, 1926; and J. Mueller, "A Contribution to the Problem of Libidinal Development of the Genital Phase in Girls," *Int. J. Psa.,* Vol. 13, 1932.

by ideas of incorporation, their object relations to be permeated with identifications, and their structure to be archaic. For this reason we should expect the aims of a girl's "pre-oedipal" attachment to her mother to coincide with those of such of her pregenital instincts as were directed toward an object and to display the same characteristics. An investigation of the pre-history of the oedipus complex means an investigation in the case of both sexes of the transition from pregenitality to genitality, and, in addition to this, an investigation in the case of the female sex of the transition from a maternal object to a paternal object. We are predisposed to believe that these two developmental achievements on the part of the female sex must—if not completely, at all events for the most part— coincide with each other.

A few years ago I made an inquiry [7] into the pregenital antecedents of the oedipus complex (in both sexes), and of the three case histories which I reported at length two were of women patients. I am glad to be able to point out that they too confirm what Freud has now formulated, namely the importance of the girl's pregenital attachment to her mother. I will quote the words in which I then briefly summarized the history of these two women; and in one of the two cases I must recall some of the material, since I shall want to refer to it later on in my discussion of theoretical problems.

(1) Pregenital (first oral, then anal) attachment to the mother; . . . later, illness regarded as castration; turning toward the father; substitutive demands made upon him, with a transposition of the mother's characteristics and of the patient's ambivalent feelings toward her onto the father; an oedipus complex colored by this; the sadism provoked by frustration; the fear of castration, which originally applied to the mother, displaced onto the father.

(2) Pregenital (first oral, then anal) love of the mother; from the outset, disappointments from the mother; aggressive reactions against her and increased fear of losing her love; repression of aggressive impulses; turning to the father possible only in imagination—real men being in fact only a screen for the figure of the mother; the sadism once again a reaction to frustrations; the fear of castration, which originally applied to the mother, later displaced onto the father.

I will now quote from the first of these two cases the following material, which relates to the passing of the attachment to the mother.

The patient had suffered from an intestinal complaint at the age of three, which brought to an end a previously existing "anal-erotic association" with her mother. We discovered that not only her incontinence but also the nature of the stool, which was unformed on account of diarrhea, wounded her narcissism severely. . . . It happened that her father reproached her mother, saying: "Whatever did you give the child to eat?" or some such words, whereupon the little

[7] O. Fenichel, op. cit.

girl came to the conclusion that her mother had made her ill—i.e., sensual enjoyment with her mother made her ill, incontinent, castrated her: "It would have been better to obey my father, who always disapproved of it." The mother was the witch who seduced one and gave pleasure, but the pleasure was fatal. The idea that her mother had given her something bad to eat brought us to the analysis of her oral attachment to her mother, which existed before the anal period. . . . From the idea of poisoning a series of transitory oral symptoms led back to the idea of drinking pus. . . . Thus the pregenital attachment to her mother ended with the verdict: "What we did was wrong." . . . The patient had an increasingly strong feeling that her mother was a *vampire* and meant to suck her dry for her own pleasure. The only thing that could give rise to this idea of "sucking out what was inside" was the encouragement which her mother gave her to bring out her well-formed stool. Her mother had thus robbed her of her well-formed stool and therefore, according to the familiar symbolic equation, of her penis. . . . In the same way as it had dawned on the patient then that her mother was "sucking her dry," so she now felt that her father's intellectual type of character, with its aloofness from the instincts, implied a "robbery of her finest capacities," a new kind of drying up.

I shall now try to give an account of what I have seen since then in some relatively deeply analyzed female cases, and I shall afterward consider in what way this material can help us in discussing the problems that have been raised by Freud in the meantime. It is obvious that the material of these analyses, all of which (from the very nature of the problem raised) lasted for several years, can only be very incompletely reported and somewhat schematically selected and arranged.

## II

A cyclothymic female patient who suffered from various characterological difficulties showed a predominance of a feminine castration complex of the "revenge" type [8] both in her whole life history and in her present-day behavior. During her depressive phases these aggressive impulses against men were turned against her own ego. On many occasions they were actually put into practice by means of faulty actions (parapraxes). At such times the patient could scarcely pick up a knife without cutting herself. To begin with there was very little said about either of her parents. (She had left their house permanently when she was still quite young.) Even in her recollections of childhood her brothers and sisters and strangers played a larger part. But that she had a powerful normal oedipus complex to master was proved, among other things, by a re-

[8] K. Abraham, "Manifestations of the Female Castration Complex," *Selected Papers*, London, Hogarth, 1948.

markable screen memory of having once played football with her father and of the ball having hit her in the abdomen. She used to tell this story while she was still a child and used to add a boastful lie to the effect that she had fallen down in a faint. This was a fantasy of being made pregnant by her father. Material of this kind accumulated, and when the patient was asked about her mother she merely said that she never had much to do with her and that her mother had not been really fond of her. Thus to begin with I regarded this unsatisfactory relation with her mother as the necessary second half of the oedipus complex. The patient was dominated in her unconscious mental life by two ideas—(1) "I want to rob the man of his penis" and (2) "I want to have a child by my father." It was therefore plausible to connect these two impulses by way of the equation of "child" with "penis" and to assume that the original form of the violent fantasy that was directed against her ego during her depressions was: "I must obtain by violence the gratification (i.e., the penis) that my father will not give me." In view of the diagnosis of the patient's case it was not surprising to discover further that *oral* traits of the most varied kinds emerged clearly in both the characterological and the erotic side of her life. The discovery (which was only made by the patient after she had been a considerable time under analysis) that she really felt sexual excitement more in the region of her mouth than in her genitals, together with a dream of giving birth to kittens by spitting them out of her mouth, provided the first evidence of the oral substructure of her sadistically colored oedipus complex.

Suppressed aggressiveness had also been the predominant character trait of her later childhood. There was not a single person with whom she could get into real contact. (I shall come to the exceptions later.) She constructed a typical "family romance." [9] She had a fantasy that she did not belong to her parents but really came out of the primeval forest and had been forcibly removed into the civilized world, where she could never feel at home. Certain physical peculiarities underlay this fantasy, as well as the exaggerated stress laid by her environment upon neatness and cleanliness and especially upon care of the hair. The girl withdrew sulkily into fantasies belonging to the world of this family romance; she felt—and, as we shall hear, certainly with some justice—lonely and unloved. "They've taken everything away from me," was what she constantly felt at that time. What she really meant by this "everything" she was unable to say—perhaps the paradise in which she had lived in the primeval forest. The formula "they've taken everything away from me" could therefore be completed by interpretation: "and I'll get it back again—but I mustn't—I must punish myself for impulses like these." Her childhood moods of longing were continued up to the present day and were thus accessible to analysis with relative ease. She sought ever

---

[9] S. Freud, "Family Romances," *Coll. Pap.*, Vol. V.

more clearly for the primeval forest, where she felt at home, in the region where town and country meet—in the quiet suburban streets. She had a longing, too, to get away from the great city onto the land. A screen memory of a visit to the country showed her with an aunt who was fattening up geese: this was almost like the primeval forest! (Note the oral character of this lost paradise.) Looking more closely at the men who played a part in the patient's later life, it was possible clearly to distinguish a type which, though it seemed to have taken over some traits from her father, was much better characterized by the fact that it must have something "rustic" or "rural" about it. And apart from this there were plenty of rural ideals. One day when she was talking of these things the patient told me how in her earlier years people were always asking about her accent and inquiring whether she came from some particular part of the country—let us say Swabia—since she had a slight Swabian accent. This was most remarkable, for none of her family came from Swabia. In this emphasis upon the factor of speech there is once again an oral factor involved, though for the moment it is quite unintelligible. In her later years she found relief during her depressive periods by going for walks in the suburbs, plunged in melancholy daydreams. It was as though she were seeking for her lost home in the country or in a suburb, where people still loved her and spoiled her orally. It was especially good if there were rain and storms when she was on these walks, for then in her imagination she was defying her father and all the world. The smell of wet meadows and fields made her intoxicated with joy. Her dreams and associations to this showed that the deeper aim of this smell-erotism was a narcissistic love of the smell of her own wet hair: "You scold me because my hair's untidy; but once, somewhere in the primeval forest, or in Swabia, there was someone who knew how to value it, who loved it and fed me!" These primal ideas completely dominated the patient's character and behavior, especially in her love relations with men. At this time I was prepared to discover some such real basis for these fantasies as that her father before his marriage had lived on the land in Swabia. But the actual solution came from a totally different direction. In the patient's descriptions of her walks in the suburbs interest began to be concentrated more and more upon one particular district. At last she gave some associations which showed that as a very small child she must often have been in this precise district. Associations of smell emerged in this connection. A picture appeared of a particular drugstore in the district and finally a recollection of a big advertisement in the drugstore which depicted a Negress washing a little girl's hair. After I had pointed out that this must be the origin of the fantasy that hair was specially cared for in the primeval forest, there suddenly appeared a recollection of a nurse belonging to her early childhood who had completely vanished from her memory. She was an old woman of peasant origin, probably from Swabia, who had washed her hair in her early years but had no doubt also taught her to speak and had fed her and had carried out for her all the usual services of a child's nurse.

I must now add a few words on the patient's attitude to the care of children in general. Every idea relating to this subject was submitted to a special repression. She could not put up with children because they had to be looked after. The fact that she had relatively little feeling about her own child was due to her having had it looked after by complete strangers during its early years. (It is true that there were other reasons for her attitude to the child. During her pregnancy she felt convinced that she was going to die in childbirth. At that time bearing a child meant to her in itself committing a crime deserving of death: we shall presently hear why.) The repression which had fallen upon the figure of the nurse was in harmony with the fact that her function was so severely repressed. For a long time the patient would not believe that behind this dislike there lay a preference. She was at last convinced by a dream in which she was cleaning a man who had dirtied himself. The man represented an acquaintance toward whom at the time she had motherly feelings. Now the patient used in every relation to replace passivity by activity. All her strivings after objects tended—as was to be expected from the nature of her illness—to be accompanied by simultaneous identifications. We could therefore, without more ado, equate the desire expressed by her in the dream to look after children with a desire to be looked after. And we now knew what it was that the sulky girl who felt so lonely was really thinking: "Treat me as badly as you like! I'm not *your* child at all. I'm the child of the old nurse who was always so kind to me." This thought and this maternal idea were older than her oedipus complex and gave it its character.

Another problem now arose. If there had really been a primal period of happy pregenital love of the nurse, when, why, and where had it broken down? It looked as though this completely buried homosexual primal period had had a highly dramatic collapse, and that turning toward her father could from the nature of things afford no substitute, since her fixation both to the nurse herself and to the method of gratification which she provided was too intense. When this question was put before the patient, she produced a paramnesia which made things substantially more intelligible. She asserted that the nurse had been dismissed at the time of the birth of a younger sister, who was born when she herself was four years old. But she added that the nurse had evidently returned soon afterwards, since she now recalled that the woman had been particularly active in looking after the new baby, which had made her, the patient, jealous. Apparently she had been re-engaged later, as nurse to the younger sister; and this would explain why the patient had felt so much injured. It turned out, however, that this was not the case. The nurse had in fact never been dismissed; but it was quite likely that she was more concerned with the new baby, who was then in great need of her care, than with the patient. The explanation of this paramnesia was only forthcoming when Freud showed how it is that girls often blame their mothers for discharging a nurse too soon.[10] Nevertheless it gave us the evidence for a connection between the patient's decisive disappointment in love and the birth of her younger sister. It gradually became apparent, from memories and dreams, as well as from her behavior in the analysis, with what immeasureable fury she must have detested the new baby. The hatred with which she saw her beloved nurse devote herself to the new arrival was ground enough for her determination "to have nothing more to do with looking after children." No doubt at the time she left nothing undone to get back the love she had lost. She identified herself with the infant and began to wet herself and probably to dirty herself again. She developed the liveliest fantasies of how one sets about producing a baby oneself. What was remarkable and at first inexplicable was that, though the whole of the analytic material reflected from this period a wild hatred against the whole world, the figure of the nurse seemed to be excepted from the hatred. All that the patient seemed to have felt toward her was a deep longing, just as though she had really been turned out of the house by the mother. At this stage of the analysis she, the active "revenge" type, began to develop, both in her love life and in her behavior in the transference, an intense girlish longing for a grown-up protector: "You all abandon me; but in the far-off distance there is a nurse who is my real mother and who loves me. If she were here she would feed me again and put me on the chamber, and would teach me how to set about getting myself a child (or a penis) instead of feces." Hence arose a wild ambition to produce things, which she manifested in many different spheres.

This discovery of the patient's pre-oedipal love of her nurse raised a number of problems. In the first place it was necessary to ascertain whether and how its passing had led to the oedipus complex which I described at the beginning of this account. Secondly there was the question of the structure of this love—the relation between longing and hatred in it. And thirdly we had to ask whether what we already had before us was really the girl's pre-oedipal attachment to her mother, and whether the bodily mother, who was after all in the house as well, really had no significance.

The ambivalence of the patient's relation to the penis has already been indicated in what has been said about her castration complex. She could only get satisfaction in sexual intercourse if she lay on top of the man. One day she discovered that while doing this she used to keep her big toe rigidly stretched out.

[10] S. Freud, *New Introductory Lectures on Psycho-Analysis*, pp. 166–167.

What interfered with her sexual behavior more than anything was a dread that the man might become frightened of her. She would then begin to commit the parapraxes to which I have already referred. In spite of her active nature and of the characteristics that I have just mentioned, she shrank from activity in all sexual matters: if she caught hold of a man she felt she might hurt him. The fantasy of robbing someone of a penis for herself was later replaced by the attenuated fantasy of looking at a penis. Transference dreams showed that she was filled with a desire to be taken by a man into a urinal. This directly recalls the wish to be put on the chamber by the nurse; and there was also an allied idea of watching the nurse at her business. She recalled that one summer —she must have been about five at the time—she went into the closet with a little boy even younger than she was and made him show her his penis—which, incidentally, he did not want to do. This recollection was accompanied by a series of further memories of this same summer, which showed that it had been an important chapter in her life, though we were still ignorant of what special event it was that had occurred in it. A number of details about her longings for the country and its smells found their explanation in the particulars of this summer holiday. Although she had a longing for most of the things that she remembered in the garden at this period, she had a pronounced phobia in later years of the smell from the blossoms of one special tree that had stood in the garden. This phobia went so far that she refused to leave the house during the season at which this tree was in flower. The analysis showed that the smell of the tree took the place of the smell of the outdoor toilet—the same one that she had gone into with the little boy. Other associations suggested that the little boy's penis was only a harmless version of the more alarming penis of a big man which she must have got to know at that time; and finally it became highly probable that for the first time in her life the little girl must that summer have seen a man micturating (or an exhibitionist) in the neighboring wood. She had behaved to the little boy in accordance with her original impulse: "I'll get hold of that for myself!" The discovery of these things now brought up another unexpected memory. During that same summer her little sister had fallen seriously ill and it became necessary to carry out the operation of trepanning. So once again there was a connection between other people being preferred to her and death wishes against her little sister. And these became still more violent, since her two parents, who had wanted a son, began to treat their baby daughter as a boy, allowed her to run about in trousers, and so on. Thus the patient could justly feel: "It's owing to her that I've lost my penis." The event of her sister's severe illness at this time was no doubt the cause of the patient's enormous sense of guilt and her intense aggressiveness against her own ego.

We still knew nothing of the change in the sex of her objects. The analysis of the transference left no doubt as to who the patient's first male love object was. She had always said that, while no one else bothered about her, there was *one* of her relatives who was nice to her—her grandfather. He used to take the child on his lap, comfort her in her enigmatic depressions, and play with her. She was very much chaffed over these relations of hers with her grandfather. Her longing to be taken into the closet by a man went back to him; and this fact showed that he had become a successor (and very much of a successor) to the nurse. "If no one else will give me what the others have robbed me of, he will; and if he doesn't give it to me, I shall have to take it for myself." Already—after the summer I have described—this "it" was thought of by the patient as a penis, and what turned out to be a momentous scene now emerged in her memory, in which she repeated with her grandfather what she had attempted with the little boy. While she sat playing on his lap, she began to undo his fly buttons so as to pull out his penis. But just as the little boy had been unwilling, so now she met with an energetic repulse from her grandfather. This was responsible for her later fear, which I have already mentioned, of her aggressiveness toward men. And this event too had what might be described as its homosexual pre-oedipal antecedents. The discovery was preluded by a dream in which she was playing with some silver balls on a Christmas tree. "Christmas," as is always the case in dreams, meant the fulfillment of the deepest wishes of childhood. What, then, were the balls with which she wanted to play? The associations told us that they were breasts, and the patient then remembered that as a very small child she was always occupied with the buttons on her grandmother's blouse. She wanted to see the breasts, just as later she wanted to see the penis. Her sister had been suckled by a wet-nurse, and the analysis left us in no doubt that the patient had watched this and had been envious. Thus the breast of the wet-nurse, who was certainly condensed with the other nurse, corresponded to the penis of the micturating man, and her grandmother's breast to her grandfather's penis. There was undoubtedly, therefore, a series of object cathexes passing from the nurse (grandmother, wet-nurse) by way of the grandfather to the father. These antecedents gave to her relation to her grandfather from the very first its characteristic sadistic traits, and to her relation to her father (dating from after the failure of her assault upon her grandfather's penis) its note of inhibited activity and of depression. Her oedipus complex had a substratum of oral sadism, derived from her earlier attachments to women: "Women first gave it to me and then robbed me of it in order to give it to someone else; and now men refuse to let me have it; so I must rob them of it."

The last piece that was missing from our understanding was again provided by a dream: "An elegant lady is emptying a chamber-pot." For a period during her later life it had been her ideal to be a "lady"—a complete contrast to what she had been before and after. It was the companion picture to her persistent masculine longing. These contrasts were explained as deriving from the contrasting demands made upon her by her father: on the one hand she was to be a boy, but on the other hand she was to be an elegant lady. At all events, there could be no doubt that a "lady" is the opposite of a "peasant-woman"; she comes, not from the primeval forest, but from the city, and she ought not to have anything to do with "chamber-pots." The lady was her mother, about whom nothing at all had been heard in the analysis for a long time. From now onward more and more memories of her began to emerge. In the patient's recollection she appeared as both strict and elegant. Certainly she had paid very little attention to the children. The feelings of passive longing, which had predominated in the transference before the nurse was discovered and which had then vanished, now reappeared in an extremely intensified form. Alongside the longing, rage and anxiety were so manifest that there could no longer be any doubt as to the answer to the riddle which had hitherto been left open of why it was that she had only felt longing and no hatred for the nurse. It was an attempt at solving a conflict of ambivalence which had originally referred to her mother. All the positive impulses were displaced onto her ideal mother, the nurse in the primeval forest; only the negative feelings were left for the picture of her real mother. The fact that the patient's femininity was buried so deeply under repressions was linked to the fact that her relation to her mother lay equally far below the surface. It is true that the feeling which dominated the whole of her later childhood, the feeling that her mother hated her, seemed in part to have an objective basis: her mother brought up her younger daughter as a son and apart from that took very little notice of her children. But in part that feeling was undoubtedly the projection of immense hatred of her own, which had brought to an end her original love. Once more the patient saw before her, in indistinct pictures charged at once with impulses of hatred and longing, the body of her mother, big with child. The hatred which she had then felt was responsible for her feeling convinced later on, when she herself was with child, that she was bound to die.

I have not yet touched upon two subjects which are of importance in connection with our problems: infantile masturbation and ideas of incorporation.

The first of these, as we know, is the essential executive activity of infantile sexuality in general; the patient's ruminative longings for the ideal primeval forest situation quite clearly betray themselves as derivatives of an old masturbation fantasy. Her ideas of having lost an irretrievable happiness and her hostility toward the environment that had robbed her of it also point in the same direction. But it is not always possible to unearth in every precise detail the character, subject matter, and end of infantile masturbation. The only thing of which it was possible to arrive at a clear memory was a picture of someone coming to see whether the child had her hands outside the bedclothes. But we were able to learn more of two derivatives of equivalents of masturbation: bedwetting and thumb sucking. The former continued to occur at a comparatively advanced age; and it was soon possible to bring into relation with it the patient's tendency to shut herself up in her feelings, always to remain indifferent and to betray no emotion—which was in such complete contrast to her exhibitionist pride in production. Continence of emotion, and especially continence of tears, meant continence of urine. A later governess compelled her when she had wetted herself for the first time—or so she seemed to remember—to fasten her wet drawers outside her satchel, where they were visible to everyone. She must have been about eight years old. The dread of having all her productions laughed at, which inhibited her inclination to showing off, dated from this occasion. It turned out later that this memory was a condensation of two events. She had indeed been punished for wetting herself, as I have described, in her ninth year; but this had only happened because this governess had made the remarkable rule that the children must be completely dressed before going to the lavatory—a rule against which they naturally rebelled. But there had already been a more important period of enuresis when she was about four, soon after the birth of her sister. At that time no doubt the principal business of the enuresis had been to attract love and attention to herself by identifying herself with the infant. So that there was all the greater disappointment when it had an opposite result. She therefore felt: "If I hadn't been robbed of my Paradise, I shouldn't have to wet myself now." When she was five, as I have described, fantasies of having lost her penis were added to those of having lost her Paradise; and she was now prepared with the judgment that must have governed her when she went to school with the wet drawers: "If I had my Paradise I shouldn't wet myself. So since you've robbed me of it, it's you yourselves that are responsible for my wetting myself."

The fear of disgracing herself, which inhibited her pleasure in showing off and which thus had as its content alike loss of the penis and incontinence, was (together with the inhibition of aggressiveness that has already been described) the main cause of her later sexual disturbances. Clearer material dealing with the relation between infantile enuresis and frigidity will come to light in cases I shall discuss later on. In any case, it was evident in the present patient's case too that there was no contradiction between fear of incontinence and fear of her own aggressiveness. If we bear in mind the rage into which a child must get if it is laughed at for incontinence, we cannot fail to see the connection between the idea that "I must control my feelings because otherwise I shall be laughed at for being uncontrolled" and the idea that "I must control my feelings because otherwise I shall be so furious that I shall make a mess." The patient remembered in the analysis that on one such occasion when she began to cry with rage she was laughed at still more on account of her tears; she then felt a compulsive impulse to tighten all her muscles, because, unless she did, the house would fall down. This can, of course, only have meant: "because otherwise I shall do something bad in my rage." When she unbuttoned her grandfather's trousers to look at his penis (or rob him of it), this rage, which she had acquired in the course of her training in cleanliness, had already become a component part of her sexuality. And there was no doubt of why this had been bound to happen. It was on account of the anal-urethral fixation which the care taken of her in the nursery had left behind in her and whose interruption by the birth of her younger sister had produced the enuresis. From this too we can see what it was that had caused the splitting of her mother-imago into a bad mother and a good nurse: namely, the different way in which the two women had behaved during the training in cleanliness. The nurse had been patient and given her encouragement; hence too her longing for the nurse's way of talking and her later idea: "If only she were to put me on the chamber again, I could produce a child." But her mother had been much stricter; hence it was that the later governess with her remarkable educational principles revived her old feelings of hatred that really applied to her mother. But the dream of a lady emptying a chamber-pot was expressing her original longing for an "anal association" with her mother.

With the oral repressions the case was just the same as with the anal-urethral ones. The patient had been a great thumb-sucker till quite late in her childhood and her desires for continence included a wish to be free of this bad habit. This threw light upon the origin of the child's poetic productions, which I have not yet mentioned but which played an important part. She was most eager to show off her products as evidence that she *did* possess a penis, but was unable to do so for fear of being incontinent. The production of these "gifts" began in this way. Before going to sleep she used to listen to the rhythmic beating of her pulse and imagined she could make out words in it. These words were, of course, those spoken by the encouraging nurse, who was still speaking to her by means of introjection. After I had pointed out to her how much this surrender at night to the rhythm of her own pulse-beat recalled masturbation, she produced emotional recollections of her pleasure in the rhythm of sucking. The fantasy accompanying this must have been her longing for an oral union with the mother-figure. Now the patient had been a very great deal tormented over her thumb sucking, especially by the later governess. Her thumb was smeared with bad-tasting stuff—this was the real basis of a number of ideas on the incorporation level of being poisoned—and she was threatened with having it cut off. As chance would have it, soon afterward, in her eighth year, she was really obliged to have an operation on her thumb. Later on she used not only to cut herself in her parapraxes, but developed a dread of genital injury which was built on the exact model of a male castration anxiety; that is, it had as its content the idea of a limb being cut off. And in our present patient this was to be explained by the fact that what she had really been afraid of happening to her thumb was transferred in her thoughts to an imaginary penis.

Thus all of her impulses for mastery, which in her neurosis were turned against her own ego, seemed in the last resort to aim at oral incorporation. When she saw her baby sister at the nurse's breast, she must evidently have recalled the heavenly experience of being fed by her old nurse and perhaps behind that her own period at the breast; and she threw this reproach at these mother-figures: "You don't feed me enough!" And although later on, in her "family romance," she disowned her mother, yet she still retained in it precisely her magical bond with the nurse-mother who had fed her. Together with the food which she gave her, the "good mother" had given her herself; and the patient now had her within her, spoke her speech and heard her voice at night in her own pulse. Her later depression shows that this effort at introjecting the "good mother" and rejecting the "bad mother" had failed. A strict maternal superego, an incorporated "bad mother," turned all the patient's aggressive inclinations against herself. Her fantasies and fears of illness and her behavior during real illnesses showed with especial clearness the fantasy of there being some poisonous maternal material in her inside.

By way of summary it may be said that in this analysis it has been possible to uncover a long, intense, and complicated "pre-oedipal" attachment to the patient's mother behind an attachment to her father, which was conspicuous, was a formative agent both of her neurosis and of her character, and was governed by the castration complex. The aims of this attachment to her mother were of the polymorphously perverse kind which are aroused by nursery care. Besides a strong skin erotism (a longing for warmth and the care of her hair), urethral and anal erotism were prominent; but the erotogenic zone which, when all is said and done, dominated the whole picture was the oral one. The relation was highly ambivalent and colored throughout by sadistic traits. Her powerful exhibitionist instinct and the associated love of showing off proved in essence to be attenuated versions of her sadism. A fantasy of having a child with her mother could be explained to some extent as being derived from the idea of being able to bear a child with the help of the nurse. But in this relation it was the mother-figure who was the procreator and the patient who bore the child, not the reverse. No definitely phallic aims could be discovered in this attachment to her mother. Her hostility to her mother, which was seen in her turning away from the female sex and (by way of her grandfather) turning toward the male one, had numerous causes. Foremost by far were the frustrations imposed upon her at the birth of her younger sister. Her discovery of her lack of a penis, which she made soon afterward, had a decisive influence on her change of object, but was perceived entirely upon the model of her earlier frustrations. The blame for her being castrated was unambiguously put upon her mother. Here the objective events came to the patient's help, since her mother treated the baby sister as a boy. But her fantasy of retaliation was only for a short time directed toward women. After the episode with her grandfather it was transferred wholly onto men and from there governed the patient's characteristic behavior.

### III

A woman in her thirties suffered from various kinds of anxiety attacks and from frigidity. In this case it was in the first instance particularly difficult to recognize the importance of her pre-oedipal period, owing to the signs of an intense oedipus complex being quite specially emphasized. The patient's father had been a remarkable man in every respect; and he constantly let his daughter see that he himself was in love with her. Her mother had died while she was in her fifth year, so that she had grown up alone with her father (and a sister who was three years her junior). She was attached to him in the closest friendship, and once, when she was a grown-up girl, she had suggested to him that they should adopt a child so that she could have one in common with him. During his lifetime she quite failed to have a real relation with any other man; and after his death her relations to men were disturbed in many ways. The first reason for these disturbances turned out to be a fear that she would inevitably die when her first child was born. Since an analysis of this fantasy showed that her mother had died in childbirth, this anxiety too seemed only to point to the oedipus complex; for in cases where a mother has died prematurely that complex is often manifested in an indissoluble link between the concepts of "sexual gratification" and "death." [11]

The first complicating factor to be discovered was that this attachment to her father was thoroughly ambivalent. The father had been of an obsessional neurotic type, unpredictable and himself ambivalent, treating his daughter alternately with extravagant signs of affection and sudden outbursts of rage, and insisting upon the scrupulous fulfillment of a number of educational principles. He had thus given her grounds enough for this ambivalence. The patient recollected in analysis a day on which her father (who had been to the oculist for some trifling reason) came home with a bandage over one of his eyes. She was fright-

[11] M. Bonaparte, "Die Identifizierung einer Tochter mit ihrer verstorbenen Mutter," *Int. Z. Psa.*, Vol. 15, 1929.

ened to death, as though she herself had done her father some injury. From this point there developed an intense and in part unconscious interest in her father's "illnesses." Her general interest in all medical questions had already been traced back to an intense visual curiosity, and it now became plain whose "illnesses" it was that she wanted to see—namely her father's.

Now her father did in fact suffer from a mysterious disease—a hernia. He wore a truss and fidgeted about a great deal round his abdomen, though without giving any explanation to his daughters, who cannot have failed to notice much of this. A mysterious object which came up in the patient's dreams as having something to do with sexuality turned out to be a heat-pad, which her father used to apply to his abdomen. She had equated his rupture (his big abdomen) with his genitals. Just as her medical interest showed her unconscious wish to *see* her father's genitals, so her fright over his injured eye showed her wish to *damage* them. (Incidentally, I believe that, even without active castrating impulses such as these, many little girls regard male genitals as a "growth," as some kind of disease, and consequently develop an interest in a number of diseases.) Confirmations of this interpretation came little by little from all directions. Once (she was about seven or eight at the time), when a little boy younger than herself came on a visit, the children had to be separated because she kept on all the time taking the little boy to the toilet so as to help him there. And the various occasions of the anxieties which had brought the patient to analysis (and which I shall not further discuss in this paper) all went back to opportunities for seeing a penis in some symbolic form. It is true that in her love life she succeeded in fact in looking at a penis without feeling anxiety; but this was due only to her frigidity, which isolated reality from her actual unconscious sexuality with its libidinal cathexis. I intend to describe in another paper the way in which this patient's scoptophilic instinct was bound up to an enormous extent with fantasies of introjection, so that whatever she looked at was from that very fact introduced, in her imagination, into her own body. I need only say here that this "ocular introjection" involved the destruction of the object; looking at something was a euphemism for destroying it and making it her own. But the oral substructure of this ambivalent oedipus complex could no longer be overlooked. Fantasies and dreams relating to the mouth and to eating became more and more prominent. And finally the whole oral anamnesis which the patient brought to the analysis had to be brought into relation with her sexuality as a whole. In her infancy she had suffered from a gastric and intestinal disorder as a result of which she had had to go hungry; and to this corresponded the constant and inordinate oral craving which she felt all through her later life. For instance, in the period which followed this illness, she was in the habit, when she had finished drinking a bottle of milk, of flinging it to the ground and smashing it. This may safely be understood as meaning: "What's the good of an empty bottle? I want a full one!" As a baby, she was extremely voracious. The fear of losing their love which dominated her relations with people corresponded to this oral fixation. Her oral greed later passed over into the greed for seeing something which I have already mentioned. (Among other things she was a passionate reader.) Her expectation that objects that she stared at would jump into her eyes (or into her mouth) was a dread of retribution; "If I bore into something with my eyes, it will bore into me." We can therefore provisionally formulate the fantasy contained in her oedipus complex as follows: "My mother is dead. Now I can do what I like with my father. I will have a really good look at his genitals. That will be just as though I were to eat them up. So he will be destroyed and get inside my body." Analytic experience has taught us how closely identifications are related to fantasies of introjection. The former are effected by means of the latter. Thus it is easier to understand than it would be to demonstrate in detail that the patient's analysis now uncovered a whole series of character traits and modes of behavior which went back to the idea of identifying herself with the penis—of herself as a whole *being* a penis. All of her object relations were—as we are accustomed to find with oral characters—permeated with identifications. And this was always especially visible where sexual relations were concerned. Once when one of her lovers turned out to be impotent, her reaction was masculine to such a degree that it could be formulated as: "We are impotent." *Affaires à trois* played a great part both in her fantasies and in her actual love life. She liked her lover to be with another woman in her presence, enjoying this in empathy with him. It was unimaginable to her, and quite intolerable, that her lover could visit another woman in her absence. She had the feeling: "After all, he can't possibly do it without me!" In moments of affection she aimed always at cuddling up into the man's body as though she were part of it. If her lover left her, she had a "wounded feeling" in her back, as though she had been attached to him by means of her back and had now been torn away. Finally, when dreams came up of "men who have a baby hanging on their abdomen instead of a penis," there could no longer be any doubt of her identifying herself with the penis. The fantasy of hanging onto a man's abdomen like a penis was thus a sort of father's body fantasy.* It was the counterpart to the fantasy of eating up her father's penis: a fantasy of herself in the form of a penis being eaten up by her father. For the man who had a baby on his abdomen instead of a penis reappeared. But now he had a great many of these children; he had them stuck into his belt or was holding one of them high up in his hand and was going to do something unpleasant to him

---

* *"Vaterleibsphantasie"* in the original, in allusion to the more usual *"Mutterleibsphantasie,"* "womb fantasy." *"Mutterleib"* means "womb," or literally, "mother's body."—Trans. note.

—like Great Agrippa in *Struwelpeter*. It was the *"Kindlifresser"*—the Ogre of Berne.*

But little by little the patient's oral-sadistic and identificatory impulses toward the penis began to show characteristics which could no longer be explained in terms of the penis but must have originated at an earlier period. A passionate curiosity to witness experiments in physics applied especially to phenomena which in some way or other involved the sucking up of a fluid. No doubt this expressed a desire to see a man micturating. Nevertheless I gained an impression that it was more a question of the act of sucking than of the behavior of the fluid, and this corresponded to the patient's original oral-sadistic desires. Her fantasies of "sucking in" and of "being sucked in" revolved around ideas of solid bodies becoming two-dimensional and of pictures becoming solid bodies. I shall have more to say about the meaning of experiences like these, which were determined by the eidetic characteristics of the patient, when we come to examine the relation of her scoptophilic instinct to identification. For the moment I will only say this: being sucked in meant being taken into a body; whereas the opposite process, a picture become animate, meant "extrajection," an object coming out of the body. I shall not now enlarge upon the complicated analysis of the patient's infantile phobias, which she had to a large extent forgotten and which were the basis of her present-day anxiety ideas. This analysis led us to the situations in which the little girl, when she was about three or four, first made the acquaintance of a penis. A penis being taken out of his trousers by a man who is going to micturate seemed to her just like a two-dimensional picture becoming a solid body—a body which had previously been introjected being given back to the external world. It was an act comparable to birth or defecation. The possibility of being thus able to produce a penis like a piece of feces (and of making it disappear again) brought a hope that she herself might still get one some day. We shall later come to know the pregenital prototype of this idea.

The idea in which the patient was equated with an introjected object inside the body was strengthened and given fresh anchorage by the equation of the penis with the contents of the abdomen. But that cannot have been its first origin. The relation between the patient and the penis must have had pregenital antecedents in her relations to food and feces. The discussion of this subject must be begun with a few remarks on the analysis of her frigidity. She was not entirely devoid of excitement, but the excitement disappeared when it had reached a certain height. It was not hard to show that the patient was *afraid* of the increase of her own excitement. But what was it that she feared? She had had a bad habit when she was a child in her gymnastics class. When she was swinging with her hands holding the rings she used as a regular thing to let

* A well-known sculpture of an ogre on a fountain in Berne.—Trans. note.

go suddenly and fall to the ground. Kindly encouragements and punishments from the mistress were equally without effect. Now the patient was peculiarly susceptible (in other circumstances as well as in this one) to equilibrium erotism. There can thus be no doubt that while she was swinging she had particularly strong erotic sensations and in all probability corresponding fantasies. Her sudden letting-go was thus a forerunner of her frigidity. When the excitement had reached a certain height, she was *obliged* to let go, however much she might want to hold on, because an increase in the sexual excitement would have involved an event that was too bad. Much to the astonishment of both of us, the analysis left us in no doubt as to what this event was. It was bedwetting. At one stage of her childhood she had gone through a period of bedwetting, though it could not be established, to begin with, when and for how long. But a dream which she had at this point of the analysis came to our assistance. It showed her mother, with her forefinger lifted, scolding her for wetting her bed. So it must have been during her mother's lifetime: and her frigidity corresponded to the unconscious thought: "If I give way to my sexual enjoyments I shall wet myself and my mother will be angry."

It now became possible to unravel a further piece of the sexual fantasy that had accompanied the bedwetting. At that time a large curtain with a number of tassels hanging from it had been visible from her bed. This was the original of the "Ogre" with all the penis-children hanging from his belt. In her fantasy this curtain seemed to come toward her. Perhaps it really did, when the window was open and the wind blew in. The curtain then became a man: what was two-dimensional became a solid body. This supremely powerful curtain-father visited her in bed to eat her up or to do something else to her that was voluptuous or terrible. But the same curtain also appeared to her with lifted finger, to see whether she had been good or had wetted herself. The curtain that visited her was not only her father but her mother as well: the sexual violation that she longed for was also the punishment that she had to expect for past guilt. Not only a man with many penises but a woman with many breasts appeared to her in a dream. More and more womb ("mother's-body") fantasies emerged. In botany the patient's interest was centered especially upon chestnuts and in zoology upon kangaroos. The remarkable and unintelligible "father's-body" fantasies must have been sequels to these "mother's-body" fantasies. The penis of her father had merely taken over a function previously performed by the body of her mother. Proof that this was really so came from the interpretation of a strange feeling that she had. When she formed a picture of an erect penis, it always seemed to her terribly cold: something quite cold was going suddenly to force its way into her body. In general she was frightened of cold in various ways and her most frequent anxiety equivalent was shivering. The origin of this cold feeling could now be seen: it was cold like that when her mother came in and suddenly pulled back the bedclothes to see whether she had wetted herself.[12] Thus what the man did to her with his penis was the same as the punishment which she had feared from her mother.

What was this punishment? And what was she to be punished for? Not for wetting her bed but for the fantasies that accompanied it. And if the punishment had something to do with being eaten up then the deed for which it was imposed must have something to do with eating up.

The whole of the patient's sense of guilt was bound up with her sister, who was two years younger than she; and she had grounds for her sense of guilt. Her oral greed and her corresponding fear of losing her mother's love brought it about that she was unable to tolerate being obliged thenceforward to share her mother's love with a rival and to see her sucking from the bottle. She made quite a number of attacks on her baby sister. Once she snatched the bottle out of her mouth, drank it up and then pushed it back empty down the baby's throat so that she nearly choked. But I must here add something that was brought out by the analysis on the subject of the patient's reaction to her mother's death. This occurred when she had already formed, or begun to form, her oedipus complex. She recalled one summer in her childhood as the only one when she had been really happy. To her surprise and shame she realized that it was the one following her mother's death. But it had been only for a short time that she was able to enjoy the happiness of anticipating that she would now take her mother's place. That happiness was disturbed both by a severe sense of guilt—as we shall hear, she had wanted to kill her mother on account of her pregnancy even before reaching the oedipus age—and by real disillusionments—a governess came into the house and the patient became a little girl once more. But in addition to all this her happiness was also disturbed by her inability to bear the loss of her mother and her endearments. Her mother had died without having forgiven her for her bedwetting or her crime against her little sister. In every sexual act she anticipated her mother's vengeance. It was the man's function to carry out that vengeance, just as he was also obliged to compete against the loss of affection which she had suffered by her mother's death. Her mother had died from rupture of the gall bladder. The little girl must have heard this. At every point in her associations and dreams ideas used to come up of bladders filled with liquid, which suddenly burst. It became clearer and clearer: the bladder bursts through being pierced open by some cold, metal object. This cold object is a penis. Her father had forced open a bladder inside her mother's abdomen with his penis. I mentioned earlier that quite at the begin-

---

[12] The cold feeling was strengthened by a condensation of this memory with something else: her notion that the cold packs used when she was ill with fever were punishments.

ning of the analysis we found that the patient equated her father's genitals with his hernia. She would have liked to look at the hernia. We know that "looking at" means "destroying" and "eating up." Only now was it possible to link up this remarkable impulse of the patient's with her mother's death: "I should like to pierce open the bladder so that its contents run out." Moreover, there must have been some connection between this and her being afraid of wetting herself during sexual gratification. She must have heard the word "bladder" used as well in connection with her enuresis, and at that time she could certainly not distinguish between the urinary bladder and the gall bladder. Thus behind all of this there lay one thought in common: "In sexual intercourse a bladder in the abdomen is pierced open and liquid spurts out."

Where did this fantasy come from? It must have been pictured originally in the active form, and for that reason was also greatly feared in the passive one. This idea of crushing in an abdomen, of destroying or eating up its contents, in order, no doubt, to put oneself in their place and so be able in turn to suffer the same experience oneself—all of this originated from an exceedingly early period. Her mother had been pregnant of her younger sister when the patient was two. It was the sight of her pregnant abdomen that had given her this destructive fantasy. What she had originally wanted was to destroy her unborn sister in this way. In view of her age at the time, we may without hesitation assume that she had the so-called "oral" fantasy of pregnancy: that is, she supposed that her mother had become pregnant by eating and had now formed the baby in her abdomen in the same way as feces. Thus her idea of forcing her way into the abdomen so that its contents should spurt out was at the same time an expression of an anal desire, and the idea of eating the contents was a coprophilic one of some sort of wallowing in feces along with her mother. (Another root of the idea of something sharp forcing its way into the body so that fluid material comes out was found to lie in the enemas which her mother had given her.)

It will be seen that we have arrived at the primitive purposive ideas of oral sadism which have been stressed so often by Melanie Klein.[13] Nor can there be any doubt of the reality of such wishes or of their sexual basis. The only question is whether when Melanie Klein makes such formulations as that the contents of the body that are to be robbed and eaten up are "the father's penis, which is presumed to be in the mother's body," etc., she is not far too greatly underestimating the integral mode of thinking at these levels and far too ready to base it upon a terminology that belongs to the adult world.

Three factors seems to have been responsible for the fact that these impulses

[13] See, for instance, M. Klein, "Early Stages of the Oedipus Conflict," Int. J. Psa., Vol. 9, 1928; "Personification in the Play of Children," Int. J. Psa., Vol. 10, 1929; and "Infantile Anxiety-Situations Reflected in a Work of Art," Int. J. Psa., Vol. 10, 1929.

of the patient's, which were originally directed against her mother's womb, came subsequently to be bound up so inseparably with her sexual life. (1) As a result of the measures which her mother took against her enuresis, a sense of guilt became attached to everything sexual; at the same time they remobilized other feelings of guilt that were already present in connection with purely aggressive impulses and linked them to the sexual ideas; this sense of guilt was enormously intensified by her mother's death. (2) The analysis showed beyond any doubt (though I cannot here go into the matter in detail) that soon after her sister's birth she witnessed one or more primal scenes; she concluded from these that her father was lying upon her mother and was afraid that he would crush in her abdomen; this made it possible to mobilize the fantasy that she had previously developed of the "burst bladder" and connect it with the sexual act. (3) These impulses at their very first appearance (as well as later in her behavior toward her sister after she had been born) were of a sadistic-sexual character; they only represented in a special form an intense, primitive, pregenital libidinal impulse directed against her mother.

In order to make this last point intelligible, I shall return once again to the sexual disturbances of the patient's adult life. We have heard that they were based on a fear of wetting herself during the sexual act. And this in turn was feared because as a child she had expected to be punished severely by her mother, to have her abdomen pierced open—the very thing that she now feared from the man. Other material pointed to another fear; if she wetted herself during the sexual act it would reveal the secret of a bodily inferiority for which she was herself to blame. The fantasy ran something like this: "If a man has intercourse with me he will notice that I have no penis" (enuresis and lack of a penis are once again equated) "and the secret of a fearful misdeed of my childhood will be revealed." So that in its day bedwetting was regarded by her not only as something for which her mother would punish her by "piercing open her bladder" but also as a distressing sign that her bladder had already been pierced open. Once, in her impatient curiosity, she had dug around with her fingers every day in the earth in a flower pot so long that she had destroyed the growing plant. She was afraid that in the same way, by digging around in her own body, she had robbed herself of the possibility of another penis growing. Which was really responsible, then, for her lack of a penis (her pierced-open bladder)—her mother or her masturbation? The idea of self-injury through masturbation is certainly only the internalization of what was originally an external fear. The idea "My mother punishes me" must cover another one: "My mother is seducing me into masturbation." When the analysis had reached this point and the patient was in a really bad condition (she began to have transitory depressions), her behavior in the transference suddenly altered. She began to complain very bitterly: the analysis, which was supposed to be a method of cure, was only making her worse; the analyst was keeping her away from real life; it was unforgivable that she should still be going on with it; she had long ago given way to the analyst and become completely subservient to him, and was doing everything he wanted, although it was ruining her. Finally there were open outbursts of rage, in the course of which she produced two or three remarkable associations, which she herself felt were nonsensical. She thought the analyst was only entangling her in his toils so as to drive her to suicide in the end. She felt inclined to shout at him, as the worst possible term of abuse, a vulgar word for the female genitals. I pointed out to her that the idea that the analyst was entangling her in order to drive her to ruin was reminiscent of stories of seducers who end by sucking their victims dry like vampires. The patient replied that she believed she had sometimes had feelings of the same sort toward her father. Upon which I asked whether she had really wanted to abuse her father with the word for the female genitals. No, there could be no doubt that what we had here was a mother-transference from the deepest levels. The analyst, who was seeking to make sexual gratification possible for her, had now mobilized ancient fantasies of being seduced by her mother. Fantasies of sexual play with her mother, which no doubt had a real basis in nursery care, had altered their character since the birth of her sister and her experiences of the primal scene. They now pictured that her mother had only seduced her into pleasure in order to be able, for the purposes of her own pleasure, to dig into her abdomen and eat up its contents. (Here we can see a projection of her own wishes.) That, she felt, was why she had become incontinent—and soon afterward she added "and was without a penis." Every man who came near her, even though he was really only a curtain, was going on the one hand to discover what her mother had done and on the other hand to repeat it.

Thus her feelings of guilt in connection with her infantile masturbation were successfully uncovered, and it even became possible for her to recollect and re-experience details of her sensations at the time. With the help of material that we had already obtained, we were now able to consider the questions of where and how this masturbation had been carried out. In this connection we found various indications that, in part at least, its scene of action had been the vagina or at all events the vaginal orifice. Fantasies concerning an antithesis between "front" and "back" only contrasted the rectum and the genitals to begin with. But as it became clearer that these allusions referred to a front opening and a back opening, an attempt was made to regard this as a contrast between the anal and the urethral functions. Dreams then began to emerge, which were incomprehensible at first but became clearer later, of two kinds of substances— an "unsuccessful," brown one, out of which nothing good could come, and a "good," white, magical one, out of which anything could come. The brown substance belonged to the back opening; it was thus feces, which is not a child. The white substance, on the other hand, belonged to the front opening; it was the raw material for a child. It was a question, so the patient's fantasy ran, of holding back the white substance, like urine; if one let it run out, one was lost. Just at this time there was a large amount of material about being "pierced open genitally" and about the patient's medical interests. We were driven to suppose that on some occasion she had had her genitals inspected by a doctor and that she had connected this with her bedwetting. But in that case the white substance could only represent a discharge. The patient responded to this hypothesis by adducing a memory which had already come up earlier that when (while she was masturbating as a young girl) she had discovered the vaginal orifice, she had quite definitely experienced the event as a rediscovery.

There can thus be no doubt that the oedipus complex proper, which seemed to dominate her life, owed its special form entirely to a transference of traits from her pregenital relation to her mother onto her genital relation to her father. During her puberal years she had, for instance, a masturbation fantasy which was heavily charged with guilt of a Moor violating her in a corset shop. This was a screen for the oedipus complex, but it also had pregenital antecedents. "Corset" turned out to be a screen expression for the idea of "crushing in a big abdomen" and the "Moor" was her father in the form of the Ogre. (It is true that he also stood for one of the men whose penis she had seen for the first time and who was an assistant in a coal shop and for that reason appeared as a Moor.) The uncovering of these deep levels of her relation to her mother made it for the first time possible to understand a number of events in her later life. One of the most intense love relationships that the patient ever had showed some special features which positively refused to fit in with the picture of a father-transference. But they could now be explained on the basis that this love object had been chosen, more directly than any other, according to the deeper prototype afforded by her mother.

What were the aims of the patient's love for her mother in the present case? What was most striking was their enormous ambivalence. On the one side there was a longing for affectionate treatment (what was in essence skin- and equilibrium-erotism); and on the other side there was an immense and almost wholly oral sadism. A striking part was played later by an additional factor, her scoptophilic instinct, which we have recognized as an attenuated form of her oral and urethral erotism. It is possible to speak of phallic wishes directed toward her mother in so far as she had a fantasy of piercing open her abdomen; that fantasy was doubtless governed by the *oral* motive to that impulse. It is not clear whether we can speak of her having had a wish for a child at this time. In any case, if there *was* any such idea of a child, it covered the older idea of feces and milk. A number of clear causes can be seen for having turned away from her mother. The first and most severe of these was once again here the patient's mortification over the birth of a new baby sister. But this alone had not been enough to bring about a separation from her mother. The second factor was the warning or punishment given to her by her mother for enuresis (which was equivalent to a prohibition of masturbation). This no doubt owed its effectiveness to the fact that she became aware at the same time of her own lack of a penis (this was the third factor) and regarded this as a punishment imposed on her by her mother: for at that period her mother herself, being equated with the abdomen (or capacity to bear a child) and the penis, was undoubtedly still regarded as phallic. At that point she began to transfer onto men with a penis the impulses and fears which had so far applied to her mother. The fact that just then (the fourth factor) her mother died had two effects. At the superficial levels the process of shifting onto her father such cathexes as still remained on her mother was accelerated; he now became her sole love object and had to stand for both her parents. In her depths, however, there was an intensification of her oral attitude and in her unconscious many of her pre-oedipal longings for her mother were retained behind the attachment to her father, and from these her neurotic disturbances arose.

## IV

Another woman patient had come to analysis on account of her masochism. (She could only get sexual gratification if she was beaten or indulged in fantasies to that effect.) Her masochism turned out to be almost entirely restricted to the sexual sphere in the narrowest sense of the words—unless one chose to describe as masochistic the fact that she was in fact unsuccessful in a number of departments of life in which she had the highest ambitions. This burning ambition was so much in the foreground of the whole picture of her character that I suspected from the first that it was a modification of particularly intense urethral erotism. Her failure was directly co-ordinated with her ambition. That is to say that she was not interested in the actual subject of the activities in question, but was only dominated by the idea of what she was going to achieve and what people would think about it—to such an extent that it interfered with her efficiency. Her ambition was also linked to an exaggerated sense of justice, and this fact suggested that it originated from some competitive situation. Her fellow competitor had in the first instance been her sister and the thing they were competing for was her father's love. The patient was still fixated upon her father to an extraordinary degree after she was grown up. She hesitated for a time between marrying a man who was *like* her father and one who was *un-*

*like* him. The fact that she ultimately chose the latter was far from being a sign that she had overcome her attachment to her father; it was rather the contrary. If she had chosen the man who was like him, it might have meant that she was really substituting him for her father, whereas the actual choice made it possible for her unconsciously to make light of her marriage and remain devoted to her father. Everything that could be learned of her father's personality was calculated to make his daughter's character intelligible. He had encouraged her ambition in every conceivable way but had never been satisfied by her achievements. He egged her on in the most exaggerated fashion to try to be first in every single situation. Yet he made her feel that he failed to take her seriously, that in general children could achieve nothing and that their worries were mere trifles compared with the serious troubles of grown-up people. My patient had realized at a relatively early age that her father, who had only the two daughters, had passionately wanted a son, and that what he was reproaching her with was not so much being a child as being a girl. The aim which he was constantly holding up before her and at the same time pronouncing unattainable was, in essence, that she should one day become a boy.

On the one hand, therefore, her competitive struggle with her sister was saying: "Which of us two can sooner become a boy and so be better loved by our father?" But on the other hand there were also spheres of competition which seemed to show no markedly masculine features. For instance, the patient had a burning ambition in the matter of the upbringing of children. She was perpetually comparing her own children with her sister's and, indeed, with all that she came in contact with. Which children make the better impression? Which of us will be the better thought of in the capacity of mother? When I suggested to her that this competition must have had a prototype in her childhood, she began by replying in scornful and skeptical tones that when she was a little girl she had not had any children on whom to display her educational talents. But a moment later she remembered her dolls and that she had waged a precisely similar war with her sister in regard to them as she now did in regard to her children. The questions had then been: "Which of us has the better dolls? Which of us keeps them cleaner? Which of us can play with them better?" In those days she had accidentally (by parapraxes) broken some of her sister's dolls. She had been haunted all her life by feelings of guilt over this, as though she had killed real children; she had smashed dolls of her own, too, by way of self-punishment, and so on.

But what was the meaning of "looking after the dolls better"? So far as the analysis could show, it meant two things. In the first place it meant being able to be clean. In next to no time—do what she could about it—the patient's dolls were dirty and in rags. She was constantly being reproached about this, and her mother (her father paid no attention of any kind to the little girls' games) was always holding up her sister to her as a model. But "bringing up children" also meant something else, which seemed at first to have no sense in childhood: namely, bearing children. She showed an exaggerated sympathy on one occasion for a childless woman; and this led us to see that, behind a wish that all women should have bad children, there really lay a wish that they should have *no* children. Dreams, arising out of day's residues connected with ambition and bringing up children, showed convincingly that the woman who counted to the patient as being best at bringing up children was the one who had the greatest number of children: a woman with four children was worth more than one like the patient (and also her mother) with only two. The next step was to find the infantile roots of this ambition to bear children. Once again there were two. One of these led to her mother and combined the ambition to bear children with the ambition to be clean. Her mother had evidently carried out her earliest training in cleanliness with unusual strictness and with libidinal interest. But even up to a relatively late period she had insisted upon inspecting her daughters' stool every day—which was enough to account for a "competition in child-bearing" between the sisters. A second root led us to the wish for masculinity which I discussed earlier. "Bearing children" meant the same as "producing." The patient sought to win her father's love by means of products of every sort which she showed him. This was precisely what he kept urging her on to; and this was precisely where she gained the conviction that she lacked the necessary wherewithal for attaining that aim—namely a penis.

Thus her ambition, doomed as it was to perpetual failure, included longings alike of a masculine kind (her penis envy) and of a feminine kind (her interest in bringing up children), dictated in both cases by a high degree of narcissistic demand for appreciation. We were still ignorant of how these two kinds of longings were interrelated; but it was certain that urethral and anal fixations must have been concerned.

Masculinity and femininity were strangely condensed, not only in this concept of "production" but in other regions of thought as well. The patient showed marked ambition in the matter of illness. I must at once explain that this had no connection with the masochism from which I started this account and to which I shall later return. "Being ill" was far from meaning to her "suffering" or anything of the kind: her unconscious idea of it was very much more infantile than that. "Being ill" meant to her "being something special": only very big and important people got "real illnesses." How this view of hers originated will become clear as soon as we learn something of the domestic habits that prevailed in her parents' house. Her father was neurasthenic: he was always supposed to be ill, had to have a special diet and regarded his afternoon nap as sacred. Everything revolved around consideration for her father's ill health. Yet this same father, oddly enough, showed nothing but ridicule and contempt for his children's illnesses. He regarded every illness as a way of playing truant from school and every pain as exaggerated. So it was just the same with illness as with production. Her father insisted all the while on what an enormous amount of love a "really" sick person deserved, but declared at the same time that it was impossible for the patient ever to achieve a "real" illness.

Quite early in the analysis the patient had once told me when and how she had first seen a penis. This memory had always remained conscious; yet she had no notion that the event had been of importance for her later life. When she was three or four she had been sitting with her nursemaid on a bench in the park when a man sitting beside them had taken out his penis and begun playing with it. The nursemaid immediately led her off, saying that the man was a swine and adding something about the police. The patient only remembered feeling astonished at the strange big thing the man had. The first dreams that contained allusions to this scene convinced her that she must also have thought: "Why haven't I got one too? I should like to have one too."

The linking of this event with her ambition for being ill led to the analysis of her beating fantasy. She used to imagine herself intentionally annoying a man (or sometimes a woman) more and more till he suddenly burst into an unbridled rage and began beating her with a stick. In analysis the accent was shifted from the stick onto the rage. It became clear that the patient was anxious to see what a man was like when he suddenly got into a rage. Furthermore "getting into a rage" was revealed as meaning "getting red." In her dreams she saw epileptic men suddenly falling down in convulsions in the street. There was no doubt she wanted to see an excited man; and that meant she wanted to see a man suddenly get red or ill. Her sexual longing made her wish that the scene in the park could be repeated; she had presumably thought that what she saw on the man was some kind of "tumor," an illness, but nevertheless something desirable. "I should like to be as ill as my father and be able to impress him with it" must therefore be interpreted: "I should like to have a penis like my father, and then he would love me more." But the analysis of the beating-fantasy led still further. The prototype of the person who did the beating was a man who had entirely disappeared from her memory: he was the father of a boy she knew, who was in fact liable to sudden fits of rage, who easily got excited and then went red in the face. The patient knew at the time that he often used to beat his son but she had never witnessed such a scene. The thought occurred to her that a girl she knew who had exhibited genitally and anally deserved to be punished by being beaten; and this led us to see what sort of behavior she would use for making the man excited. The masochistic fantasy concealed an exhibitionistic one, and the complete fantasy ran: "I should like to exhibit and look on while a man gets excited about it and then be beaten for it." What I have already said will be enough to show what a strong exhibitionist component there was in the patient's sexuality and character. What we call "ambition" was distorted exhibitionism: "Look how good I am at getting (producing) children!" "Look how seriously ill I can be!" "Look how clean I can be!" These were the three mottos by which her whole life seemed to be ruled. In this connection I may add a further detail apropos of her pride in being ill. From the day of her first menstruation, she felt happy in an exhibitionistic way over the fact that she bled a great deal and (in contradiction to her exaggerated cleanliness) she contemplated the discharge with joy and pride. Her pride in blood was a repudiation of an earlier dread of it.

The patient had spoken of a girl who had exhibited and of a boy who had been beaten. She thought it was her beating-fantasy which had first brought these two things together. But it now appeared from the analysis of some dreams that the boy who had in fact been beaten had also exhibited in front of her by urinating. The two children had had urinating games, in which presumably the patient had been laughed at because she had no penis. No details of these games were any longer obtainable, but enough was established to show that an identification with this boy who had in fact been beaten by his father lay behind the patient's longing to be beaten. An originally phallic impulse had been repressed, to this effect: "I should like to do the same as what the man in the park did" (or be as ill as he was). When we consider the patient's great dread of blood, the meaning of her beating-fantasy seems to emerge. Not only did it cover the prohibited idea of the man getting excited (i.e., the appearance of the penis), but it also repudiated castration. Thus her full sexual fantasy, of which the being beaten formed only a part, ran: "I will display a penis, like this boy and that man, so that my father may be fond of me. I will not believe that I have been castrated for doing this and shall never have a penis any more. That is not so. People are only beaten for things like that."

Since we are not here discussing the psychology of the perversions, I will only add a few sentences to show how much condensation lay in the patient's wish to be beaten. In connection with her love for her father, she was faced with the tasks of getting rid of the penis as the root of all trouble, of getting rid of her strongly anal instinctual undercurrent (on account of her exaggerated training in cleanliness), of avenging herself on her preferred sister, and of tolerating her father's contempt. In her beating-fantasy the objectionable penis was replaced by the beating hand, and the anus by the skin of the buttocks; in the unconscious fantasy the beating really applied to her sister, and it was only secondarily turned against her own ego; and the sexualization of the process of being beaten made it more possible for her to tolerate her father's real contempt. Her masturbatory activities had been continued throughout her whole childhood without any period of latency. It was the perverse distortion of her original fantasies which enabled her to overcome her sense of guilt, though in spite of everything it remained considerable (cf. her overcompensatory pride in blood). She had certainly been prohibited from masturbating by her mother. I should like to point out that, though in the patient's memory she had always carried out masturbation with her clitoris, the analysis showed that it had an autoerotic forerunner that was carried out "further back" and which was thus probably of an anal character. Some isolated memory traces pointed in the direction of her having also practiced masturbation in the vagina or at the vaginal orifice.

In the interpretations that have been made at the level of the oedipus complex we have been regarding the patient's feminine (or anal) ambition as a distortion of her phallic impulses. We were certainly justified in doing so, but we are equally justified in suspecting that this phallic oedipus complex had pregenital antecedents in which exhibitionism and anal erotism played the leading parts. The patient said that her mother had tormented her with regulations about orderliness and cleanliness all through her childhood. Though her whole life was permeated with anal-erotic traits, our first discussions of the subject had aroused the strongest resistance, and for a long time she had endeavored to repudiate the very existence of anal erotism. The idea "my father *shall* see how ill I can be" must have had behind it the older idea "my mother *shall* see how well I can produce things." It gradually became clearer that the competitive struggle with sister-figures was concerned by no means only with her father's love but also with her mother's. Any woman of whom she had a high opinion had only to speak to her for her to feel recognized and happy, but if this same woman diverted her attention, in however unimportant and transient a fashion, to someone else of her sex, the patient at once felt miserable and became filled with a violent hatred for which she could find no sort of rational basis. It was a repetition of a competitive struggle between schoolgirls about an adored mistress; and this in turn was a new edition in puberty of the infantile competition for her mother. It will be remembered that the beating-fantasy sometimes had a woman as its conscious object. And although the patient asseverated, in identification with her father, that she despised women, it happened more and more frequently that women made their appearance as authorities whose recognition she warmly solicited and whose judgment she greatly feared, for instance in connection with the upbringing of children. During this phase of the analysis she withdrew a good part of her transference interest from the analyst and turned it onto women, as though she were saying to him: "You can't fit in with my

transference fantasies since you're not a woman." The contempt that she felt
for her mother in real life had arisen relatively late; for she did it in imitation
of her father, and was saying to him: "I'm not like Mother; I'm one of the men-
folk." The contempt covered a deep admiration for her mother as a competitor
whom she could never catch up with. (When she herself became a mother, she
was clearly competing in her ambition not only with sister-figures but with her
mother too.) But the contempt also covered a deep admiration for her mother
as someone whose love she was determined to capture for herself (without regard for her father) and to divert from her sister. Just as she had sought to
impress her father with her "productions" and "illness," so at an earlier date
she had sought to impress her mother. The forerunners of her masculine "productions" had been anal ones. One wonders whether her masculine wish to be
ill, which was later replaced by the wish for masturbation and for bearing
children, may also have had a pre-oedipal forerunner.

At the end of the patient's second year or at the beginning of her third her
sister had a severe illness. It had not, as in our first case, led to trepanning of
the skull; it was an abdominal complaint. It seems very likely that as a result
of this illness her mother had centered her care and affection upon the sister—
not only immediately after it, but throughout her childhood. No doubt this illness—in contradistinction to all the patient's own illnesses—had been "taken
seriously." She had connected with her sister's illness some notions which were
hard to put into words of changes of a sexual kind. Her later pride in having a
menstrual discharge went back, as was shown by her dreams, to her joy at being
as ill as her sister, whose diarrhea was evidently represented by her own later discharge. Her father, who had to have his special diet, was therefore suffering,
like her sister, from an abdominal complaint. So that all these people who
had "an illness down there"—her sister, the man in the park and her father—
seemed to be preferred to her. No doubt, too, her exhibitionistic longings dated
from this period: "I want my abdomen to be examined like my sister's." Thus
"I should like to be able to show myself off like my sister" was the forerunner
of the fantasy which lay unconsciously behind her perversion: "I should like to
be able to show myself off like the boy who has a penis but is beaten."

In the present case the pre-oedipal attachment to the mother does not stand in
such clear contrast to later times as in the two cases I have already discussed.
Nevertheless here too it has been shown that the characteristics of the patient's
oedipus complex and the marks left upon it by its pregenital antecedents—
her ambition, her competitive envy, and especially her pride in being ill—were
transferred from her mother onto her father. The aims of the impulses that
were directed toward her mother were above all anal-exhibitionist and probably

also urethral-exhibitionist, besides being influenced by skin-erotism and, strongly, by scoptophilia.[14] Her attachment to her mother was characterized by strong ambivalence. The way for its end was prepared by the deep mortification she felt when her mother transferred her interest from her onto her sick sister, and also by the strictness with which her mother trained her to cleanliness. The end was actually set in motion by her observing the man's penis in the park, which she immediately took as a repetition of her sister's illness and thus of a snub from her mother. The latent content of her chief sexual fantasy—a longing to be able to exhibit phallically—and her idea of being castrated for that offense suggests a further probability. It seems likely that when she became aware of her own lack of a penis she formed a notion that she had once possessed a penis but that it had been taken away from her through her mother's neglect or through the measures her mother took at the time of her training in cleanliness.

## V

My fourth case is one with which I hope to deal at greater length elsewhere. I shall therefore content myself here with bringing out briefly some of the material which seems to be of interest in the present connection. It concerns a woman whose entire infantile instinctual life was dominated by her relation to her mother. Her father left the family circle while she was still in her second year; so that the men who were of importance to her in her later sexual life corresponded from the very first to a maternal prototype, without any complications from her oedipus complex proper. Her case was an instance of the "oral symptom complex" which was recently described by Wulff [15] and which appears to lie between manic-depressive disorder, drug addiction, and hysteria. The main part of the patient's libido was concentrated upon the function of eating, and periods of gorging alternated with periods of almost complete abstention from food. The former were in the nature of orgies, and evoked intense feelings of guilt in the patient, as a result of which she felt ugly, fat, bloated, and altogether degenerate and diseased. If she abstained from food, this sense of her own unworthiness (which corresponded to a feeling of severe bodily damage) could be to some extent mitigated. As a rule, however, these feelings of being damaged were so strong that they governed all her relations with other people. She was in an exaggerated state of social anxiety: she must know or guess in advance what other people thought of her. She had an immense desire to be loved so as to be able to increase her self-confidence and compensate for the reproaches of her

---

[14] In this account I have disregarded the indications of sadistic impulses, which were also present in great number, and which, after they had been turned against the patient's own ego, dominated her manifest masochistic sexual fantasy, on the ground that they were of less importance for the general picture than in the former cases.

[15] M. Wulff, "Ueber einen interessanten oralen Symptomenkomplex," *Int. Z. Psa.*, Vol. 18, 1932.

superego. But this never succeeded: she was always obliged to arrange things so that she was abandoned and her unworthiness thus confirmed. In this state she felt that she herself was the lowest of all God's creatures and that everyone else was inestimable and ideal. Strangely enough, however, after these disappointments—for a time at least—things might be reversed. At such times she would detect and scarify everyone else's weaknesses with quite remarkable acuteness and spite; and she would then ridicule the ignorance and baseness of other people in almost exactly the same words which as a rule she used against herself.

Two historical prototypes of this behavior were discovered with little difficulty. Her voracious eating, which made her so ugly and ill, had the meaning of a regressively distorted masturbation from which as a child she had dreaded the same consequences. The complete lack of interest in all genital processes which she showed at the beginning of the analysis, her assertion that she had never masturbated, as well as the perpetual motor restlessness of her hands, pointed toward this connection, which was confirmed in the course of the analysis, particularly by the analysis of her dreams. The first object which she had treated in the ambivalent manner I have described had been her mother. She produced her spiteful caricatures of other people relatively seldom, and they became morbidly prominent only after she had suffered a disappointment. But in the case of her relation to her mother this attitude predominated consciously. She reproached her with being stupid, incompetent, unhealthy, and often even with being ugly, in a way that was clearly without any objective justification. And in spite of this she produced quantities of memories and, more particularly, of symptomatic acts which allowed of no doubt that at one time she had loved her mother dearly.

Since identifications with her mother cropped up in every direction—for instance, she had taken up the same profession as her mother—it seemed more and more probable that the reproaches which she heaped upon her mother were identical with her self-reproaches. These were directed, as in melancholia, against introjected objects; [16] only in her case the introjection had remained partial—reproaches against the object were still retained alongside the depressive self-reproaches. In her early childhood she had had several illnesses, and she was very unwilling to think back into that period. "All my unhappiness," she felt, "dates back to that time; since then I've been ugly and useless—and I don't want to think back into it." The analysis showed beyond a doubt that it was during that period that her struggle against masturbation (and bedwetting) had raged. Her mother had forbidden it, and she attributed her lack of a penis (which she realized then or somewhat later) to this activity. For that reason she deter-

[16] S. Freud, "Mourning and Melancholia," *Coll. Pap.*, Vol. IV, London, Hogarth, 1948.

mined to turn away completely from the genitals and started back along the path of oral repression, which had already been marked out by fixations.

Her reproaches against her mother now began to group themselves more and more round this period of illness and began to take the shape of complaints that her mother had not looked after her properly when she was ill. It was evident, therefore, that what she was really reproaching her mother with was her prohibition against masturbating. At the same time, this reproach must have undergone a twofold transformation: first into a fantasy of being seduced and secondly into thoughts that corresponded to her knowledge that her mother too was without a penis.

At first it was: "My mother did not look after me properly." But it then became: "My mother looked after me in some sort of ugly and vulgar way." It was a long time before we could discover what this really meant. The family had lived in fairly modest circumstances, and to the patient's recollection this seemed like a sordid outrage on the part of her mother. They had been restricted for space, and the "ugliness" evidently consisted in the fact that she had often had occasion to see her mother performing various toilet operations, and so on. The neighbor's children used to come to visit them, and started sexual games; and this had been the occasion on which she had come to know the penis. "My mother was so bad," she complained, "that she let me come into contact with these bad children." This could only mean: "You have no right to forbid my masturbating, since it was you yourself who seduced me into it. If I've become ugly and useless, the fault is yours." There was a particularly tormenting memory of her mother feeding her up unceasingly and with endless patience when she was run down after her illness. The patient thought she remembered what a burden she had felt it. Though her reason told her that her mother could only have been led to behave in this way by feelings of concern about the patient, she nevertheless felt this feeding up as something decidedly evil that her mother had carried out in order to torment her. When we bear in mind that later on all of her wishes and anxieties were expressed in terms of eating we can safely say that this reproach too must have meant: "It was wicked and wrong of my mother to seduce me into sexual pleasures, and so bring about all my unhappiness."

Her fantasy of having been seduced by her mother was intended to assuage her own feelings of guilt. But it also covered another, deeper reproach: "My mother did not love me enough." She showed by various pieces of behavior that the reproach "My mother tormented me with her perpetual feeding" should be regarded as a case of "representation by the opposite." There lay concealed behind it the reproach "My mother didn't give me enough to eat." The demands which the patient made for love, and which I cannot here discuss in detail, were extraordinary. We discovered, too, in the analysis what the actual deprivation of love was which she had suffered in her early childhood, and which had raised her demands to such a pitch. When she was two years old, her parents had been divorced. The circumstances were such that her mother had been greatly distressed. At this time her mind had no doubt been chiefly occupied with her own sorrow and she had been very much self-absorbed. It is true that she carried out her duties to her children in a self-sacrificing manner, but she evidently did so without feeling any inclination to enter into their interests more closely. So that the patient's reproaches could be summed up altogether in some such formula as this: "My mother didn't love me enough or protect me enough. As a consequence I lapsed into masturbation and have ruined my whole life. The hatred that I feel for my mother on that account is a grave crime, which requires expiation." I have already mentioned that her later self-reproaches reproduced in detail the original reproach that had been aimed against the object—a mechanism familiar to us in melancholia. The important feature in all this from the point of view of our present context is the child's triumph over discovering that her mother too was without a penis. This was shown by the way in which all the ugliness and the inferiorities which corresponded to her own lack of a penis were now attributed in precisely the same way to her mother as to her own ego. And this in turn naturally caused a still further intensification of the feelings of guilt and of her self-reproaches.

The patient's feeling that she was unspeakably ugly was rationalized by a recollection that grown-up people had often called her ugly when she was a little girl. She had cried a great deal, and had been given an appropriate nickname on that account. They used to show her the picture of a frog in a book of fairy tales and tell her that she looked like that when she cried. The frog looked to her unspeakably ugly. She felt convinced that she looked exactly like it, and hated herself and the world. The analysis showed that once again incontinence of tears stood for incontinence of urine; and her recollection of being laughed at for crying was only a screen for the fierce battle she had waged with her mother over her bedwetting. "I'm so ugly because I cry so much" was a distorted version of the idea "I'm ugly because I can only urinate in an ugly way and not like boys."

We were just in process of working through the feelings of being abandoned which she had had as a child but had now forgotten, when there emerged a memory of her feeling of loneliness as she lay in bed longing to be loved, while her mother, instead of coming to her, sat by herself in the room and cried. Her mother had cried a great deal during this period of her depression. There can be no doubt that while the little girl was reproached with crying she must have thought: "You've no right to reproach me with that. You cry just as much, and then you look just as ugly as I do." But if my interpretation is correct and in-continence of tears means "being castrated," then the patient was also saying: "You can't reproach me, for you've become just as worthless and ugly (that is, penisless) as I am—and evidently on account of the same crime." No doubt this contemptuous sexual estimate of her mother, which corresponded to the patient's spite later in life, originated at a relatively late date—much later, at all events, than her feeling of not being sufficiently loved (or not loved in the right way) by an omnipotent mother.

In this case too the aims of the patient's attachment to her mother (though I cannot now give the detailed evidence for this) were of a predominantly oral-sadistic character. What seems more especially to call for notice here is the pa-tient's motives for turning away from her mother—the motives which led to the prominence of the hatred in her ambivalent attitude to her mother. These were: her feeling (which had a sound objective basis) of being left by her mother and not sufficiently loved by her, the prohibition against masturbating (repre-sented in the struggle about bedwetting), and her discovery of her own lack of a penis. This discovery and the bodily feeling appropriate to it were subsequently —in the form of a fantasy of revenge—extended to her mother and to the whole world.[17]

## VI

Making use of this material, I shall now proceed to discuss three groups of questions: (1) concerning the instinctual aims of the pre-oedipal attachment to the mother, (2) concerning the reasons for the passing of that attachment, and (3) concerning the infantile erotogenicity of the vagina.

If we cast our eyes over the chaos of sexual aims and anxieties that is re-vealed by the analysis of the periods with which we are dealing, all that we can say about them in general is that they display "polymorphous perversity" But here, as always, an insight into the stages of libidinal organization makes it pos-sible to bring order into the polymorphous perversity of infantile sexuality. Whatever erotogenic zone is at the moment dominant sets its mark on the little girl's longing for her mother. Freud himself has stressed the fact that in a girl's sexual attitude towards her mother oral, (anal-) sadistic, "and finally even phallic" impulses appear in succession.[18] In the cases we have been considering, the oral and sadistic attitudes are on the whole by far the most prominent. The earliest period, in which object impulses in general are developed, in relation to the

---

[17] I should like once more to emphasize the fact that a complete picture of this case could only be given after a consideration of the patient's oral pre-history, as well as of her introjective processes and their consequences.

[18] For what follows, see once more S. Freud, "Female Sexuality," Coll. Pap., Vol. V.

mother, seems to have left behind the deepest traces. Freud is entirely convincing when he remarks that all these impulses, including the oral ones, are first experienced *passively* and that subsequent activity seeks to repeat and master that experience. Nevertheless, later, subjectively passive aims seem to arise owing to the activity being turned back once more onto the ego. This prominence of the primitive oral aims in the impulses directed toward the mother also explains why all the attributes that characterize primitive orality are found in them to a greater degree than in later heterosexuality: not only ambivalence, but also the features that mark the preliminary phases of object relations—"partial love," ideas of incorporation, and the characteristics of identification associated with those ideas. It seems as though, wherever the oedipus complex in a woman seems to show particularly strong signs of a substructure derived from an antecedent relation to her mother that has not been dealt with, we can also say that her orientation is particularly oral. Alongside of (or covering) these oral impulses we habitually find (together with skin erotism) anal and urethral impulses. (The last of these [bedwetting] appears with such regularity that it seems surprising that Freud should not have mentioned it specially.) Phallic traits are not found with anything like the obviousness of the pregenital ones. For the urethral impulses cannot by any means be regarded as being in the first instance phallic. They attach themselves to the phallic impulses when once penis envy has become established, but by that time the process of turning away from the mother has also started. In the material before us the wish to have a child with the mother was of an anal rather than a phallic kind. It is certain that in these cases clitoridal masturbation was practiced (and forbidden) during the period of attachment to the mother. It could not be shown, however, that it was accompanied by fantasies of wanting to penetrate with the clitoris into some hollow organ of the mother's. Only in the case of my second patient, who wanted to burst her mother's "bladder," were there signs of anything of the sort; but, precisely with her, the oral-sadistic character of this fantasy (a wish to eat up the contents of the mother's body) was quite specially prominent. Thus our expectation seems to have been fulfilled that the pre-oedipal period would approximately, though not completely, coincide with the pregenital one. Not one of my cases gave evidence of the father appearing as a rival who interfered with the patient's love of her mother—not one, that is, gave evidence of a well-defined negative oedipus complex as a forerunner of the positive.[19] Further evidence is necessary to show whether this is merely a chance finding or whether on the contrary, as I am inclined to suspect, a fully developed negative oedipus complex is relatively exceptional. The

[19] A. Lampl de Groot believes that this occurs habitually. See "The Evolution of the Oedipus Complex in Women," *Int. J. Psa.*, Vol. 9, 1928.

main impression left is that wherever one comes across this early love for the mother one also meets with features which are familiar to us as being specifically pregenital.[20]

There are defensive anxieties corresponding to the instinctual aims that are in operation. The predominantly oral character of the latter finds its counterpart in the numerous oral anxiety ideas (stressed by Freud as well)—ideas of starving, of being poisoned, and so on, culminating in the idea of being eaten up. No doubt we often meet with anxiety ideas of this kind as a distortion of castration anxiety. (The case of the Wolf Man is an instance of this.) [21] Nevertheless, it can scarcely be doubted that in such cases the distortion follows regressive paths, and that there is a primitive fear of being eaten up, belonging to the oral period, which is only reactivated later for purposes of distortion. Freud says he has not found this fear in a direct form in women: "The fear of being eaten I have so far found only in men; it is referred to the father." I must say at once that in my opinion a chance in Freud's selection of material must be responsible for his astonishment at always finding this fear (which must certainly apply originally to the mother) displaced onto the father, even in the case of men. For some considerable time past, I have been able to observe this fear in its original form—directed, like the similar material in so many fairy tales and legends, toward the mother—as the principal anxiety idea in a number of male neuroses. I have also been able to uncover the condition upon which the clear emergence of this fear evidently depends: the birth of a girl in the little boy's family or environment.[22] His knowledge that there is a child in his mother's pregnant abdomen clearly leads him to the conclusion that women are man-eaters. The dread of "intrauterine castration" follows from this. I will not pursue this branch of the subject further, but return to the question whether it may not be that girls suffer from a corresponding anxiety. It is true that none of the oral anxieties included in our present material express the idea of being eaten up so undisguisedly as the male cases. But the idea of being sucked up by her mother, which occurred in a case that I have previously reported,[23] and the idea presented by the second of my present patients that her mother would pull out the contents of her body and devour them, seem by no means far removed from the idea of being eaten up. And, in general, the anxiety idea of being robbed of the contents of one's body, which is certainly not a rare one and is also to be counted among the anal anxieties, has its place in this connection, since it is

---

[20] This does not imply that I feel any doubt that the change of object occurs typically during the phallic phase—in the sense that being put at a disadvantage through lacking a penis only produces a strong effect where there is a phallic orientation.

[21] S. Freud, "From the History of an Infantile Neurosis," *Coll. Pap.*, Vol. III, London, Hogarth, 1948.

[22] O. Fenichel, "The Dread of Being Eaten," No. 18 in this volume.

[23] O. Fenichel, "The Pregenital Antecedents of the Oedipus Complex," No. 21 in this volume.

usually linked to the idea that the contents of the body after being stolen will be eaten up. It represents a dread of reprisals for corresponding desires felt by the subject toward her mother, and its widespread occurrence has with justice been repeatedly stressed by Melanie Klein.[24] I will once more, however, repeat my opinion that one must be very cautious in putting the contents of these instinctual fantasies into words. The physical prototype of these ideas is in my view the child's training in cleanliness, in the course of which the mother does actually demand the contents of the child's body. If this subject were to be fully considered—which is impossible here—it would be necessary to take account of all the phenomena of introjection: that is to say, the aim of incorporating the object and the subject's fantasy that the contents of his own body—whether feces or an organ—are identical with some object in the external world and have found their way into his body by being eaten (or by an enema, or by being breathed or rubbed in, or by being looked at). The fear of being robbed of the contents of one's body is related to the fear of an enema, for which Freud has found such a novel explanation and which played a part in one of my cases. But the anxieties centering round the subject of continence seem to be far more important than this. The patients expected that their mother would damage them most severely as a punishment for being wet (or dirty); but they also thought that they would damage *themselves* by bedwetting or that the bedwetting was a sign of their having already damaged themselves. These last ideas were connected with fears of being punished by the *introjected* mother and also corresponded to the notion of being *magically* robbed of the contents of their body.

Finally, as a result of the prohibition against masturbating, various fears of injury to the genitals became attached to these pregenital anxieties—a subject which I shall touch upon later. All of these ideas have in common a covering motive of fear of loss of love.

In the same way, according to Freud, the fantasy which occurs so frequently in women of having been sexually seduced by their father covers a deeper idea of having been seduced by their mother, which can relate to actual manipulations carried out by their mother while looking after them in infancy. These real manipulations cause no less anal than genital stimulation, and, along with the displacement of attachment from the mother to the father, a parallel displacement may perhaps have taken place from pregenitality to genitality. An interesting counterpart of the straightforward displacement of the seduction fantasy onto the father is presented by a case published by me in 1930.[25] There the displacement did not take place to begin with, and the patient's father appeared as her protector and savior from the seductive wiles of her mother, who was pic-

[24] M. Klein, *op. cit.*
[25] O. Fenichel, *op. cit.*

tured in the pregenital shape of a vampire. Her father was imagined as giving her back what her mother as a seducer had robbed her of; nevertheless later on he himself became, if not a seducer, at least a producer of illness and a castrator.

With regard to phallic activity in reference to the mother, Freud wrote: "The sexual activity of this period culminates in clitoridal masturbation; probably the child accompanies this with images of her mother, but whether she really imagines a sexual aim and what that aim is my experience does not make clear." In my cases the ideas seem to have been of a purely pregenital kind. The idea of having a child with the mother was clearly present only in my first case; but there the mother-figure was thought of as the donor and the patient herself as the bearer of the child, which was pictured anally. It is true that I occasionally came across the idea that a newly born baby sister was a child of the little girl and of her mother, but it was always possible to regard it as being no more than a reaction formation to the wish that "this should be my child and not yours." The interest in producing a child seemed in the pre-oedipal period to be wholly anal.

In turning to the problem as to the motives for the change in object, I shall begin by considering for a moment what in general are the reasons that determine a step forward in mental development. (1) What determines the transition from one stage of libidinal organization to the next higher?—say from the oral to the anal-sadistic, or from that to the phallic? (2) What brings about the "passing of the oedipus complex" [26] and the beginning of the latency period? As regards the first of these questions, we must above all remember that a transition of this kind never takes place suddenly but that the phases pass over from one to another by degrees. Thus, for instance, at some particular time a person may already in the main be open to genital excitement, but his instinctual executive functions may still be predominantly anal, and so on.[27] The essential cause of the changes between the phases is to be looked for in somatic events. (The instinctual *sources* change.) But no doubt factors of experience play a part as precipitating causes and are responsible for many deviations from the normal. The clearest example of this is the effect of seduction, which either stimulates a higher libidinal position precociously or acts so strongly as a repellent from it that it cannot be reached even later. But in general it is the case that all gratifications tend to make the subject hold fast to a libidinal position and all frustrations tend to make him leave it. Moreover, traumas of any kind, even though they show no special signs of being either gratifications or frustrations of the predominant instinctual impulse, nevertheless create fixations at the libidinal posi-

[26] S. Freud, "The Passing of the Oedipus-Complex," *Coll. Pap.*, Vol. II, London, Hogarth, 1948.
[27] See, for instance, B. Bornstein, "Phobia in a Two-and-a-Half Year Old Child," *Psa. Quart.*, Vol. 4, 1935.

tion concerned. What above all precipitates the forward movement are such prohibitions which suggest that the gratification of the present instinct involves some
danger (e.g., of loss of love or of castration). Experiential factors of a social kind
support or inhibit the biological factor.

Similar conditions no doubt apply to the passing of the oedipus complex, but
the distribution of emphasis is different. Presumably the oedipus complex too
must come to an end for phylogenetic reasons—as Freud says, "it falls out like
the milk teeth." In boys it occurs incontestably owing to the fear of castration.
But, as we know, particular experiences are responsible for the nature and content
of the castration anxiety as well as for its consequences. It would certainly be
wrong to ask whether the superego (or the idea which is at the basis of its
formation: that it is dangerous to gratify the instincts) originates in the biological imperfections of man or in the experiencing of prohibitions in childhood. Obviously the two factors must operate together; but their relative strength
is of importance. If babies were not so helpless and if they had not experienced
any traumatic anxiety, no doubt they might later have no dread of instinctual
gratification. But the fact that they *have* this dread, and the way in which they
have it, is determined by their education and its prohibitions. The fundamental
antithesis in the mental life of man still remains the one between the instincts
and the prohibitions of the external world. In any case, the social components
have a greater share in the bringing about of the latency period than in the
changes of the libidinal organization.

Is the transition in little girls from their attachment to their mother to that
to their father more like the former or the latter process? Undoubtedly the
former. The fact that women are in the end attracted by men is certainly biologically determined, and the loss of their homosexual beginnings is comparable
to that of their milk teeth. The occasion for the change is supplied by the disappointments inevitably experienced from the mother. Freud has made it clear
that these are not of equal importance for both sexes, but that those which
affect only the female sex must be given the most weight. (In spite of their disappointments, little boys do *not* turn away from their mothers.) The important
factor, then, is the castration complex—the perception by the girl of her own lack
of a penis. The earlier disappointments have only an auxiliary significance. These
bring it about that the new disappointment too is regarded as the fault of the
mother. In my present material the birth of a younger sister and the training in
cleanliness played the chief part in this connection. But *how* all this is to happen is once again influenced by the particular form that all these experiences
have taken—just as the experiential factors, which give occasion to inhibitions
in development, to fixations, and to regressions, exercise a formative influence in
the transition from one phase of the libido to the next higher one. It is only

necessary to bear in mind how greatly the effects of training in cleanliness and the prohibition against masturbating vary in different circumstances.

Normally, the change of object brings about a change in sexuality but not its disappearance. But in practice, all the same, it seems sometimes to amount to its disappearance. Freud relates the girl's turning away from her mother (which in his view is also a turning from activity to passivity) to things which we had hitherto connected with the beginning of the latency period: "Frequently, with the turning away from the mother there is a cessation of clitoridal masturbation, and very often when the little girl represses her previous masculinity a considerable part of her general sexual life is permanently injured." Very often, but certainly not always. On theoretical grounds, one would expect rather that vaginal masturbation would from now on take its place. It is true that we do not find this. But we do quite often see—and we must regard it as the normal event—that henceforward clitoridal masturbation is continued to the accompaniment of feminine fantasies relating to the girl's father; only then do feelings of shame originating from the oedipus complex become attached to it, and fears of genital injury from her father—in short all those things that we have hitherto thought of and described as the normal oedipus complex of girls. And it is only after these conflicts that the latency period sets in. In the first three of the cases that I have been discussing here the early period of attachment to the mother was followed by an intense sexual attachment to the father, and in two of those cases masturbation undoubtedly persisted. If after a girl has turned away from her mother a large part of her whole sexuality seems to vanish, the disappointments that she has suffered from her mother must obviously have had more effect than they should. In that case the social factor of educative prohibitions has attached itself to the biological factors with complicating results and has interfered with their functioning.

I will now proceed to a detailed comparison between the motives which Freud has assigned to pre-oedipal hostility and the material of my present cases. As we know, pre-oedipal hostility arises when the negative components present in all pregenital object relations become much intensified owing to frustrations. Freud enumerates these motives as follows: (1) First, there is jealousy, whether of the father or of other people. Three of my four patients were dominated by jealousy of a sister: with the first two it arose at the birth of a new baby, while in the third case her rival was older than herself. In the fourth case (as well as in the two others on which I reported previously) [28] this motive was absent. Its place was taken either by being fatherless or by fear of illness. In none of these cases was there evidence of a pronounced negative oedipus complex as a

[28] O. Fenichel, op. cit.

forerunner of the positive one. (2) The wishes directed toward the mother remain ungratified because they are incapable of gratification and are indeed without an aim. (This, incidentally, might have an opposite effect.) The fact that some of these fantasies (for instance, the one which has been stressed by Melanie Klein) are biologically incapable of fulfillment has a place here. This would seem to be a purely biological factor; once again the point is to discover its relative importance in comparison with the other factors. (3) The decisive factor is the castration complex. My material conclusively confirmed the fact that as a rule when a little girl first perceives a penis she at once feels it as a narcissistic mortification and holds her mother responsible for it. The effects of penis envy can be very various, according to the history of the subject's masturbation. "A defiant persistence in masturbation," says Freud, "would appear to open the way to masculinity." I have also seen cases in which the patient displayed a defiant persistence of this kind, but at the same time turned away from her mother completely, and developed a strongly feminine oedipus complex, while the fantasies attached to the latter were then gratified in the masturbation in which she persisted. (On the other hand, my third case showed that a persistent masturbation with *manifest* feminine fantasies may in fact serve a *latent* wish to exhibit the penis.) When Freud says that "resentment at being prevented from free sexual activity has much to do with the girl's detachment from her mother," it must be added that this is also true where the subject's free sexual activity is of a feminine character and takes her father as its object and has jealousy from the oedipus complex as a new and additional motive for hatred of her mother.

The prohibition against masturbating and the castration complex spoil the pleasure of sexuality. How do they accomplish this? By causing anxiety. This is clearly shown by the analysis of feminine frigidity. Here again gratification of genitality, which has remained infantile in the unconscious, is felt as a danger to be avoided: a danger, in the first place, of loss of love but subsequently of damage to the genitals. The latter has been described as a fear of the penis being torn off or split, and so on. My material shows us that fears of this sort too have their pre-oedipal forerunners. My first patient was afraid, in quite a masculine way, that her thumb might be cut off; the second one was afraid that her abdomen might be pierced or cut open; the third and fourth, it is true, were only afraid they might be laughed at or ridiculed. But all four were afraid these things would happen if they wetted themselves; and the foremost fear expressed in their frigidity was that if they were sexually excited they might wet or dirty themselves. This general agreement in all the cases I have observed cannot be accidental. The point is not mentioned in Freud's paper.

In his later set of lectures, Freud has this to say about frigidity: "The sexual frigidity of women . . . is still a phenomenon which is insufficiently understood.

Sometimes it is psychogenic, and, if so, it is accessible to influence; but in other cases one is led to assume that it is constitutionally conditioned or even partly caused by an anatomical factor." [29]

It will be seen that in this formulation Freud does not enter into the special forms of anxiety which frigid women couple with the idea of the sexual act, for the "psychogenic" factor receives no further treatment from him. The widespread occurrence of frigidity squares above all with the fact that not only the particular prohibition against masturbating but the whole education of women is calculated to suggest to girls that sexuality is something bad—that at bottom it is something dangerous. This social factor, in fact, seems to me more important than the anatomical one.[30]

Thus the factor chiefly responsible for directing the girl's development along other paths than the boy's is the different effect produced on her by the sight of the genitals of the opposite sex. "My father must give me back the penis which my mother robbed me of" remains the *Leitmotif* of the change of object. At a later date, Freud remarks, castration is often regarded as a punishment for masturbation and its carrying out is ascribed to the father, and he adds that neither of these ideas can be primary ones. This is certainly true of the idea that it is the father who carries out the punishment. But if a girl made the discovery of the penis after having received a prohibition against masturbating, is it not possible that the thought might immediately arise in her mind that her mother had taken the penis away as a punishment for her masturbation? This seems indeed to have happened in my second case. And this is the point at which to add that in some circumstances the sight of an adult *woman's* genitals can also produce a traumatic effect upon a little girl. In such a case the adult female genitals, in contrast to the girl's own, are regarded as a devouring mouth and are calculated to mobilize the old pregenital anxieties afresh. The oral anxieties, as I have already said, serve as a defense against oral-sadistic aggressiveness, which in its turn is a reaction to real or imagined oral slights. I may recall the part played in my case histories by oral envy and, perhaps, the way in which my first patient wanted to seize her grandmother's breast by force because she imagined it was being held back from her.

Freud writes: "We believe that we may justly assume that for many years the vagina is virtually nonexistent and possibly remains without sensation until puberty. It is true that recently an increasing number of observers have been inclined to think that vaginal stirrings are present even in those early years. But the essence of female genitality must center in childhood in the clitoris." [31] The

---

[29] S. Freud, *New Introductory Lectures on Psycho-Analysis,* p. 180.

[30] S. Freud, " 'Civilized' Sexual Morality and Modern Nervousness," *Coll. Pap.,* Vol. II.

[31] S. Freud, *New Introductory Lectures on Psychoanalysis,* New York, Norton, 1933, p. 161.

new findings in connection with the pre-oedipal attachment to the mother speak strongly in favor of the correctness of Freud's view. If there were a vaginal period of female infantile sexuality which is habitually so much repressed that we cannot see it as a rule in our analyses, we should nevertheless expect regularly to find traces of it revealed by these fresh advances into the hitherto unknown depths of femininity. The new findings show that a vaginal stage of libidinal organization could only occur during the period of the established oedipus complex with the father as object; but it is precisely at this period that we so frequently find clitoridal masturbation. How is it, then, that the existence of vaginal masturbation is nevertheless confirmed by observers? [32] In view especially of my experience in my second case and of the memory traces in the third, I must agree with the views of these observers. Infantile vaginal masturbation, or at least sexuality of the vaginal orifice, does exist. Early infantile masturbatory manipulation does occur in this region, and is accompanied by the fantasy of having some object inserted there. How does this fit in with the apparently contradictory statement of Freud? There is only one possibility. Vaginal sexuality is not an invariable but an occasional phenomenon; it does not dominate any stage of libidinal organization but, like other wishes associated with skin and mucous-membrane erotism, accompanies anal and oral receptivity. It may be that the erotogenic zone belonging to this "genital receptivity" is restricted to the region of the vulva and vaginal orifice. But in that region it undoubtedly occurs; this is proved by little girls having a discharge. There is no question that it bears the mark of orality and anality, and indeed is scarcely to be distinguished from the latter; in conflicts between pregenitality and genitality it stands on the side of pregenitality.

Freud writes again: "The sexual life of women is regularly split up into two phases, the first of which is of a masculine character, whilst only the second is specifically feminine." [33] If this means that girls feel sensations in their clitoris and want to pull at it and rub it, but that after discovering the penis they find that boys are better off in this way than they are, and that it is only after and as a result of this discovery that they learn to take men as their love object instead of women—if this is what is meant by Freud, then he has brought evidence in favor of it which may well be called uncontradictable. But if it means that the girl's fantasy of inserting this highly sensitive organ into a hollow organ habitually precedes the desire to have something inserted into a hollow organ of her own, then, according to my present findings, it seems questionable. What makes decisions on this point so difficult is that clitoridal erotogenicity and masculinity (wishing to penetrate) are by no means always connected with

[32] See the material contained in the paper by J. Mueller, to which I have already referred.
[33] S. Freud, op. cit., p. 159

each other. Analytic observations leave no doubt that clitoridal masturbation can also be accompanied by feminine-receptive fantasies.[34]

[34] Since the completion of this paper a number of works on the same subject have appeared in the psychoanalytic periodicals. I have not been able to consider them here; but it will be obvious from what I have already written that my attitude to some of the views expressed in them is highly critical.

## TWENTY-FIVE

# Analysis of a Substitution of Names Made Twenty Years Before[*]

THE fantasy of having been seduced as a child by an adult, which is much more frequent than actual seduction, is considered by Freud to be one of the "primal fantasies," and he discovered that the meaning of this fantasy was the apologetic denial of autoerotic activity and oedipal wishes. The fantasy makes it possible to indulge oneself in sexual thoughts without guilt.

This was confirmed in the analysis of a minor parapraxis, undertaken twenty years after it happened. The patient was a man with a quite unusually strong sexual inhibition which corresponded to an unconscious fixation on his mother. The analytic material had already suggested that his incestuous wishes and feelings of guilt had found a condensed expression in the unconscious fantasy of having been seduced by his mother into sexual activity. At first the patient could not accept this interpretation. Shortly after, he came to speak of a remarkable lapse of memory which had happened to him in a religious class when he was a small boy. He had been asked about the story of Joseph and had not been able to remember the name "Potiphar." When the teacher had pressed him for an answer, he, believing he had at last remembered the right name, had called out "Tatacky!"—to the great amusement of the whole class. The patient immediately went on to say that he still knew the explanation of this peculiar substitutive formation. He had tried to remember the name "Potiphar" by thinking of the word *"Pfote"*; [†] when questioned by the teacher, what had come into his mind, instead of *"Pfote,"* had been its synonym *"Tatze,"* and he had made out of it "Tatacky."

[*] First published in *Imago*, Vol. 20, 1934, pp. 231–234.
[†] *"Pfote,"* German for "paw."—Trans. note.

It turned out that the patient still did not know who Potiphar was. He thought that Potiphar's wife had beheaded Joseph, and with this he betrayed a castration fantasy. But then he noticed that he had mixed up Potiphar's wife with Salome. The analyst, he assumed, would translate "beheading" by "castration," but assuredly the story of Potiphar's wife had nothing to do with the penis. I answered that it certainly had something to do with sexuality, and told him the story of Potiphar's wife. Yes, he said, now he remembered the story, but they certainly did not tell the children that in school! I thought it more promising not to engage in a discussion on the subject, but to ask for further associations. He now told me that "Tatacky" was the name of a shopkeeper whose sign he used to read on his way to school. It was thus plausible that when he thought of "Tatze," the name which was similar to it and which he had read shortly before should come to his mind. I then said that the word "Pfote," of which he had to think in order to learn the name Potiphar in the first instance, must also have prevented him from remembering the name; thus the "Pfote," that is, the hand, must be objectionable. The patient hastened to deny this: he argued that in that case the substitute word "Tatze," which was identical in meaning, would not have occurred to him either. Moreover, he then said—in complete contradiction to reality—that the difference between Potiphar and Tatacky was not so great: in both words, almost the same letters occurred (!), only the "Po" is lacking in "Tatacky." So then, I replied, the "Po" must be objectionable. "Now I know," said the patient, displeased, "where you are headed; you must certainly be thinking of 'Popo.'" * Well, I could produce good evidence for the correctness of my interpretation. If the "Pfote" in "Potiphar" had been simply replaced by "Tatze" the substitutive word could only at best have been "Tacky." The patient, however, reduplicated the syllable "Ta" and made it "Tatacky," thus betraying the unconscious alteration which he had made in the original word. The objectionable reduplication which would have changed the name into "Popotiphar" was displaced to the substitute word.

Now we could guess what went on in the little boy's mind when he heard the story of Potiphar's wife. It aroused in him a wish to be treated as Joseph was. His mother, too, should seduce him; and he imagined that seduction would take place by a contact of the "hand" (Pfote, Tatze) and the "Popo," either by the mother's hand touching his bottom, or vice versa. This fantasy, however, had to be repressed because of castration anxiety, and together with it the name "Potiphar."

Somewhat later, the patient reported the following dream:

*I am invited to visit Hindenburg. Then I am with his wife in the children's room, I am proud of it, but I am afraid that I may make a fool of myself. Then*

---

* "Popo," child's word in German for the buttocks and anus.—Trans. note.

*a fountain pen gets broken there in the children's room, and everything is flowing with ink.*

The patient's association to the dream situation was the officers' dining room in the war, where the danger of disgracing oneself, he said, was very great, particularly when not only the superior officers but their ladies were present; one had to be on the watch not to give offense in any way. He remembered a lieutenant there who had an affair with the colonel's wife. How disagreeable his situation must have been for him! If he was nice to his ladylove, he insulted his superior; if he was not, he insulted her, and she might then betray him to her husband. When I pointed out that he was back again to the story of Potiphar, he turned to the second part of the dream. He said that the fountain pen was probably a penis symbol. On my suggestion that he should associate to this, he began—apparently without taking cognizance of my comment about the Potiphar story—to remember stories of his school days. In school they had smeared about with ink; though he did not take part in this, he felt guilty when the others did it. He remembered the peculiar smell of the school ink, and the prank of putting carbide into the inkwell, which produced a stench and gas. He now remembered a hitherto forgotten piece of the dream: *"Out of the fountain pen there came compressed air with peculiar noises."*

Now we knew what the fountain pen that broke in the children's room was. (We may assume, without further ado, that Hindenburg represented the patient's father, and his wife the mother.) In point of fact, he had often soiled his pants even as an older boy and had been punished for it. The "disgrace" with which he is threatened in the presence of adults cannot be anything else. If the anally conceived story of Potiphar is linked up with this disgrace, the double meaning of the seduction fantasy, as at once an apology for incest and incest, becomes clear. On the one hand, it is an apology in the sense that it is not he who has soiled his pants, but his mother who has seduced him into it; on the other, it gives him an opportunity to think about anal contacts with his mother, for which perhaps the soiling may in fact have given occasion. The shame which he felt in reality at the time was to be canceled out by his seduction fantasy. It is true that this did not quite succeed. For not only did the shame necessitate his forgetting the word "Potiphar" which reminded him of all this; it also forced him again to "disgrace himself," in that the whole class burst into laughter over the word "Tatacky."

# TWENTY-SIX

# On the Psychology of Boredom*

PSYCHOANALYTIC literature furnishes us with only one work concerning the remarkable field of phenomena presented by boredom. I refer to Alfred Winterstein's paper "Angst vor dem Neuen, Neugier und Langeweile." [1] We shall have frequent occasion in what follows to refer to this paper, which nevertheless leaves many problems unsolved. Probably the word "boredom" covers very different states of mind and psychological attitudes. In my present essay I make no claim to completeness, but only hope to characterize a particular kind of boredom.

Let us take our point of departure from Lipps' [2] definition of boredom, which Winterstein also quotes. "Boredom," he says, "is a feeling of unpleasure arising out of a conflict between a need for intense mental activity and lack of incitement to it, or inability to be incited." Let us add that, besides the need for intense mental activity there is always at the same time an inhibition of that activity. This inhibition is experienced as such—one does not know *how* one ought or wants to be active. It is because of this conflict that incitement from the outside world is sought. Let us add further that the "lack of incitement" often does not correspond to external reality, as is indicated by the addition of the words "inability to be incited." Just as boredom is characterized by the coexistence of a need for activity and an inhibition of activity, so is it characterized by a craving for stimulus and dissatisfaction with the proffered stimuli. Thus the central problem of the psychology of boredom lies in the *inhibition* both of the urge to activity and of the readiness to accept the longed-for incitatory stimuli.

From a purely descriptive point of view, the state of mind of boredom is perhaps best characterized as "an unpleasurable experience of a lack of impulse."

* First published in *Imago*, Vol. 20, 1934, pp. 270–281.
[1] A. Winterstein, "Angst vor dem Neuen, Neugier und Langeweile," *Psa. Bewegung*, Vol. 2, 1930.
[2] T. Lipps, *Leitfaden der Psychologie*, Leipzig, Engelmann, 1903.

This formula poses a problem which must first be solved. We assume that the state of tension of the psychic apparatus is heightened by internal and external stimuli, and that this increased tension elicits impulses, that is, trends whose aim is to re-establish an absence of tension. Thus we should expect instinctual urges to be unpleasurable and instinctual gratifications pleasurable, that is to say, impulses ought to be unpleasurable and lack of impulses pleasurable. The problem that pleasurable impulses do nevertheless exist has often been discussed.[3] The corresponding problem of the existence of unpleasurable lack of impulses seems to be presented in the phenomena of boredom. But boredom, as our definition shows, is not just a lack of impulse, but also a "need for intense mental activity." The lack of impulse by no means coincides with a lack of tension. The problem is rather, Why does this tension not result in impulses—why does it, instead of manifesting itself in the form of instinctual impulses, require "incitements" from the outside world to indicate to the subject what he is to do to decrease his tension?

Naturally, a craving for stimulation that turns toward the external world is also encountered outside the realm of boredom. It arises the moment the small child recognizes that there emanate from the outside world stimuli which can be used for instinctual gratification. Once the subject has experienced pleasurable stimuli, a state of instinctual tension in him brings with it a longing for those stimuli. This longing is accompanied by a recalcitrance toward available objects or stimuli which are unsuited to bring about discharge, and if more suitable ones are not available it leads to introversion, fantasy activity, and, finally, to actual neurotic phenomena due to a damming up of libido. Can such a state of craving for adequate objects, and unpleasure at available inadequate ones, be called "boredom"? Correctly speaking, no doubt, it cannot; yet it often is. We are accustomed to say of objects and stimuli which do not afford us the "aid to discharge" which we legitimately expect of them that they "bore" us. (We shall return to this point later on.) But a person who "is bored," in the strict sense of the word, is searching for an object, not in order to act upon it with his instinctual impulses, but rather to be helped by it to find an instinctual aim which he lacks.

The instinctual tension is present, the instinctual aim is missing. Boredom must be a state of instinctual tension in which the instinctual aims are repressed but in which the tension as such is felt; and therefore one turns to the external world for help in the struggle against repression. The person who is bored can be compared to someone who has forgotten a name and inquires about it from others.

---

[3] S. Freud in *Three Essays on the Theory of Sexuality*, London, Imago, 1949, and in "The Economic Problem in Masochism," *Coll. Pap.*, Vol. III, London, Hogarth, 1948.

This formula, which is correct but not specific, makes at any rate one or two things comprehensible, as, for instance, the inability to be incited. When a bored person looks for "incitements" because he has lost his instinctual aims through repression, it is understandable that, on the one hand, he will offer to incitements which could really bring about the desired relaxation of tension the same resistance as resulted in the repression of his instinctual aims, and, on the other, that if the "incitement" provided by the external world is too distantly related to the original instinctual aim, there can be no displacement of his cathectic energy onto the new activity offered to him.

He who wards off an instinctual demand finds himself involved in a conflict; his id wants instinctual action, his ego is against it. The same conflict repeats itself in relation to the stimuli coming from the external world. The id makes for them as an "instinctual substitute," while the ego, even though it wants to discharge its tensions, does not want to be reminded of the original instinctual aim, and seeks a "diversion" or "distraction" of its energies which are fixated on the unconscious instinctual aim. Thus, in so far as the original instinct persists, the subject resists diversion and distraction; but he also resists substitutes which are too closely related to the original aim.

We know of various conditions of high tension accompanying repressed instinctual aims. In such cases we expect to find a condition which differs very considerably from boredom. Everybody knows the general internal restlessness, and most often motor restlessness too—the state of "fidgetiness"—seen in such cases. Yet though this state of restlessness is very different from the manifest quiet of boredom, we recognize that the two conditions have an inner relationship. States of boredom of this kind are the same thing, in *tonic binding,* as motor restlessness is in a *clonic* condition, as it were. We are left with the question, What circumstances give rise to such a tonic binding and when does it appear in the shape of boredom? For it is clear that even tonic bindings of acute instinctual tensions with repressed aims themselves take various forms.

The question whether these considerations are valid for all forms of boredom may be left open. They are certainly so for a certain pathological type of boredom which can be clinically investigated. Our understanding of this type will be rendered easier if we begin by making a few remarks about the relationship between boredom and monotony.

A monotonous external world is often felt by the subject to be boring. It provides no new stimuli, it does not of itself increase his inner tensions. Monotonous stimuli send him to sleep. When the outer world does not excite him he withdraws his libido from it. Often, however, it is precisely monotonous stimuli which can arouse specific excitations in him. We have only to think of the effect of monotony in praying or in primitive dances, etc. Here monotony obviously

serves the same purpose as it does in the case of monotonous stimuli employed
to induce sleep, viz., to get the subject to withdraw his libido from an external
world that has become monotonous; but in this case the aim is to increase his
narcissistic libido to a corresponding degree. This task is facilitated by the special
properties of such monotonous stimuli, for they are in fact stimuli and different
from the absence of stimuli. Monotonous stimuli, especially when they are
rhythmic, clearly help to bring on particular kinds of states of excitation, namely
excitations which have a certain narcissistic quality, states of ecstasy. Not only
strong monotonous and rhythmic external stimuli, but weak ones as well, have a
sexually excitatory effect (and one, moreover, in which it is the excitation itself
rather than the exciting object which is the focus of interest for the subject). In
the small child, in whom sexual excitation is not yet properly differentiated from
sexual gratification, these stimuli have a sleep-inducing effect; later on they may
also cause an increased desire for gratification. Thus if it is asked whether such
stimuli act in a quieting or a disturbing way, the question would be wrongly put.
For they can do both. Which they do depends upon what the relation of the
excitation to the gratification is.

In analysis, monotonous rhythms, as experienced in a single sensory field or in
all together—and most frequently in sensations of balance and space—are met
with in the form of memory traces of infantile sexual excitations. The subject's
perception of his own pulse rhythm plays an important part here; and the significance of fever as a sexual stimulus is connected with this.

In certain circumstances, monotony does not simply induce sleep or ecstasy but
has an intensely unpleasurable effect. One may suddenly have the impulse to
interrupt the monotonous stimulus at once. This unpleasure is comparable to
the unpleasure that is experienced when some sexual activity which has reached
an advanced stage of excitation has suddenly to be broken off. In such a case,
therefore, the monotonous stimulus has generated sexual excitation whose course
has been disturbed. A disturbance of this kind may come from within and have
a psychological origin. This happens with people who can only tolerate a certain
degree of sexual excitation without anxiety, especially if the excitation is of an
infantile character, as is obviously the case with this type of excitation due to
monotony. On the other hand, the disturbance may come from without; for the
increasing excitation has need of increasing stimuli, too, or of the prospect of
some kind of end-pleasure, so that the monotony of the continuing stimulus, by
not thus increasing, proves inadequate.

A great deal of light is thrown on these matters by the analysis—whether carried on at the time or in later years—of the effects upon neurotic children of
noises at night. Sounds like, say, a dripping tap or snoring put the child into
a state of excitation or of anxiety and give it "unpleasure from interruption."

When we discover excitations or fears of this kind we rightly think at once of experiences in the nature of a primal scene. But in making this interpretation we must not forget that excitement, anxiety, and restlessness can also correspond to those situations in which the child, having on one occasion experienced a primal scene, expects its repetition in vain. In such situations of nocturnal expectation the child has the same conflicting attitude toward the external world as we have seen to be the case with the adult who is bored. His instinct demands that the external world shall repeat that sexually exciting spectacle and so end the intolerable tension of his expectation; but his ego, which fears the tremendous excitement of the primal scene more than it fears the disagreeable tension of expectation, demands of the external world that it shall divert his attention, put on the lights, and reassure him and turn his mind away from all the horrors of his night fears and excitations to sober reality.

Excitation, anxiety, and interruptive unpleasure are very closely linked here and are liable to take one another's place. It is a familiar fact that it is precisely in this field of phenomena that the smallest quantitative changes in their configuration can turn sensations of pleasure into anxiety. But states which can only be subjectively experienced as "boredom" are also very close to both. We can often observe, for instance, that "unmusical" people who are "bored" by listening to music go over into a state of anxiety or unpleasure of the kind described. The "boredom" of the long nights of which many sufferers from insomnia complain has the same painful quality.

In boredom of this kind, then, while subjectively the intense conflictual excitation seems to have disappeared, there are signs to show it is actually there. In this respect, boredom seems to be a variant or subdivision of "depersonalization," where the libido is usually by no means withdrawn from internal perception but where it is only opposed by an anti-cathexis which is mostly shown by an increased self-observation.[4]

Boredom makes some children cry. Such crying and restlessness break the tonic binding of cathexes, and then what these children call boredom is hardly distinguishable from manifest restlessness and fidgetiness. That children call it boredom shows the relatedness of these conditions. Thus, the meaning of this boredom may be schematically formulated as follows: "I am excited. If I allow this excitation to continue I shall have anxiety. Therefore I tell myself that I am not at all excited, that I don't want to do anything. Yet at the same time I feel I do want to do something; but as I have forgotten my original aim I don't know what I want to do. The external world must do something to relieve me of my

---

[4] Cf. O. Fenichel, "Organ Libidinization Accompanying the Defense against Drives," No. 14 in this volume.

tension without making me anxious. It must make me do something, and then I shall not be responsible for it. It must divert me, distract me, so that what I do will be sufficiently remote from my original aim. It must accomplish the impossible: it must afford me a relaxation of tension without instinctual action."

This meaning of states of boredom was particularly clearly demonstrated in a patient whose whole analysis was dominated by intense transference-resistances. These resistances took one of two forms: continuous motor restlessness or boredom. Analysis showed that these two conditions, outwardly so different, were only different expressions of the same latent psychic situation. The patient called his motor restlessness "being angry." He was continually angry with his analyst, at times furious at him; but all he had against him was that he had not miraculously cured him overnight. His associations were completely inhibited, and he raged at his analyst for not changing this by a magic word. This "being angry" was accompanied by marked general restlessness and by tormenting subjective feelings of the intolerability of his present emotional state, such as we see in persons with strong disturbances of the libido. Light was shed on the meaning of his behavior by a glance at his sexual life. He suffered from an acute libidinal disturbance by which, when he was with a woman, he began intercourse in a normal fashion, and even experienced normal sensual pleasure until the excitation reached a certain degree; then—often before the penis was inserted, at times after—came a sudden change. He experienced intense unpleasure of a general sort, did not know what to do next and became "angry" with the woman because, he felt, she should do something to free him at once from this disagreeable situation. In matters other than sexual ones he also displayed a masochistic character, continuously demonstrating his unhappiness, and being "angry" at those present because they were not overcome by pity for him and did not immediately perform some miracle to liberate him. Analysis showed that his constant excitation, which was exacerbated in the sexual sphere, repeated infantile situations of lying in bed with his mother. Having repressed his active phallic wishes toward his mother, he expected her to intervene in such a way as on the one hand to give him guiltless sexual gratification and, on the other, to divert him from his sexual thoughts. Characteristically, this action which he expected from his mother, and later from everybody, was conceived of as an oral gratification. Now on certain days this patient's masochistically colored excitement was replaced by a state of "boredom." Though he could not associate on these days either, his feeling was quite different. He experienced no intolerable tension; allegedly he experienced "nothing at all," but continually asserted that analysis and everything to do with it was so boring that he did not feel like saying anything, or even know what he should say, and that he would soon give up the analysis. The manner in which this state alternated with the one described above left no doubt that it was primarily a successful defense against the *expectatory excitement* with which the patient on other occasions awaited the magic (oral) intervention of the analyst which he craved. I shall communicate here a small association experiment carried out during one of these days to demonstrate that the excitation which was at other times manifest was still present, but in tonic binding. When the patient declared he was bored, he was asked to follow with particular conscientiousness the fundamental rule of psychoanalysis, and to be sure not to suppress any idea that occurred to him as "too boring." The patient began by relating that he was looking into the corner of the room and thinking, What if a cobweb were there? One could take a broom and brush *up and down* the wall, *always up and down.* Besides, he had a toothache; he had come directly from the dentist, who had run his drill *up and down* his teeth. His attention was called to the fact that the dimensions of sensations in the mouth are often misrecognized; therefore the idea of brushing the wall showed that psychologically he was still at the dentist's, not at the analyst's, and that in his fantasy the analyst was doing something exciting in his mouth. "Now only nonsense comes to my mind," the patient continued; "I could say any random word, for instance, 'light switch' or 'chamber pot.'" "Light switch" and "chamber pot" are means by which adults attempt to quiet an anxious child at night. Thus the patient's state of mind could be interpreted as follows: "I have anxiety, do something quieting (or disquieting) in my mouth!" The boredom which the patient experienced denied his excitation in the same fashion that depersonalization does.

It may be asked whether what is characteristic of this kind of tonic binding of anxiety in boredom is that the instincts involved have a passive aim which, having been warded off, returns in the shape of undefined demands upon the external world for "incitement." We should answer this in the negative and be more inclined to think that this mechanism may be giving us a view of a transformation from activity into passivity in *statu nascendi:* the subject seeks to be freed by means of a *passive* experience from a tension which set in because he was afraid of his own *active* impulses.

We cannot deny that all this does not solve the questions we have raised, namely, What makes "tonic binding" possible, and how is the tonic binding of "boredom" distinguished from other states? When does motor restlessness arise, and when a feeling of lack of impulse and a craving for diversion?

We cannot offer a final answer to these questions. All we can say is that every tonic binding, hence also boredom, fends off *more* than motor restlessness does—it fends off the motor impulses themselves. But this again is no fundamental answer; for just as there are persons who, when they are in states of dammed-up libido which cannot possibly be characterized as boredom, are completely inactive physically, so are there persons who, when they are bored, dash about and do all sorts of things. "Blasé" people are noted for undertaking many more or less nonsensical activities out of "boredom." The so-called "spleen" * of the Englishman is of this nature. This is a variant of boredom in which the bored ego does not wait for the stimuli of the external world, but thinks up its own "substitute actions," which shall on the one hand release the tension—that is, represent his instinctual activities—and, on the other, "divert" him from them and deny them. The paralysis of the motor system is thus neither the sole nor the essential characteristic of boredom. It may be absent; and in any case something else is necessary as well. This is the mechanism which we have described as akin to depersonalization, whereby a person can manage to conceal from himself completely the presence of extremely high inner tension. It is well known that people endowed with imagination are rarely bored, and those given to boredom are unable to produce daydreams or are inhibited in doing so. (The patient I have described above had no fantasy life at all.) Obviously, a rich imagination enables a person to unburden himself to a certain extent in daydreams, whereas the want of such a means of outlet calls for a massive anti-cathexis to block his internal perceptions.

Is the internal perception of one's own excitation lacking in such a state? We have already mentioned outbursts of crying from boredom, although we had to add that we could not consider them as characteristic of that state. Obviously the transition from fidgetiness to boredom is fluid; but extreme cases of the latter are characterized by the very fact that the subject himself believes that he has a certain degree of lack of excitation, which is precisely what he calls being "bored."

We have answered in the negative the question whether instincts which, when their aim is frustrated, give rise to the kind of boredom we have in mind are mainly instincts with a passive aim. But perhaps there is another instinctual content which is more characteristic for this. May it not be that what comes most into play is aggressive instincts on the one hand, and, on the other, narcissistic needs? The relationship between boredom and fluctuations of self-regard and "moods" cannot be overlooked. There are also cases of "periodic boredom" which at once leave no doubt of their affinity with the manic-depressive cycle. Such forms of boredom show every stage of transition to definite types of depression. We are acquainted, too, with certain kinds of defense against depression (or equivalents of the same) in which the subject strives to make headway against the depressive lowering of his self-regard by seeking "diversion" in the external world. The addict makes for stimuli there which, thanks to their chemical composition, can in fact introduce alterations in his feelings of self-

* "Spleen" as meant in the Continental sense of "eccentricity," not in our sense of "bad temper."—Trans. note.

regard; and the psychopath with an "instinct for wandering" leaves the place of his abode when his depression comes on, in order to find "distraction" through a change of environment.

Does this affinity with depression contradict our earlier views about the psychogenesis of boredom? By no means. The boredom which is related to depression finds its place as a special case of the pathological form of boredom which we have been describing. As had already been said, this is always a matter of an instinctual tension which, while its aim is repressed, is nevertheless perceived, although it is denied, and from which the subject hopes to be rescued by an intervention from the outside world; in the present instance the tensions arise from the narcissistic needs of an injured self-regard, and from all those instinctual oral-sadistic demands which are familiar to us in the psychogenesis of depression. From this standpoint it can be understood why it is that among the activities which bored people turn to for "diversion" eating, drinking, and smoking occupy a favored position, and how a pathological boredom can set in long before the emergence of an addiction or a neurosis with "impulsional behavior" and the like. But we do not suppose that narcissistic needs and oral-sadistic impulses are the *only* things whose damming up can lead to boredom.

It is now easy to understand the relationship between boredom and loneliness. If the situation of a bored person is correctly described as a state of instinctual tension of which he is not conscious but which seems dangerous to him and to cope with which he expects the help of stimuli from the external world, then it is clear that the etiological conditions of boredom and loneliness must be identical. Their relationship to masturbation, like that of neurotics with a phobia of being shut away, is of two kinds. The bored person, like the lonely one, may be afraid of the actual temptation to masturbate and combat it, so that what he is conscious of is not his masturbatory impulses, but a craving for diversion from them instead; or he may attempt to escape a burdensome instinctual tension, whose aim is completely unconscious to him, by resorting to repeated acts of masturbation. There are many threads, too, connecting boredom and compulsive masturbation.[5]

Let us recall in this connection Ferenczi's "Sunday neuroses."[6] There are "Sunday neurotics" whose symptom is merely that on Sundays, or during vacations, they *are bored*. So long as they are at work, these people succeed in what the bored person strives for in vain, namely "to divert themselves" from their state of pent-up drives. When the diversion is not possible, the tension makes itself felt and the hitherto latent "boredom" becomes manifest. As a rule, mem-

[5] See O. Fenichel, *Perversionen, Psychosen, Charakterstoerungen*, Vienna, Int. Psa. Verlag, 1931.
[6] S. Ferenczi, "Sunday Neuroses," *Further Contributions to the Theory and Technique of Psycho-Analysis*, London, Hogarth, 1950.

ories of childhood Sundays play a role here; for the damming up of drives was artificially increased on those days, by the children, with their high instinctual appetites, being more than ever prevented from giving vent to them.

Now that we have sketched the mechanisms of a pathological form of boredom, the question is, are they the essential mechanisms of boredom in general? How does a differently structured "normal" boredom look? It arises when we must not do what we want to do, or must do what we do not want to do. This "innocent" boredom appears at first to be entirely different from that so far described, but one common property is easily recognized: *something expected does not occur.* In pathological boredom it fails to occur because the subject represses his instinctual action out of anxiety; in normal boredom it fails to occur because the nature of the real situation does not permit of the expected de-tension. (This is why, when a tired person is prevented from going to sleep he regards the external world which prevents him as boring.) It is difficult to predict, however, when a frustrating external world will mobilize aggressiveness in the subject, when it will be tolerated by him, and when it will be experienced as "boring." One should not forget that we have *the right to expect* some "aid to discharge" from the external world. If this is not forthcoming, we are, so to speak, justifiably bored. To characterize this situation, Winterstein quotes Field Marshal Ligne: "I am not bored, it is the others who bore me." [7] This is why anyone who is "affectively blocked" or otherwise equipped with strong characterologically anchored anti-cathexes—as is, for instance, a particularly correct or otherwise rigid person—is so boring. His emotional aloofness does not correspond to people's instinctual expectations of one another. Often such people are anxious lest they prove boring, and we must say that their anxiety is well founded. Analysis of this anxiety shows that this quality of boring people, so feared by the patient himself, may harbor a great deal of sadism.

A factor which undoubtedly has an important bearing on the nature of boredom, and one which has not as yet been mentioned, is its relationship to *time.* The very word *"Langeweile"* * indicates that in this state there are always changes in the person's subjective experience of time. When we experience many varying stimulations from the outside world, the time, as we know, appears to pass quickly; but should the external world bring only monotonous stimuli, or should subjective conditions prevent their being experienced as tension-releasing, then the "while is long." Because of this basic phenomenon of subjective time-experience, the sensation which has given the whole experience

---

[7] A. Winterstein, *op. cit.,* p. 550. The original statement is, "Nicht ich langweile mich, es sind die andern, die mich langweilen." A literal translation would therefore read, "It is not I who bore myself, it is the others who bore me."

* "Boredom"; literally, "long while." In German the word itself thus expresses the relation between boredom and time.

of tedium its name seems to be but a secondary consequence of the mechanisms described. However, the possibility cannot be rejected that primary disturbances of subjective time-experience facilitate a coming into play of those mechanisms. This is the case with people who have sexualized their sensation of time,[8] and it is also frequently the case in certain types of anal character especially. In the light of these facts we can agree with Winterstein's description of certain anal characters as particularly disposed to boredom, and with his relation of the phenomenon of boredom in general to that of "being stingy with time." [9]

The rest of Winterstein's remarks on the disposition to boredom is also in agreement with our views. He writes: "Two types may be distinguished here: the person who is blasé, who has become dulled through overstimulation, who craves pleasure but is unable to enjoy it (such boredom may have a physiological foundation); and the person who escapes from painful boredom in work, because he finds everything boring which is not fulfillment of a duty." These two types appear to us as being simply two variants of a chronic damming up of libido which takes the form of tension while the instinctual aim is repressed. The first type is the orgastically impotent individual who is in a state of longing because he is unable to enjoy pleasure. (We do not believe that his "dulled state" is due to "overstimulation." In our opinion the psychogenic damming up of his libido is the cause both of his longing for stimuli and of his becoming dulled.) The second type is the "Sunday neurotic" mentioned above. We believe that in both cases boredom has a physiological foundation, namely that of the damming up of libido.

[8] Cf. J. Hárnik, "Die triebhaft-affektiven Momente im Zeitgefuehl," *Imago*, Vol. 11, 1925.
[9] A. Winterstein, *op. cit.*, p. 552.

## TWENTY-SEVEN

# Defense against Anxiety,
# Particularly by Libidinization*

FREUD's [1] recent views concerning anxiety, this cardinal topic of psychoanalytic investigation, may be summarized as follows. To begin with, anxiety is the manner in which the ego experiences an increased tension of need in the id, when no adequate possibility of discharge is present in so-called "traumatic situations." But later on the ego learns to experience the unpleasure of anxiety in cases of danger as well—that is, in situations which might become traumatic; and whereas it formerly experienced the unpleasure in a passive way, it now behaves actively toward it, setting off by means of a signal of anxiety the various mechanisms designed to meet the danger.

There is no absolute distinction between "anxiety in the traumatic state" and "anxiety signal." They are connected together in the first instance by the fact that the anxiety which is actively developed by the ego as a signal obviously arises because the ego's insight into the presence of danger establishes in the id, or rather, in the somatic apparatus, the same conditions which obtain in the traumatic state, except that they are less in degree; furthermore, it must be realized that the intention of producing an "anxiety signal" often fails, in that, in the presence of dammed-up libido, the acute signal often has the same effect as a match in a barrel of gunpowder. The major anxiety attacks of anxiety hysteria, for instance, leave no doubt that the ego, in giving a signal, has set off something which, thanks to a pre-existing latent damming up of libido, it can no longer control.

This possibility that what should *protect* against a traumatic state, under cer-

* First published in *Int. Z. Psa.*, Vol. 20, 1934, pp. 476–489.
[1] S. Freud, *The Problem of Anxiety*, New York, Psa. Quart. Press and Norton, 1936.

tain conditions *elicits* one, makes it necessary for the ego not only to effect an instinctual defense by producing anxiety, but to make other arrangements as well to ward off the unpleasure of anxiety.

Naturally, the human being wants to avoid every kind of unpleasure. But an anxiety signal which is kept as minute as possible, and which protects against a greater unpleasure, ought nevertheless to be approved as a useful institution by the reality principle. It is only the uncertainty as to whether the signal may not become something else, and something more disagreeable than was intended, that explains the enormous expenditures of anti-cathexes which, as we know, are deployed in order to hold down anxiety. There is hardly a single phenomenon which comes under our notice in the field of psychology which does not in one way or another betray a purpose of this sort. Basically, every shape in which an anti-cathexis appears, except when it itself appears as anxiety, must be considered to be a defense against anxiety; for if such a binding by an anti-cathexis of the warded-off instinctual energies should fail, then, being dammed up, these would produce anxiety. This holds most clearly for phobic mechanisms, which avoid anxiety at the price of a limitation of the ego. It holds in general for neurotic symptoms; for, although these are not manifestations of anti-cathexis, yet—in so far as they are symptoms and not instinctual gratifications—anti-cathexis has a share in them, and their suppression brings about anxiety. It holds, above all, for all kinds of chronic characterological elaborations of instinctual conflicts in terms of reaction formations, and—to use Freud's phrase—for "those inconsistencies, queernesses, and foolishnesses of people . . . by the acceptance of which they save themselves repressions," [2] or, more exactly, by which they spare themselves acts of after-expulsion—that is, other, more acute and more expensive defense forms—and thus anxiety attacks as well.

The rational effect of the anxiety signal would be defense against *danger,* by fight or flight. But there exists a "fear of fear," owing to the danger that the ego might be overwhelmed by the anxiety it has itself used as a signal; and therefore, there are also fights and flights which are directed only against the *experience* of anxiety, and do not alter the objective or supposed danger. These anti-cathexes are, to begin with, security measures against the occurrence of anxiety experiences. But as in all other anti-cathexes of the reaction-formation type—that is, those which have to keep down a contrary unconscious attitude—we encounter overcompensations here as well. As is known, the attempt is not only to "disprove" anxiety, as for instance, in perversions; as Demosthenes did with his organ inferiority, so do some people overcome their anxiety by doing and seeking out precisely what they had anxiety about initially. Naturally, not all succeed equally in this, and the still extant anxiety hiding behind such at-

---

[2] S. Freud, "Neurosis and Psychosis," *Coll. Pap.,* Vol. II, London, Hogarth, 1948, p. 254.

tempts at repression, or rather denial, of anxiety, may be betrayed by quite a few symptoms, symptomatic actions, or dreams.

The small child's frequent anxiety is, to begin with, due to biological circumstances. He cannot gratify his needs by himself, because he cannot yet act, cannot yet intervene effectively in the external world. The absence of help from the external world when instinctual needs present themselves thus leads to frequent traumatic situations. This was demonstrated by Freud,[3] and it has been confirmed on concrete examples, particularly by Melanie Klein [4] and by Nina Searl.[5] These traumatic situations, however, only create the *possibility* for the conception that drives are dangers, because the judgment "danger" is always the memory of a traumatic state that has been experienced. But whether or not an ego which has already acquired an improved mastery of the external world will really be afraid of drives as dangers—that naturally depends upon what vicissitudes the child's drives have undergone during his first years of childhood owing to his experiences at that time. Without the biological precondition mentioned above, this pathogenic conception could not exist; but in order that such a conception be formed, there must be added to it socially determined external frustrations, for these determine the special form of the two major anxiety contents—loss of love and castration—and cause the damming up of libido, which permits anxiety signals to turn into major anxiety attacks in anxious children.

Now, we know that the transition from the pleasure principle to the reality principle is not a once-and-for-all act, but a prolonged process. The absence of a fully formed reality principle in early years causes the child to view objects only in relation to his own instinctual life, and this leads to a fantastic misapprehension by him of the external world, so that he expects punishments from it which correspond to his own view of his instincts as dangerous. These supposed dangers, which are of such great significance for the theory of anxiety and of defense against anxiety, and which hang over the child owing to his projective misapprehension of the external world, have been repeatedly described to us, above all by Melanie Klein, and our other English colleagues. We take exception only to their terminology, to their designating these dangers as the "threats of the particularly strict and still entirely sadistic early infantile superego." The child expects the evil *from outside;* objectively, there is no such threat, but the child *thinks* that there is such an objective threat. Freud wrote: ". . . the anxiety of zoophobia is transformed castration anxiety, therefore a real anxiety, a reality fear, fear of a danger actually threatening or believed to do so." [6] The idea that

[3] S. Freud, *The Problem of Anxiety.*

[4] The pertinent points of her previous studies are summarized in her *Psychoanalysis of Children,* New York, Norton, 1932.

[5] Cf., for instance, N. Searl, "The Psychology of Screaming," *Int. J. Psa.,* Vol. 14, 1933.

[6] S. Freud, *The Problem of Anxiety,* p. 39.

one might be devoured by the *real* mother is attenuated too, if the child continuously sees the mother, who is actually friendly; just as the phobic patient, according to Helene Deutsch's observations, must have the people whom he unconsciously hates by his side, not to increase his hatred by looking at them, but to lessen it by being called to reason, as it were, by reality.[7] Why and how reality is misapprehended in imagination still needs to be thoroughly studied; there is no doubt that in fact not only projections, but introjections also, rule the psychic life of early childhood, and that at this time already introjects may threaten the rest of the ego; nevertheless, such anxiety is essentially outward-directed, and these "precursors of the superego" are to be clearly distinguished from that decided new acquisition which accompanies the decline of the oedipus complex and which builds a differentiating grade in the ego.[8] A precise comprehension of the pregenital world, which is so remote from verbal thinking, is made more difficult if its contents are represented as "oedipus complex" and "superego," which are terms pertaining to later stages of development. In spite of this—or perhaps even because of this—it should be stressed that we are indebted to Melanie Klein for a clinical discovery, the theoretical significance of which has not yet been nearly sufficiently appreciated. (Only by relating it with Freud's "pre-oedipal phase" [9] can this be done.) I refer to her discovery that in both sexes, and with more lasting significance in women, there arise in early childhood—in the so-called oral-sadistic period—object trends whose aim is to enter forcibly and with destructive intent into the mother's body and to devour its contents; and that furthermore, this wish gives rise to retributive fears, that it is these anxieties which blur the small child's picture of reality, and that the child now tries in many ways, fantasying in a confusion of projections and introjections, to combat this anxiety.[10]

Among the methods already used early in life by the small child to ward off such anxieties, two stand out primarily: identification with the object of anxiety, and flight into reality.

Identification as defense against anxiety (which was the subject matter of a paper by Anna Freud at a congress [11]) cannot be understood without further clarification. It may be made more plausible by two considerations that are related to each other. In the first place, identification is the oldest method of coming to terms with the world of objects in general; for this reason every wish to alter

---

[7] H. Deutsch, "The Genesis of Agoraphobia," *Int. J. Psa.*, Vol. 10, 1929.

[8] S. Freud, *The Ego and the Id*, London, Hogarth, 1947.

[9] S. Freud, "Female Sexuality," *Coll. Pap.*, Vol. V, London, Hogarth, 1950.

[10] M. Klein, "The Psychological Principles of Infant Analysis," *Int. J. Psa.*, Vol. 8, 1927; "Early Stages of the Oedipus Conflict," *Int. J. Psa.*, Vol. 9, 1928; "Personification in the Play of Children," *Int. J. Psa.*, Vol. 10, 1929; "Infantile Anxiety-Situations Reflected in a Work of Art," *Int. J. Psa.*, Vol. 10, 1929; *The Psychoanalysis of Children*, New York, Norton, 1932.

[11] A. Freud, "Ein Gegenstueck zur Tierphobie der Kinder," paper given at the 11th Int. Psychoanal. Cong. Author's report in *Int. Z. Psa.*, Vol. 15, 1929.

subsequent object relations of a higher order may lead to identification if it precipitates regressions.[12] Not only are internal anxieties defended against by being projected onto external anxiety objects, as happens in a phobia; external anxiety objects, too, are struggled against, and when this is done by introjection it leads to an identification with them. In the second place, acting the role of the object of which one is afraid is but a special case of the mechanism described by Freud, which consists of a subsequent active repetition of unmasterable passive experiences in the mass of excitation.[13] The prerequisite of such a solution seems to be that the ambivalence which comes to expression in the identification with the anxiety object should have been already extant before. We have only to think of the role of ambivalence in the infantile return of totemism, so clearly described by Freud.[14] But the child not only acts like the animal of which it is afraid; it feels that it belongs, so to speak, to its totem. Identification and object love are here not yet completely separated. The child's feeling toward the animal is expressed by a "we," and it loves narcissistically every representative of the species with which it has identified itself. In this fashion, castration anxiety may lead not only to cruel actions against a third person, by way of identification with the castrator, but even to passive-homosexual pleasure in being castrated, by way of a sort of "identificatory love" toward the castrator.

Flight to reality, too—for instance, the clinging to the real mother, which is to protect the child from the mother it misapprehends in imagination—leads to a dependence on, that is, to a kind of love for, the person whom one feared. Just as there is a prophylactic counterattack, so there is also a prophylactic love toward him whom one fears.

What is called the "libidinization" of anxiety is of two sorts. One is a defense against anxiety by developing a pleasure in anxiety. The other is the development of dependence, love, or sexual attitudes in those respects where previously there was anxiety; and this is a combination of the two methods of identification and flight into reality.

Secondary libidinization of a mechanism designed to ward off instincts occurs outside the realm of anxiety also. This happens both when, with the persistence of the pathogenic conflict, that which is defended against returns in the defense, and when a secondary gain comes about by the ego's managing to derive secondarily some kind of libidinal pleasure from behavior which originally subserved a defense against the instinct. An example of the first is a compulsion whose original meaning of atonement retires ever further behind its instinctual meaning as

12 Cf. O. Fenichel, "Identification," No. 10 in this volume.

13 See in the first instance S. Freud, *Beyond the Pleasure Principle*, London, Hogarth, 1948; furthermore, also "Female Sexuality," *Coll. Pap.*, Vol. V.

14 Cf. S. Freud, "Totem and Taboo," *The Basic Writings*, New York, Norton, 1952.

the neurosis progresses; [15] an example of the second is the "compulsive play," so frequent in obsessional neurotics, in which the patients experience a certain conscious pleasure.[16] The normal anal pleasure in retention seems to be in general such a "libidinization" of a defense against the original pleasure in expulsion.

*Pain* too is an unpleasure which is used by the ego as a signal to prevent greater evil. And pain, too, is then defended against, because of its unpleasurable character, and not rarely by "libidinization." [17] Concerning the pleasure of pain, which is analogous to the pleasure of anxiety, we know that it rests in the first instance on a physiological foundation, on erotogenic masochism; it rests on the fact that the general proposition, that excitations of *any kind* are also sources of *sexual* excitation—that this proposition holds for pain as well.[18] Now if, owing to certain instinctual vicissitudes, an anxiety compels the overcoming of a sadistic impulse by turning it against the ego, then this erotogenic masochism may, under certain circumstances, become the theme from which a fateful development toward the "libidinization of an unpleasure" may start. What happens in the "pleasure of anxiety" is clearly exactly analogous to this. Just like any other excitation, the excitation of anxiety may also become a source of sexual excitation. However, just as with pain, this is possible only so long as the unpleasure remains within certain bounds—as we see, for example, in the case of empathy with the heroes of tragedy. When, now, an intense anxiety has to be overcome, the methods of *active repetition of passive experience,* or of *prophylactic anticipation of what is feared,* by which subsequent more intense unpleasure is avoided, can also bring into use the "erotogenic pleasure of anxiety," just as happens in masochism; and as a result, anxiety may to a certain extent be enjoyed. This, as in masochism, is a secondary process of adaptation. There is absolutely nothing to support the hypothesis proposed by Laforgue, that pleasure in anxiety is the primitive form of all pleasure in general.[19]

Let us now return to our other question: How does dependence on, love for, or sexual behavior toward, what were originally objects of anxiety, come about? How can anxiety be avoided in this fashion?

As a boy, a certain patient was good friends with all the animals in the zoo and displayed his familiarity with them to all the visitors with exhibitionistic pride. One day a jackdaw, which would come and be fed by him at his call, pecked his hand. This only increased his pride; he felt even closer to the animal and exhibited the wound. It is readily seen that both of the mechanisms discussed

[15] S. Freud, *The Problem of Anxiety.*
[16] Cf. O. Fenichel, *Perversionen, Psychosen, Charakterstoerungen,* Vienna, Int. Psa. Verlag, pp. 9 ff.
[17] Cf. in this respect, S. Freud's discussion in *The Problem of Anxiety,* p. 120.
[18] Cf. S. Freud, *Three Essays on the Theory of Sexuality,* London, Imago, 1949.
[19] R. Laforgue, *Libido, Angst und Zivilisation,* Vienna, Int. Psa. Verlag, 1932.

were involved simultaneously in the boy's predilection for the unconsciously feared animals: He identified himself with these animals, and felt himself to be one of them; and he fled from the feared animals of his fantasy to the harmless animals of reality.

Similar to this is the attitude which is important in the psychology of examinations: "I am not only not afraid of the examiner; I am friends with him." There is no doubt, nevertheless, that these mechanisms of "libidinization of anxiety" make it possible for a deeply feminine instinctual attitude toward the father to appear in a form compatible with masculine ideals.

Thus, we have a threefold layering before us: An instinct is defended against by anxiety, and the defense against this anxiety in turn brings once more to light that was originally defended against. Naturally, the passive homosexuality of the third layer is then no longer identical with that of the first one.

Exactly the same happens as regards the return of active instinctual impulses for the purpose of defense against anxiety. When a child plays all the time at being a wild animal, so as to escape from the fear of being devoured, this anxiety may in its turn be a retributive anxiety due to drives that were originally oral-sadistic. Their oral-sadism, however, has then changed its character in passing through the phase of retributive anxiety.[20]

There are people whose whole character is formed by this kind of anti-cathexis. They constantly do things about which, without knowing it, they in fact have anxiety, in order precisely to spare themselves anxiety by such prophylactic behavior. In doing this they also gratify to some extent—once more without knowing it—the original instinctual impulses, for the warding off of which the anxiety was actually developed. These are reactive, ungenuine characters, whose anxiety must be first mobilized in the analysis.

The phenomenon here outlined in general terms is particularly frequent in the realm of sexuality: The sexual behavior of a person, which from a purely descriptive point of view is in line with his instinctual disposition, is separated from the latter by an interpolated layer of anxiety, and is therefore unfree and ungenuine and serves in the first instance to ward off anxiety.

Freud has stated that there exist forms of homosexuality which represent an

[20] One is here reminded of the "instinctual conflicts" which were described by F. Alexander as being as much productive of neuroses as are the "structural" conflicts. ("The Relation of Structural and Instinctual Conflicts," *Psa. Quart.*, Vol. 2, 1933.) A castration anxiety, for instance, which makes masculinity lie fallow, elicits strong unconscious femininity; this in turn is defended against by an outwardly masculine behavior, etc. These situations are analogous to those we have in mind. We would only add that it seems incorrect to set them up as counterparts to cases of pathogenic "structural conflicts." It is *always only* structural conflicts that are pathogenic, and the conflicts of bisexuality would never lead to neuroses (for in the unconscious contradictions stand unordered side by side), did they not also correspond to a "structural" conflict, in that one of the drives partaking in the conflict stands closer to the ego.

overcompensation of an original hatred.[21] There are other reactive forms of homosexuality also, namely, identification with the other sex, for the purpose of denying fear of the other sex.

The patient who had the adventure with the jackdaw, though not a homosexual, had a strong feminine orientation. He loved women only with a sort of identificatory love, in that he tried continuously to show them in a somewhat exhibitionistic manner: "Look how I can empathize with you, indeed, how there is no difference between you and me." A relatively late traumatic observation of the feminine genital had fatefully influenced this boy's development. He experienced what he saw as something completely strange. He condensed all his previous castration fears in his fear of this strange thing, which he apprehended as orally dangerous, and now had to come to terms with it. This he managed by denying with his total behavior his knowledge, "women are something different from me," and asserting instead, "women are exactly like me, I need make no frightening discoveries about them, I am perfectly familiar with all feminine matters " Here we have an identification with the anxiety object which alters the subject's sexual behavior. What appears to be a genuine drive was really in the first instance a defense against anxiety.

Many features of love-life serve at the same time to avert an existing sexual anxiety through overcompensation.[22] Cases like the following are familiar to all of us. A woman patient suffered from a severe manifest anxiety, based on various infantile sexual experiences, about being abandoned. Just as an anxious child cannot go to sleep when a protecting person is not present, she, even as an adult, had continually to secure for herself some kind of connection with other people in order to avoid severe anxiety. She invoked the most intense resistance against psychoanalytic therapy by being interested in nothing else but making sure that the analyst "stood by her." It will be readily understood that this young woman could not say "no" to men who courted her, and indeed, that when she was alone she could not refrain from courting men. She seemed to have a rich sex life, but the external sexual activity of the adult meant to her nothing else but what the hand of the mother means to the child, who has to hold onto it when in bed in order not to succumb to the temptation to masturbate: it was a means of defense against anxiety, a way of keeping real sexuality under repression.

The case of another woman patient was not so simple. This patient was by no means frigid, yet she had a number of severe neurotic disturbances of a cyclo-

[21] S. Freud, "Certain Neurotic Mechanisms in Jealousy, Paranoia and Homosexuality," *Coll. Pap.*, Vol. II.

[22] Considerable material of this sort will be found, for instance, in M. Schmideberg, "Some Unconscious Mechanisms in Pathological Sexuality and Their Relation to Normal Sexual Activity," *Int. J. Psa.*, Vol. 14, 1933.

thymic type, and her symptoms and character showed that she had not yet solved her conflicts of the oral-sadistic stage. In contrast to her other serious worries, she worried little about her sexuality. In this field everything seemed to be in order: she had intercourse frequently and with various men, having a predilection for playing the role of the seductress. At the same time she treated the men with a motherly, loving tenderness and consideration. The harmless and friendly character of her entire sexual behavior was so pronounced that it was easy to recognize in it a reactive formation against aggressive tendencies. The way in which she arrived at this reactive formation was through an identification with her mother, who, though she was otherwise often strict and frustrating to the child, had nursed her with a self-sacrificing devotion all through a long-drawn-out illness. The patient's sexual behavior thus meant: "I don't want to hurt men; on the contrary, I want to be as kind to them as Mother was to me when I was sick." Analysis left no doubt that the patient considered this illness as a sort of punishment that had been meted out to her for her aggressive impulses, and thus she regarded her mother's kindness, which deviated from her usual behavior, as a forgiveness. She had warded off some terrible fears of a retributive sort, which were activated by her illness, by clinging to the now kindly mother who nursed her, and later on she had identified herself with her mother's attitude.

In later childhood, when disappointed or grieved by older playmates, she sought out younger ones whom she could protect. Her loving behavior appeared thus as a defense against both aggressiveness and anxiety.

Further analysis uncovered yet another way in which the patient markedly corresponded to that structural picture which we have in mind when we diagnose "pseudo-nymphomania." [23] With a part of her ego she was still at the stage of partial love; unconsciously, the thing which primarily or exclusively interested her about men was their penis. All her tenderness was at bottom addressed to it; and so were her aggressiveness and her terrible fear of destructive retribution. What her loving, tender behavior was meant to deny was her oral-sadistic ideas of incorporation and the anxieties that went along with them. We indicated above that she chose the men to whom she was tender according to the narcissistic type of object choice, in order to treat them as she was treated by her mother; and we must now amplify this statement by saying that fundamentally it was the penis of these men with which she identified herself. Once, in telling me that her father had gone out riding, she said "I was very proud of my horse," instead of "my father."

Her later love relation to her father was altogether shot through with identificatory characteristics. Her longing was to feel toward his penis: "I have a share

[23] Cf. O. Fenichel, *Perversionen, Psychosen, Charakterstoerungen*, Vienna, Int. Psa. Verlag, pp. 48 ff.

in it; it is something I am at home with: it is 'our' penis." Thus her attitude toward her father's masculinity was exactly like that of the previously discussed feminine male patient toward the lack of a penis in women: her loving tenderness denied the anxiety-arousing difference in him.

Further analysis gave us a glimpse into the deeper layers of her oral-sadistic aggressiveness and fear of the penis. This attitude was acquired in relation, not to her father, but to her mother. The foundation of her whole character was an intensely ambivalent oral tie to the mother. She displayed a strange interest in the dead, in graveyards, and everything connected with these; in her postpuberal period she spent hours daydreaming in the graveyard. She imagined the dead to be very "friendly." As was to be expected, the analysis revealed that underlying this interest was an interest in the "inside of the mother's body." Behind the friendly, tender interest in the dead was hidden an intensely sensuous interest in this object. The idea of sitting peacefully on a grave, that is, "of being united in love" with a woman "underground," was a successful way of disproving her enjoyable death wishes against the mother and her corresponding retributive fear of death, in precisely the same fashion in which she later on disproved by her tender behavior to men her analogous anxieties in regard to them. Her fear of death originated from the time of her previously mentioned illness, in which she thought she might die. This had mobilized immense retributive anxieties on account of older oral-sadistic drives which will not be further discussed here. That her mother, against whom she otherwise wanted to enjoy revenge for the frustrations imposed by her, should have been so friendly to her precisely at this time, and should, by her tenderness, have served the patient as protection against her death fears—this made it possible for her to use tenderness, and sexuality in general, as a defense against anxiety later on in life.

The patient's sexual behavior was thus altogether built like a neurotic symptom. There was no doubt that in its depths what found expression was the repressed libido, which had been preserved in her unconscious in its original oral-sadistic form. But after the intervention of the repressive forces, this expression was no longer oral-sadistic, but genital. The genital form in which her sexual behavior became manifest was due to a mechanism of defense against anxiety that was composed of "identifications" and "flight to reality." Her genital behavior did not correspond to genital drives, but to a mixture of oral-sadistic drives and anxieties which were warding them off. The anxiety was defended against with the help of precisely this genital tenderness. It was "libidinized." The patient loved and spoiled the objects of which, actually, she was afraid. It was therefore no surprise when, in the course of the analysis, the accidentally fortunate quantitative conditions were disturbed and the patient became temporarily frigid.

Certainly a case of the sort just discussed presents nothing out of the ordinary in itself. It is no different fundamentally from those well-known cases of men who lead an externally rich sex life, but only, in reality, in order to disprove their internal fear of impotence—or, in general, like those cases where the most varied external sexual activities are carried on only for the sake of bolstering up a threatened self-esteem. Nevertheless, the case permits us to make a comparison between "reactive" sexuality, which defends against anxiety, and spontaneous sexuality. The difference is usually obvious. Occasionally, when the quantitative relationships are fortunate, the difference is less pronounced, but even then it remains most significant from a theoretical standpoint. When a human being whose sexuality has remained basically infantile defends against the anxiety opposing it by externally adult sexual behavior, these sexual activities can in principle never bring real gratification. The person is orgastically impotent. If the defensive ego attitudes are divided into those in which the instinctual energies defended against are freely discharged (the sublimation type), and those where they are held in check by an anti-cathexis but persist unchanged in the unconscious (reaction-formation type), then we must state that though the defense against anxiety effected by the method of libidinization described here makes certain discharges possible, it always belongs fundamentally to the second type. The dreaded infantile sexuality persists in the unconscious. Reactive sexual behavior, thus, does not differ from other forms of behavior having the character of a reaction formation. It is, like the latter, overstrained, aim-inhibited, self-contradictory, energy-consuming, and therefore inexpedient.

Reactive sexuality is a *secondary formation*. Were it mistaken for the primary, somatically determined sexuality, a bad theoretical confusion would soon arise.

"Libidinization of anxiety" has played a great role recently in psychoanalytic literature. This it is which has moved me to try to clarify the true state of affairs. If we now take another look at this literature, we cannot but see that the danger of confusion mentioned above has not always been avoided. One of our colleagues speaks of the "psychological meaning of sexual intercourse," because she found pregenital defenses against anxiety at work in patients during intercourse.[24] Colleagues who find in orally fixated patients that the penis had the unconscious significance of the breast and was used to solve oral-sadistic conflicts and anxieties, maintain that the libidinal cathexis of the penis originates from the longing for such a solution.[25] In some writings one almost gets the impression that libido is regarded as nothing more than a means of neutralizing anxiety; the fact that libido is a biological, somatically determined force is forgotten.

---

[24] German Psychoanalytic Society, 1931.
[25] E. Bergler and L. Eidelberg, "Der Mammakomplex des Mannes," *Int. Z. Psa.*, Vol. 19, 1933.

We find some of this even in the works of Jones. He writes, for instance: "The typical phallic stage in the boy is a neurotic compromise rather than a natural evolution in sexual development." [26] It is true that when he refers to the "phallic phase," he means the "deutero-phallic" period—castration anxiety and its consequences; that is, for instance, not the impulse of phallic penetration, but the inhibition of this impulse. Nevertheless, it seems as though the tracing of the involved relationships between genitality and pregenitality, particularly the tracing of the anxieties which persist from the pregenital period and of their further vicissitudes, has led him into considering genitality as being essentially a product of the *struggles* centering around pregenital anxiety. Freud has explained that at the time when the whole interest of the young boy is centered in his penis, he will, on hearing sexual prohibitions of any sort, but particularly prohibitions against masturbation, expect punishment to be carried out on his penis, in accordance with the law of talion; and Freud has furthermore shown that the dynamic value of the castration anxiety that arises in this fashion is derived from the very circumstance that the penis is so highly cathected at this period of life.[27] It is the somatically determined *libido* which accounts for the intensity of the *anxiety* which is engendered by the intervention of education. According to Jones, the state of affairs is just the reverse. "Libidinization" not only of what one is afraid of, but also of what one is afraid *for* is a means against anxiety. The penis is highly cathected *because* castration anxiety predominates at this time; "the narcissistic cathexis of the phallus is secondary in nature." The situation is not that the young boy has anxiety about his penis because he loves it as an organ which is rich in somatic sensations, but that he loves it because he has anxiety about it and therefore he must take particular care of it. But whence, then, the anxiety? Now, it is a fact that the English school of psychoanalysis has taught us much that is worthy of note about those pregenital anxieties which derive primarily from oral sadism. There is no doubt that here the old is always still present behind the new in psychic development, and thus that castration anxiety, too, is always associatively connected with those anxieties. But instead of describing these paths from pregenital to genital anxiety as being, as it were, accidental, Jones sees in castration anxiety *only* a developmental product of the earlier anxieties, and regards the phallic phase as being solely a consequence of castration anxiety.[28]

---

[26] E. Jones, "The Phallic Phase," *Papers on Psycho-Analysis*, 5th ed., Baltimore, Williams and Wilkins, 1948, p. 466.

[27] See, for instance, S. Freud, "The Infantile Genital Organization of the Libido," *Coll. Pap.*, Vol. II.

[28] I will refrain from discussing numerous analogous examples from our literature. Let one stand for many: Nina Searl maintains that a libidinization of the respiratory organs arises in order to counteract the justified fear of a damage to this region, which has its origin in the experience of crying attacks of early childhood. (N. Searl, *op. cit.*) There is no doubt that organs and functions about which one is anxious may be libidinized as a matter of overcompensation. But the erogeneity

The questions here discussed become particularly important in problems concerning the psychogenesis of perversions. These are libidinal phenomena which serve the purpose of keeping under repression drives of another sort, which are considered dangerous. It seems plausible, therefore, to think that here something is sexualized because it is feared. This is Glover's view,[29] to which one would give credence, should one encounter, for instance, a scissor-fetishist. Or again, we are accustomed to see in pedophilia a being in love with one's own childhood. But there are other forms of pedophilia too, which are analogous to the femininity of that male patient who defended himself by it against his fear of women. Just as there are many patients who cannot speak to children and cannot find contact with them because they are afraid of children, in whom they see their own repressed childhood, so there are pedophiles also, who love children because they want to give such a fear the lie and want to prove to themselves and to others that they are not afraid of children. It is thus possible that in such a reactive love of children what is libidinized is the very thing that was once feared. Glover believes that this is actually the case, and that perversions correspond to libidinizations at just those points where once there were childhood anxieties. But fetishism, which is invoked by Glover, seems precisely to prove the opposite. If a leg and foot fetishist recalls that when, as a child, he saw a little girl with short skirts he had the experience of an "injunction to remember"[30] which ran as follows: "I must remember this forever, that girls, too, have legs"—then we understand that he had at that moment come to an opposite decision, namely: "With the aid of this sight, I can forget that girls *have not got* a penis." Thus he does not sexualize where he experiences anxiety, but sexualizes that which contradicts his anxiety. Infantile sexual gratifications which seem to refute an anxiety occurring at the same time are naturally particularly well suited to serve as the foundation of fixations.

Indeed, it is characteristic of perversions that the infantile partial instinct which becomes manifest in them is *not* identical with those sexual attitudes which are feared and defended against. In perversions, there operate factors which pull away from adult sexuality, together with such as pull toward infantile sexuality. The factor of the overcoming of anxiety by libidinization may play a role as a subdivision of the second group. But if libidinization is regarded as the sole decisive factor, then the first group of factors are totally overlooked. These always culminate in *castration anxiety*. Glover objects to this view on the ground that

---

of a region, which is a biological property, cannot be reduced to such a mechanism altogether; it must be kept in mind that the anxiety which is here defended against was itself destined to defend in turn against yet earlier somatically determined erotogenicity.

[29] E. Glover, "The Relation of Perversion-Formation to the Development of Reality-Sense," *Int. J. Psa.*, Vol. 14, 1933.

[30] O. Fenichel, "The Economic Function of Screen Memories," No. 11 in this volume.

its explanation of perversions is too uniform. Unjustly so. Castration anxiety *is* uniform, for it does indeed have the same effect in all perversions, namely, that adult sexuality has to be replaced by something else; but what that sexuality is replaced by is *not* uniform. It depends on the attraction exerted by the various partial drives, and here libidinization for the purpose of overcoming anxiety may be one factor among others.

But libidinization for the purpose of overcoming anxiety must not be brought forward in too isolated a fashion, even among the fixating factors. Otherwise the impression arises that the somatic basis of the partial drives, and the well-attested observation that these can undergo fixations through constitution or through experience, can be underplayed in favor of a single new discovery. When, for instance, Glover states that "many of the so-called spontaneous sexual activities of childhood are already, in principle, perversions," that is, serve to overcome anxiety, then this arouses concern for the basic discoveries of psychoanalysis concerning infantile sexuality as a phenomenon which arises from somatic sources.

To the question, "How can the ego affirm the perverse impulse?" the answer, "Because, thanks to libidinization, the affirmation of what is feared averts anxiety," is certainly not correct in principle. One would have to say, rather, something like, "Because this affirmation can eliminate precisely the factor which makes instinctual gratification appear to the patient as a danger." Eidelberg's answer seems to me utterly unsatisfactory. He says, "This difference in the behavior of the ego seems to be determined by the fact that the ego's infantile megalomania receives far greater scope in the formation of a perverse activity, than it does in the formation of a neurotic symptom." [31] To us it seems that the process occurs in the reverse order: when the ego succeeds in finding this fortunate way out of an instinctual conflict, so that its endangered sexual pleasure is maintained at the price of a change of aim in the sense of a return to old fixations, then its childish delusions of grandeur are also thereby enhanced and become more clearly manifest.

Psychoanalysis deals with extremely complex states of affairs; if it is to attain a general survey of these states of affairs, it is important that it should base the arrangement of those complexities on correct co-ordinates. For instance, in masochistic phenomena there is a pleasure in unpleasure. This must not lead us astray into throwing away the pleasure principle, which gives us the first and most secure orientation concerning man's modes of behavior, but should only prompt us to explain this exception to an otherwise valid principle in a psychogenetic manner. Similarly, there is a "defense against anxiety by libidinization." This state of affairs again could confuse us, because our point of departure for the

[31] L. Eidelberg, "Zur Theorie und Klinik der Perversion," *Int. Z. Psa.,* Vol. 19, 1933.

understanding of all the instinctual conflicts of man is that, on the contrary, it is anxiety which lends force to the defense against drives, against "libido." But this conception is of crucial importance for the scientific and theoretical position of psychoanalysis, since the biologically determined nature of sexuality, the instinct as a demand for work made by the body upon the psychic apparatus,[32] is the bridge between our science and biology. Here, too, the solution is to comprehend libidinization as a defense against anxiety, as a secondary phenomenon, as a consequence of the "principle of multiple function," [33] which leads to a somatically determined urge taking over yet other functions as well in the psychic economy. To consider defense against anxiety as the chief function of libido would lead us away from our entire mode of thinking and would threaten the character of psychoanalysis as a natural science. There were primary instincts before there was a defense against anxiety with the help of instincts; and it was those primary instincts whose non-gratification gave rise to anxiety and which were themselves warded off by the development of anxiety.

[32] S. Freud, "Instincts and Their Vicissitudes," *Coll. Pap.*, Vol. IV, London, Hogarth, 1948.
[33] R. Waelder, "The Principle of Multiple Function: Observations on Over-Determination," *Psa. Quart.*, Vol. 5, 1936.

# TWENTY-EIGHT

# Psychoanalytic Method[*]

THE word "psychoanalysis" has many meanings. Many misunderstandings are traceable to the fact that the various meanings have been confused. It means: (1) a therapeutic method for neurotic diseases; (2) a psychological method of research; (3) a science which has arisen from the results of this method of research. As an example of the confusion of these various meanings I may cite the reproach that is so often directed at psychoanalysts to the effect that they are intolerant. Actually, we are of course by no means intolerant with reference to method. It has never been asserted that psychoanalysis is the sole means of curing neurotics. On the contrary, there are many counterindications against psychoanalysis, and no psychoanalyst will deny that there are neuroses for which other psychotherapeutic methods are more appropriate. But so far as the *science* is concerned, we *are* "intolerant." A scientific hypothesis may be refuted; but so long as it is not refuted, no one can demand of those who have established a principle on the basis of research that they should be tolerant toward the assertion that the opposite is likewise true.

Wherein lies the origin of the ambiguity of the concept of psychoanalysis? It can be explained on historical lines. Psychoanalysis began as a therapeutic method. Unexpectedly its application brought further discoveries, so that Freud then became aware that with this therapeutic method he had also discovered a method of research; and then gradually the results of the new method of research became synthesized into the new science.

As a method of research psychoanalysis is comparable to the use of a new instrument, such as the microscope. Anyone who has not himself looked through the microscope may, for instance, criticize logical contradictions in the utterances

* This paper was first presented at Prague in January, 1935. Dr. Fenichel's manuscript has been translated into English, in conformity with the other papers, but no attempt has been made to give it the final form Dr. Fenichel might have given it if he had prepared it for publication.

of a user of the instrument, but not the facts which the latter asserts he has seen.

The method has grown empirically. Only according to empiricism and through the application of it did the theory evolve. Today our task is an easier one: with the theoretic insight at our disposal we can explain and justify our method. But please do not forget that if I now proceed to explain to you theoretically how the psychoanalyst goes ahead, I am reversing the situation for the sake of the presentation: in reality, the analyst Freud "went ahead," and then gradually discovered what happened psychologically.

To understand this we may begin with the first findings which Breuer and Freud published in 1897. The significant phrase then was, "Hysterics suffer from reminiscences." What was meant by this was that hysterical symptoms, and we can add today, all other neurotic symptoms also, are determined in the past of the individual, and represent a piece of his past life in a distorted form, without the person in question knowing it. Neurotics are people who, at some time, have undergone certain experiences which they have not experienced to the full, such as emotions which have arisen in them and have never been completely expressed. When the affects are not discharged at the right place and at the right time, they burst forth at the wrong place and at the wrong time in a distorted form as neurotic symptoms.

If this is correct, then the next most important problem to be stated is: Under what conditions are experiences not experienced in full? What prevents adequate discharge?

The experiences in question were sometimes strong and stirring, so-called traumata. In such cases we can imagine that it was simply the overdose of excitement that made normal discharge impossible. But sometimes the experiences to which the "strangulated affects" could be assigned were not in the least traumatic, but very banal everyday occurrences. In the attempt to explain this, Breuer's and Freud's paths separated. Breuer was of the opinion that perhaps the experiences which were not experienced to the full were those which happened to the individual in a certain exceptional state, a so-called hypnoid state. Freud, on the contrary, asserted that he could find no indications of such an exceptional state in any of his patients, and offered another explanation, which became the foundation of psychoanalytic theory: the experiences which were not experienced to the full were those which the individual did not *wish* to experience to the very end. He saw that in the organism there was a force which resisted certain experiences, whether they be conditions of excitement or memories or perceptions; and under certain conditions these defensive forces were strong enough to circumvent the experience, but not strong enough to prevent the disturbance of mental equilibrium which made itself unpleasantly felt elsewhere.

This marked the introduction of the so-called "dynamic" principle. Neurotic symptoms can be explained as the result of a struggle between opposing forces, forces which may be deduced from their effect: on the one hand there is the normal tendency to discharge all excitations, and on the other hand there are "opposing forces" which try to make discharge impossible.

Innocent occurrences, against which something within the individual struggles, have always turned out to be representatives of something less innocent. What neurotics seek to ward off are regularly certain instinctual experiences which they have learned to fear. Outwardly the experiences against which the individuals defend themselves seem to be unobnoxious, but actually they are either situations that tempt the rejected instinct, or situations that recall an unconscious expectation of punishment for the instinctual activity in question, or some similar thing—in short, representatives of an instinctual conflict.

What is significant is that the neurotic manifestations themselves offer us proof that that which has been rejected has not been fully rejected, but seeks to obtain distorted expression without the knowledge of the individual. A simple example which shows that the same conflicts are to be found in normal people as in neurotics is seen in the so-called parapraxes, or slips of behavior. In them a tendency which the individual does not want to express nevertheless regularly finds expression against his will.

Psychoanalysis is a psychology that strips disguises. It does not believe in pretended motives, and seeks to deduce from people's behavior their hidden, true motives.

In parapraxes and neurotic symptoms the repressed nevertheless does find expression. From the standpoint of the psychologist who wants to become acquainted with the repressed, the repressed itself, with its constant tendency to obtain discharge, with its so-called "upward drive," is an ally; the repressing forces of the ego, however, which seek to prevent expression of the repressed, set themselves against these strivings as "resistances."

And now I should like to state theoretically how psychoanalysis operates as a therapeutic method. We have heard that neuroses are expressions of a conflict between rejected instincts and defensive forces of the ego—in the last analysis, of anxiety. For the most part, symptoms represent a breaking through of the rejected instincts, a breaking through *in spite of* the opposing will of the ego; sometimes they are merely the expression of the defensive struggle itself. From this we may conclude that a neurosis would be cured if we succeeded in removing the defense. But how is this to be achieved? Dissolution of the defensive measures would not do away with the instincts themselves. Do we then suppose that a healthy person, who no longer defends himself against all his unconscious instincts, is going to gratify them? Not at all! The change which follows, if we succeed in removing the defense, is not limited to permitting gratification to the instinct which had previously been rejected. The situation is better described as follows: The child who had reached the conclusion that his instincts were dangerous and had to be rejected, was still a small child and had no more effective defense methods at his disposal than those which later led to neurosis. Just because the instinct had been "rejected" in childhood, it remained unchanged in the unconscious, and did not participate in the further development of the personality. But the rest of the personality had in the meanwhile built its childish instincts into the instinctual structure of the adult, and had further learned to apply other, more effective methods of defense where the indication was *not* to yield to these instinctual impulses. Only the repressed instinctual component did not participate in this development. If we succeed in doing away with the repression, what was formerly excluded once again finds contact with the total personality. The instincts, now released from repression, change their character and achieve a capacity for satisfaction and for control in the intervals between instinctual excitations.

I should prefer to demonstrate all this to you by examples, but our time is limited. Therefore, we shall now turn to a more important question. It is the aim of psychoanalysis to remove pathogenic defenses. How is this aim to be attained? You will recall that the repressed seeks to express itself—if no obstacle prevents it from such expression. The initial efforts of the analyst are devoted to eliminating such obstacles. He does this with the assistance of the so-called "basic rule." This may be stated as follows: The patient, or the test person, is requested to say out loud everything which goes through his mind, without any selection. The meaning of the rule will immediately become clear if we recall what we do in our ordinary conversations when we do not follow such a rule. We feel impulses to tell the person to whom we are speaking all sorts of things, but do not yield to these impulses because a certain conceptual goal, the thought of what we wanted to tell, permits us to select from among the impulses, so that we suppress that which does not belong to the topic under discussion. In everyday life, what we say or do is determined by certain conceptual goals. By means of the basic rule an attempt is made to eliminate all these conceptual goals. If the selective conceptual goals of the ego no longer determine the topic, what is expressed can be determined only by one other force: by tensions and impulses within the organism which await the opportunity to attain expression. The point to which we first seek to bring the patient is to learn to eliminate the conceptual goals. He is not to tell us selected things. In fact, he is not to be active at all; he is to do nothing except make an effort not to prevent giving expression to impulses which rise within him.

"To tell everything" is much more difficult than one imagines theoretically.

Even the individual who most conscientiously tries to adhere to the basic rule fails to tell many things, because he considers them too unimportant, too stupid, or too indiscreet, or for some other reason. There are many who never learn to apply the basic rule, because their fear of losing control is too great, and before they can give expression to anything, they must examine it to see exactly what it is.

It is, therefore, not so simple for the unconscious to find expression when we request the patient to obey the basic rule. The injunction to bring no conceptual goals into play obviates "resistances" of the ego, assuredly, but not all of them. The very deepest resistances—to be exact, those which originated in childhood and which are directed at unconscious instinctual outbursts—cannot be swept out of existence by a stipulation to "tell everything." The result of this is that the utterances of a patient obeying the rule are not simply a reflection of the unconscious that now becomes conscious. The picture is rather one of a struggle between certain unconscious impulses, which undoubtedly reveal themselves relatively more clearly than in ordinary conversations, and certain resistances of the ego, which similarly are unconscious to the subject, or become apparent to him in a distorted form.

Now, what does the analyst do?

(1) He helps the patient to eliminate his resistances as far as possible. He does this by every means employed by man to influence his fellow man, including persuasion and suggestion. But fundamentally he does it by calling the attention of the patient, who is either completely unaware or insufficiently aware of his resistances, to their effect.

(2) Knowing that the utterances of the patient are really allusions to other things, the psychoanalyst tries to deduce what lies back of the allusions and to impart this information to the patient. He does this when there is a minimum of distance between allusion and what is alluded to, and thereby makes it easier for the unconscious to break through by lending the patient words to express that which he feels coming to the surface.

This procedure of deducing what the patient actually means and telling it to him is called "interpretation." From what we have just said, it follows that "interpretation" means helping something unconscious to become conscious by naming it just at the moment it is striving to break through. This explains why we can only interpret at one specific point, namely, where the patient's actual, immediate interest and attention is momentarily centered; that is, we can interpret only on the so-called surface. The actual, shocking, infantile instinctual impulses are so deeply repressed that in the beginning we are of course not concerned with them, but with their derivatives, never with that which is being defended against, but always with the defensive forces. We have been asked why we are unable to apply our theoretical knowledge to shortening the regrettably long time analyses take: if we know that the basis of a neurosis is the so-called "oedipus complex," why not tell the patient immediately that he loves his mother and wants to kill his father and cure him with this information? There was once a comparatively large school of pseudoanalysis which held that the patient should be "bombarded" with "depth interpretations"; and in psychoanalytic literature, too, we come upon statements to the effect that a speedy "depth interpretation" can overcome the patient's anxiety. But we now understand why such efforts have nothing in common with psychoanalysis. The unprepared patient can in no way connect the words he hears from the physician with his real emotional experiences. Such an "interpretation" does not interpret at all.

How can the analyst know what the words of the patient actually allude to? His "resistances" have twisted his utterances into unrecognizability. In the analyst's interpretative work, his task is to undo and make retroactive the distortion caused by resistance. There are many methods of bringing distortion about; and they give rise to many interesting psychological questions. Let me enumerate a few examples of the techniques employed in distortion:

(1) Specific links may be missing in the associations of the patient, as, for example, the specific quality of affects, or specific recollections, or specific attitudes that are to be expected in certain situations. When the analyst observes such hiatuses, he knows that the censoring forces of the ego have been busy with their scissors.

(2) We know that affects which have once been suppressed express themselves in some other place. If a man must swallow his anger at his boss, he may easily become enraged at his wife. Therefore, when the analyst observes that an affect is incommensurate with a given situation—whether it be too strong or whether it be inappropriate in quality—he knows that he is dealing with a derivative of something that was originally quite different.

(3) Whatever the patient says, not only in words, but also in his movements, his attitudes, his slips—in fact, in all his modes of expression—is associatively bound up with the unconscious, to which it alludes. And these associative connections are, in turn, of various kinds:

(a) The connection with the unconscious may be seen in the fact that what is said and what is meant represent parts of an entity. So long as the analyst does not know what the entity is, he cannot surmise what is meant. The more the analyst knows about the history of his patient, the better is he able to understand. Neurotic symptoms, especially, often become understandable through their historical connections only. Here is an example: An obsessional neurotic suffered from a compulsive doubt as to whether he should sleep with his windows open or shut. Instead of sleeping, he spent the night opening the windows, then closing them, *ad infinitum*. The symptom could only be explained by a historical episode. During his puberty, the patient had once slept with a friend; and at that time there had been a similar conflict. But the conflict had not been in the mind of the patient; it had been between himself and his friend. One of the boys wanted the window open, the other insisted upon its being closed. This information made the symptom comprehensible. It meant, "Shall I defend myself actively against my friend, or shall I passively submit to his will?"

(b) It is known that things which are similar to one another are associatively connected with one another. As we may assume that the unconscious strives for expression again and again, the best way for the analyst to find out what is actually meant is to look for a common factor in the various utterances of the patient. Frequently, it is the interplay or the contradiction between the patient's various statements, or between his words and his gestures, or his words and his feelings, that puts the analyst on the right trail. At times the very manner in which the patient relates something or experiences something must itself be interpreted, and is the expression of a specific unconscious thought. Remarkable, too, is the fact that everyone shares a common reservoir of expressions which serve to distort meaning; i.e., what is known as *symbolism*.

It is understandable that the interpretative work of the analyst does not consist in stopping to examine every utterance of the patient and saying to himself: Did he omit something here? Is his remark only a fragment of some complete train of thought? Perhaps I must find some historical connection in it. What is the connection between the patient's utterance and what he said five minutes ago or yesterday? Is the patient's facial expression in harmony with or in contradiction to what he is saying? Is what he has just mentioned to be found in Freud's table of symbols? Is his affect commensurate with his utterance? And so on. By the time the analyst has considered all these points, the patient will have gone on to something else. No, discovering what the patient really means does not involve the conscious analysis of all possible distortions, but an intense empathy with the personality of the patient. In performing this part of his task, the tool of the analyst is his own unconscious.

With this confession, have we denied the scientific character of the psychoanalytic method? How can the analyst, working with his intuition, actually know if that which he has surmised is really correct? Let us postpone the answer to this question for a few minutes.

We have already said that an interpretation can only be effective if it is given at the moment when the distance between what is said and what is meant is at a minimum. How can the analyst know *when* to interpret? He must constantly have a sense of the strength of the resistances operative at any given moment.

Resistances find expression in manifold ways. Everything that prevents the patient from producing material derived from the unconscious is resistance. It is impossible to tabulate the various ways in which resistance can be expressed. The patient may stop talking, or he may talk so much that a common factor cannot be deduced from the recital. What he says appears to deviate further and further from what he actually means; it seems to be extensive rather than deep. (If we call the patient's attention to this, he may justly reply, "You asked me to say *everything* that comes to my mind. If my associations tend to spread out in all directions, should I therefore abandon the basic rule of analysis?" The answer is simple: the patient must follow the basic rule as closely as he can. If, however, no common factor develops, the analysis is confronted with an antecedent problem before what is actually meant can be surmised. *Why* do the patient's associations extend in all directions? Both the analyst and the patient have to find out why the patient is in the throes of this particular resistance, and also why the resistance is expressed in this specific form.) The patient forgets certain things, certain important events of the day before, or something that has already been discussed in the analysis. He criticizes misunderstandingly every comment of the analyst; he feels a sort of unpleasure in his relationship to the analysis. All these are forms of resistance which are easily recognizable as such. Some resistances, however, operate far more secretively. For example: A patient appears to be doing a good analysis; that is, he is making progress in understanding the forces working within him; he experiences the connections between things; he digs up new childhood recollections; and yet there is no change in his neurosis. This is necessarily due to the operation of a secret resistance which, however, may assume many forms. Progress in the analysis may only be apparent; actually, the patient's attitude during the analysis—an attitude which has not itself been analyzed—may even nullify the effect of the treatment. He may, for instance, have a feeling of doubt. He may feel, "that would be all very fine if it were true; but I don't know if it is true." Or the patient may have understood what the analyst and his own associations show him, but specific attitudes of resistance have enabled him to keep this new knowledge quite separate from his real life. It is as if he had said to himself: "This is all valid only as long as I lie on this couch; the moment I get up, it doesn't count." Or a patient may accept everything the analyst tells him as a matter of mere courtesy; but it is just this courteous attitude which protects him from having to relive to the full his instinctual conflicts, and which therefore is the first thing that has to be analyzed. Then there are intellectual resistances, in which patients try to refute the theoretical validity of psychoanalysis instead of seeking to clarify their own mental life. Some patients, again, become enthusiastic supporters of psychoanalysis in order to avoid applying it to themselves.

You will readily understand that an acute resistance, one that is directed against the discussion of some particular topic, is far easier to handle than "character resistances." These are attitudes which the patient has previously developed in order to maintain his repressions, and now exhibits to the analyst. These attitudes must first be broken down before the repressions can be resolved.

With that we come to the most remarkable and most significant form of resistance, the treatment of which is usually the core of the analysis: the "transference" resistance, as it is called. Understanding the contents of the patient's unconscious from his utterances is relatively the simplest part of the analyst's task. Handling the transference is the most difficult. Now just what do we understand by "transference"?

It seems very natural that in the course of an analytic treatment the patient should produce powerful affects. They may be expressed in anxiety, in joy, in an increase of his inner tension beyond the point of endurance, or in a happy feeling of complete relaxation. And they may also take the form of specific feelings towards the analyst: a strong love, because the physician is helping him, or bitter hatred, because the analyst forces him to undergo unpleasant experiences. But the problem becomes more complicated when a specific affect is in contradiction to what is happening in the analysis, as, for example, when the patient hates the analyst for helping him, or loves the physician for putting an unpleasant restriction upon him. Even more complicated is the problem when the patient obviously misconstrues the real psychoanalytic situation, and either loves or hates the analyst for something which, in the opinion of the analyst, is nonexistent. Such misconstruing of the actual psychoanalytic situation is a regular occurrence in almost every analysis. Ever since Freud pointed this out, it has not been very difficult to understand it theoretically. We know that the analytic situation induces "derivatives of the repressed" to develop, and that at the same time a resistance operates against them. Now, these "derivatives" do not always appear in the form of recollections or abstract impulses, but often as highly concrete emotional needs directed toward the person who happens to be present at the time. The resistance then sees to it that the patient develops a tendency to be blind to the true situation. He misunderstands the present in terms of the past. Instead of discussing the past, he strives—without recognizing the nature of his action—to *relive* the past, and to relive it more satisfactorily than he did in childhood. He "transfers" past attitudes to the present.

In an analysis, transference has a twofold aspect. We have already stated that it must fundamentally be considered as a form of resistance. The patient defends himself against discussing his infantile instincts by reliving them. On the other hand, the transference attitude offers the analyst a unique opportunity to observe directly the past of his patient, and thereby to understand the development of his conflicts.

What, then, is the behavior of the analyst when the patient proceeds to "transfer"? In principle, his behavior toward this new attitude of the patient is exactly the same as toward other attitudes of the patient: the analyst interprets it. In the patient's attitude, the analyst sees a derivative of the unconscious and tries to show this to the patient "ad minimum," starting from the surface.

In practice, however, this task is far more difficult than any other type of interpretation. Were the analyst to behave as the patient's parents had previously done, he could not help him, for then what had once occurred in the patient's childhood would merely be repeated. And were the analyst to behave in a contrary way, he would not be able to cure the patient either, for then the physician would only be fulfilling the patient's resistance wishes. The analyst, therefore, may do neither the one nor the other. If he felt flattered by the love of the patient and responded in kind, or if he were hurt by the patient's feeling of hate —in short, if he were to react to the affects of his patient with counteraffects (as happens in life) he could certainly never again show his patient the infantile origin of these impulses, for the patient would justly respond to these interpretations in some such way as this: "No, I love you or hate you, *not* because unresolved love or trends of hate are operating within me, but because you have actually behaved in a lovable or a hateful way."

Thus the task of the analyst is plain. He may in no way play along with the patient. His work is to hold a mirror up to him, so to speak, a mirror in which the patient can observe his own behavior. But this image of the patient must not be blurred by affects and the corrective words of the analyst.

There are several reasons why analytic institutes demand that all analysts shall themselves first have been analyzed. One of the reasons is that in psychoanalytic courses it is not possible to give clinical demonstrations. Consequently, the future analyst can only learn analytic technique by personal experience. A second reason is that the analyst's own repressions would make him overlook certain things in his patient, or see them in an exaggerated way, and therefore falsify their significance. Much more fundamental is the third reason. It is not easy to face the innumerable and various affects with which patients bombard the analyst without reacting with counteraffects—whether conscious or unconscious. The unconscious tendencies of the analyst to express his own unresolved love and trends of hate in transference work must, therefore, be eliminated through a training analysis.

Now we comprehend that logical and consistent interpretative work, both within and without the framework of the transference, can be described as edu-

cating the patient to produce steadily less distorted derivatives until his fundamental instinctual conflicts are recognizable. Naturally, this is not a single operation which results in a single act of "abreaction." Rather is it a chronic process
—the so-called process of "working through"—which shows the patient again
and again the same conflicts and his customary way of looking at them, but from
new angles and in new connections. We have already stated what the final result is. With the gradual dissolution of the pathogenic defenses, the forces that
have previously been repressed again find contact with the total personality. New
and more effective instinctual defenses, which do not cause neuroses, can be applied by the adult ego when all the dammed-up infantile instincts have been
converted into mature instincts which find normal, regular satisfaction.

Before concluding, I must say a word about a problem which I have put off
until now. How do we know that our interpretations are correct? A familiar
objection that is frequently made against psychoanalysis is that the interpretations are arbitrary, that the analyst more or less interprets his fantasies into the
patient. He makes things easy for himself: if the patient says "yes" to an interpretation, that is taken as proof of its validity; if he says "no" he thereby shows
a resistance to the interpretation, proof positive of its validity. As for scientific
certainty, there simply is no evidence of it.

What is the real situation? As a matter of fact, it is true that usually we
accept the "yes" of a patient as confirmation, but under certain circumstances do
not regard a "no" as refutation. Freud very rightly called our attention to an
analogous situation: that of the magistrate. The confession of an accused is generally valid as proof of the crime, although it must be kept in mind that the confession may be a falsified one; but a denial on the part of the accused is by no
means proof of innocence. The difference between the accused and a psycho-
analytical patient is merely that the former consciously conceals the truth, the
latter unconsciously.

Hence neither a "yes" nor a "no" in reply to an interpretation is a final clue
as to its validity or its falsity. It is rather the manner in which the "yes" or "no"
is expressed. Certainly there is at times a "no" that merely represents a final attempt to maintain an attitude which has become untenable; there is a variety of
signs by which such a patient betrays, immediately after uttering his "no," that
he has been inwardly affected by the interpretation and feels that what the
analyst has called to his attention really exists within himself.

But in general one can say that if a patient really counters an interpretation
with a "no," the interpretation was wrong. That does not necessarily mean
that it was wrong in content, that for instance the instinctual distortion which
the analyst surmised and imparted to the patient had never been operative; the
interpretation may have been correct in content, but incorrect dynamically or

economically, that is, given at a moment when the patient could not grasp its validity, nor get any further with it. A "yes" on the part of the patient may be simulated out of either politeness or negligence or fear of the consequences of a contradiction or something else, whereas the patient's behavior may show us that inwardly he is saying "no."

To put it differently, it is not a matter of the words used by the patient in answering an interpretation. We recall again what the purpose of the analyst is in giving an interpretation. He seeks to intervene in the dynamic interplay of forces between the repressed which strives for discharge and the repressing forces, to change the balance of the forces in favor of the repressed. The degree to which this takes place is the criterion for the validity of an interpretation. It is the patient's reactions in their *entirety,* not his first "yes" or "no," which give the answer. A valid interpretation brings about a dynamic change in the patient's entire behavior, which cannot escape recognition.

Freud once compared psychoanalysis with a jig-saw puzzle, in which the aim is to construct, out of the fragments of a picture, a complete picture. There is but one correct solution. So long as it is not discovered, one can perhaps recognize isolated bits of pictures, but there is no coherent whole. If the correct solution is found, there can be no doubt as to its validity, for each fragment fits, beyond question, into a general whole. I wish that I could show you a completed case, how a final solution reveals a unified coherence in which every hitherto incomprehensible detail has at last found its place, and how the patient's actual emotional behavior has changed exactly according to this coherence, as was to be expected. Unfortunately, such a demonstration would require many evenings.

We are frequently asked for statistics on the therapeutic results of psychoanalysis. They are difficult to give. Their appearance depends, first of all, on which cases have been selected. There are many neurotic conditions about which there is great uncertainty as to the possible success of a psychoanalysis, but where it may nevertheless be attempted. If we decide to include such cases, the statistics naturally look much worse than if we present statistics on specially selected cases. A second difficulty is the circumstance that different physicians understand very different things by "cure" and "improvement." I once attempted to collate statistically ten years' work of the Berlin Psychoanalytic Institute, and established very severe criteria for the task. The results, which were published, certainly bear comparison with those of any other statistics on medical treatment. There is no doubt that psychoanalytic therapy leaves much to be desired. There are failures and there are cases where one has to be content with partial success. But there is no doubt that in psychoanalysis, which is the only radical method, we have the best method for the treatment of the neuroses. Its chief disadvantage is

the great expenditure of time and money which it requires. Its advantage, however, of which we are proud, and which psychoanalysis alone possesses, is that
it is built upon scientific insight, and that the therapy is at the same time a
method of research which affords still further scientific insight—an insight
which will be useful not only in the treatment of neuroses, but in far wider
fields of practical application.

## TWENTY-NINE

# On Compulsive Doubt about News of Death*

WE CONSIDER the frequent compulsive doubts about news of death as an expression of ambivalence: he who has death wishes against others cannot but mobilize these upon receiving news of a real death; and the struggle between the death wishes and the striving to suppress them is the unconscious content of the compulsive doubt. Since the settlement of the compulsive doubt by reality is a desirable way out for all compulsion neurotics, it is understandable that incontrovertible confirmations of news of death are so often received with a "Thank God!" and we recognize in it a grotesque break-through of the repressed from repression. On closer study of such cases, we find the following complicating psychic state of affairs, which appears to be typical.

After the receipt of the news of death, the old unconscious death wishes appear in the following form: "I have already often thought that 'X' was dead, without its having been true. Therefore, now too only my own bad thoughts suggest this to me. But previously I myself never believed in the reality of these thoughts, I only played with them, and did not speak of them to anyone. Now that I believe I have received the news of death from the outside, it is a much more serious matter. If the man is really dead, then everything is all right. But I have a bad conscience, because I have often thought of this death; therefore, it would be possible this time too that I have been mistaken, that I misheard or misread it. Should I mention anything about this death, my bad wishes would become apparent, I would be compromised, and would have to be punished." Therefore, the confirmation of the news of death rightly elicits a "Thank God!" for it means: "It is objectively true—I am not the kind of bad man who thinks up this sort of a thing when it is not true."

* This brief paper was translated from a German galley page, dated 1935, found among Dr. Fenichel's papers. A check of the journal literature shows that it was never published.

*THIRTY*

# Concerning the Theory of
# Psychoanalytic Technique *

## I

IN DISCUSSING the "theory of technique" it is unfortunately still necessary to discuss the justification of this concept. There exist some views about the "irrational" nature of psychoanalytic technique which oppose any attempt at constructing a theory of its technical principles. One of these views, for instance, was expressed recently by Reik.[1] Since the instrument of psychoanalytic technique is the unconscious of the analyst (the "relay" conception), and since intuition is indispensable for apprehending what goes on in the patient, he wants to leave everything in that technique to the unconscious and to intuition. But in view of the fact that the subject matter of psychoanalysis is the irrational, such conceptions must in the final analysis lead to that method itself being regarded as irrational, losing every characteristic of science and becoming pure art.

*Per contra,* we argue as follows. We have a dynamic-economic conception of psychic life. Our technique, too, which aims at a dynamic-economic change in the patient, must follow dynamic-economic principles. It must always remain true to the mode of thinking underlying psychoanalysis, and must order our behavior issuing from intuition (which is of course indispensable) according to rational directives.

Freud was the originator of the concepts "dynamics" and "economics" in psychic life. His whole method of studying neurotic phenomena, as well as his papers on technique,[2] leaves no doubt that he considered analytic interpretation,

---

* Discussion of H. Kaiser's "Probleme der Technik," *Int. Z. Psa.,* Vol. 20, 1934. First published in *Int. Z. Psa.,* Vol. 21, 1935, pp. 78–95.

[1] See T. Reik, "New Ways in Psycho-Analytic Technique," *Int. J. Psa.,* Vol. 14, 1933.

[2] S. Freud, "Papers on Technique," *Coll. Pap.,* Vol. II, London, Hogarth, 1948.

as well as the procedure of the analyst in general, as an intervention in the dynamics and economics of the patient's mind, and thus he demanded of interpretations more than that they should be correct as to content. It was he who asserted that only a procedure which used *resistances* and *transference* could be called psychoanalysis; [3] that is, only a procedure which intervened in the dynamics and did not merely give "translations" of the patient's allusions, as soon as the analyst understood to what they alluded. The formula that the analyst should make the unconscious conscious might lead to such a misunderstanding. Indeed, it is possible that the statement of a symptom's meaning will at times make it disappear; but it need not. Mere topological conceptions do not suffice to explain what determines whether an interpretation does or does not have this effect. Whether it does or not is determined by whether or not a repression (more correctly, an instinctual defense implying continued expenditure of energy) is actually eliminated. But what eliminates a repression? The dynamic conception views the psyche as a continuous struggle between mental trends which seek discharge and the defensive and selective forces of the ego, between the instinctual cathexes and the anti-cathexes of the ego. That the latter too arose from the former does not interest us here. In reviewing an already existing neurotic conflict, we see that it takes place between an unconscious instinctual demand and the defensive forces of the ego, which are supplied with "anti-cathexes," and which manifest themselves in the treatment as resistances. (Kaiser's designation of the energy used by the forces defending against drives as "narcissistic libido," is *per se* correct, but apt to be misleading. To avoid discussions about the genesis of this libido, it is probably better to use for these energies the term "anti-cathexis" introduced by Freud.) What we have to do is to intervene in this interplay between drive and resistance. In so intervening, we need not, and even cannot, reinforce the drive. The repressed drive is our ally in our work; it strives of itself toward consciousness and motility. Our task is only to see that no resistances bar its way. Were it possible to brush aside the resistances, the repressed would appear on its own. This *dynamic* conception of interpretation —that our task is to seek out resistances and to uncover them so that the repressed manifests itself—must be supplemented by the economic conception that our task is to tackle the economically most important and strongest resistance in order to achieve an actual and economically decisive liberation of libido, so that what was tied up so far in the struggle of repression shall be available to real gratification. The infantile sexual impulses which have been repressed then find contact with the ego and change, for the greater part, into genitality capable of orgasm, the rest becoming capable of sublimation.

[3] S. Freud, "The History of the Psychoanalytic Movement," *The Basic Writings*, New York, Random House, 1938.

The "theory of technique" is but a commentary on these propositions. These propositions should be taken seriously; and it cannot be denied that there are many factors in the analytic situation which tempt the analyst not to take them seriously, but, sooner or later, to "drift" and to use the only-an-art conception of analytic technique, making the inevitability of a certain lack of system in the analysis an excuse for letting himself float along in a planless way—that is, letting himself interpret purely intuitively what occurs to him, or at best, to his patient.

## II

It is Reich's merit to have especially warned us against this procedure. His proposals for the reform of the technique derive mostly from a serious view of the *economic* conception, namely, from an insight into the fact that our task is to liberate the energy tied up in the repressive struggle and to change repressed infantile sexuality into adult sexuality capable of orgasm, by eliminating repression.[4]

There are a number of "technical formulas" transmitted by tradition from Freud, inspection of which shows that what Reich's proposals on technique are saying is, "Consider whether you are really always applying the true Freudian technique." One of these formulas is, "Work always where the patient's affect lies at the moment." To the thoughtful analyst this clearly does not mean: "Work where the patient *believes* his affects lie." The analyst must always *seek out* the points where at the moment the conflict is decisively centered. Another example: "Interpretation begins always at what is on the surface at the moment." Taken correctly, this can only mean that it makes no sense to give "deep interpretations" (however correct they might be as to content) as long as superficial matters are in the way. For this reason one cannot, as Melanie Klein wants,[5] "get into direct contact with the unconscious of the patient," because to analyze means precisely to come to terms with the patient's *ego,* to compel the patient's ego to face its own conflicts. If we, for instance, know that a compulsion neurosis has regressed, out of castration anxiety, from the genital oedipus conflict to the anal-sadistic stage, we cannot use this knowledge for discussing "immediately" the genital oedipus conflict; the only way to it is by working through the anal-sadistic conflicts. This is obvious. But it is also necessary always to keep in view the hundreds of analogies of everyday life. The defensive attitudes of the ego are *always* more superficial than the instinctual attitudes of the id. Therefore, before throwing the patient's instincts at his head we have first to interpret to him that he is afraid of them and is defending himself against them, and why he does so.

---

[4] See W. Reich's *Character Analysis,* New York, Orgone Institute Press, 1949.
[5] M. Klein, *The Psychoanalysis of Children,* New York, Norton, 1932.

Here is another formula: "Interpretation of resistance goes before interpretation of content." Every resistance hinders the patient from digesting a contentual interpretation, that is, an utterance of his unconscious trends so that it effects a dynamic change. Thus there is no point in trying to do this before the obstacle is out of the way. Since not all resistances are manifest, however, the analyst must continuously seek out and work on the momentarily acute resistances, first, by separating the patient's judging ego from his resistance-determined behavior; secondly, by getting the patient to experience the latter as arising from his resistance; thirdly, by finding the occasions of the resistance; fourthly, by explaining why the resistance takes precisely this form; and fifthly and lastly, by telling him against what it is directed. Freud has, moreover, repeatedly discussed and demonstrated by examples that not only the content of what the patient says but his modes of behavior, his "accidental" actions, and his manner and bearing are all also the subject matter of the analysis.

There are, it is true, some other traditional formulas as well, which at first sight seem to contradict Reich's views. There is, for instance, Freud's warning against making a kind of "stock-taking" of the situation from time to time during the course of the analysis, in order to clarify the structure of the case for oneself, because in this way one only gets a biased view of it; one should rather respond to the patient's unconscious with one's own unconscious and wait until a structural picture arises of itself.[6] Again, there is his comparison of analysis with a jig-saw puzzle in which one piece after another is observed at random as each presents itself "by accident," until one finds how they fit together.[7] Then, too, there is the formula: "The patient determines the theme of the session."

The apparent contradictions of such formulas are resolved if we keep in mind that the psychoanalytic technique is a *living art,* in which rules never have more than a relative validity. Surely Freud's views, if represented correctly, mean that the analytic technique must guard against two extremes, both equally incorrect: on the one hand, one must not analyze too much according to a rational plan, by intellect alone (the concept of "relay," the analyst's own unconscious as his instrument—"he who wants to analyze must be analyzed"); and on the other hand, one must not be too irrational, because to analyze means to subject the irrational in man to reason. (Otherwise psychoanalytic technique would be unteachable. The frequently used comparison between analytic and surgical technique is here indeed in place; for analytic technique, too, one needs endowment and intuition, but these, without training, do not suffice in surgery either.)

Reich's view is that interpretation has never been as yet consistently thought

---

[6] S. Freud, "Recommendations for Physicians on the Psycho-Analytic Method of Treatment," *Coll. Pap.,* Vol. II.

[7] S. Freud, "The Etiology of Hysteria," *Coll. Pap.,* Vol. I, London, Hogarth, 1948.

through and followed out as a dynamic-economic process. Instead of using their insight into the dynamics and economics of psychic processes to build up their technique in a planned and systematic way, analysts succumb to indolence and lack any system. In their work, despite their better knowledge they take the task of interpreting resistances to mean that they are to interpret whatever the patient is talking about. In Reich's opinion, the reason why the analyst usually fails to work "where the affect really is" is that it simply does not occur to him to look for the affect where it should be sought—namely, in characterological behavior. Characterological behavior acts as a kind of armor-plating which covers the real conflicts, and this aspect of it is not taken seriously enough. Indeed, were one to take the rule "to work where the affect actually lies" seriously, it would mean that as long as the leading characterological resistance was unbroken, one would work on no other subject matter, and discuss no other theme with the patient but this. The more "the affect" is "frozen" into an "attitude," the less does the patient know about it, and the more important is it to work on this *first,* so that the contentual interpretations which the analyst will make later on shall not be wasted beforehand. Though the comparison with the jig-saw puzzle is correct, that game too can be played systematically and according to a plan, by not examining the pieces as they accidentally present themselves, but looking every time for the pieces which would fit. The psychic material of the patient has a certain stratification. His resistance attempts to conceal this stratification. The analyst, nevertheless, must discover this stratification and follow it exactly in his interpretations, and he must recognize when material whose content belongs to a deeper stratum emerges only in order to ward off more superficial material. Otherwise, he will be confronted with the dreaded "chaotic situation," in which material from every stratum of the mind is produced in disordered comminglement. Thus Reich thinks the principle "begin always at the surface," too, should be taken more seriously and carried out more consistently than hitherto. Such a consistent procedure demands primarily that material—including dreams—which does not serve the momentary purpose should be left untouched, in order not to "fire away" uselessly the work of interpretation. "The patient determines the theme of the session," not by what he says, but by showing the analyst where his economically crucial resistance lies. This theme the analyst must then compel the patient to work through, even if the latter would rather talk about something else.

I should like to insert a few critical comments at this point. With those principles of the so-called "Reichian technique" which I have attempted to represent here, I am in complete agreement—qua *principles.* I consider them as correctly deduced from Freud's theoretical and technical views.[8] I also agree with Reich

[8] They have been excellently formulated already by W. Reich in his study "On the Technique of Interpretation and of Resistance Analysis," Chapter 3 of *Character Analysis.*

that in our everyday work all of us often infringe on these principles, and that in this respect no amount of self-control is too much. The contradictory judgments which have been made in analytic circles about the so-called "Reichian technique" —some saying, "It is nothing new, but only exactly what Freud does," and others saying "It is so different from Freud's analysis, that it ought not to be called psychoanalysis"—can be explained in this way: In so far as these principles are merely elaborations of Freud's views, they are "nothing new"; in so far as they are *consistent elaborations* of it, they *are* something new.

The agreement in principle with Reich which I have just expressed is only limited, on the one hand, by two minor theoretical objections, and on the other, by objections, not against the essence of his views and principles, but simply against the manner of their application on particular points.

The two minor theoretical objections are:

(1) The psychic material in the patient does not have an orderly stratification. Reich's assertion to the contrary is schematic and disregards complicating details. The regularity of the stratification is just as regularly broken through—in different people to different degrees—even when there have been no incorrect analytic interpretations. The phenomenon which geology calls "dislocation" is a general one and consists in materials originally layered over, or side by side with each other, being mixed into each other by various natural events; consequently, the sequence in which the material presents itself to the geologist who drills into the earth is not identical with the age of the layers in question. The material is only "relatively" ordered. In the same way, to my mind, the relatively correct views of Reich on the "consistency" of interpretation must not be taken for absolute either. For there are *spontaneous chaotic situations* too; indeed, there are people whose character neurosis presents a picture which cannot be diagnosed by any other term but "chaotic situation." Moreover, "dislocation" continues to take place during psychoanalytic treatment. And the fluctuations of everyday life, which cannot be disregarded, also lessen this "consistency" to some extent.

(2) If we are to pay particular attention to "frozen resistances," to habitual actions and attitudes, we must not only know that they express resistance, but get to understand their meaning. Naturally, even only to call the patient's attention to his resistive attitude is better than to overlook it completely. But there is no doubt that we shall succeed the more easily, the more completely we understand the concrete meaning of such a resistive attitude. The discovery of this meaning in turn will be facilitated by every piece of knowledge we gain about the individual patient's past history. We are thus faced with a vicious circle: His past history becomes accessible only through resolving these attitudes—and resolving these attitudes requires knowledge of that history. In my opinion, this vicious circle is best resolved by the analyst's setting out from the beginning to learn for his own information (without major "interpretations") as much as

possible about the patient's past. I think that it is always a good thing to use the first period of analysis for *collecting material*. The more *information* one has, the better armed one goes into the actual struggle with the resistances. We do not always succeed in such an initial collection of material; nor is such failure any reason for giving up an analysis. I believe, however, that we should not deliberately by-pass occasions for collecting such material. It seems to me that Reich, in the intention of doing nothing else but work consistently upon the point around which for the moment everything turns, often leaves aside material which, if he had regarded it, would precisely have helped him to understand the point in question. I have especially often had this impression in connection with "by-passed dream analyses." In free associations, we often have the experience to which Freud has called attention,[9] viz., that what the patient says becomes comprehensible only from what follows after it. Therefore, until what is to come after *has* come after, we cannot, I think, know what material we ought to leave aside.

Naturally, there are many situations in which absolutely *every* interpretation of a dream is contraindicated, namely, when "dream interpretation" *per se* has some other unconscious meaning for the patient which the analysis has not yet apprehended. But where this is not the case, I believe that it is precisely through correct dream interpretation that an attitude of the patient can often be understood. After all, the dream is a commentary on the patient's ego-attitudes of the previous day. Among the latent dream thoughts there are always some which are close to the conscious attitude but yet contain an additional element or show the attitude in a relationship which the patient has not thought of on account of his repressions. To interpret a dream does not mean telling the patient, "You want to sleep with your mother"; it may also be "to infer latent dream thoughts and by means of them to show the patient the actual nature of his present behavior and its intentions." Latent dream thoughts, however, cannot be inferred without getting the patient's associations to the elements of the manifest dream. If the patient does not associate, we give up the attempt at interpreting and try to apprehend this resistance. If, however, he does associate, his attention is thereby not necessarily fatefully diverted from consideration of his characterological behavior of the moment; it should rather be possible to use his associations precisely to lead him to that point.

I have called these two objections "minor objections," because they do not undermine Reich's principles, but only make them less absolute. The question now is how these principles are applied. This will vary with each case, and particularly with the personality of the analyst. In spite of Reich's assertions that

---

[9] S. Freud, "Recommendations for Physicians on the Psycho-Analytic Method of Treatment," *Coll. Pap.*, Vol. II.

there is no such danger, I believe that the "shattering of the armor-plating" could be done in a very aggressive way, but that both the aggression and the consequent disintegration of the armor can be *dosed,* and indeed, that it is the task of the physician to make this procedure as little unpleasurable as possible for the patient. The first thing we must be clear about is that the consistent tackling of the patient's character traits wounds his narcissism much more than any other analytic technique. Not only does the degree to which patients can tolerate such wounds vary, but also the degree to which analysts can or should inflict them. As analysts we should in principle certainly not be afraid of "crises" (the surgeon isn't afraid of blood either when he cuts); but that is no reason for inviting such "crises" in every case. On the contrary, I believe that our aim ought to be the *gradual* reduction of the existing insufficient neurotic equilibrium. We are familiar with the resistance of some patients, who long for a "trauma" and expect cure not from a difficult analysis, but from the magic effect of a sudden explosion. There is an analogous longing for a trauma on the part of the analyst also. Let us beware of it!

The conviction that a consistent working through of character resistance is the one and only correct method may make one overlook the fact that experiencing this kind of analysis may itself become for the patient a *transference resistance*. This would naturally be an even more superficial one than the "character resistance" and would have to be dealt with first. In one case, a patient, who in his fear of experiencing sexual excitation, always fell away, at a certain height of excitation, from his active masculinity into a receptive orality ("at this point I dare go no further, you do it for me"), experienced and enjoyed the "activity" with which the analyst pursued his current "attitudes," etc., as the fulfillment of his receptive longing, and this he did without the analyst noticing it. In another case the unconscious content of the neurosis of a woman patient was her rebellion against her father, who throughout her childhood reproached her for her traits and mimicked them. To have begun her treatment with an attempt at a "consistent attitude analysis"—a procedure which became highly necessary later on —would have led to an immediate breaking off by her of the analysis.

### III

Kaiser's study, "Probleme der Technik," [10] agrees in many points with Reich's views, so that the agreements and criticisms so far expressed here apply, for the greater part, to it also. I also agree with some objections which Kaiser makes against Reich; for instance, as to the impossibility of advising beginners not to use character analysis if it is the right technique.

Kaiser, however, goes further and states that analysis should be carried out

---

[10] H. Kaiser, "Probleme der Technik." See * footnote, p. 332.

entirely without "content interpretations." This proposition seems to me to be inimical. In one place, Kaiser says that if one has first given a warning against "too early" or "too deep" interpretations, there is not so very much difference between whether one does in the end allow a "content interpretation" or not. But the difference is very great, if this "in the end" is correctly understood. In order to do this we must first discuss the theory of "content interpretations."

According to Kaiser, "content interpretation" contradicts our understanding that the aim of psychoanalytic work should be to eliminate resistances, not to reinforce unconscious drives. He maintains that if our task is to work on resistances, then we must not interpret anything but resistances. If the repressed does not appear after an interpretation of resistances has been made, then our job is not to "name it," but to consider this a proof that the interpretation has failed, that it was not differentiated enough. Though he does not deny that under certain circumstances "content interpretations" may also eliminate repressions, he believes that theoretically this cannot be explained except in a roundabout way, namely, that without the analyst's knowledge and intention, such an interpretation too can direct the patient's attention to "resistance ideas," and can correct them by this change in the direction of his attention. He denies that an "anticipatory idea" might be at work here, or more correctly, that an interpretation could have the same effect as the indication given by the teacher of histology to the student as to what he will see in the microscope, without which the student's eye, which is not yet set for microscopic vision, would not see anything—which is actually Freud's view of the essence of interpretation. He considers this impossible (though his "resistance analysis," too, consists in nothing but calling the patient's attention to something whose presence has so far eluded his attention), and argues as follows: "A repressed impulse is neither in the Pcpt.-Cs. system, nor in the Pcs. system. Even the most exact and most apposite anticipatory idea we might give to the searcher could not facilitate his search as long as he is searching in a space which does not contain the object sought; and the patient cannot look into his unconscious."

This argument collapses if we realize that "content-interpretation" does not designate unconscious instinctual impulses, but preconscious derivatives of them.

But what are the contents of consciousness and of the preconscious? First of all, perceptions (and the phenomena of feeling accompanying them); then memory traces (ideas, etc.) mobilized by new perceptions—these memory traces differing according to the instinctual excitation of the moment. That is, they consist of instinctual impulses. The defense against impulses consists in this: that they—or rather, their undistorted ideational representatives—are thwarted in their striving toward consciousness by deep strata of the ego by means of anti-cathexes of every kind. The anti-cathexis creates a barrier in front of the preconscious. The defensive struggle demands a *permanent expenditure* of psychic energy. The impulse that has been warded off continuously produces *substitutive formations;* that is, it uses other ideas (impulses) that are associatively connected with it, which break through to consciousness, in order to discharge its energies. It *reinforces* preconscious formations that are innocent in themselves, thus forming them into those "mixed formations" between preconscious and unconscious, which have been discussed by Freud. Against these—as derivatives of the repressed—the defensive trends of the ego can still be directed just as much as against the unconscious impulse proper.[11] The fate of these derivatives—that is, whether they become conscious or are also repressed—depends on a variety of factors; namely, on all those which influence the dynamics and economics of the interplay between drive and defense. In general, one may say that the greater the degree of its distortion the more easily does the derivative become conscious. Analytic therapy may be described as a general education of the ego toward tolerating increasingly less distorted derivatives.

We cannot ever "interpret the unconscious." Stekel and his followers, who "fired interpretations" at their patients, attempted this. A "too early" or "too deep" interpretation, one which names something unconscious, but no preconscious "derivative"—something, therefore, that the patient cannot find however much he searches—is no interpretation. The adherents of "content interpretation"—and among them Freud—do not interpret repressed drives, but their preconscious derivatives. Moreover, since defense and what is defended against are forever interwoven, they do not believe that they can always name what is being defended against without also naming with it the defense. The details of defense are just as unconscious to the patient as the details of what is being defended against. In "interpreting a resistance," too, one cannot reveal more to the patient than what he is able to discover in himself by self-observation. What is remarkable, however, about psychoanalytic interpretations from the economic angle is that, whether one interprets a resistance or a derivative of the repressed, one does not interpret only that portion of what is being defended against which has already penetrated into the preconscious, but just a *little bit more*—a bit that the analyst already senses but the patient not yet. How does it happen that by so being interpreted, this little bit more actually breaks through? Naturally, this procedure, too, has not increased the "cathexis of the repressed" but weakened the "anti-cathexis of resistance." It remains true that one cannot do anything but break the resistance. But this can be done in various ways, and "naming," even if it is only by the "method of indication," seems to us the *via*

11 S. Freud, "The Unconscious," *Coll. Pap.,* Vol. IV, London, Hogarth, 1948.

*regia*. Of course, this naming has to take place at the right point and in the right way. Where is this point, what is this way, and how does the naming become effective?

In order to understand this, let us consider first the theory of the basic rule of psychoanalysis. What do we want to achieve by it? In every person there is an uninterrupted struggle between instinctual impulses which strive toward consciousness and motility, and the forces of the ego, which refuse untimely instinctual demands and, directed by purposive ideas, admit only what is pertinent to present action or speech. By means of the basic rule, we want to eliminate first of all the thousands of "resistances" of everyday, which on all ordinary occasions are what make life and mutual communication possible at all. But if it were really possible to eliminate all "purposive ideas" and concentrate attention only on noting what emerges of itself, we should not even then get to see the repressed. True, most "resistances" would be eliminated, but precisely not the resistances of repression, which are the strongest in intensity; for these are by definition not amenable to the conscious will of the ego. What we see are the results of the struggle between unconscious impulses and unconscious defenses of the deep layers of the ego. What do we do then? When we "interpret resistances" to the patient—no matter whether we do so by shifting certain resistive ideas into the focus of his attention, or whether we are only able to tell him at first that something in him rebels against abiding by the basic rule, or against the interests of his analysis in general—we are always demanding of him that he should *discover* something in himself; that is, we do exactly as the teacher of histology does. If the indication "you have a resistance" (an indication which is naturally not given in these words) leads the patient, who did not know this till then, to notice that something in him is indeed rebelling against the analysis, then we have given an effective interpretation. For this reason, such a statement to a patient does not seem to me by any means as ridiculous as some recent discussers of technique consider it to be. What is important is to give this indication in such a way as not to be a reproach against the patient, but a direction of his attention to something preconscious which he had not before noticed (and to a "something more"). The resisting ego, however, rebels against accepting such indications of the real nature of preconscious derivatives. This is what Freud has in mind when he says that our daily practice continually proves that besides the main censorship, between unconscious and preconscious, there is yet a second censorship between preconscious and conscious. *To begin with, we only work against this second censorship.* We have various means of doing this. These means are the same as those at the disposal of people for inducing other people to do something disagreeable: first, by convincing the patient that what is disagreeable is *useful* (the patient wants to be cured and the therapist explains to him that it is necessary for the cure); second, by making use of his libidinal tie to the maker of the demand (his "transference of affection"). Freud says with good reason in his *General Introduction to Psychoanalysis* that we use all means of suggestion (which is nothing but "using the libidinal tie") to induce the patient to produce and recognize "derivatives." [12] The defensive ego, which, limited in its reality function, cannot itself notice what is going on—which does not "direct" its "attention" to it—is as a rule bribed to behave in this way by a "secondary gain," by a sort of premium.[13] In that case we must try to uncover these premiums. If we cannot do that, we must at least let the patient experience the insufficiency of his ego's reality function. (This is the "directing attention to resistive ideas.") This happens in that the ego's observing part is made to stand away from its experiencing part and is thus able to condemn it as irrational, and such a condemnation results in a change of the dynamics of defense. These events and the reason for them seem to me to have been best described in a study by Sterba.[14] I readily agree with Kaiser that this standing away and this calling to attention can be better achieved if one has learned to study ever more sharply and exactly all the details of conscious defensive attitudes. Yet it must happen that as the patient's experiences of his defending anxiety become accessible to him, his attention is also directed to the *contents* of his anxiety, which gradually appear in consciousness in the form of derivatives. The latter, however, originate in early days, and can no longer be separated from what is being warded off. If the derivatives of the warded-off material are named as well, and *at the right place*—that is, where the naming leads to the patient's being really able to discover the derivatives in himself—then this, by producing an external perception which is in consonance with those derivatives in their nascent state, brings about a removal of the resistance and an entrance of the derivatives into consciousness. The "something" which we add here is thus also swept by this consonance into consciousness.

The assertion that content interpretations should only be given "at the end" means, to my mind, merely that they should not be given so long as the patient cannot discover their representatives in his preconscious, because obstructing resistances prevent their entrance there. I cannot convince myself that the interpretation quoted by Kaiser: "Note please how you behave toward me . . . Can you understand it any other way but that you are actually very angry with me . . . ?" is as wrong in principle as he believes. Kaiser argues that what is brought to consciousness by such an interpretation is not the warded-off affect which we seek, but an "innocent version of it," something about which one

12 S. Freud, *A General Introduction to Psychoanalysis*, New York, Liveright, 1935, 1948, p. 391.

13 S. Rado, "An Anxious Mother," *Int. J. Psa.*, Vol. 9, 1928.

14 R. Sterba, "The Dynamics of the Dissolution of the Transference Resistance," *Psa. Quart.*, Vol. 9, 1940.

can think and talk without disquiet; and that such an interpretation, instead of mediating the experience of the affect, mediates the experience of a reassurance, which takes away the real seriousness of the affect and is thus a resistance. No doubt this can happen. If it does, we are then dealing with an "obstructing resistance," which must be recognized and interpreted as such. But I cannot see why this should always or even often be the case. A "reassurance" need not, by any means, always have this resistive meaning. A certain "taking distance" from the affect—which has the air of "Here I can permit myself to let all the affects come, because I do it only as an experiment and I am not really aiming at the analyst about whom I feel the emerging affect"—need not, by any means, imply a lack of seriousness in the whole discovered affect; on the contrary, it can increase the tolerance of the ego and thereby considerably facilitate the discovery of the presence of very serious affects. I believe that on this point Kaiser is guilty of *an underestimation of reason*. He is right when he warns against analytic pseudo-interpretations, which offer the patient more or less the same as the reading of Freud's writings, namely, dynamically ineffective knowledge. But he exaggerates this concern, when, because of it, he refuses to *use reason* in self-observation. One can make quite effective discoveries in oneself, discoveries which leave no doubt as to the reality and affective vividness of the discovered material, without wanting to *act it out* in reality at the moment. A few words should be said here about the nature of "acting out." It is often welcome as a means to the patient's self-knowledge, and at times it is even indispensable. But if it is not followed by a sufficient analytic "working through" it is also a great danger and a resistance. A "reliving" of affects without the self-judging ego taking a sufficiently detached attitude is at least as dangerous as that isolation which limits the experience to the judging ego's "cognizing" the affect. The impulses which were repressed must be *experienced* as actually existing (and as, at the moment, inappropriate—as in the "transference"); but they need not for this reason be acted out. We often succeed in subjecting the experience of them to intellectual judgment while they are still in *statu nascendi*. Indeed, I believe that to succeed in this is the real goal of psychoanalytic interpretation— "to remember with affect, and to recognize what is remembered as truly operative in the present."

The difference must be somehow related to what Kaiser calls the "genuine break-through of instinct." There is no doubt that the patient must make affect-filled new discoveries, or rather, rediscoveries in himself. Transmitting of "knowledge concerning the unconscious" is no analysis. But must the elimination of the judging ego go as far as Kaiser demands, when he gives the following as a characteristic example of what he is after: "Then he addresses the analyst by the name of a person out of his past . . ."? Can we not read here between the lines a "longing for trauma" on the part of the analyst, to which reference has already been made? I think so, and I think it although in another place Kaiser warns against "sham break-throughs" and knows very well that the task of analysis is not to entice out unconscious material, but to get the ego to work over the unconscious which it has recognized. Therefore it makes no sense to interpret unconscious drives when there is no ego capable of digesting it; in such cases we have first to establish such an ego. For this reason all sham break-throughs, just like all "acting out" in general, must be unmasked to the patient as manifestations of resistance as soon as it is once more possible to discuss things reasonably with him. Kaiser thinks that the phrase used by Freud to demonstrate the success of a psychoanalytic intervention, "Thus the patient often relates without any difficulty . . . ," does not show that the phenomenon of genuine instinctual break-through is being indicated here. But I believe that that is precisely what is being indicated; or perhaps, more correctly, what is indicated is not a phenomenon of an instinctual break-through but of a real removal of repressions, in that the patient now recognizes impulses and affects which were so far barred for him, and can judge and control them. It seems to me that Kaiser underestimates, in favor of a "traumatic" conception, the gradual increase of extent to which "derivatives" become admissible, owing to persistent interpretation of these "from the ego side" and the concomitant gradual increase of the power of the ego, when he writes: "At any rate, it is a fact that changes in the patient which may be considered as an advance in the direction of real cure, are observed only after the occurrence of phenomena of the described sort," namely, after more or less traumatic instinctual break-throughs. Therefore, the fact that when he "gave content-interpretations with apparently good effect" he "never achieved comparably intensive break-throughs of drives" as when he "refrained from using any content-interpretations," does not seem to me a proof that that good effect was only "apparent." Kaiser believes that nothing is gained therapeutically if one brings a patient to convince himself that he has criminal impulses, but that he must experience this impulse, and experience it in such a way that he has to suppress it quite consciously if he is not to become criminal. We, on the contrary, believe that it suffices if he experiences it to such an extent that he has no doubt about its original reality. The actual situation, however, may be so evident to him at the moment of experiencing the impulse that it needs no particular suppression to avoid criminal behavior.

I cannot agree with Kaiser's criticism of the "procedure of interpretation and indication" either. To my way of feeling, there is nothing artificial in the analyst's behavior if, when he wants to demonstrate something to his patient, he does not simply assert it, but puts the evidence for it so clearly before the patient that he must draw the correct inference himself. If the patient answers this with an

"Aha, you're thinking again that . . . ," then that is a new resistance which must be analyzed; that this can happen is, however, not a sufficient reason for rejecting the procedures of interpretation and "indication" in general. Kaiser's assertion that "the therapeutic effect will be just about nil" is altogether contrary to my observations. Undoubtedly there is such a thing as a discovery of affect which is the opposite of experiencing, but there is also a form of discovery which leads to experiencing, and indeed may be identical with a certain kind of experiencing. If the "indicatory procedure" makes it possible for the patient to fend off the affect anew, as Kaiser describes it, then we recognize this and must not make the interpretation before that resistance is removed. But there is a "taking distance" from the affect which seems to me, in contrast to Kaiser, to be desirable. The judging ego of the patient should stand at a distance from its affect and should recognize it as untimely, while remembering its origins affectively. A break-through of affect without such "taking distance" is—as Freud once well put it—"an outright mishap." Kaiser's comment, that "after a 'genuine instinctual break-through' there is nothing left for the analyst to explain or clarify or add to the contents expressed by the patient" makes us suspect that he actually does not recognize this "mishap" for what it is, that he neglects the process of "working through" and does not understand its essential role in the true elimination of repressions, so that he is aiming at a sort of "neo-catharsis" instead of analysis. "Working through" is an essential constituent of psychoanalytic work and consists in rediscovering what one has found in one place in many others. For instance, in resistance analysis we have to undermine every single one of the many resistance positions; we do this by stressing the characteristics which are common to them all, unmasking them as variants of a single core. The "attitude" in question is represented in various single complexes of ideas, just as is the unconscious instinctual demand discovered in analysis. The undermining of these complexes by working through is no different from what the work of mourning does, since the idea of the mourned-for lost object is also represented in many connecting ideas.[15] For Kaiser the demand to "start always from what is at the moment on the surface" also entails a contraindication of any "content interpretation." He says "Only he will escape drawing this conclusion who counts as belonging to the surface the 'contents' brought forth by the patient in any given analytic hour. Such a conception of the surface, however, appears extremely unpsychological. Supposing a patient, impelled by an urge to make the analyst impatient, relates an experience from his fourth year of life in an affectless and boring manner, then it is the affectless and boring manner of presentation, not the content of the narrative, which belongs to the surface." Very good; but if the patient at a later stage of his analysis relates an experience

[15] See S. Freud, "Mourning and Melancholia," *Coll. Pap.*, Vol. IV.

from the fourth year of life with appropriate affect, then the content, as well, of this narrative can belong to the surface. And if he misjudges a detail of this experience, the correct judging of which might lead, for instance, to the understanding of a present attitude, so that the naming of it takes the patient by surprise, then this content belongs to the surface.

Kaiser is thus unwilling to use reason on the two points where it is legitimate to use it: namely, in order to make certain experiences accessible to the patient on the one hand, and, on the other, to get him to judge his affects and stand at a proper distance from them. This *underestimation* of reason is in contrast to Kaiser's *overestimation* of it at other points. "To interpret resistance" is for him identical with indicating the existence of resistance ideas. But this undoubtedly necessary indication of a resistance does not amount to an interpretation of it if the patient cannot also understand why his attention was diverted from the mistaken ideas—namely, because he had anxiety—and why he had anxiety and when and how he acquired it. To indicate the mistaken ideas is not yet to correct them, as long as the cause which made the patient think mistakenly is not eliminated. The reduction of character resistances to "mistakes in thought" is the best example there is of the overestimation of reason in the work of interpretation. This becomes also particularly clear where Kaiser equates "compulsion" and "rationalization." The incorrect thinking of the compulsion neurotic is not a consequence of his ego's having been "distracted" by some forces from the act of thinking, so that this might be altered by his attention being called to the incorrectness of his thought. It is because he has wanted to escape from instincts which are unpleasurable to him, into thought which is remote from instincts; but that which was defended against broke into the defense and the function of thought itself became "sexualized" and thereby pathological and distorted. The nature of "transference resistance," too, seems to me to have been misrepresented by Kaiser. Transference becomes resistance not only by being "rationalized" but, in general, because its transference character is not conscious. The tendency to satisfy a repressed drive on a substitute object is, in and of itself, a compromise between the drive, which seeks gratification, and a resistance, which prevents it from getting to the object proper. In analytic therapy, therefore, transference (except for its positive, affectionate form, which to begin with facilitates the overcoming of other resistances) becomes fundamentally a resistance, and must be recognized and worked through as such.

What Kaiser does is nevertheless in keeping with the principles of Freudian analysis, and he corrects many mistakes made by other analysts through an insufficient regard for the dynamic and economic factors. But his study exaggerates in its distribution of emphasis, and it contains a latent danger, which if this emphasis is continued might become manifest: the neglect of the factor which is crucial for Freud's psychoanalysis, namely, the unconscious and its specific characteristics.

The history of psychoanalysis brought it about that we became acquainted with the unconscious before the conscious and with the repressed before the ego. Nowadays the psychology of the ego stands in the center of our investigation. All those fine differences in the consciousness of man, which have been studied by the non-analytic schools while they have so far, of necessity, been neglected by psychoanalysis, now come within the sights of analysis, too. No doubt the psychoanalytic technique stands to gain much from this through the refinement of "resistance interpretations." Let us remember, for instance, how convincing Kaiser is when he constantly emphasizes, side by side with the instinctual needs of the id, the need of the ego to maintain its level of self-regard. But let us not forget, either, that the preceding exploration of the unconscious makes it possible for the psychoanalyst to approach the phenomena of the ego, the differences of consciousness and the phenomena of self-regard, in a fundamentally different manner from other schools: psychoanalysis must explain these phenomena too as arising from an interplay between unconscious—and in the final analysis, biological—instinctual tendencies, and influences of the external world.

Kaiser contrasts "resistance analysis" with "interpretative procedure" (and "indicatory procedure"). What he means by "interpretative procedure" is clear: he means that "content interpretation" which he rejects and which we have discussed at sufficient length here. Nevertheless, "interpretative procedure" is applied all around. But anyone who would really not admit any interpretative procedure of any sort could not, I believe, be called an analyst. Because if the means of analysis consist in a surmounting of resistance and a use of transference, then the principles by which it sets these means into motion are to be found in the fundamental rule of analysis and in interpretation.

*THIRTY-ONE*

# A Contribution to the Psychology of Jealousy*

## I

A PERSON who suffers an instinctual frustration experiences intense unpleasure, and we take it as a matter of course that he should feel hatred against the frustrating object. Nor does it seem to us a problem that he should feel *envy* toward another person who is more gratified than he—that is, that he should identify that person with himself and experience the more bitterly the contrast between this empathy of his imagination and the unpleasant reality and, out of this contrast, should develop aggressive tendencies against the luckier one. Jealousy is obviously a combination of this envy with that hatred, and so it does not seem to raise, at first sight, any specific problems.

The psychoanalytic literature of this topic has shown, however, that things are actually by no means so simple.[1] Two striking features of jealousy already indicate this to a superficial glance. In the first place, jealousy is by no means always greatest where previously being in love and (genital) gratification were greatest, as would have to be the case if jealousy were a simple reaction of frustration. It appears, on the contrary—and on this all authors agree—that people who are particularly inclined to jealousy are precisely those who are incapable of deeper love, who change their objects continuously and readily, and who can become jealous even of objects toward whom they were fairly indifferent before they had occasion to become jealous. In the second place, if the situation

* First published in *Imago*, Vol. 21, 1935, pp. 143–157.
1 S. Freud, "Certain Neurotic Mechanisms in Jealousy, Paranoia and Homosexuality," *Coll. Pap.,* Vol. II, London, Hogarth, 1948; E. Jones, "Jealousy," *Papers on Psycho-Analysis,* 5th ed., Baltimore, Williams and Wilkins, 1948; R. Sterba, "Eifersuechtig auf . . . ?," *Psa. Bewegung,* Vol. 2, 1930; J. Riviere, "Jealousy as a Mechanism of Defence," *Int. J. Psa.,* Vol. 13, 1932.

were simple, one would expect that the unpleasurable reactions to a frustration would tend rather to be repressed, as are all other unpleasurable experiences. On the contrary, however, jealousy has in general the propensity *to be obtrusive,* it easily becomes a *supervalent idea.* The psychology of supervalent ideas is familiar: the persistence of jealous ideas in consciousness must serve to repress something else, it must—as screen memories do—bring the jealous person a certain advantage in the economy of his libido.

As regards the fact that it is people who are, in a sense, incapable of love who become most readily and most intensely jealous, we may begin with the following observation: The mixture of depression, envy, and aggressive tendencies with which a loss of love is responded to, betrays a particular *intolerance* for such a loss. We know that fear of loss of love is strongest precisely in those people for whom to be loved is more important than to love, that is, precisely *not* to those who have most fully attained genital primacy. The fear of loss of love is strongest precisely in those people to whom loss of love really is the worst that can befall them—to whom it means not only a sexual frustration, but also a severe impairment of their self-regard and under certain circumstances a dissolution of the ego. To experience loss of love as a narcissistic injury has been stressed by Freud as a very general characteristic of jealousy.[2] We are, therefore, dealing with persons in whom narcissistic and erotic needs are insufficiently differentiated from each other. It is well known that this differentiation is always to some extent blurred in people who are in love, for their self-regard, like that of small children, depends once again on the behavior of their loved object. (This is why all people in love are inclined to be jealous.) A chronic impairment of this differentiation is seen, however, above all, in certain orally fixated people, the regulation of whose self-regard remains continuously and more or less exclusively dependent upon the external world. Just as the infant needs external material supplies in order to survive, so do they need "external narcissistic supplies" in order to maintain their self-regard.[3] An "internal regulation of self-regard" (as carried on, say, by the relationship between ego and superego) has not, or has not sufficiently, developed, or has been regressively lost in favor of an "external" regulation. This is the same disposition as that which underlies the "oral" or "self-regarding" neuroses, that is, in the first place, manic-depressive phenomena, addictions and other impulsional neuroses, and the "masochistic character." Naturally, there are quite varied subtypes among the people whose

---

[2] S. Freud, *op. cit.*

[3] The first description of these phenomena of regulating self-regard was given by S. Rado, in "The Psychic Effects of Intoxicants," *Int. J. Psa.,* Vol. 7, 1926, and continued in "The Psychoanalysis of Pharmacothymia (Drug Addiction). I. The Clinical Picture," *Psa. Quart.,* Vol. 2, 1933. Cf. also the discussion of self-regard in O. Fenichel, *Perversionen, Psychosen, Charakterstoerungen,* Vienna, Int. Psa. Verlag, 1931.

self-regarding regulation is fixated on primitive levels. Here, the "instinctual" persons, who want to acquire by force the indispensable supplies which the wicked outside world withholds from them, stand out in sharp contrast to the "masochists," who attempt to repress the same tendency to use force, and who plead instead, through their suffering, for those supplies. (Their pleading may be directed at their own superego, as well as at external objects; moreover, their repressed aggressive inclinations usually return from the repression, anxieties of various kinds seek to prevent them from receiving what they long for, and other complications may also arise.) The fact that a firm hold on *possessions* (which vouchsafe bodily integrity) fulfills the same function for self-regard as do "external supplies," opens a different chapter which cannot be discussed here. Let it only be said that a society whose ideology makes one marriage partner appear as the property of the other, for this reason increases the psycho-economic usefulness of jealousy.

If we now turn to the second-mentioned striking characteristic of jealousy and ask what the secret libidinal-economic advantages offered by jealousy to the jealous person are, we find that Freud and the literature of the subject up to date give us definite answers to this. The first discovery was that the excessive affect arose because the situation which precipitated the jealousy recalled a similar earlier one, which had been repressed. The excess of affect was due to the contributions which come from the repressed, and the prominence in consciousness of the *present grievance* helped to keep the *past* one in repression. The jealousy had its origins in the relations of the siblings to one another, or, still more, in the oedipus complex. Undoubtedly this historical information holds for *all* jealousy. But we should like to know on what it depends whether the breakdown of the oedipus complex, which is, after all, experienced by all people, does or does not leave behind it a disposition to jealousy. This must already depend on how the oedipus complex and its breakdown have been experienced at the time, so that the reduction of jealousy to infantile situations only displaces, but does not solve, the problem. Here Freud went further by adducing the jealousy of paranoia for comparison. Jealousy is, after all, a sort of "normal prototype" of delusions of jealousy, just as mourning is of depression.[4] What is fundamental for the psychology of delusions of jealousy, must—to a correspondingly limited extent—hold for normal jealousy also.

As we know, Freud found that in paranoid cases jealousy is used to defend against two kinds of impulses. "Projected jealousy" keeps the patient's own impulses to unfaithfulness out of consciousness, and delusional jealousy does the same for his homosexuality. Probably both these motives play some part in every case of normal jealousy as well. If impulses to unfaithfulness about which one

---

[4] S. Freud, "Mourning and Melancholia," *Coll. Pap.,* Vol. IV, London, Hogarth, 1948.

feels guilty are successfully dealt with by projection, that is certainly a libidinal-economic advantage which can explain the obtrusiveness of a supervalent idea. Concerning the share of unconscious homosexuality in non-delusional jealousy, I need only remind the reader of Sterba's fine study,[5] or of a female patient observed by me who had a perverse preference for sexual intercourse à trois, with a burning jealous fear that her man- and woman-friend might come together in her absence too.[6]

The problem which requires further discussion is, then, the relationship of the three factors discovered by Freud (historical determination, unconscious impulses to unfaithfulness, unconscious homosexuality) to what has been said concerning the fear of loss of love and the fixation of self-regard on primitive levels, which coincides with an "oral fixation."

The fixation of the regulation of self-regard on primitive levels can also be called a *narcissistic* fixation. But it is true that the term "narcissistic" has several meanings. Naturally it is not implied that the state of such people, whose dependence on objects is enormous, should be likened to a "narcissistic state"—e.g., a catatonic stupor—which knows no objects, or that they should be compared to what Freud describes as "the narcissistic type."[7] People who are thus excessively dependent on objects are "narcissistic" only in the sense in which "On Narcissism: An Introduction" designates the wish to be loved as a narcissistic aim, in contrast to the wish to love.[8] Their "narcissistic need," their need to maintain their self-regard, is greater, and the methods they use to gratify it are more archaic, than those of more "genital" people. But projection, too, which characterizes the paranoid mechanisms contained in jealousy, is an archaic mechanism which points to a persistence or revival of a relatively narcissistic stage. The homosexual object is closer to the narcissistic object, that is, to the subject's own ego, than is the heterosexual object. The psychoanalysis of paranoia has taught us how close the mechanisms of projection and introjection are to each other. In both, the boundaries between ego and non-ego, usually so solid, once again disappear. Where there is projective thinking there is introjective thinking too. Introjection occurs in connection with all the erotogenic zones, but primarily, as we know, with the *oral* one. The "external narcissistic supplies," too, about which we have spoken, are thought of on the deepest level as oral supplies. They also are related to "introjection."

The interplay between oedipus complex, impulses to unfaithfulness, and unconscious homosexuality on the one hand, and narcissistic intolerance for loss of

[5] R. Sterba, "Eifersuechtig auf . . . ?," *Psa. Bewegung.*
[6] Cf. my study "Further Light upon the Pre-oedipal Phase in Girls" [No. 24 in this volume].
[7] S. Freud, "Libidinal Types," *Coll. Pap.,* Vol. V, London, Hogarth, 1950.
[8] S. Freud, "On Narcissism: An Introduction," *Coll. Pap.,* Vol. IV.

love on the other, has already been clarified by Jones.[9] He describes the narcissistic dependence on his object of the person disposed to jealousy (for instance: "To him love is a therapeutic cure for a morbid state of affairs . . ." [10]); but he pays less attention to the fact that here an interaction of constitution and infantile experience brings about a fixation on a primitive (oral) mechanism of regulation of self-regard than he does to the contentual aspect of the matter—viz., that it is always severe and early feelings of guilt which are designed to be eliminated by "external narcissistic supplies." [11]

Subsequent to Jones's paper there appeared Riviere's, which also dealt with the problem discussed here.[12] I shall consider this study only after presenting material from a case of my own. From the theoretical considerations so far presented, we bring the following expectation to our clinical considerations, viz., that the relation between jealousy and oral introjective fantasies must be much closer than has so far been brought out.

## II

A woman on the brink of her climacteric relapsed into a severe neurosis from which she had been free for many years, with phenomena of depersonalization, anxiety, and various conversion symptoms. She was able to give the precipitating cause of her relapse: The symptoms reappeared after her husband became impotent. Thus the symptoms seemed to be the consequence of discontinuation of libidinal gratification. This impression was reinforced by the transference behavior of the patient. At the time of her illness she had undergone the most varied psychotherapeutic treatments, and her behavior left no doubt that what she expected of the doctor was friendly advice, "showing her a goal in life," recognition, friendship—in brief, that now she believed she had lost her husband's interest, she wanted to buy herself a substitute for it from a doctor. But her anamnesis already brought a surprise. Her first statement that the relapse fol-

---

[9] E. Jones, "Jealousy," *Papers on Psycho-Analysis.*

[10] *Ibid.*, p. 334.

[11] Jones rightly stresses that in these people the great longing to get something from the love object is usually opposed by a fear of the fulfillment of this longing, a fear which is determined by infantile experiences. Often it is only such a conflict which brings about repression in the first instance, and with it the fixation of the mechanisms of this stage. A restless flight from object to object may result from a fear of receiving something from it—a reception which is dreaded in a magical way as involving self-destruction. Such a flight is the more easy for these people, since they do not have any real individual relation to their object; they only long for this "magic reception" from it, and consequently they easily change their object. Nevertheless, the conclusion Jones draws from this state of affairs seems to me most dubious: "Much more marital infidelity is of neurotic origin than is generally supposed; it is not a sign of freedom or potency, but quite the reverse" (*op. cit.*, p. 338). The neurotic "fear of ties" is less frequent than are "neurotic ties," attended by a fear of the longing for a change of object—a longing which is certainly not pathological but biologically normal.

[12] J. Riviere, *op. cit.*

lowed immediately upon the impotency of her husband proved incorrect. For a long while afterward the patient was free of symptoms, both while her husband was still making unsuccessful attempts at intercourse, and after he had given it up and no longer approached her sexually. When the patient began to suspect that her husband was secretly going with another woman, she immediately developed the conviction that he was still fully potent with her. She produced an intense and torturing jealousy which until then had been quite unknown to her, and it was only in conjunction with this jealousy that her old neurotic symptoms reappeared. Equally surprising was her information that she had always been frigid throughout her many married years, and therefore had never cared about intercourse with her husband. During all these years she had to masturbate periodically with certain fantasies in order to attain a sexual detension. These fantasies will be discussed below.

It may, therefore, be true that the changes in her marital relations had deprived the patient of a gratification. But the lost gratification must not be taken in a crude somatic sense as a discontinuation of sexual intercourse; it is rather that the behavior of her husband—and his unfaithfulness more than his impotence—must somehow have devaluated in her eyes the masturbation which before that had gratified her.

We shall come closer to the understanding of the nature of the patient's lost gratification if we analyze what the *substitutive* gratification was which she now strove for. This showed up first of all in her transference behavior. The patient demanded from the analyst energetically and clearly very much attention and friendship as something she had a right to. She explained that it was only when the analyst talked to her that she once again felt worthy of respect; at home, among her anxiety-filled thoughts and the ideas of depersonalization, she felt completely worthless. Finally, she stated quite directly that she came to the doctor in order to be thus "maintained" by him, and if he would not give her the advice she wanted, she would know how to get it, for instance, by going to another doctor. After analytic hours in which she felt that the analyst had talked too little, she would go to a pastry shop and console herself by eating a cake. The words and friendliness of the analyst meant to her an oral "supply from without."

Furthermore, the patient's symptoms showed the same thing. Both her depersonalization and her anxiety appeared primarily when she was alone. She experienced depersonalization as a feeling of "split," as though she were simultaneously two different people. In that state she experienced extensive alienations of her body; in particular, her hands appeared strange to her and she did not know what to do with them. In the same way, her fear of being alone proved to be a fear of the temptation to masturbate. Our surmise is now reinforced that the husband's behavior had, in an as yet incomprehensible way, changed the masturbation, which before that had been gratifying, into a danger. And this must somehow be connected with the fact that in her masturbation oral impulses found expression, and that in it she somehow represented two different people simultaneously. This so far unknown *infantile character* of her masturbation, of which she was afraid, must have been relatively reinforced by the behavior of the husband.

The anxiety states, which clearly appeared in situations of temptation for this unknown infantile sexuality, could be decreased or even banished by the patient, by a kind of "housewife's neurosis," which must thus represent a "substitute" for the masturbation which had become impossible. The patient felt better if she could cook, scrub, and "put things in order" all through the day. The sadistic component involved became clear in her attempts to force upon everyone else her principles of order. Traits of this anal-sadistic attitude had, it is true, been present all along. She had, for instance, completely dominated her younger sister, made all her decisions for her and imposed her own mode of thinking upon her. When the younger sister, after an analysis, would not put up with this any longer, the patient responded with a burning and conscious hatred. What was new was that this anal-sadistic behavior now vented itself in the particular domain of housewifery and, especially, that it became a means to fend off anxiety.

At the same time the patient's *jealousy*—which is our primary interest here— increased to an extraordinary extent. Thoughts about her husband's unfaithfulness, brooding over when, where, and how he was seeing his lady friend and what he did with her, forced themselves upon her in a compulsive way with torturing and ever-increasing intensity. She was compelled to imagine details of that sexual intimacy, and she declared finally that she could not tolerate having to think about her husband "giving his penis" to another woman. This expression was striking, but not unexpected, after what we had learned about the oral longings of the patient to *get* something from the love object. Her already described transference behavior had shown that she expected from the analyst what her husband had withdrawn from her, namely, a bolstering up of her self-regard through words (giving advice). Thus, unconsciously, she thought of her husband's penis also as an "oral supply," of this sort. What remained remarkable was that she did not feel bereft of these supplies by the impotency of her husband, but only by another woman's receiving what she did not.

Now there was a story of "unfaithfulness" in the patient's period of puberty. Her father had begun an affair with a maid and her mother had discovered it. The mother made a great fuss and cried a lot, and when her daughter asked what was the matter, she poured out her heart to her. The patient's housewife's mania, described above, revealed in the first place a pronounced identification with this maid. The first interpretation of the role of the triangle fantasy in her sexual life thus again pointed to the oedipus complex, and the first interpretation of her jealousy—that is, of her intolerance of triangular situations—to the repression of that complex. The thought that her husband might be with another woman was intolerable because the husband, by being unfaithful, became a father-figure. The patient, afraid of retribution, felt: "Now I get what as a child, identifying myself with the maid, I did to my mother."

But the mobilization of the patient's oedipal wishes, and of the anxieties opposing them, does not yet explain why the sexual act in general was conceived of by her as "getting" and indeed, as became increasingly clear, as "a robbing of what is not given freely." The discoverable details of the patient's actual oedipal experiences showed that this conception already existed in her early childhood, but they did not suffice to explain it. She repeatedly went with her father on long carriage drives, in the course of which he occasionally left the carriage to urinate. In doing this he was not always careful enough in front of the little girl (as, for instance, on some occasions when he was drunk). The patient's dreams and memories indicated that she had always reacted at that time with an intense, "I want to have it!", and in this situation the association "lonely forest—robbers," played a role.

We are now able to give a first answer to the question as to how her husband's unfaithfulness gave a more infantile character to the patient's masturbation which had until then afforded her gratification, so that it had to be repressed and replaced by neurotic symptoms. It mobilized her oedipus complex; she was now being treated as her mother had been in her childhood. Nevertheless, we shall find a deeper answer if we turn to the fantasies which accompanied her gratifying masturbation before she relapsed into illness.

At puberty the patient had often talked about sex with her girl friends. One of them told her of having seen a farm hand having intercourse with his girl standing up. This image brought the patient into extreme excitement and stayed with her throughout her life. Her masturbation fantasies from then on always pivoted about somebody's watching a couple having intercourse. Soon the fantasy was added that the man had left the watching woman for the other woman. Clearly the prerequisite for the patient's excitation was to empathize simultaneously with both women, with the robber and the robbed one. This discovery permitted the analysis of the "split" feeling of her depersonalization, which was a masturbation equivalent: she was split into a robber-woman and a robbed woman. The unconscious masturbation fantasies which had been reinforced by the husband's unfaithfulness may be formulated more or less as follows: "I want to take my father from my mother, as the maid did. When I have a husband, what happened to my mother will happen to me."

Now the patient hated her mother at the time of her analysis just as intensely as she did her sister. She reproached her incessantly. Her mother was responsible for everything, had brought her up badly, had neglected her, etc. The strained violence of her hatred left no doubt that it was a reaction formation: The patient had to repress a deep love toward her mother. The reproaches against the mother could but mean: "She left my wishes for love unfulfilled," though we cannot as yet state what actual disappointments the patient had had from her mother. Naturally, the formula of these disappointments must have been: "She had taken something from me, to give it to others." In this respect, then, the husband who goes to the other woman represents not the father, but the mother. Characteristically, the patient's anxiety about whether the analyst was "giving her enough" went over into an anxiety whether he would stand by her in her present-day quarrels with the mother. The analyst increasingly became an "intermediate figure" between the patient and her mother (or her husband), just as the man in the triangular fantasies faded increasingly into the background as against the basic idea: *a woman takes something away from another one.* The elaboration of the patient's penis envy in connection with her carriage drives with her father, already stood in the shadow of this idea. "I take another woman's food away from her," or, more precisely, "If they take my food away, I will get it back by robbing (my mother's body)"—this was the unconscious meaning of her triangle fantasies, and the repression of those oral-sadistic impulses was the unconscious meaning of her jealousy.

In her latency the patient had been a particularly naughty child. Numerous memories and family anecdotes report how no adult could put up with her. Once when she left on a trip with an uncle he brought her back because her intolerable behavior had made the trip unbearable. All this "badness" turned out in the analysis to be attempts to extort love. Newly emerging memories showed that a tendency to kleptomania—a tendency which was to be expected in such a mental structure—was also present. She recalled first that she had stolen chess pieces from her father, who was a passionate chess player, and had thrown them into the toilet. Later on she remembered that she had done the same with various belongings of her mother's. The meaning of these actions was: "You are not to occupy yourselves with these things, but with me." Throwing the things into the toilet went back to her hatred against her younger sister, whom —in accordance with an anal theory of birth—she had wanted to remove again in this fashion. The meaning of all these actions was: "I get for myself what is withheld from me. I take revenge for the love that was taken from me. I want to get back what I lost."

It is certain that the patient's enormous penis envy, too, was worked out from this oral-sadistic standpoint. But it is equally certain that the schema of this mode of reaction had originated before this, in her pregenital relation to the mother. When, in analyzing a dream, we talked about the anal instinctual impulses of children, the patient suddenly hallucinated an intensively strong taste —and knew that it was the taste of feces; and although she could not remember anything of the kind, there could be no doubt that she had engaged in coprophagic activities in order to "get back what she had lost."

Though no historical details about the origins of the patient's oral-sadistic fixation were ascertained, we can summarize the situation as follows: *robbing* (or, turned against the ego, being robbed at the same time) became for her a *condition of love*. Her jealousy was, in the final resort, oral-sadistic wishes directed toward her mother, and permitted the reappearance in the defense of what was defended against. The jealousy she directed against her husband had, on a deeper level, a *homosexual* meaning, and furthermore, the unconscious significance of the obtrusive ideas of jealousy was *oral introjection*.

The patient's original pre-oedipal tie to her mother was disturbed, in a typical manner, by the birth of her younger sister, and by her discovery of the penis. Her reaction to this disturbance, however, was not a simple turning to the father, but first of all a fixation of libidinal excitation in general to the fantasy, "I am being robbed, and I rob." The fixation onto this fantasy is the "pregenital coloring" which the patient brought into her genitality, and which she transferred from her mother to her father; it was because of this that all her love relations remained on the level of partial love. The stimulation of her oedipus complex at puberty by the episode of the maid—an episode which she elaborated in terms of her robber fantasy—together with her girl friend's story about the voyeur scene, which was suited to act as a "screen experience" for the more or less contemporary episode, put the final seal on her fixation to that oral-sadistically conceived triangle situation. Her jealousy, her feeling that any triangular situation was intolerable, and yet having always to think of such a situation, corresponds to an attempt to repress her own oral sadism and nevertheless to gratify it. The motive of her repression was fear of retribution. This was naturally reinforced when the patient felt that she had *actually* been robbed of something.

Turning now from these findings to the previously mentioned case of Mrs. Riviere, we are at first astounded by the far-reaching agreements between them.

In Mrs. Riviere's case too, the severe jealousy of a woman proved to be connected with a predominant unconscious fantasy—the manifest derivatives of which took most varied forms—that she must steal something from, and thereby badly damage, a beloved person. The "triangle situation" included the patient herself, the object from whom she had stolen, and what she stole. One of the patient's transference fantasies concerned the possibility that her analyst's husband might die. She wanted to rob the analyst of her husband in order herself to possess her. In her fantasy, death was a form of robbery and meant to her a twofold possibility of obtaining gratification for herself: first, by gaining possession of what she wanted and secondly, through the suffering she inflicted upon the beloved person whom she had robbed. In this case too, the pre-oedipal origins of this oral-sadistic fixation could be demonstrated by the analysis of the leading masturbation fantasy, which was: A naked young woman is being examined by a doctor, while another woman stands at the back of the room. The young woman who is being examined represents the patient, the woman in the background her mother, from whom she takes away the father. The patient's outbursts of jealousy occurred when real or transference situations brought the realization of the fantasy within the realm of possibility, and thus increased the amount of the anxiety which opposed it. The fact that here the father, that is, the father's penis, is treated as a possession of the mother is explained by Mrs. Riviere with the help of the idea of "the father's penis in the body of the mother." Thus the patient's wish-fantasy was to become the sole possessor of the mother, and to rob her body of its contents. In her unconscious the patient never reached a full object relation to men; her genital heterosexual wishes played a secondary role compared to her homosexual oral sadism.

So far, the agreement between this case and ours is indeed striking. So much so that we could consider all that we have so far said as a confirmation of Mrs. Riviere's view, that it can be assumed that in people in whom jealousy or compulsive unfaithfulness are essential traits of their personality, loss of love and craving for love do not so much have a genital character, but rather arise from the longing to take possession of partial objects in order to incorporate them. This makes the relative unimportance of objects and their frequent change comprehensible.

We have, however, theoretical objections against some of the inferences drawn by Mrs. Riviere from these findings, which deserve discussion:

Mrs. Riviere repeatedly designates jealousy as a defense—as a protective measure of the ego. This is understandable in so far as jealousy represents an *intolerance* for triangle situations, and thus seeks to *avoid* them. It is a striving to avoid the very situation which is longed for unconsciously. Where this attempt at avoidance originates from is clear: Like all infantile instinctual defenses, it comes from the anxiety which opposes the idea of the instinctual action—in our case, from a fear of retribution for the patient's oral sadism. (Though the jealousy implies not only defense against the triangle situation, but also the return in a distorted form, in spite of the defense, of what is defended against.) If we thus consider jealousy as an (unsuccessful) attempt to defend against an instinctual fantasy, then it seems to us to make little sense to designate the instinctual fantasy itself which is being defended against as "defense" also. But this is just what Mrs. Riviere does. Now it is true that we know that the instinctual aims onto which a person, after having passed through the phases of infantile sexuality, remains "fixated," are not simply identical with the "constitutional" instinctual aims of the id, but that compromise formations are already involved in the shaping of which the ego, which defends against drives, has also had a hand; nevertheless, we must naturally consider such unconscious instinctual aims, the defense against which has been the business of the ego, to be first and foremost an expression of the pleasure-craving id (upon which the defensive or selective ego has only exerted a modifying influence). Mrs. Riviere, on the contrary, considers the fixation onto the fantasy as being itself a defense in the first instance and maintains that this fantasy owes its significance in the life of the patient to the fact that she had succeeded in transforming the fantasied situation, which was composed of wish and anxiety, into a situation of security and defense. The patient's mother was in reality a very kindly person, who had suffered many losses, but had loved the child only the more for that. For this reason Mrs. Riviere maintains that the patient—whose sexuality was curtailed by her retributive anxiety which opposed her oral sadism—could only become sexually excited when she reminded herself, by stressing her triangle fantasy, of the reassuring experience: "I did bad things to my mother as a child, too, and nothing happened to me." According to this, therefore, the cause of the fixation would be an attempt to *disprove* the retributive anxiety (and not the original oral-sadistic fantasies themselves, which in childhood had occasion for particular gratification, and which were the very ones which were opposed by her fear of retribution). Were Mrs. Riviere right in thinking that the patient's triangle-fantasy served the purpose of convincing herself that she could rob without having to fear punishment, then we would expect that on those occasions on which the realization of the triangle fantasy came within the bounds of possibility the patient would joyfully reach for it, and, indeed, that only on these occasions would she experience really undisturbed sexual pleasure. But we see the opposite, namely, that it is just then that the patients retreat and develop jealousy and neurotic reactions. Why? The only answer Mrs. Riviere has to this is that a defensive measure pitted against retribution anxiety can fail too, if the anxiety becomes excessively strong. Is it not much simpler to regard—as we are accustomed to do elsewhere—the fixation onto the oral-sadistic fantasy as an interplay of constitutional factors with particular gratifications (or frustrations), which the child experienced at the oral stage of libido organization—that is, as an "id phenomenon"—and, in contrast, to regard jealousy as an (unsuccessful) ego-measure? (Though admittedly—as the perversions demonstrate—fixations come about at these very libidinal positions which are suitable to disprove a simultaneous anxiety of the ego.) To attempt to regard the presence of a libidinal impulse—and one, at that, against which the ego, filled with retributive fear, puts up the most impressive measures of defense—as being *first and foremost* a measure taken by the ego to ward off anxiety—to attempt, that is, to regard it as a defense, seems to me to commit the error, all too frequently found in psychoanalytic literature, of overestimating the role of the libido as a means of defense against anxiety (a role which it does in fact play), and of underestimating its nature as a biologically given phenomenon—an error about which I have spoken in detail elsewhere.[13] To continue: Mrs. Riviere calls the retributive anxiety which is a constituent of the jealousy, unconcernedly, a fear felt by the ego toward its superego. In this she follows Melanie Klein in terminology, and she can show that precisely in the case of her patient the contrast between the real, benign mother and the horrific images of the "introjected mother" was particularly great. Mrs. Riviere points out that such a benign mother, whose kindness gives little occasion to the child for external aggression, increases proportionately the intensity of the aggressions committed by the early "superego." It is this early superego, threatening the patient from inside, against which the patient must protect herself. In the triangular fantasy she flees from this superego to the real mother, who can be robbed with impunity ("flight into reality"). We question neither that children's fears, so grotesquely contradictory to reality, originate from projections of their sadistic impulses, nor that in their genesis introjections too play an essential role, but we do maintain that it is characteristic for these very "retributive anxieties" that the child does actually expect the evil to come *from outside,* and that therefore since he has projectively misunderstood the external world, his actions are inhibited more by external anxiety than by anxiety coming from his conscience.[14] The fact that, as Freud has already stressed,[15] the feeling, "I myself am to be blamed for the loss of love" is a constituent of jealousy does not prove that jealousy is a symptom of an unconscious accusation directed by the superego against the ego. A lowering of self-regard through loss of love is conceivable without participation of the superego, particularly in orally fixated people, whose level of self-regard depends from the beginning on external supplies of love.

One word about the often-cited idea of "the father's penis in the body of the mother." Our patient too, like Mrs. Riviere's, seemed to have this idea. There is no doubt that she longed to receive from her mother the penis which she saw on her father, and she betrayed an unconscious desire to get it out of her body. Indeed, this attitude is frequently observed. There seems to be no question as to the existence of this idea; all that is questionable is whether this image has

---

[13] O. Fenichel, "Defense against Anxiety, Particularly by Libidinization," No. 27 in this volume.
[14] *Ibid.*
[15] S. Freud, "Certain Neurotic Mechanisms in Jealousy, Paranoia and Homosexuality," *Coll. Pap.,* Vol. II.

always to derive from a fantasy about parental intercourse, in which the father's penis is supposed to remain in the mother's body, or the like. In this respect, it seems to us, authors are often guilty of not correctly estimating the level of integration of this stage or time, in that they use too much "adult logic" in their attempt to understand pregenital modes of thought. If, for entirely different reasons (namely, because in the pre-oedipal time, the mother is the only essential object), the little girl has the habit of demanding all it wants from the mother, and if, furthermore it brings along from its pregnital time an oral-sadistic tie of the sort, "I want to destroy something, to get what is withheld from me," then its penis envy too will be elaborated in terms of this pre-existing schema. In fact, in cases where this idea is particularly pronounced, we find that it was always preceded by other great disappointments from the mother (whether these were objective or merely subjective), to which the penis envy has then associated itself and which have ended in the fantasy of "tearing it out of her body." These disappointments are first and foremost pregnancies of the mother, but also conflicts about training in cleanliness and weaning. It must not be forgotten that the fantasy of contents of the body being taken away originates from the feces, in regard to which it was actually experienced; I need only remind the reader of the meaning of enemas as pointed out by Freud.[16]

The integrated reaction of a little girl to the sight of the penis is, then, a working over of this sight in terms of previous experiences. The (father's) penis enters only as the last and often decisive link into series of introjects, milk, feces, child, penis, about which the little girl feels cheated, and for which, when corresponding fixations are present, she can retaliate by oral (pseudo-phallic-) sadistic procedures against her mother.[17]

[16] S. Freud, "Female Sexuality," *Coll. Pap.*, Vol. V.
[17] Cf. O. Fenichel, *Perversionen, Psychosen, Charakterstoerungen*, pp. 57 ff.

* * * * * * * * * * * * * * * * * *

## THIRTY-TWO

# A Critique of the Death Instinct*

IT IS not possible to treat exhaustively the tremendous problem of masochism and of the "death instinct" in a brief contribution. I shall therefore limit myself to the discussion of a few aspects of it which seem to me important.

The original division of instincts into ego instincts (hunger) and sexual instincts (love) possessed two advantages, namely, (1) that it was popular, and (2) that in accordance with traditional biological thought it contrasted the interests of the individual with those of the species. In addition, it fulfilled a definite function in the developmental history of psychoanalysis. Freud's great discovery was *repression,* that is, the fact that one part of the personality struggles against another. What was being defended against was, as psychoanalysis recognized, sexuality. But what was carrying on the defense was fear of punishment or an aesthetic or moral interest of the ego, that is, impulses which could be lumped together with "hunger" as "ego instincts." The function of the older instinctual theory, therefore, was first of all to reflect the fact of repression. The reason for Freud's turning at the time so sharply against Jung, whose "libido" concept asserted the unity of ego instincts and sexuality, was that at that time the assertion of such unity amounted to a denial of repression.[1] Thus an ego instinct wards off a sexual instinct: two kinds of instincts are in conflict with each other. This view was *not* in contradiction with the assertion that originally the neurotic conflict was conceived as one between the instinctually determined individual and the instinct-frustrating external world. For there was no doubt that it was only under the influence of the external world that the ego instinct had turned against the sexual instinct. The ego instinct subserved self-preservation. If self-preservation had not been menaced by the apperception that an in-

* First published in *Imago,* Vol. 21, 1935, pp. 458–466.
[1] Cf. S. Ferenczi, Review of Jung's *Wandlungen und Symbole der Libido, Int. Z. Psa.,* Vol. 1, 1913, pp. 396 ff.

stinctual activity threatened it, the ego instinct would have had no reason to turn against a sexual instinct. But this apperception originates from the frustrating external world.

This first theory of instincts was overthrown by the discoveries concerning narcissism. In Freud's paper "On Narcissism: An Introduction" [2] we learn what were the findings in normal and psychotic psychology which suggested to him that what had so far been called "ego instincts" were also, to a greater or lesser degree, fed by sexual energy, which can later be once more turned toward sexual aims, or which can be withdrawn anew from them into the ego. The circumstance that the older theory of instincts reflected the theory of repression prompted Freud to do all he could to preserve it. He attempted the assumption that the ego instincts were cathected by two qualitatively different kinds of energy, by "interest," or ego-instinctual energy, on the one hand, and by a "libidinal contribution" which constituted narcissism, on the other. This view did not hold for long. The recognition of such displaceable "libidinal contributions" was incompatible with the view that in the repressing and the repressed—or, in our present nomenclature, in the ego and the id—two basically different kinds of instinct were at work.

The new classification of instincts now proposed by Freud [3] to replace the old one which had thus failed has two roots, one speculative, the other clinical.

The speculative root lies in the "conservative" character of the instincts, which becomes tangible in the so-called "Nirvana principle." Every instinctual excitation represents a state of tension and every instinctual gratification brings a relaxation of tension. Thus instincts tend toward a relaxation of tension, toward a "state of rest." We conceive of the entire psychic apparatus on the analogy of a reflexive apparatus (though one equipped with delaying complications). It experiences external stimuli that excite it as disturbances for which it strives to find motor discharge as quickly as possible (or later: which it attempts to bind by anti-cathexes). If this conception is justified, then one can say that the aim of the psychic apparatus is absence of excitation, "Nirvana." In *Beyond the Pleasure Principle* Freud has clearly and convincingly demonstrated that this tendency to discharge excessive excitations or to bind them is under certain circumstances stronger than the pleasure principle, and that in traumatic neuroses, children's play, and transference it even leads to unpleasurable repetitions of unpleasurable experiences. There can be no objection against preferring to call this "Nirvana" "death," since inorganic substances differ from organic ones precisely in that they are not excitable. The problem for speculation was, how-

---

[2] S. Freud, "On Narcissism: An Introduction," *Coll. Pap.*, Vol. IV, London, Hogarth, 1948.

[3] First in S. Freud, *Beyond the Pleasure Principle*, London, Hogarth, 1948, then in *The Ego and the Id*, London, Hogarth, 1947.

ever: Does this consideration hold for all instincts or only for some? There is in the realm of life a phenomenon which appears to be completely contrary to the "Nirvana" principle: it is the "craving for stimulation." The "craving for stimulation"—that is, the endeavor, not to eliminate stimuli as much as possible (or at any rate not to *liquidate* them as soon as possible), but to seek them out—is most marked in the sexual instincts. Thus, for one portion of the instincts these considerations about "death" seem not to obtain, or to obtain less directly, than for the rest.

The clinical root is the existence of aggressiveness. Aggressive tendencies of all sorts constitute quite a high percentage of all human instinctual impulses. In part, they have a reactive character; i.e., they are responses to frustrations, and their aim is to eliminate frustrations from the world. In part, however, they appear closely linked with certain sexual impulses, and in particular with those instinctual sexual aims which predominate in the early stages of libidinal organization, and are called by us "pregenital" aims. Finally, they seem also in part to appear spontaneously, independent of sexuality. In addition there is the riddle of *masochism,* namely, the fact that under certain conditions the pleasure principle—the *leitmotif* which on all other occasions enables us to orient ourselves in regard to human actions—seems to be suspended and the person manifests self-destructive tendencies.[4] Furthermore, clinical experience shows that all manifestations of masochism are exchangeable with sadism—that aggressiveness which is so close to sexuality. Where masochism appears, analysis (as Freud has shown [5]) demonstrates that a sadistic impulse has undergone the vicissitude of "turning against the self." Undoubtedly the opposite of this also occurs: externally sadistic behavior may hide unconscious masochistic aims.

These speculative and clinical roots were then welded together by Freud into the new instinctual theory, according to which there are two qualities in the psyche, a self-destructive one, the "death instinct" (which can be "turned outward" and can thereby become an "instinct of destruction"), and the object-seeking eros which strives for higher unities. Since there is in reality neither a pure self-destruction, nor a pure object-seeking which intends no discharge of tension, this theory conceives of all actual psychological phenomena as various "degrees of fusion" of the two assumed qualities.

I should like to preface some critical considerations about this theory with the following remarks:

The problem of the classification of instincts is solely a *heuristic* issue. In "Instincts and Their Vicissitudes" Freud clearly states that one can introduce as

---

[4] Cf. S. Freud, "The Economic Problem in Masochism," *Coll. Pap.,* Vol. II, London, Hogarth, 1948.
[5] S. Freud, *Three Essays on the Theory of Sexuality,* London, Imago, 1949, pp. 45–46; "Instincts and Their Vicissitudes," *Coll. Pap.,* Vol. IV, p. 70; "A Child Is Being Beaten," *Coll. Pap.,* Vol. IV, pp. 189–190.

many kinds of instincts as one pleases, and why this is so. Our task is not to prove what kinds of instincts there are, but to ask: Which classification of instincts enables us to grasp various actual psychological phenomena most easily and with least contradiction? Setting out from this formulation of the problem, there arise several objections against the theory of the death instinct.

From the point of view of scientific theory, it seems to me characteristic of psychoanalysis as a scientific psychology that it integrates itself with biology and regards mental life only as a special case of life in general. It explains psychological phenomena as the result of an interplay of biological needs and influences of the external world. "Instinct" is the concept which reflects for us those "biological needs"; therefore it is an indispensable bridge between our science and biology. The concept of an instinct, as presented in Freud's "Instincts and Their Vicissitudes" [6] must remain our directive: instinctual need is "the demand made by the body upon the psychic apparatus." It begins in a somatic "instinctual source," which makes the psychological system excitable, and which with the aid of sensory stimuli it actually excites; the instinctual action then results in changes at this source which are equivalent to a "discharge" of the excitation— that is, to a relaxation of tension. A "death instinct" does not fit in with such a definition of instinct. True, Freud has attempted to answer the question as to its biological source by trying to co-ordinate the erotic phenomena with the processes of biological assimilation and the destructive phenomena with processes of dissimilation.[7] But dissimilation in the cells—that is to say, an objective destruction—cannot be the source of a destructive instinct in the same sense that a chemically determined sensitization of the central organ through stimulation of the erotogenic zones is the source of the sexual instinct. For according to the above definition, instinct aims at *eliminating* the somatic change which we designate as the source of the instinct; but the death instinct does not aim to eliminate dissimilation. For this reason it does not seem to me possible to set up the "death instinct" as one species of instinct over against another species. We should rather attempt to regard all the actual phenomena which are denoted by the concept "death instinct" as dependent not on a species of instinct, but on a *principle,* which originally obtained for *all* instincts, but in the course of development has, under certain influences (in the final analysis, those of the external world), been obliged to undergo several modifications in several respects. Indeed, the concept of the "Nirvana principle" as a point of departure does in fact permit a unitary view, not only of all psychological processes, but also of all life processes in general. Let us remember that it is the very group of instincts which most clearly exhibits a craving for stimulus, a longing for objects, and

---

[6] S. Freud, "Instincts and Their Vicissitudes," *Coll. Pap.,* Vol. IV, p. 64.
[7] For instance, cf. S. Freud, *The Ego and the Id,* p. 57.

a striving toward higher unity—namely, the sexual instinct—which also most clearly shows a striving toward discharge, toward "rest" after excitation. It cannot be that the "Nirvana principle" holds for one kind of instinct, while the "craving for stimulus" holds for another; the craving for stimulus must be derived on genetic-dialectic lines from the Nirvana principle, as a principle which is at the present day antithetic to the Nirvana principle. (When an infant that craves sleep is awakened by somatically determined hunger, it follows in the first instance its Nirvana principle in wanting to assuage its hunger and continue to sleep. When it later on recognizes that an intervention of the external world is necessary to this end, then it strives for this intervention and longs for the external world. The first craving for stimulus does not seem to be in contradiction to the Nirvana principle, but to act in its service. The aim of increasing the stimulus is an *intermediary* on the way to the goal of freedom from stimulation; it is not a characteristic of one kind of instinct in contrast to another. The genetic relationship between the Nirvana principle and the craving for stimulus is a very interesting chapter which requires detailed study. The existence of the craving for stimulus, however, must not lead us into the mistake of overlooking the fact that it is in the sexual instincts that we can best study the "longing for quiescence" and the "conservative nature of the instincts.")

The concepts of "instinctual fusion" and "instinctual defusion" [8] also invite criticism. Freud assumes that in the early stages of the development of instinctual life, the two kinds of instincts are not as yet well fused with each other, while the fusion is most successful in the so-called genital stage of libidinal organization; every regression of the libido brings with it a defusion of instinct and every progression a new fusion. But if we assume that in this conception the death instinct and eros are related to each other like acid and base, then we would have to assume that in an "unfused" state there would be much free eros as well as much free destructiveness, while in a "fused" state, there would be none of either, but rather neutral quiescence. In point of fact, however, in the so-called defused conditions, there is relatively much destructiveness and little eros, while in the so-called fused states there is relatively much eros, and little destructiveness. Thus the concepts of fusion and defusion do not seem to reflect the situation very well. The actual state of affairs is that in certain phases, aggressive and libidinal trends always appear together, and cannot be separated at all—so much so, indeed, that they arouse the suspicion that at these stages there is still an integrated condition out of which libido and aggression are only differentiated later on. This is the case with the so-called pregenital organizations, and particularly the oral ones, in that their aim is *incorporation,* which eliminates the

[8] Introduced in *ibid.,* pp. 57 ff.

independent existence of objects. Is it the most adequate way of representing this state of affairs of the indivisibility of aggression and libido, to say that these indivisibly connected qualities are "defused"?

In psychoanalysis we are accustomed to conceive of various phenomena belonging to the higher stages of development as products of a differentiation from a common original state. Does not the circumstance that both the libidinal object relations and the hate-filled destructive desire of adults can be demonstrated in analysis to derive genetically from oral incorporative tendencies suggest that love and hate originate from a common integral? Are there compelling clinical observations which contradict such a plausible assumption? If not, then what Freud calls "fusion" would be "a progression in differentiation," and what he calls "defusion" would be "regression toward the integral, and together with it a reoccurrence of that destructive quality which was peculiar to the primitive stages." The answer to the question whether ambivalence is a biological characteristic or a reaction to experienced frustrations, would then vary with the definition of the concept "ambivalence." What is without doubt biologically determined is the fact that the earliest instinctual relationships to objects, which first arise with the apprehension of the existence of an objectual world, strive for an objective annihilation of that world. The affective reaction of "rage," which follows frustrations, is rooted in this fact. But that such a primary destructiveness (which is not yet distinguishable from libidinal excitation and is certainly not *subjectively* aimed at a destruction of the object, but only at "a cessation of the unpleasurable situation") is due to a turning outward of a destructive tendency originally directed against the own ego, does not seem to us in any way proved. True, the developmental history of the differentiation of libido and aggression, and, as regards the former, the observable rise to independence of the intermediary aims, as also the history of the establishment of that instinctual consideration for the object and the tendency to organization and synthesis which constitutes the growth of love—these things have not yet been written about; nor is the subject exhausted by Abraham's correct observation [9] that the decisive consideration for the object evolves at a definite point of development within the anal phase. (Jekels and Bergler's [10] attempt at a developmental history of love does not seem to me to be useful, not only because it postulates this problematic classification of instinct, but, more important still, because it neglects both conflicts within the ego and biological instinctual needs.)

But do not the clinical facts of depression, and of the superego in general, compel us to assume the existence of a death instinct? According to what has

<hr/>

[9] K. Abraham, "A Short Study of the Development of the Libido, Viewed in the Light of Mental Disorders," *Selected Papers*, London, Hogarth, 1948, p. 432.

[10] L. Jekels and E. Bergler, "Uebertragung und Liebe," *Imago*, Vol. 20, 1934.

been said above, the clinical facts, which have been correctly seen by Freud and by the adherents of the theory of the death instinct, compel us only to state this: that primitive instinctual life has a powerful destructive coloring; that this coloring is maintained throughout the "vicissitude of turning against the ego," and is reinforced in every libidinal regression. The clinical facts do not, however, posit anything concerning the genesis of this coloring. They say nothing about this destructiveness having been originally directed against the own ego, nor about its being of a different quality from a second, also-existing, contrary instinct. The strong suicidal tendency of depressions on the one hand reflects the powerfulness of the destructive impulses directed against the (introjected) object, and, on the other, is an attempt by the ego to attain a discharge which is unattainable and to placate a superego which is implacable. "Moral masochism" and similar phenomena also only show us once again alterations of instinct through experiential vicissitudes and regressions, in periods in which archaic destructiveness was still excessive; but they do not show us anything about its genesis. Therese Benedek maintains that the theory of instinctual defusion is indispensable for the explanation of certain phenomena of oral sadism. According to her only the instinctual defusion accompanying pathogenic regression can explain the sadistic nature of orality, which did not as yet belong to it at the time of the oral stage of libidinal development.[11] According to our psychoanalytic experience, however, the sadistic destructive rage of some small children who have encountered oral frustrations is indeed enormous.

It seems to us that Freud himself has implied that the opposition of love and hate is not a primarily given opposition of qualities, but one which is a developmental product, when, in discussing the processes of the apparent change of libido into hate and vice versa—as seen in some cases of mild homosexuality and in delusions of persecution—he explains that without assuming an energy "free of quality," which is per se neither eros nor destructiveness and which can associate itself to either kind of instinct, "we cannot manage at all." [12] In this he is certainly right. But does not such an assumption play the same role for the new theory of instincts as did narcissism for the older one (even with the help of the auxiliary hypothesis that "quality-free energy" originates from "desexualized eros")? If quantities of energy can be displaced from the sexual instincts to the ego instincts, and vice versa, then—so it seems to us—sexual and ego instincts must derive from a common origin. Does not the same hold for eros and destructiveness?

If we should decide in favor of such an assumption, many difficulties would disappear, among them in particular those which arise from an anthropomorphic

---

11 T. Benedek, "Dominant Ideas and Their Relation to Morbid Cravings," *Int. J. Psa.*, Vol. 17, 1936.
12 S. Freud, *The Ego and the Id*, pp. 61–62.

conception of Eros and Thanatos. To give an example: In one passage, Freud explains that the store of energy of the ego comes for the greater part from de-sexualized eros, but also contains some quantities of death instinct (both these kinds of instinct are active in the id as well as in the ego, so that this new theory of instincts can by no means—as some authors have wrongly understood—do what the old one could not, namely, reflect the opposing forces at work in repression). He then writes: "By thus obtaining possession of the libido from the object-cathexes, setting itself up as the sole love-object, and desexualizing or sublimating the libido of the id, the ego is working in opposition to the purposes of eros, and placing itself at the service of the opposing instinctual trends." [13] Does not psychoanalytic experience teach us that such "regression to narcissism" represents "a substitutive gratification" of a sexual instinct which has suffered external frustration, and that it therefore conforms to the "purposes of eros"? Or does it make sense to say that the id (that is, the compendium of all the instincts) "defends itself" against eros by satisfying its demands? [14]

We must agree with Reich that the death-instinct theory gives many opportunities for unfortunate misuses.[15] The first such misuse is that wherever the analyst comes upon phenomena of masochism, self-punishment, and so forth, he is inclined to fall back on the death-instinct theory and to stop analyzing, thinking that he is faced with a primary biological fact which cannot be further analyzed, instead of proceeding here too to search for determining experiences in the patient's life.

A second danger of the death-instinct theory, as Reich has also correctly stressed, is that it may mislead one into overlooking the relationship between the individual whose instincts are engaged and the external world which prohibits his instincts and through whose influence some of the energy of instinctual origin is used to suppress the rest of it. We have already said that in the older classification of instincts into ego instincts and sexual instincts neurotic conflict was conceived of as a conflict between two kinds of instincts. But we also said that this did not militate against the view that the conflict was originally one between the individual and the external world, and we have shown why this is so. When now the conception that in the neurotic conflict two kinds of instinct struggle with each other was abandoned, it was able to return in a more dangerous variant, namely, in the theory that neuroses rest upon a conflict of two kinds of instinctual qualities, a self-destructive one, the death instinct, and an "erotic" ego which was afraid of its death instinct. Such an interpretation would mean a total elimination of the social factor from the etiology of neuroses, and would amount to a

---

[13] *Ibid.*, p. 65.
[14] *Ibid.*, p. 65.
[15] Compare W. Reich, "The Masochistic Character," *Character Analysis*, New York, Orgone, 1949.

complete biologization of neuroses. And, in fact, Rado takes this view at the present day.[16] He maintains that anxiety is a "masochistic phenomenon," that is, that anxiety always arises only when a hidden self-destructive instinct is at work and is rightly feared. Rado, it is true, believes that to say this is not to deny the influence of the external world. He thinks that he is doing no more than assert that frustrations only become effective by the roundabout way of first changing the frustrated instinct into a masochistic one. Thus the neurotic conflict would no longer be played out between the instinct and the defense against it determined by the external world, but between the self-destructive and the self-preservative instinct. There is no doubt that this conception—which, by the way, does not use the term "death instinct"—draws a false inference from the theory of the instinct of death.

When we consider that there is no psychological impulse in which no joining of what is separate or separation of what is joined takes place, it becomes clear how futile it is when various authors try to demonstrate "the effectiveness of both eros and death instinct" in specific psychological phenomena. The most extreme example of this has recently been seen in the dream studies of Jekels and Bergler, who consider, among other things, that the activity of dream censorship is a proof of the existence of the death instinct.[17]

After such polemical comments against the assumption of the death instinct, may I be permitted to make the following remarks: A biological generalization of the Nirvana principle—a conception like that of the biologist Ehrenberg, which has several meeting points with Freud's theory of the death instinct—seems to me to be very profound and impressive.[18] That life is "a course toward death" seems to me to do fundamental justice to the nature of the phenomena of life. The young organism is full of prospective potentialities. Every stretch of life it passes through crystallizes out of it "structure" which makes it "rigid," limits its prospective potentialities and brings it nearer to the inorganic. In the beginning of life, the prospective potentialities are at their height and structure is minimal; at the end of life there are no more potentialities but mere structure $=$ death. Once one has thought through such a conception of life it is easy to see in psychological processes, too, only a special case of life processes in general.

It is thus far from my intention to deny either the facts or the philosophical depths underlying Freud's hypothesis. It seems to me, however, that both these facts and the assumption of "a course toward death" should be apprehended otherwise than by assuming the existence of two kinds of instincts which are opposed to each other from the start, the aim of the one being relaxation of ten-

[16] S. Rado, "Fear of Castration in Women," *Psa. Quart.*, Vol. 2, 1933.
[17] L. Jekels and E. Bergler, "Triebdualismus in Traum," *Imago*, Vol. 20, 1934.
[18] R. Ehrenberg, "Psychoanalyse und Biologie," *Auswirkungen der Psychoanalyse in Wissenschaft und Leben. Krisis der Psychoanalyse*, H. Prinzhorn, ed., Leipzig, Neue Geist Verlag, 1928.

sion and death, that of the other, increase of tension and binding into higher unities. In my critique I have limited myself to the theory; I have not attempted, by reference to the literature of the subject, to support my view that this hypothesis has not proved heuristically useful in the science of psychoanalysis and has brought much more confusion than progress.

# THIRTY-THREE

# The Scoptophilic Instinct and
# Identification*

## I

IN THE following paper it is not my intention to present anything fundamentally new: I have sought merely to connect and comment upon certain facts which are already familiar in psychoanalysis.

One such well-known fact is the influence exercised upon our psychic processes by the symbolic equation: to look at = to devour. When someone gazes intently at an object, we say that he "devours it with his eyes," and there are many similar phrases. Psychoanalytical writers have been struck by this unconscious significance in one form of looking in particular. Strachey in his paper on reading begins by examining its pathology (the inhibitions of reading and the passion for it) and goes on to show that the participation of the unconscious mind in reading always represents the idea that the sentences, words, or letters read are objects being devoured by the reader.[1] On a previous occasion I quoted in confirmation of his view the following significant lines by Morgenstern:

> Korff brought out a mid-day newspaper
> and anyone who read it
> found himself full up. . . .†

Another conclusion which Strachey draws is that the idea of devouring, which in the unconscious underlies that of reading, actually represents a form of sadis-

* First published in *Int. Z. Psa.*, Vol. 21, 1935, pp. 561–583.
[1] J. Strachey, "Some Unconscious Factors in Reading," *Int. J. Psa.*, Vol. 11, 1930.
† *Korff erfindet eine Mittagszeitung,*
  *welche, wenn man sie gelesen hat,*
  *ist man satt. . . .*—Trans. note.

tic incorporation, with all the qualities which we associate with other ambivalent oral incorporation tendencies. This interpretation throws immediate light upon certain types of libidinal reading. If reading represents an act of incorporation, it explains the passion which so many pregenitally fixated persons have for reading in the water closet. It is an attempt to preserve the equilibrium of the ego; part of one's bodily substance is being lost and so fresh matter must be absorbed through the eyes. Some persons of an oral-erotic disposition are prompted by libidinal impulses to read whenever they are eating, but here the matter is more complicated. We must assume that their oral erotism, when stimulated, requires a twofold satisfaction.

We have other evidence to show that looking has the unconscious significance of devouring. The wolf in Little Red Riding Hood declared, first, that he had such big eyes, the better to see his victim and, next, that he had such a big mouth, the better to eat her up. Probably every psychoanalyst could produce analytical material in support of this equation.[2]

In magic the act of looking has various meanings, of which devouring is only one; the lore of magic knows many methods of putting a spell upon a victim by means of a look. By the magic glance one renders him defenseless, generally by paralyzing him or otherwise making him incapable of movement. My readers will recollect that snakes are said to fix with their gaze animals which they wish to devour, so that the victims walk into the snake's jaws of their own accord; anyone who encounters the basilisk's eye is turned to stone, and similarly the "true" hypnotist (as the attraction of the uncanny prompts people to conceive of him) lays a spell on his victim by fixing upon him an irresistible gaze. In all these cases the eye, or the glance, is a sadistic weapon. Freud[3] and other writers[4] have pointed out that this is because the eye is used to symbolize the penis. But in many cases it is quite clear that the sadism which has its source in the eyes is *oral* in character. Curiously enough, this is sometimes the case precisely when the phallic significance of the eye is unmistakable. The snake fascinates its victim in order to devour it. The most familiar instance of erection symbolism in relation to the eye is to be found in Andersen's story of the Tinder Box, where we read of dogs with eyes as large as saucers, as soup-plates, and as the Round Tower at Copenhagen. Now what anyone fears about a dog is, of course, that it may bite or devour him. It is noteworthy that in all such magic

[2] It was on the strength of such material that I wrote as follows: "There are many cases of anxiety hysteria in which we can detect violently destructive tendencies operating with relatively great strength. This often comes to expression by way of the equation: looking = devouring," *Hysterien und Zwangsneurosen*, Vienna, Int. Psa. Verlag, 1931, p. 49.

[3] The first reference to this idea occurs in *The Interpretation of Dreams*.

[4] In Volume 1 of *Int. Z. Psa.* there are papers on the symbolism of the eye by Eder, Ferenczi, Rank, and Reitler, in all of which attention is drawn to the phallic symbolism of the eye. There are also references to its vaginal significance, a point to which we shall recur later.

procedures as I have mentioned the eye plays a double part. It is not only actively sadistic (the person gazing puts a spell on his victim) but also passively receptive (the person who looks is fascinated by that which he sees).

One particular type of enchantment by the glance of the eye is specially interesting in connection with what I shall say later. In this case the victim is neither paralyzed, transfixed, nor devoured, but is compelled to *imitate* all the movements which the magician makes. Freud once said that fairy tales were "the descendants of legends, come down in the world," and we may certainly say the same of children's traditional games.[5] There is a well-known game in which the children sing:

> "Adam had seven sons,
> Seven sons had Adam.
> They did not eat, they did not drink,
> They looked at each other without a blink,
> And they all went like this. . . ." *

At the last line one of the children makes some sort of fantastic movements and the others have to copy everything that they see him do. Again, in Kipling's story, the gigantic snake Kaa dances its "hunger-dance" in front of the monkeys and they imitate it until finally they jump into its jaws. Any collection of examples of "imitative magic" contains instances of this kind. In psychoanalysis we are familiar with the term, coined by Liebermann,[6] "magic gesture" which we apply in cases where the purpose of a neurotic symptom is that someone else should copy it. The person who magically compels others to imitate him is, in fact, making use of the expedient of demonstration. If the hypnotist, that uncanny character, can compel the person he gazes at to do anything he chooses, this is certainly only a further elaboration of the original idea that he can compel him to imitate the gestures which the hypnotist himself makes.

To turn now to quite a different field: We take it as a matter of course when we say that a child who has witnessed his parents' sexual activities in a "primal scene" identifies himself with that which he sees, and we are agreed that this identification has important consequences for his whole life; but we seldom reflect on the relation between looking and identification.

---

[5] Cf. E. Schneider, "Kinderreigen," *Z. Psa. Paed.,* Vol. 6, 1932.

* *"Adam hatte sieben Soehne.*
*sieben Soehne hatte Adam.*
*Sie assen nicht, sie tranken nicht,*
*sie sahen einander ins Angesicht,*
*und machten's alle so . . ."*—Trans. note.

[6] H. Liebermann, "Ueber monosymptomatische Neurosen," author's abstract, *Int. Z. Psa.,* Vol. 10, 1924.

Here is another point. In his book on looking-glass magic [7] Roheim devotes several pages to the enumeration of magical customs and beliefs connected with looking-glasses. Why is a looking-glass so suited to be a magical property? In the first place, it confronts everyone with his own ego in external bodily form, thus obliterating the dividing line between ego and non-ego. And, secondly, it gives the scoptophilic instinct a very special chance; "looking-glass magic" is another instance in which looking is associated with changes in the relation between ego and non-ego.

Let us sum up our conclusions so far. In the unconscious, to look at an object may mean various things, the most noteworthy of which are as follows: to devour the object looked at, to grow like it (be forced to imitate it), or, conversely, to force it to grow like oneself. What is the connection between these relations?

## II

In order to answer this question it will perhaps be a good thing to recall briefly what we know of the scoptophilic instinct in general. As Freud has shown in his *Drei Abhandlungen,* this instinct is a component of the sexual instinct. In adults it serves the purpose of inducing sexual forepleasure and this in a typical way, since all end-pleasure requires contact with the partner, whereas an object which is only seen remains at a distance. Since sight is the sense by which human beings are mainly guided, we must regard it as the chief agent in the production of forepleasure, though, at the same time, we must remember that it is precisely in the realm of sensuality that the so-called lower senses are most prominent. (Whether, when subserving the scoptophilic instinct, the eye is to be regarded as an erotogenic zone, as it is for instance when rubbing the eyes is equivalent to masturbation, is a point which I do not propose to examine here, because it would sidetrack us unnecessarily into the domain of physiology.) At all events the scoptophilic instinct, like other component instincts, is liable to repression and may give rise to fixation. Freud has devoted a special paper to a description of the neurotic symptoms which ensue from the specific forms of repression of this instinct.[8] And today we know that these may result in equally specific neurotic character traits: especially among obsessional neurotics do we find persons suffering from a typical inhibition in looking, who, instead of seeing objects, make contact with the world around them only through concepts and words or by way of the other senses. The original scoptophilic instinct generally betrays itself here in some sort of "return of the repressed from under

---

[7] G. Roheim, *Spiegelzauber,* Vienna, Int. Psa. Verlag, 1919.

[8] S. Freud, "Psychogenic Visual Disturbance according to Psycho-Analytical Conceptions," *Coll. Pap.,* Vol. II, London, Hogarth, 1948.

repression."[9] I would mention in this connection a characteristic phobia because, although it is of wide occurrence, it has met with relatively little notice. I refer to the inhibition of the capacity for recognition, the inability to recognize people's faces. Patients suffering from this inhibition have always repressed a specially strong instinctual impulse to look at people. Possibly Berta Bornstein's interpretation applies in all such cases. She holds that it is always a question of displacement from below upward and that what the patients really do not wish to see is the distinguishing marks of sex.[10]

What is the aim of the scoptophilic instinct? I think there can be no possible doubt that it is *to look at* the sexual object. Freud adds: to look at the genitals of the desired person or to watch him or her performing the functions of excretion.[11] We need only take at random any phenomenon from the sphere of the scoptophilic instinct, or watch children who are deriving libidinal gratification from looking, in order to know what accompanies or conditions pleasurable looking: one looks at an object in order *to share in* its experience. This comes out specially clearly in the psychoanalysis of scoptophiliac perverts. Anyone who desires to witness the sexual activities of a man and woman really always desires to share their experience by a process of empathy, generally in a homosexual sense, i.e. by empathy in the experience of the partner of the opposite sex. Exhibitionists, too (who unconsciously are always active scoptophiliacs as well), enter by empathy, during their perverse activities, into what is actually, or what in their magical fantasy they conceive to be, the experience of their objects. Freud arrived at this conclusion long ago,[12] and Landmark has emphasized the universal significance of this fact for object love in general.[13] Very often sadistic impulses enter into the instinctual aim of looking: one wishes *to destroy* something by means of looking at it, or else the act of looking itself has already acquired the significance of a modified form of destruction. Thus, for instance, the compulsion so frequently met with in women to look at the region of a man's genitals is really a modified expression of active castration tendencies. It seems, then, that there are two tendencies which always or often determine the goal of the scoptophilic instinct: (*a*) the impulse to injure the object seen, and (*b*) the desire to share by means of empathy in its experience. Here "empathy" is a complicated psychological process which cannot immediately be reduced to a short formula. But at any rate it has something to do with the mechanism of *identification*.[14]

[9] O. Fenichel, *Perversionen, Psychosen, Charakterstoerungen*, Vienna, Int. Psa. Verlag, 1931, p. 170.
[10] B. Bornstein, "Zur Psychogenese der Pseudodebilitaet," *Int. Z. Psa.*, Vol. 16, 1930.
[11] S. Freud, *Three Essays on the Theory of Sexuality*, London, Imago, 1949.
[12] *Ibid.*
[13] J. Landmark, "Ueber den Triebbegriff," *Imago*, Vol. 20, 1934.
[14] O. Fenichel, "Identification," No. 10 in this volume.

### III

Now let us consider the position. Every pregenital component of the sexual instinct is in part autoerotic and in part directed toward objects. In so far as pregenital instinctual impulses are directed toward objects, their object relations are primitive and the primitive object relation, the precursor of love and hate, is *incorporation*.[15] Thus incorporation may be associated with any erotogenic zone. Thus there is a strong inherent probability that this holds good of the scoptophilic instinct. The underlying tendency may be formulated as follows: "I wish what I see to enter into me." Now this certainly does not *necessarily* mean that the eye itself is thought of as the avenue of introjection. So there are two problems with regard to this process of "ocular introjection," which takes its place with oral, anal, epidermal, and respiratory introjection; (1) Are the two aims "I desire to incorporate that which I see" and "I desire to participate in the experience of that which I see" identical? and (2) Is there such a thing as incorporation through the eye?

All that we know of the relation between empathy, identification, and introjection makes it very probable that we should answer the first question in the affirmative. Empathy is always conditioned by identification and it seems that we have already good grounds for believing that all identification takes place through an act of introjection.[16]

Analytic experience points to an affirmative answer to the second question also. We have a particularly good illustration of this point in fantasies of head pregnancy, in which *the eyes* play a part. For instance, one patient as a little boy was convinced that children could grow inside a mother's head, because, whenever he looked closely into his mother's eyes, he could see there the image of a child. It is a common saying that the eye is the "seat of the soul." This phrase in itself is not sufficient proof of the existence of fantasies of "eye impregnation" or of processes of ocular introjection. It is, of course, primarily suggested by physiological facts (the participation of the eyes in the play of the features), but none the less these fantasies and processes may have something to do with it.

It is scarcely possible to doubt that there is such a thing as incorporation through the eye (for we know that incorporation may be associated with any erotogenic zone). The only question is how frequent such fantasies are and what is their significance in the whole course of libidinal development.

When a child is present during a primal scene and identifies himself with his parents, we might suppose that two successive acts have taken place: First, the

---

[15] K. Abraham, "A Short Study of the Development of the Libido, Viewed in the Light of Mental Disorders," *Selected Papers*, London, Hogarth, 1948.

[16] S. Freud, "Mourning and Melancholia," *Coll. Pap.*, Vol. IV, London, Hogarth, 1948. See also the many publications on the subject which have appeared since Freud's work.

child *perceives* (and we must, of course, discriminate between perception and introjection, i.e. the fantasy of taking possession of and assimilating oneself to the object—a point to which we shall recur). And, secondly, he *identifies himself* with that which he perceives. But here two separate problems present themselves. In the first place, it is doubtful whether these two acts are in reality so distinct as they are when viewed in the abstract. Is it not possible that there is a mode of perception which amounts to identification? Are not the subsequent manifestations of "ocular introjection" possibly the residue or resumption of a more primitive mode of visual perception, when the objective external world was as yet not so much perceived as taken possession of, by a process akin to identification, and then subjectively elaborated? And in the second place we must ask: with what unconscious fantasies and physical prototypes of mental processes is this identification with the object seen associated?

## IV

Let us begin with the first problem. When looking has become libidinized, so that the aim of the person who looks is not perception but sexual gratification, it differs from the ordinary kind of looking. Libidinal looking often takes the form of a fixed gaze, which may be said to be spastic, just as the act of running, when libidinized, is spastic. (Libidinization has the effect of impairing an ego function.) [17]

Now the *magic* glance of which we have already spoken is always supposed to be a "stare." (The eye of the basilisk or of the hypnotist.) Moreover, in libidinal looking in general the motor function plays a greater part than in ordinary looking. The process is more active: the world does not approach the eye but the person looking makes an onslaught with his eye upon the world, in order to "devour" it. But, it may be objected, is it really otherwise in the ordinary, physiological act of seeing? Freud [18] and the exponents of perceptual psychology are agreed that even this process is not so much passive as active and that only the centrifugal impetus of cathectic energy from within the organism enables a sense organ to function, so that it can, as it were, sample the outside world. It is, then, impossible to discover any fundamental antithesis between libidinal and ordinary seeing. Evidently the position is that that which is characteristic of every act of seeing merely becomes more manifest when the seeing is libidinized. Moreover, the stronger motor element is in evidence not only in libidinal seeing but equally in every mode of "archaic" seeing, so that the scoptophiliac would seem to have regressed wholly or in part to a more primitive mode of seeing. Bally points out the importance for psychoanalytical theory of in-

---

[17] S. Freud, *The Problem of Anxiety*, New York, Psa. Quart. Press and Norton, 1936.
[18] S. Freud, "A Note upon the 'Mystic Writing-Pad,'" *Coll. Pap.*, Vol. V, London, Hogarth, 1950.

vestigations in the field of optics, and what he says is briefly this: [19] There is a primitive mode of looking or of visual representation. This original mode of seeing cannot be divorced from motility: there is as yet no sharp distinction between perception and ideation; seeing is a piece of active behavior by means of which one enters into the object seen. When we say that seeing cannot be divorced from motility, we mean, of course (since the control of the motor function depends on the deep-seated sensibility which directs it) [20] that that visual perception cannot be separated from kinesthetic perception; in seeing, our whole body undergoes change. The object seen is at first not sharply differentiated from one's own body—and this is true originally of the whole object world by whatever sense it may be perceived; perception and the consequent motor reaction are still one and the same thing.[21] All primitive perception is a taking part in what is perceived. It is only later that perception as a separate process is differentiated both from the behavior with which we react to what we perceive and from thought ("experimental action"), in which use is made of the data acquired by perception.[22] Goldstein has reported that patients suffering from cerebral lesions, who could apparently read well, became incapable of reading if anyone held their heads still. They had accustomed themselves to trace with their heads the forms of the letters that they saw and to read kinesthetically with the help of their own movements, in order to compensate for the defect of a central function.[23] The organic disturbance of a cerebral function had caused these patients to regress to an earlier phase. Thus in libidinal seeing certain characteristics of *primitive* seeing are reproduced; that is to say, the motor and kinesthetic faculties play a greater part than in ordinary seeing. And, since in psychic development a lower phase always persists to a certain extent behind a higher one, *every* act of seeing still retains something of these characteristics.

The first relation of a human being to the object world is invariably that of primary identification,[24] i.e. imitation of the external world as perceived. Here, however, another factor comes in: it is only by means of the co-operation of the motor system that full perception is possible; observation takes place *by way of* identification.

[19] G. Bally, "Die Wahrnehmungslehre Jaenschs und ihre Beziehung zu den psychoanalytischen Problemen," *Imago,* Vol. 17, 1931.

[20] O. Fenichel, "Organ Libidinization Accompanying the Defense against Drives," No. 14 in this volume.

[21] In connection with this point and what follows cf. S. Spielrein, "Kinderzeichnungen bei offenen und geschlossenen Augen," *Imago,* Vol. 17, 1931.

[22] Even at a later period, however, each separate thought is seen on closer examination to have its origin in that stratum where there is still only imperfect differentiation, not only between thought and action but also between both these processes and that of perception. Cf. P. Schilder, "Ueber Gedankenentwicklung," *Z. Neurol. Psychiat.,* Vol. 59, 1920.

[23] Cf. J. Steinfeld, "Ein Beitrag zur Analyse der Sexualfunktion," *Z. Neurol. Psychiat.,* Vol. 107, 1927.

[24] O. Fenichel, "Identification," No. 10 in this volume.

This brings us to the problem already alluded to of the relation of perception to introjection in general. It would certainly be incorrect to regard these two concepts as identical or to define perception as a variety of introjection. One does not become like every object which one has seen. Nevertheless the relation between perception and introjection must be a close one and we can surmise its nature. Perception and secondary identification are two separate products of what was originally a single process. Freud long ago recognized that primitive perception is akin to introjection.[25] Simmel holds that the oral erotogenic zone, the first organ of incorporation, is also the organ of our earliest perceptions, so that all the organs concerned in subsequent perception derive some of their qualities from this, their original predecessor. He defines the eye and the ear as "organs of introjection for the elaboration and satisfactory assimilation of optical and acoustic perceptions."[26] In fantasy also the eye and the ear are conceived of as organs of sex designed for the reception of the object. (We must observe that, all the same, they seem less suitable for such representation than another sense organ, the nose, for in olfactory perception the introjection of minute particles of the objects is actually *real*.)

The fact that libidinal seeing is a partial regression to these archaic forms of seeing explains how it is that, as we have already noted, the aim of the scoptophilic instinct regularly includes elements of sadism and the desire to incorporate the object.

## V

Let us now turn to the second question: With what fantasies of "physical prototypes of mental processes" is incorporation by means of the eye associated?

The present study is really the outcome of certain clinical observations bearing on this point. They relate to two cases, one of which I propose to discuss in some detail.

The general outline of the first case was as follows:[27]

A young girl had suffered as an infant from a gastric affection, on account of which she had been put on a starvation diet. This engendered in her peculiarly strong oral cravings. In the period immediately following this illness she had contracted the habit of throwing her bottle, when she had finished the milk in it, on the floor and breaking it, a gesture which I construe as an expression of some such thought as this: What good is an empty bottle to me? I want a full

[25] Compare in this connection Freud's remarks on the "purified pleasure-ego," in "Instincts and Their Vicissitudes," *Coll. Pap.*, Vol. IV.

[26] E. Simmel, "Praegenitalprimat und intestinale Stufe der Libidoorganisation," author's abstract, *Int. Z. Psa.*, Vol. 19, 1933.

[27] This survey of the structure of the case has already been given in my *Perversionen, Psychosen, Charakterstoerungen*, p. 50. A discussion of the theoretical problems involved will be found in a paper entitled "Further Light upon the Pre-oedipal Phase in Girls," No. 24 in this volume.

one! As a little child she was very greedy. The oral fixation manifested itself in an intense dread of a loss of love and passionate clinging to her mother. It was therefore a great disappointment to her, at the age of three, when her mother became pregnant. The patient wanted to do exactly the same to her mother's enlarged abdomen as she had previously done with the empty bottles: to destroy it, to devour its contents, and doubtless to take their place herself. After the child's birth, the patient snatched her baby sister's bottle from her mouth, drank up the contents, and thrust it empty so far down the infant's throat that she was almost choked. It was no wonder that, when the patient discovered the existence of the penis, which she did about this time, she perceived it in terms of "the child in the abdomen" and wished to tear it out (or push it in), eat it up, and put herself in its place.

Her mother's death, which occurred when the patient was five years old, strengthened the oral fixation and completed for good and all the displacement onto her father of the attitude which had originally characterized her relation to her mother. For a very short time the child was happy in the expectation that she would now take her mother's place. This happiness was shattered not only by a heavy sense of guilt (for long before the oedipus phase she had wanted to kill her mother because of her pregnancy) but by real disappointments (a governess came to live in the house and the patient found herself once again in the position of a little child). But there was something more: her own (oral) incapacity to bear the loss of her mother and her mother's tenderness. The true oedipus complex, the love fixation to her father, which now rapidly established itself and stamped its impress upon her later life, derived its unconscious specific form entirely from a transference of her pregenital relations with her mother to the genital relation with her father. This was characterized either by the fantasy of tearing out the penis (the child) and devouring it; or again, by the fantasy of being attached to or enclosed in her father's abdomen and being devoured herself, so that, lying in the body which was at once paternal and maternal, she was secure from the fear of any further loss. And finally she fantasied that she was wholly transformed into her father's penis and shared in his masculinity. All her later attachments to men were modeled on this prototype and permeated by impulses toward identification as well as by the idea of being a tiny creature nestling against the love object. During the years of puberty she had the following masturbation fantasy, accompanied by a crushing sense of guilt: she was raped by a Negro in a corset shop. This fantasy at once concealed the oedipus complex and embodied its pregenital antecedents. For "corset" proved to be a screen word for the idea of "getting rid of a large abdomen," and the "Negro" represented the father, the ogre who devoured little children, stuck them into his belt, and let them dangle there.

In this account I have done far less than justice to the patient's strongly developed scoptophilic impulses. These took two principal directions: (a) phenomena connected with physics and (b) reading.

The first was easy to interpret. Her father had shown and explained to her various experiments in physics. Thus her leaning toward that branch of science was primarily a leaning toward her father. She always took a particular delight in experiments in which she could watch the rise of fluids. This had a genital significance and represented in the first instance the unconscious wish to watch her father urinating. Again, anything connected with reflection in mirrors had a special interest to her. She had once seen some "living pictures" in a "Tanagra" theater; these dainty little midgets stood in her unconscious for the penis. Moreover, she had an uncle who was an oculist and possessed an ophthalmoscope. She conceived the idea that this was a magic mirror with which one could see through a person's eye right into his body. She constantly asked to have the way the mirror worked explained to her and to be allowed to look through it. (But she was never permitted to do so.) In her imagination another of her uncle's instruments was inseparably associated with the ophthalmoscope and was also an object of absorbing interest to her. This was his large magnet with which, he said, he could draw things out of people's eyes. She was enormously interested in all medical matters, partly as a result of her interest in the oculist's instruments. We may say provisionally that the main object of her scoptophilic instinct was the penis. At the same time she had the idea that the eye gave access to the interior of the body.

Accidents were another object of her curiosity and she wanted to be able to witness them. On one occasion, when her father came home with a bandage over his eye, her excitement was intense: here was a combination of her two great interests—an accident and something to do with the eyes. She always wanted to see "illnesses" in general; it was easy to recognize that this was a case of active castration tendencies and that for her "seeing" also signified "injuring."

We seem to have traveled a long way from problems of identification. We see that a certain person's scoptophilic instinct really signifies "I want to see how someone is castrated," or "I want to see how I could castrate somebody," but it does seem incredible that this could also signify "I want to be castrated myself."

Yet, improbable as it seems at first sight, there was one element in the situation which indicated that this was the true interpretation. I mean the part played by identification throughout the patient's life.[28] The whole aim of her tender impulses was to be a tiny creature nestling close against the large body of a man. Her unconscious, and to a certain extent her conscious, love life was principally

28 Cf. my more detailed account of this case in the paper already referred to.

conditioned by masculine sympathy with her sexual partner. On one occasion, when her lover failed in coitus with her, her reaction expressed itself in the words *"We* are impotent." Another time, when she heard that a man friend had had sexual intercourse with another woman, she involuntarily thought "How could he? He cannot possibly do it without me." When her lover was absent from her for some time, she felt "as if she had a wound" in her back, as though she had been joined to him there and were torn away from him.

It is quite evident that the patient's strong scoptophilic instinct, of which the aim was to *see* the penis, had for its counterpart the no less powerful fantasy of herself *being a* penis.

These two tendencies were represented in the fantasy of the "father's body," where she was a little child dangling from a man's belt; they finally turned out to be a superstructure, built up on a deeper stratum, where the mother was the chief love object. It was her mother's pregnancy which led her to adopt an attitude only later displaced onto the man and his penis. She had wanted to inspect her mother's pregnant body closely and to lie within it herself in place of the strange child. Here, seeing had a sadistic significance and corresponded to the fantasy to which Melanie Klein has drawn attention, in which the subject desires to penetrate the mother's body by an oral act of destruction and subsequently fears retribution in the form of a similar assault upon his or her own person.

For our purpose it is a matter of secondary importance whether the oral sadism and the tendency to identification, simultaneously manifested in this patient, had reference primarily to the penis or whether that organ simply stood for the contents of the mother's body. What concerns us here is, first, that the two tendencies were represented by scoptophilic impulses in relation to both objects; secondly, the fact that they could be discovered only by the analysis of dreams of looking and other phenomena connected with libidinal seeing; and, thirdly, the manner in which they were revealed.

The patient's dread of her own destructive impulses in relation to her mother's body and of "being devoured" herself by way of retribution came to light in a number of dreams of looking, in which female symbols, horribly distorted, were seen by her through a window or in a theater, etc. It was easy to recognize the nature of her conflict "I want to look at the inside of a body" (cf. the ophthalmoscope), "which I picture as a place of bloodshed where one is devoured, but I am afraid of it just because it is like that." In contrast to the anxiety associated with such dreams was her bliss when, by way of exception, she had an opportunity "to look at the inside of a body" without any sadistic impulse. Her delight was unbounded when, as a child, she was once shown the model of a mine and when, on another occasion, her father took her for a walk and pulled a potato out of the ground in order to show her how it grew.[29]

It is clear then that for this patient seeing represented destruction and oral introjection of the pregnant body and the penis. But we have as yet no idea how the scoptophilic instinct came to be utilized thus, whether it is really correct to speak of "ocular introjection" in this case and with what special fantasies the process was associated. The analysis of the anxiety attacks, which were the reason for the patient's coming for analysis, led directly to visual experiences. The anxiety overtook her for the first time at a meeting and at a moment which had left a vivid visual image engraved upon her mind. A speaker had worked himself up into a state of excitement and held up his arm in a threatening way. We can see at once that the gesture had a phallic significance. The analysis of it led to the patient's dread of the mother who had died so early: she felt her mother would come and punish her for wetting her bed. (The ideas of punishment and sexual gratification were here condensed in a remarkable manner.) The qualities of her mother as an agent of sexual punishment had been transferred to the penis and men in general, and the patient thought of her exclusively by means of visual images. For instance, one memory emerged in a truly dramatic fashion: she remembered how, in a state of sexual excitation, she had watched a window-curtain blowing in the wind, whereupon the dread of her dead mother's return took the form of the curious idea that the flat curtain was turning into a solid two-dimensional or three-dimensional body. The analysis of all this material involved analysis of certain childish phobias connected with looking.

As a child of five, the patient had had an attack of acute anxiety at the theater (this was the prototype of her anxiety-attack at the meeting). Later she evolved a fantasy that the people whom she had seen on the stage were now ghosts, doing evil deeds in a house opposite her own home. When they appeared at the window, they were ordinary human beings, made of flesh and blood. But by degrees as they drew back into the house, they shriveled, becoming just like pictures painted on a wall, and finally vanished altogether. Then, when they approached the window again, they gradually became substantial. Often they would slowly appear, disappear and reappear in a rhythmical sequence. Up to a certain point these fantasies were pleasurable but after that point the pleasure changed to manifest anxiety. She had forgotten them until her analysis.

Here we have again the motif of pictures becoming bodies in three dimensions. We shall connect this first of all with the idea of the return of the dead

---

[29] One of the principal factors in her delight in looking at models was the thought that, although smaller than the original objects, they were yet qualitatively exactly the same. This idea was based on the equation of child and grown-up, and also on the longing to prove to herself that a clitoris, although smaller than a penis, was otherwise exactly the same thing.

mother (ghosts are dead people), while in the rhythmically repeated appearance and disappearance we see an expression of the sexual excitation which was evidently associated with the child's idea of her mother.

Presently a new detail emerged: the ghosts had no feet, they had instead little round wooden disks. This seemed on the one hand to indicate castration thoughts and, on the other, to be an allusion to some toy. It turned out, however, that the patient had once had a book with pictures of people who had queer little wooden disks like those in her fantasy. Her first recollection about this was that she never wanted to look at the picture book. It was not until later on that it became clear that she had had a real dread of looking at it and that a marked "picture-book phobia" had preceded her visit to the theater and her fantasy of the ghosts. I was now able to tell her what she must really have been afraid of in looking at the pictures: she thought they might jump out of the flat page and become alive.

This interpretation was confirmed by a curious experience. At the time when we were analyzing this material the patient went for an excursion, when, all at once, the landscape assumed a strangely unsubstantial aspect, as if it had suddenly been reduced to two dimensions only. This sensation was accompanied by a feeling of anxiety. Her associations showed that the landscape had reminded her of a picture in a book.

Now how does a child, looking at pictures, conceive the idea that they might come to life? Doubtless the biological basis for her notion was that, owing to her strong optical interests, this child actually saw the pictures that she looked at as solid bodies. The only question is, What was the psychic significance of her experience?

It was easy to discover the most superficial of its several meanings. From the age of five she had had, hanging over her bed, a portrait of her dead mother. This was the source of her phobia: she longed for the portrait to become alive and yet she dreaded its doing so. Evidently this anxiety sprang from the oral-sadistic attachment to her mother upon which her whole sexual life was based.

Analysis showed that she had had the picture-book phobia in her mother's lifetime. But this fact does not contradict our conclusion. We have seen that her instinctual aim, with its cathexis of anxiety, was always to look at and to identify herself with a penis or a child in her mother's body, the act of looking being equivalent to the infliction of an (oral) injury. It is plain that the "living pictures" in a "Tanagra" theater were penis symbols, so too the little figures in the picture book which were stiff because they walked on wood. And it is not difficult to recognize pregnancy- and birth-symbols in the people who made themselves out of nothing, in the interior of a house (which the patient equated with a cave or the interior of the earth). But why should the optical experience

of seeing the pictures turn into solid bodies suggest so forcibly the idea of destroying and devouring or of being destroyed and devoured?

At the time when she had a dread of the picture book the patient suffered
from another form of anxiety, which was more deeply repressed and only came
to light later. She had had a toy, called a "wheel of life," a sort of embryo cinema.
It was in the form of a revolving cylinder, divided into sections, in which one
placed sheets of pictures. If one looked at these as they revolved through the
different sections, the successive positions assumed by the pictures gave them
the appearance of being in continuous motion, and also made them look like
solid figures. Here she saw with her own eyes pictures turning into solid bodies
(the prototype of her subsequent interest in the marvels of physics). It was a
phenomenon which terrified her. She recalled how she had had to turn away
her eyes in an agony of fear, because she had a feeling (based on a law of
physics) that the pictures were jumping into her head. She recalled, too, which
series gave her the most acute anxiety; it was one representing a clown, jumping
through a paper-covered hoop and tearing it. Here once more the penis- and
birth-symbolism is obvious. The picture which came forward out of the plane
surface and turned into a solid body symbolized the protruding penis or the
pregnant abdomen. And the underlying processes of oral introjection were
represented by the idea that these protruding objects were leaping into the eye
which looked at them. The expectation that pictures, steadily gazed at, would
leap into her eyes was really a dread of retribution: "That which my eyes pierce
will pierce me." But it is important to note the special form of this retribution:
"Just as I pierced it with my *eyes,* so the first thing it will pierce will be my
*eyes.*" Moreover, when we remember what identification with a penis or a child
in the mother's body signified to this patient, we cannot doubt that to force
one's way into the body through the eye represented in her mind as complete
a process of introjection as is implied to the general run of people by entering
it through the mouth.

Phantasies similar to those analyzed here seem often to play a part in the
minds of even those children whose psychic processes are less completely dominated by "ocular introjection." One patient, whose scoptophilic instinct was not
otherwise particularly marked, told me how in his childhood he had had a
dread of magic lanterns. He said "I was always afraid that the pictures would
jump out and bite me." [30]

I would mention in this connection the curiously pleasurable excitement with
which most children look through opera glasses, often, too, through the wrong

---

[30] This is somewhat reminiscent of a dream related by another patient who was afraid of magic
lanterns: "I saw a child squashed flat." I have quoted this in "Respiratory Introjection," No. 23 in
this volume.

end. Probably their experience on such occasions is identical with that which our patient described as seeing objects becoming two- or three-dimensional. It is a visual experience of the archaic type. The child sees objects approach and grow larger or recede and grow smaller, all in an uncanny way. To the unconscious this probably signifies that these objects are forcing their way into the child's own eyes or are being ejected from it. Many children make a game of advancing toward a mirror and then retreating from it, or else pressing on their eyeball and so producing a double image which approaches or recedes. Probably the same psychic mechanism is at work here. Moreover, the child's perception of his own excitation expresses itself in a general way in some rhythmic (in this case, visual) crescendo and diminuendo, and in analogous sensations conveyed to him by one or other of his senses—especially those of equilibrium and space—or by all his senses simultaneously.[31]

Analysis showed that our patient's passion for reading was closely connected with her former picture-book phobia. In the printed letters or word images she saw "substitutes" for the objects and figures previously seen in the picture book. (Here she was right from the objective as well as the subjective point of view.) Formerly her impulse was to cause the pictures she saw to turn into solid bodies, in order to devour them with her eyes, and it had consequently caused her much terror; now it was permissible for her to gratify it since she had displaced it onto a new object. Letters are substitutes for concrete objects; this is so to a very much greater extent in the mind of a child who is learning to read than in the mind of an adult. Difficulties in reading depend not only on what objects the letters symbolize, but also on how the reader intends to treat them; i.e., they are associated with the secret, sado-masochistic idea of incorporation which is attached to the act of reading.

When discussing another aspect of this case I showed that the patient's principal sexual anxiety was connected with the idea that a man (in a deeper stratum, her mother) might "make a hole in her," so that she would wet herself (because she had wetted herself). Here the act and its punishment are fused into one. Relating this idea to the scoptophilic impulses (while ignoring, for the moment, the deeper stratum) we may formulate it as follows: the penis might leap out, detach itself, make a hole in her eye and so force its way into her. Her eye itself thus acquires a phallic significance. Earlier in this paper we asked the question how this patient's two dominating ideas, "I want to *see* a penis" and "I want to *be* a penis," were connected with one another. We can now answer: by the fantasy that the penis, if seen, would force its way through her eye into her body.

---

[31] This interpretation is not incompatible with Freud's statement that the feeling one has in dreams of seeing everything "through the wrong end of an opera glass" means that the events seen happened a very long time ago ("The Interpretation of Dreams," *The Basic Writings*, New York, Random House [Modern Library], 1938, p. 399).

## VI

Material similar to that which has been discussed here occurs exceedingly often, though it may not be so patent or so powerfully cathected.

Fantasies of "ocular introjection" must be accorded the same status as the ideas of incorporation associated with the other erotogenic zones. There are still some problems in this connection which demand our consideration.

Long ago Freud recognized, and we regard it as a matter of course, that the eye is a phallic symbol and that, accordingly, to be blinded signifies to be castrated (especially as a punishment for some transgression prompted by the scoptophilic impulse). Can it be that the eye acquires this significance only through identification with a penis which is seen and thereby introjected? This can hardly be so; the *tertia comparationis*—"the most noble organ" and "the vulnerable organ"—probably suffice to explain the phallic nature of the eye. But no doubt ideas of incorporation may *reinforce* the symbolism. If the eye stands for the penis, then the eye fixed in a stare stands for the penis in erection.

In our patient's associations there constantly recurred the fairytale of the stone prince in the Arabian Nights. Over and over again in her dreams and fantasies figures of men appeared which had their prototype in this tale. The upper part of their bodies was ordinary and familiar, perhaps that of her father, while the lower part was somehow uncanny, being rigid or like that of an animal. The man with the belly of stone signified to her the man with the belly of a beast—in fact, a centaur; a counterpart was the Little Mermaid from Hans Andersen's story, who had a fish's tail instead of legs; a figure which also played a great part in her fantasy. The purpose of these fantasies was simply to repress or psychically to master her observations of the genitals of adults in childhood. Now the rigidity of the stone prince, his disability, and his immobility were stressed in a very remarkable fashion. They signified something more than erection. We recall the fact that to be turned into stone is, like losing his sight, a very frequent punishment for the scoptophiliac. A person who looks at something terrible is turned into stone (you will remember the story of the head of Medusa).[32] This means that, like the victim who encounters the paralyzing glance of a snake, he is incapable of movement. The head of Medusa and other objects the sight of which is fatal have been conclusively demonstrated to be symbols for the female genital, and so to be turned into stone symbolizes the shock of castration with which such a sight is visited, or even castration itself. Loss of the power of motion signifies loss (not only of life but) of the penis, while a stony immobility signifies (being dead and) castration. When we reflect that the object which turns people

---

[32] S. Ferenczi, "On the Symbolism of the Head of Medusa," *Further Contributions to the Theory and Technique of Psycho-Analysis*, London, Hogarth, 1950.

into stone is very often a glaring eye (basilisk, snake, hypnotist), it is natural to conclude that such an eye is another symbol for the terrible, devouring, female genital. Now we noted that the oral-sadistic eye, which seeks to devour everything, also has this fixed glare, a fact which accords well with the interpretation just given. Let us recollect further that one of the problems which I suggested at the beginning of this paper was how the eye comes to acquire an oral significance precisely in cases in which there can be no doubt of its phallic character. We begin to realize what is the idea which in the unconscious is the link between the penis and the mouth. It is that of the vagina, which is seen but not comprehended and about which the child is uncertain whether it conceals within it a penis or is a kind of devouring mouth. In the unconscious, contradictions can exist side by side. To be turned into rigid stone symbolizes not only erection but also castration, just as the eye symbolizes not only a penis but a vagina (and a mouth).[33]

The idea of being turned into stone reminds us of the strange immobility of the wolves in the Wolf-Man's dream.[34] Freud interprets this as "representation through the opposite"; i.e., the immobility stands for the vigorous movement which the child must have witnessed during the primal scene. Now there was one person who, as Freud also has noted, actually was rigid during this scene: the child who witnessed it. So, "to be turned into stone" by the sight of something means to be fascinated by it. The primary basis of this fantasy must have been the recollection of the physical feeling of actual inability to move and rigidity which comes over a person who suddenly sees something terrifying. This fascination represents the child's helplessness in face of the enormous masses of excitation experienced when he witnesses the primal scene. Further, it has something to do with the adult genitals which he observes—with both erection and absence of the penis—and indicates his identification of his own condition with both of these, and especially his expectation of castration. At all events, in the case of the stone prince, the immobility of the person who looked was displaced onto the object looked at. And a similar displacement takes place in the act of libidinal seeing, when subject is confused with object and the ego with the outside world.

There is, however, a still deeper significance in the mechanisms of introjection or identification here at work.

Why were Lot and his company forbidden to look at Sodom as it perished? Because the sight was the sight of God Himself! But no one can bear the sight of God. Why not? What is the sin in looking? Surely it is that looking implies iden-

---

[33] As early as 1909 K. Abraham drew attention to the bisexual character of the eye (*Dreams and Myths*, New York, Nerv. Ment. Dis. Pub. Co., 1913). Since then several other authors have made the same point.

[34] S. Freud, "From the History of an Infantile Neurosis," *Coll. Pap.*, Vol. III, London, Hogarth, 1948.

tification. If a man looks upon God face to face, something of the glory of God passes into him. It is this impious act, the likening of oneself to God, which is forbidden when man is forbidden to look at God. "Thou shalt not make to thyself any graven image" is a variation of the more general prohibition which forbids us to look at God.

So to be turned into stone means also to be punished for seeking to become that which one has seen and, after the fashion familiar to us in hysterical identification,[35] the idea includes that of sacrilegious identification, translated, however, into terms of the superego. And this identification is achieved by looking at the object: he who looks at that which has been castrated (the head of Medusa) himself undergoes castration. He who looks at the dead is himself struck dead. Therefore the counterpart to the dread of being turned into stone is that of being forced in some uncanny way to look at a stone (dead) man. (Cf. the "guest of stone" in *Don Juan*).[36] Again, the eyes of the dead must be closed, because otherwise they would slay with their look those who still live;[37] the underlying idea here is the same, but the sadism of the eyes is once more displaced from the person looking to the object looked at.

When we realize that, from a schematic point of view, the idea of being turned into stone represents the reaction to the witnessing of a primal scene, we can appreciate how many elements are contained in it: erection and castration, the death of the parents, and, above all, identification with that which is seen, identification which is at one and the same time a wish fulfillment and a punishment. What concerns us most in our present context is that, when we are fascinated by some sight, the fixity of our own devouring gaze (of which we have an inner perception) is not only the basis of physical feeling on which is founded the fantasy of being turned into stone but is also, in fantasy, the bridge by which identification occurs. I would add that such an experience of fascination results in more than a fixity of gaze: the whole muscular system becomes rigid (feeling of paralysis), especially the respiratory muscles.[38]

An idea frequently met with in the analysis of patients is that the moon is a "dead man" (or, in the primal scene, "a man in vigorous action") whom one is forced to look at by some fascination and yet dare not look at because, if one did, one would die and become rigid oneself. The wan light of the moon does give a very strong impression of fixity and immobility. It is said to lay a spell upon the "moonstruck" somnambulist; * obviously it is here equated with the

---

[35] O. Fenichel, *Hysterien und Zwangsneurosen.*

[36] O. Rank, "Die Don Juan-Gestalt. Ein Beitrag zum Verstaendnis der sozialen Funktion der Dichtkunst," *Imago,* Vol. 8, 1922.

[37] G. Roheim, *op. cit.*

[38] O. Fenichel, "Respiratory Introjection," No. 23 in this volume.

* In German the word *"mondsuechtig"* has the double sense of "moon-struck" and "somnambulistic."—Trans. note.

unwavering eye of the hypnotist who puts a spell on his victim. The movements of the somnambulist, like those of persons in hypnosis, are described as unnaturally stiff and wanting in freedom.[39] He is compelled to follow the direction of the moonbeams, just as a person in hypnosis is compelled to imitate the movements of the hypnotist. The characteristics of the subject's own state of fascination are projected onto the moon; it is as motionless and silent as the watching child, as dead as the child fears that he himself will shortly be. (One of the ideas associated with somnambulism is that the "moon-struck" person is in imminent danger of his life, that he might, for instance, fall off a roof. This is in accordance with the psychoanalytical observation that the dread of falling is derived from the dread of bursting as a result of the discharge of one's own excessive sexual excitation.) The moon, at which one is compelled to look, is perceived as a face, an eye, which, like the eye of God, sees everything. It too symbolizes those terrible objects of the scoptophilic instinct, identification with which takes place by means of a look and upon which are projected one's peculiar bodily sensations; they are, of course, the parents in the primal scene and, above all, their genitals. Here, as in the case of the head of Medusa, the female (maternal) elements predominate. It is clear, then, that the moon stands for an eye and that one identifies oneself with it by looking at it.[40]

Akin to the idea of being turned into stone is the childish fantasy that a grimace may "stick" or "you'll be struck like that." The uncanny feeling experienced when dead people look as if they were still alive, as if they had "stuck" in the midst of whatever they happened to be doing, has the same character. (Cf. the story of the Sleeping Beauty.) Here again we often discover the idea of identification accomplished by means of a look.

Thus we arrive at the conclusion that the rigidity of a person turned into stone stands for the fixed gaze and the rigidity of the whole muscular system of a person fascinated by something he sees, and that it signifies erection or (death and) castration. In this train of thought the essential point is that looking is conceived of as a means of identification. If we pursue it, it leads us finally to the problems of the effect of shock and of traumas in general—i.e., the victim's sudden inability to master the outside world, a reaction which is a mode of defense against excessive masses of excitation.

[39] This peculiarity has a real physiological basis, for certain types of subcortical movement become relatively more noticeable in somnambulism. However, we are here interested not so much in persons actually under the influence of somnambulism or hypnotism as in the part which these phenomena play in legend and folklore.

[40] We may compare in this connection the very full material on the subject of the moon to be found in J. Sadger, *Sleep Walking and Moon Walking*, New York, Nerv. Ment. Dis. Pub. Co., 1920 (a clinical work), and G. Roheim, "Mondmythologie und Mondreligion," *Imago*, Vol. 13, 1927.

## VII

Freud has stated that the superego is a product of introjection. Whenever conformity to the demands of another person involves *looking up* to him we have, on the one hand, a proof of the existence of ocular introjection, and, on the other, of the genesis of the superego through introjection. There are hundreds of different instances of this sort. For example, he who stumbles looks at the image of God and stands firm again. Or, we derive moral strength by looking at the picture of someone whom we desire to copy—the very word "copy" implies looking. It is certainly true that that which it is one's duty or desire to imitate must first have been perceived and that such a perception does in itself amount to an "ocular introjection." But here it is not merely a question of reinforcing one's moral courage by acquiring visual evidence that other people are moral and that they behave in such and such a way. Rather it is a question of *the magical property of a look*: through the look itself the characteristics of that which is looked at are acquired by the person who looks.

## VIII

The unconscious processes which in the history of our race have formed the basis of the plastic (and other) arts are reproduced today in the unconscious of the artist. Ella Sharpe, following up suggestions thrown out by Melanie Klein,[41] has worked out a theory as to the nature of these processes, and this dovetails at various points with my argument. She holds that the representation of objects in works of art is primarily an unconscious attempt at "making reparation" for crimes previously committed in fantasy—above all, an attempt to reanimate persons whom one has killed by means of the "omnipotence of thoughts." Such slaying or destruction is conceived of as having been effected by introjection; reanimation is achieved when the introjected object (the design of the artist's fantasy) is restored to the outside world in the form of a work of art; in other words, it undergoes projection.[42]

If it proves that this discovery is general in its application, it will be important in our present connection. For the artist looks at some object in nature, elaborates in his mind the image which he has formed of it, and then employs his power of artistic creation to turn it into a work of art. If his unconscious fantasy is really concerned with killing and reanimation, then there is no doubt that it is the original act of *looking at* the objects which is held to be equivalent to killing and devouring them and for which restitution must be made by "spitting out"

41 M. Klein, "Infantile Anxiety-Situations Reflected in a Work of Art and in the Creative Impulse," *Int. J. Psa.*, Vol. 10, 1929.

42 E. Sharpe, "Certain Aspects of Sublimation and Delusion," *Int. J. Psa.*, Vol. 11, 1930.

the work of art. It is a well-known fact that in plastic artists the scoptophilic instinct is peculiarly strong and susceptible of sublimation. The suggestion now is that in their case also scoptophilic activity signifies an introjection of the external world by a process of oral destruction.

It seems not improbable that this is actually the case. At any rate I have some confirmation of the hypothesis in the detailed analysis of the inhibitions from which a certain woman painter suffered in connection with her work. During certain periods of her analysis she became temporarily unable to work. We finally discovered that this always happened when her powerfully inhibited sadism, in particular her active castration tendencies, were mobilized either by some material which just then emerged in her analysis or by some external event. Her inhibition then manifested itself, side by side with various other symptoms designed to protect her against her own aggressive impulses; so there could be no doubt that her creative work had a secret sadistic significance. Exhaustive analysis of this inhibition showed that it was not her motor but her *sensory* powers which suffered: she became unable to see her models properly or else she felt an unconquerable disinclination to observe them accurately. She told me how strong the bodily sensation was accompanying her empathy in her model; she would imagine that her head, her hand, etc., was just like the model's, and then she needed no longer to look but was guided in her work by her own bodily sensation. When the "sadistic" periods occurred her capacity for empathy was impaired. It seems, then, that it was her identification with the object she was painting which introduced an element of unconscious sadism into the act and, once again, this identification was achieved by ocular means.

Here is one detail taken from her various sadistic ideas. The patient developed temporarily a neurotic dread of a certain aged and famous painter. We discovered that this dread was a new edition of an infantile anxiety: as a child she had had just the same fear of her grandfather, who actually had been very brutal to her, and whom she therefore conceived of as the castrator (in order to shift the responsibility from her mother, who, in a deeper stratum, was the object of her fear). When she reached puberty, she experienced a mystic attraction to the Mother of God and a corresponding aversion from Almighty God Himself, whom she pictured as terribly severe. She imagined Him to be like her grandfather. Although, even as a child, she drew and painted all manner of objects, she had never made a drawing of her grandfather. She had a feeling that it would be quite impossible for her to do so and that, if she did, he would be inexpressibly angry. We see that she was applying to her grandfather the prohibition which has reference to God: "Thou shalt not make to thyself any graven image." Various details gradually showed that to draw her grandfather meant looking at him and that looking at him meant avenging herself for the castration inflicted upon her and devouring his penis. Dread of retaliation by her brutal grandfather forced her to suppress this wish. Since the offensive wishes were embodied in the idea of painting, her dread of retribution inevitably assumed the form of a dread of being painted. This was her reason in later life for selecting a famous artist as a transference-substitute for her grandfather.

It was plain that in this patient the act of looking was equivalent to introjection; it was less obvious that her creative work represented a projection, but it was by no means incredible that it had this significance and contributed to her profound narcissistic delight when she had achieved a successful piece of work. There were times, however, when the act of painting itself appeared to have a sadistic ("anal-sadistic") connotation, the underlying idea being, "Now I have eaten him up and he is inside me; I can do what I like with him, go on tormenting him, if I want to."

The patient's dread of being painted was really a dread of retribution, and this suggests that certain other well-known facts of ethnology and folklore come into the same category. The fear manifested by primitive or superstitious persons at the thought of having their likeness taken is commonly explained as a dread of magic. The idea is that anyone who possesses a likeness of someone else has him in his power, for everything that he does to the likeness happens to the person himself. This is also the reason for the efforts which such primitive persons make to prevent a stranger's possessing himself of any part of their bodies (e.g., fingernails) or of their excrement. It is clear that they regard a likeness as part of the ego which the other person's eye (or the apparatus he uses) can take away from them, just as his hands can take away excrement. We have the best illustration of this in the idea that, as soon as the likeness begins to exercise its magical influence, the person whom it represents loses part of his personality—e.g., his reflection or his shadow.[43] When a primitive or superstitious person is looked at (has his likeness taken), he feels that something is taken away from him. Once again the eye is conceived of as an organ which robs or bites.

Finally let me remind you that man's mechanical ingenuity has actually created a "devouring eye," which looks at and incorporates the external world and later projects it outward again. I refer, of course, to the camera. When we analyze the dread so frequently displayed by children (and occasionally by grown-ups too) at the sight of a camera, we invariably find that they think of it as an eye which is going to bite off some part of them. Here the genital significance of the eye is obvious; we have found that the "devouring eye" always has this significance. One patient had had an acute attack of anxiety as a child, when he was to undergo an X-ray examination. In analyzing this anxiety it had

[43] O. Rank, "Der Doppelgaenger," *Imago*, Vol. 3, 1914.

to be admitted that radioscopy really does enable the eye to penetrate into the interior of the body, just as the patient had always wished unconsciously that his own eye might do, while his dread of retaliation made him constantly afraid that such a thing might happen to himself. But the sadism which informed these fantasies was not in fact a feature of the objective X-ray apparatus.

We have seen that being blinded and being turned into stone are the specific punishments of the active scoptophiliac. We can now add that there is a corresponding specific punishment for the exhibitionist: the eye which looks at him will bite off part of him or devour him whole. One often meets with ideas of this sort when analyzing an exaggerated sense of shame. Probably some similar notion of ocular introjection is a regular element in the sense of shame in general.

## IX

In conclusion I wish to refer to a problem of medicine, for the solution of which many more works, on quite different lines from this, will doubtless be required.

In psychoanalytical literature the problems of the psychogenesis of myopia have at various times been discussed.[44] The writers in question have taken as their point of departure the effect of myopia and have simply introduced the idea that it served some psychical purpose. What they asked was: What does the patient gain by not being able to see distant objects or by hiding his face behind a pair of spectacles? Put in this way, the question seems to me unjustifiable, and over-simple. We cannot disregard the somatic nature of the symptom. If there is a psychic factor in its genesis, we must look for it elsewhere.

It is a well-known fact that when an organ is constantly used for purposes of erotogenic pleasure, it undergoes certain somatic changes.[45] It happens that Freud was speaking of the eyes of persons in whom the scoptophilic instinct is specially developed, when he said, "If an organ which serves two purposes overplays its erotogenic role, it is in general to be expected that this will not occur without alterations in its response to stimulation and in innervation," [46]—i.e., of the physiological factors in general. From the point of view of research it is probably more useful, when studying myopia, to consider the somatic changes which take place in the eye in consequence of its being used for libidinal purposes than to regard the incapacity to see at a distance as a symbol of castration. We

---

[44] S. E. Jelliffe, "Psychoanalysis and Organic Disorder: Myopia as a Paradigm," *Int. J. Psa.,* Vol. 7, 1926.

[45] Cf. the very full material on this subject in S. Ferenczi's *Hysterie und Pathoneurosen*, Vienna, Int. Psa. Verlag, 1919.

[46] S. Freud, "Psychogenic Visual Disturbance according to Psycho-Analytical Conceptions," *Coll. Pap.*, Vol. II.

have an additional reason for thinking that we shall discover somatic-neurotic relations when we read further in Freud: "Neurotic disturbances of vision are related to psychogenic as, in general, are the actual neuroses to the psychoneuroses; psychogenic visual disturbances can hardly occur without neurotic disturbances, though the latter surely can without the former." [47]

What has ophthalmic medicine to say on the subject of myopia? We are told that it is caused by an elongation of the axis of the eyeball. This elongation is attributed partly to the external muscles of the eye and partly to general vegetative changes which alter the contour of the eyeball itself. It would seem, then, that incapacity to see distant objects has no psychic significance but is the involuntary, mechanical sequel to processes which either affect the external optic muscles or take place within the eyeballs. But what causes these processes? At all events the vegetative nervous system plays a decisive part in them, and the functioning of that system is, apart from various somatic factors, psychically determined. The question is this. We have seen that the constant use of the eye for the libidinal gratification of scoptophilic impulses causes it actively to strain in the direction of objects, in order psychically to incorporate them. Is it not possible that this may finally result in a stretching of the eyeball?

We recognize that this is putting the problem very crudely. Of course an exact knowledge of the ways in which such stretching may occur would be necessary to explain why many people in whom the scoptophilic instinct is peculiarly strong are not in the least shortsighted. There is no difficulty about the converse fact, namely, that many shortsighted people (often those in whom the symptom is most pronounced) show no sign of a marked scoptophilic tendency. There is no reason to suppose that every case of myopia is psychogenic. And, while the stretching of the eyeball may sometimes be due to the attempt to incorporate objects at the bidding of scoptophilic impulses, in other cases the origin of the disability is undoubtedly purely somatic.

[47] *Ibid.*, p. 112.

# THIRTY-FOUR

# The Black Cook*

A PATIENT's anxiety about the children's game "Is the black cook here?" gave occasion to think a little about the unconscious meaning of this game.

I know two versions of the verses of this game. The children sing either:

> "Is the black cook here?
> No, no, no.
> Three times must she march around,
> The fourth time she must lose her head,
> The fifth time you will come along!" †

or:

> "Is the black cook here?
> No, no, no.
> Three times must she march around
> The fourth time she must lose her head,
> The fifth time you must say:
> You are pretty, you are pretty, you the prettiest of all." ‡

In this game the children are "counted out" as in all counting rhymes, and the child on whom the "you will come along" or "the prettiest of all" falls, is

---

* First published in Z. psa. Paedag., Vol. 10, 1936, pp. 103–105.
† "Ist die schwarze Koechin da?
  Nein, nein, nein.
  Dreimal muss sie rummarschiern,
  Das vierte Mal den Kopf verliern,
  Das fuenfte Mal kommst mit!"—Trans. note.
‡ "Ist die schwarze Koechin da?
  Nein, nein, nein.
  Dreimal muss sie rummarschiern,
  Das vierte Mal den Kopf verliern,
  Das fuenfte Mal musst sagen:
  Du bist schoen, du bist schoen, du die Allerschoenste."—Trans. note.

out. Then the verse is repeated until only a single child is left. This is the "black cook" who is scorned in the rhyme:

> "Is the black cook here?
> Yes, yes, yes.
> Here she is, here she is,
> Fie, fie, fie!" *

The game reminds one of the more familiar "black Peter." In this, by means of a special ceremony, a child is sought out from among all and is ridiculed for having been chosen by fate. There are many indications that the ridicule is but a weakened expression of something much worse. The "black Peter" is smeared with dirt (the "black cook" too is "black" like him), and in other similar games the child chosen by fate is sent to hell. There can be no doubt that these are "ordeal" games. Out of the number of those present, one who is to be punished is chosen by a sort of ordeal. According to Reik, the proof of guilt in medieval criminal processes was like this.[1] Thus in these games a culprit must be found and punished.

Let us do as we are accustomed to in psychoanalysis, and take the words of the verses seriously. The "black cook," "the fourth time she must lose her head." The actual punishment which befalls the "cook" of the game, the scornful "fie, fie, fie," is thus obviously only a secondary, weakened punishment. What threatens her is something much worse: beheading. Why? The analytic interpretation, that beheading means castration, seems to get us no further. Let us rather assume that beheading means actually beheading. Somebody is sought who has committed a crime worthy of death.

We still remember Schneider's fine study [2] which demonstrated how often children's games and children's dances, particularly those whose texts are ununderstandable, are residues of once socially important old customs, now fallen into oblivion and sunk to the level of children's games. Here the children's game apparently repeats a court procedure, which was once a matter of life and death: a murderer or a criminal otherwise deserving death is sought by means of an ordeal.

Why does the cook lose her head only the "fourth time"? She must first "three times . . . march around." Now we seem to understand. Medieval executions were public events, at which, as is known, the condemned were very

---

\* *"Ist die schwarze Koechin da?*
  *Ja, ja, ja.*
  *Da ist sie ja, da ist sie ja,*
  *Pfui, pfui, pfui!"*—T. ans. note.
[1] T. Reik, *The Unknown Murderer*, London, Hogarth, 1936.
[2] E. Schneider, "Kinderreigen," *Z. psa. Paedag.*, Vol. 6, 1932.

often first led around the city. The death punishment was made more severe by a sort of preceding exhibition.

Is there any doubt left who the "black cook" is? "Black magic" was the name of witchcraft, practiced by witches in their witch-kitchens. He who practices black magic in a kitchen can well be called a "black cook." The children play in this game a witch trial, in which the witch is recognized by ordeal, and, after being led around town, is executed.

How and why do such serious customs sink to the level of children's games? This question is not easy to answer. It is not sufficient that the children's world is one which is not taken seriously by adults and is therefore particularly suited to conserve socially superseded institutions, the residues of which still persist in the unconscious. The further circumstance is apparently added that these residues are suitable to pedagogical application and can be secondarily revised for this purpose. What was once a serious social threat is later still useful as a threat to children. (Something similar must occur in the "sinking" of myth into children's tales.)

In our game this pedagogical use becomes particularly clear in the verse: "The fifth time you will come along!" This sounds as if the child were being told, "You know that witches, that is, bad people, are beheaded; don't be bad, because otherwise next time it will happen to you!" . . . In the other version, the seeking out of the "prettiest of all" reassures the person of his temporary innocence and of forgiveness; but he cannot be sure either whether or not the next time the ordeal will decide against him.

# Index of Names

# Index of Subjects